Taking Sides: Clashing Views on Controversial Educational Issues

It is better to debate a question without settling it than to settle a question without debating it.

Joseph Joubert

For Sonja and Daniel

STAFF

Carol Dudley	*Editor*
Brenda Filley	*Production Manager*
Charles Vitelli	*Designer*
Bertha Kinne	*Typesetter*
DB Photographics	*Cover Photo*

Taking Sides: Clashing Views on Controversial Educational Issues

Edited, Selected, and with Introductions by
JAMES Wm. NOLL
University of Maryland

The Dushkin Publishing Group, Inc.
Guilford, Connecticut

Library of Congress Catalog Card Number: 80-65112

Manufactured in the United States of America
First Edition, First Printing

PREFACE

Controversy is the basis of change and, hopefully, improvement. Its lack signifies the presence of complacency, the authoritarian limitation of viewpoint expression, or the absence of realistic alternatives to the existing circumstances. An articulate presentation of a point of view on a controversial matter breathes new life into abiding human and social concerns. Controversy prompts re-examination and, perhaps, renewal.

Education is controversial. Arguments over most appropriate aims, most propitious means, and most effective control have raged over the centuries. Particularly in the United States, where the systematic effort to provide education has been more democratically dispersed and more varied than elsewhere, educational issues have been contentiously debated. Philosophers, psychologists, sociologists, professional educators, lobbyists, government officials, school boards, local pressure groups, taxpayers, parents, and students have all had their views heard.

The aim of this book is to present opposed or varying viewpoints on a spectrum of basic issues in the field of education—questions of purpose, power, and reform. The statements assembled here are excerpted from the work of thinkers whose ideas are fundamental to the full understanding of the issue at hand. Many are seminal ideas which, since their articulation, have proved useful in further defining the meaning of education.

Questions of purpose are addressed from both philosophical and psychological perspectives by such luminaries as John Dewey, Max Rafferty, Paul Goodman, Clifton Fadiman, B.F. Skinner, Carl Rogers, Lawrence Kohlberg, Howard Kirschenbaum, Jerome Bruner, and Robert Gagné.

Issues of power and control are analyzed by historians, sociologists, political theorists, legal experts, and professional leaders, among them Patricia Graham, James Banks, Christopher Jencks, Nathan Glazer, James Bryant Conant, Mario Fantini, Albert Shanker, and Herb Kohl.

Reform and improvement issues are treated by social critics, philosophers, educators, radical theorists, and futurists such as Ivan Illich, Robert Hutchins,

Carl Bereiter, Samuel Bowles, Herbert Gintis, Arthur Pearl, and John Goodlad.

Seventeen issues are presented here for examination, from the more embracing consideration of educational and social goals, curricular organization, psychological atmosphere, moral development, and instructional methodology to the more specific concerns of opportunity equalization, educational policy formation, accountability, professionalism, student rights, compulsory schooling, and the development of alternative paths to knowledge.

Each issue is preceded by a brief introduction and is followed by a postscript which recognizes that the views offered do not exhaust all possible slants and, accordingly, points the reader toward other sources of ideas. By combining the material in this volume with the informational background which a good introductory textbook can provide, the reader should be prepared to address the actual problems confronting the schools today.

It is the hope of the editor that the reader will find challenges in the material presented here—provocations which will lead to a deeper level of understanding of the roots of educational controversy, a greater awareness of possible alternatives in dealing with the various issues, and a stretching of personal powers of creative thinking in searching for more promising resolutions of the problems. The quality of future life is dependent upon the fruitful combining of understanding, awareness, and creative thought.

In the spirit of this sentiment, I wish to acknowledge the understanding of Rick Connelly and his Dushkin Publishing Group staff while patiently dealing with my procrastinations, the awareness of editorial supervisor Carol Dudley in purging my prose of professional pedantry, and the creative thinking of my wife, Sonja, in finding alternative sites while the dining table was strewn with the fragments of this work.

James Wm. Noll
University of Maryland

CONTENTS

INTRODUCTION: WAYS OF THINKING ABOUT EDUCATIONAL ISSUES

JAMES Wm. NOLL

Concern about the quality of education has been expressed by philosophers, politicians, and parents for centuries. There has been an unresolved debate in most all geographic quarters regarding the definition of education, the relationship between school and society, the distribution of decision-making power in educational matters, and the means for improving all aspects of the enterprise.

In recent decades the growing influence of thinking drawn from the humanities and the behavioral and social sciences has brought about the development of interpretive, normative, and critical perspectives which have sharpened the focus on educational concerns. These perspectives have allowed scholars and researchers to closely examine the contextual variables, value orientations, and philosophical and political assumptions which shape both the status quo and reform efforts.

The study of education involves the application of multiple perspectives to the analysis of "what is and how it got that way," and "what can be and how we can get there." Central to such study are the prevailing philosophical assumptions, theories, and visions which find their way to concrete educational situations. The application situation, with its attendant political pressures, socio-cultural differences, community expectations, parental influence, and professional problems, provides a testing ground for contending theories and ideals.

This "testing ground" image applies only insofar as the status quo is malleable enough to allow the examination and trial of alternative views. Historically, institutionalized education has been characteristically rigid. As a "testing ground" of ideas it has often lacked an orientation encouraging innovation and futuristic thinking. Its political grounding has usually been conservative.

As social psychologist Allen Wheelis has pointed out in *Quest for Identity,* social institutions by definition tend toward solidification and protectionism. His depiction of the dialectical development of civilizations centers on the tension between the security and authoritarianism of "institutional processes" and the dynamism and change-orientation of "instrumental processes."

Similarly, the "lonely crowd" theory of Riesman, Glazer, and Denny portrays a civilizational drift from a traditional imposed and authoritarian value structure to a socialized and internalized ethic to a contemporary situation of value fragmentation. Having cracked, or at least called into question, many of the institutional rigidities of church, school, and home, people in technologically advanced societies face three basic possibilities: learning to live with diversity and change, sliding into a new form of institutional rigidity, or reverting to traditional authoritarianism.

The current situation in education seems to graphically illustrate these observations. Educational practices are primarily tradition-bound. The 20th-century reform movement, spurred by the ideas of John Dewey, A.S. Neill, and a host of critics who campaigned for change in the 1960s, challenged the structural rigidity of schooling. The current situation is one of contending forces—those who wish to continue the struggle for true reform, those who demand a return to a more traditional or "basic" model, and those who are shaping a new form of procedural conformity around the tenets of behaviorism and competency-based approaches.

We are left with the abiding questions: What is an "educated" person? What should be the primary purpose of organized education? Who should control the decisions influencing the educational process? Should the schools follow society or lead it toward change? Should schooling be compulsory?

Long-standing forces have molded a wide variety of responses to these fundamental questions. The religious impetus, nationalistic fervor, philosophical ideas, the march of science and technology, varied interpretations of "societal needs," and the desire to use the schools in social reform have been historically influential. In recent times other factors have emerged to contribute to the complexity of the search for answers—social class differences, demographic shifts, increasing bureaucratization, the growth of the textbook industry, the changing financial base for schooling, teacher unionization, and strengthening of parental and community pressure groups.

The struggle to find the most appropriate answers to these questions involves, now as in the past, an interplay of societal aims, educational purposes, and individual intentions. Moral development, the quest for wisdom, citizenship training, socio-economic improvement, mental discipline, the rational control of life, job preparation, liberation of the individual, freedom of inquiry—these and many others continue to be topics of discourse on education.

A detailed historical perspective on these questions and topics may be gained by reading the several interpretations of noted scholars in the field. R. Freeman Butts has written a brief but effective summary portrayal in "Search for Freedom—The Story of American Education" (NEA Journal, March 1960). A partial listing of other sources includes:

R. Freeman Butts and Lawrence Cremin, *A History of Education in American Culture*
S.E. Frost, Jr., *Historical and Philosophical Foundations of Western Education*
Harry Good and Edwin Teller, *A History of Education*
Adolphe Meyer, *An Educational History of the American People*
Robert L. Church and Michael W. Sedlak, *Education in the United States: An Interpretive History*
David Tyack, *Turning Points in American Educational History*
Merle Curti, *The Social Ideas of American Educators*
Henry J. Perkinson, *The Imperfect Panacea: American Faith in Education 1865–1965*
Clarence Karier, *Man, Society, and Education*
V.T. Thayer, *Formative Ideas in American Education*

These and other historical accounts of the development of schooling demonstrate the continuing need to address educational questions in terms of cultural and social dynamics. A careful analysis of contemporary education demands attention not only to the historical interpretation of developmental influences but also to the philosophical forces which define formal education and the social and cultural factors which form the basis of informal education.

In his recent book, *A New Public Education,* Seymour Itzkoff examines the interplay between informal and formal education, concluding that economic and technological expansion have pulled people away from the informal culture by placing a premium on success in formal education. This has brought about a reactive search for less artificial educational contexts within the informal cultural community which recognize the impact of individual personality in shaping educational experiences.

This search for a reconstructed philosophical base for education has produced a barrage of critical commentary. Those who seek radical change in education characterize the present schools as mindless, manipulative, factory-like, bureaucratic institutions which offer little sense of community, pay scant attention to personal meaning, fail to achieve curricular integration, and maintain a psychological atmosphere of competitiveness, tension, fear, and alienation. Others deplore the ideological movement away from the formal organization of education, fearing an abandonment of standards, a dilution of the curriculum, an erosion of intellectual and behavioral discipline and a decline in adult and institutional authority.

Students of education (whether prospective teachers, practicing professionals, or interested laymen) must examine closely the assumptions and values underlying alternative positions in order to clarify their own viewpoints.

This tri-level task may best be organized around the basic themes of purpose, power, and reform. These themes offer access to the theoretical grounding of actions in the field of education, to the political grounding of such actions, and to the "futures" orientation of action decisions.

A general model for the examination of positions on educational issues includes the following dimensions: identification of the viewpoint, recognition of the stated or implied assumptions underlying the viewpoint, analysis of the validity of the supporting argument, and evaluation of the conclusions and action-suggestions of the originator of the position. The stated or implied assumptions may be derived from a philosophical or religious orientation, from scientific theory, from social or personal values, or from accumulated experience. Acceptance by the reader of an author's assumptions opens the way for a receptive attitude regarding the specific viewpoint expressed and its implications for action. The argument offered in justification of the viewpoint may be based on logic, common experience, controlled experiments, information and data, legal precedents, emotional appeals, and/or a host of other persuasive devices.

Holding the basic model in mind, readers of the positions presented in this volume (or anywhere else, for that matter) can examine the constituent elements of arguments—basic assumptions, viewpoint statements, supporting evidence, and conclusions and suggestions for action. The careful reader will accept or reject the several elements of the total position. One might see reasonableness in a viewpoint and its justification but be unable to accept the assumptions on which it is based. Or one might accept the flow of argument from assumptions to viewpoint to evidence but find illogic or impracticality in the stated conclusions and suggestions for action. In any event, the reader's personal view is tested and honed through the process of analyzing the views of others.

The Search for Purpose in Education

Historically, organized education has been initiated and instituted to serve many purposes—spiritual salvation, political socialization, moral uplift, societal stability, social mobility, mental discipline, vocational efficiency, social reform. The various purposes have usually reflected the dominant philosophical conception of human nature and the prevailing assumptions about the relationship between the individual and society. At any given time, competing conceptions may vie for dominance—social conceptions, economic conceptions, conceptions emphasizing spirituality, conceptions stressing the uniqueness and dignity of the individual.

These considerations of human nature and individual-society relationships are grounded in philosophical assumptions, and these assumptions find their way to such practical domains as schooling. In western civilization there has been an identifiable (but far from consistent and clear-cut) historical trend in the basic assumptions about reality, knowledge, values, and the human condition. This trend, made manifest in the philosophical positions of idealism, realism, pragmatism, and existentialism, has involved a shift in emphasis from the spiritual world to nature to human behavior to the social individual to the free individual, from eternal ideas to fixed natural laws to social interaction to the inner person.

The idealist tradition, which dominated much of philosophical and educational thought until the 18th and 19th centuries, separates the changing, imperfect material world and the permanent, perfect spiritual or mental world. As Plato saw it, for example, human beings and all other physical entities are particular manifestations of an ideal reality which, in material existence, humans can never fully know. The purpose of education is to bring us closer to the absolute ideals, pure forms, and universal standards which exist spiritually by awakening and strengthening our rational powers. For Plato, a curriculum based on mathematics, logic, and music would serve this purpose, especially in the training of leaders whose rationality must exert control over emotionality and baser instincts.

Against this tradition, which shaped the liberal arts curriculum in schools for centuries, the realism of Aristotle, with its finding of the "forms" of things *within* the material world, brought an emphasis on scientific investigation and on environmental factors in the development of human potential. This fundamental view has influenced two philosophical movements in education: "naturalism," based on following or gently assisting nature (as in the approaches of John Amos Comenius, Jean-Jacques Rousseau, and Johann Heinrich Pestalozzi), and "scientific realism," based on uncovering the natural laws of human behavior and shaping the educational environment to maximize their effectiveness (as in the approaches of John Locke, Johann Friedrich Herbart, and Edward Thorndike).

In the 20th century, two philosophical forces (pragmatism and existentialism) have challenged these traditions. Each has moved primary attention away from fixed spiritual or natural influences and toward the individual as shaper of knowledge and values. The pragmatic position, articulated in America by Charles Sanders Peirce, William James, and John Dewey, turns from metaphysical abstractions toward concrete results of action. In a world of change and relativity, human beings must forge their own truths and values as they interact with their environments and each other. The European-based philosophy of existentialism, emerging from such thinkers as Gabriel Marcel, Martin Buber, Martin Heidegger, and Jean-Paul Sartre, has more recently influenced education here. Existentialism places the burdens of freedom, choice, and responsibility squarely on the individual, viewing the current encroachment of external forces and the tendency of people to "escape from freedom" as a serious diminishment of our human possibilities.

All of these basic philosophical views and many of their countless variations are operative today and provide the grounding of most of the positions on contemporary educational issues, including those presented in this book. The conservative and "liberal arts" tradition, emphasizing the humanities, the cultural heritage, and moral standards, can be easily detected in the words of Hutchins, Fadiman, and Rafferty. The progressive, experimental approach, concentrating on critical intelligence, socio-psychological factors, and social adjustment, is found in the ideas of Dewey, Goodman, Kohlberg, and Bruner. Modern behaviorism, taking cues from the earlier scientific realism, finds its way into education through the views of Skinner and Gagné. Existentialist concerns regarding human subjectivity, self-actualization, and authenticity are aired by Rogers, Kirschenbaum, and Illich.

And so these many theoretical slants contend for recognition and acceptance as we continue the search for broad purposes in education and as we attempt to create curricula, methodologies, and learning environments which fulfill our stated purposes. This is carried out, of course, in the real world of the public schools in which social, political, and economic forces often predominate.

The Struggle for Control

Plato, in the fourth century B.C., found existing education manipulative and confining and, in the *Republic,* described a meritocratic approach designed to nurture intellectual powers so as to form and sustain a rational society. Reform-oriented as Plato's suggestions were, he nevertheless insisted on certain restrictions and controls so that his particular version of the "ideal" could be met.

The ways and means of education have been fertile grounds for power struggles throughout history. Many educational efforts have been initiated by religious bodies, often creating a conflict situation when secular authorities have moved into the field. Schools have usually been seen as repositories of culture and social values and, as such, have been overseen by the more conservative forces in society. To others, bent on social reform, the schools have been treated as a spawning ground for change. Given these basic political forces, conflict is inevitable.

When one speaks of the control of education the range of influence is indeed wide. Political influences, governmental actions, court decisions, professional militancy, parental power, and student assertion all contribute to the phenomenon of control. And the domain of control is equally broad—school finances, curriculum, instructional means and objectives, teacher certification, accountability, student discipline, censorship of school materials, and determination of access and opportunity, of inclusion and exclusion.

The general topic of power and control leads to a multitide of questions: Who should make policy decisions? Must the schools be puppets of the government? Can the schools function in the vanguard of social change? Can cultural indoctrination be avoided? Can the schools lead the way to full social integration? Can the effects of social class be eradicated? Can and should the schools teach values? Dealing with such questions is complicated by the increasing power of the federal government in educational matters. Congressional legislation has broadened substantially from the early land grants and aid to agricultural and vocational programs to more recent laws covering aid to federally impacted areas, school construction aid, student loans and fellowships, support for several academic areas of the curriculum, work-study programs, compensatory education, employment opportunities for youth, adult education, aid to libraries, teacher preparation, educational research, career education, education of the handicapped, and equal opportunity for females. This proliferation of areas of influence has caused the administrative bureaucracy to blossom from its meager beginnings in 1867 into a cabinet-level Department of Education in 1979.

State legislatures and state departments of education have also grown in power, handling greater percentages of school appropriations and controlling basic curricular decisions, attendance laws, accreditation, research, etc. Local school boards, once the sole authorities in policy-making, now share that role with higher governmental echelons as the financial support sources shift away from the local scene. Simultaneously, strengthened teacher organizations and increasingly vocal pressure groups at the local, state, and national levels have forced a widening of the base for policy decisions.

In the 1980s important policy clarifications will have to be forged by this mēlange of influential groups. Among the problems inherited from the previous decade are the appropriateness of affirmative action on the basis of race, sex, and ethnicity; the growing public and professional concern over student achievement; the development of effective approaches to teacher accountability; increasing efforts to build school programs which are truly multicultural; implementation of PL94-142, the legislation designed to provide appropriate educational environments for the handicapped; further clarification of teacher and student rights; and reconciliation of the centralization-decentralization issue in light of changing patterns of school finance.

In Part Two of this book a selection of these issues is examined, following two appraisals of the institutional development of education in America by Patricia Albjerg Graham and Peter Schrag. James Banks and Orlando Patterson debate the value of the current emphasis on multiculturalism, Christopher Jencks and Nathan Glazer focus on the struggle for equalization of opportunity, and James Bryant Conant's early suggestions for greater centralization are contrasted with the views of two community control advocates, Mario Fantini and Marilyn Gittell.

In other pairings, the virtues of accountability are debated by Leon Lessinger and Robert Bundy, Albert Shanker and Herb Kohl offer differing perspectives on teacher power, and Guy Leekley and Mary Kohler present two slants on the scope of student rights. Each of these basically political wrangles reflects the general effort to reform the total approach to education in this country, which is the focus of the final portion of the anthology.

The Design of Improvements

The schools often seem to be either facing backward or to be completely absorbed in the tribulations of the present, lacking a vision of possible futures which might guide current decisions. The present is inescapable, obviously, and certainly the historical and philosophical underpinnings of the present situation must be understood, but true improvement often requires a break with conventionality, a surge toward a desired future.

The radical reform critique of government-sponsored compulsory schooling has depicted organized education as a form of cultural or political imprisonment which traps young people in an artificial and mainly irrelevant environment which rewards conformity and docility while inhibiting curiosity and creativity. Constructive reform ideas that have come from this critique include the creation of "open" classrooms, the de-emphasis of external motivators, the diversification of educational experience, and the building of a true sense of "community" within the instructional environment.

Starting with Francis Wayland Parker's schools in Quincy, Massachusetts, and John Dewey's laboratory school at the University of Chicago in and around the turn of the current century, the campaign to make schools into more productive and humane places has been relentless. The duplication of A.S. Neill's Summerhill model in the free school movement of the 1960s, the open classroom/open space trends of recent years, the several curricular variations on applications of "humanistic" ideals, and the emergence of schools without walls, storefront schools, and street academies in a number of urban areas testify to the desire to reform the present system or to build alternatives to it.

The progressive education movement, the development of "life adjustment" goals and curricula, and the "whole person" theories of educational psychology moved the schools toward an expanded conception of schooling which embaced new subject matters and new approaches to discipline during the first half of this century. Since the 1950s, however, pressure for a return to a narrower conception of schooling as intellectual training has sparked new waves of debate. Out of this situation have come attempts by educators and academicians to design new curricular approaches in the basic subject matter areas, efforts by private foundations to stimulate organizational innovations and to improve the training of teachers, and federal government support of the community school model and the career education curriculum. Yet, criticism of the schools abounds. The schools, according to many who use their services, remain too factorylike, too age-segregated, too custodial. Alternative paths are still sought—paths which allow action-learning, work-study, and a diversity of ways to achieve success.

The need for reform has prompted some critics to call for an abandonment of institutionalized compulsory schooling. Ivan Illich's insistence that the school's monopolistic hold on the definition of "success" must be broken and Carl Bereiter's compromise position on "deschooling" form the cornerstone of the selections included in Part Three of this book. Robert Hutchins and Philip Jackson, in turn, analyze the argument against compulsory schooling and find the present schools to be basically worthwhile and reformable.

In other excerpts, Samuel Bowles and Herbert Gintis attack the prevailing economic manipulations to which the schools are a party, and Harvey Scribner and Leonard Stevens call for concerted parental action to bring about improvement. The situation in higher education is appraised by Arthur Pearl and Caroline Bird, both of whom find the present regimentation unpalatable. And finally, Patrick Suppes and John Goodlad look forward to a period of expanded technological and humanistic possibilities.

Some Concluding Remarks

H.G. Wells has told us that human history becomes more and more a race between education and catastrophe. What is needed in order to win this race is the generation of new ideas regarding cultural change, human relationships, ethical norms, the uses of technology, and the quality of life. These new ideas, of course, may be old ideas newly applied. One could do worse, in thinking through the problem of improving the quality of education, than to turn to the third-century philosopher, Plotinus, who called for an education directed to "the outer, the inner, and the whole." For Plotinus, "the outer" represented the public person, the socio-economic dimension of the total human being; "the inner" reflected the subjective dimension, the uniquely experiencing individual, the "I"; and "the whole" signified the universe of meaning and relatedness, the realm of human, natural, and spiritual connectedness. It would seem that education must address all of these dimensions if it is to truly help people in the lifelong struggle to shape a meaningful existence. If educational experiences can be improved in these directions the end result might be people who are not just filling space, filling time, or filling a social role, but who are capable of saying something worthwhile with their lives.

David Attie

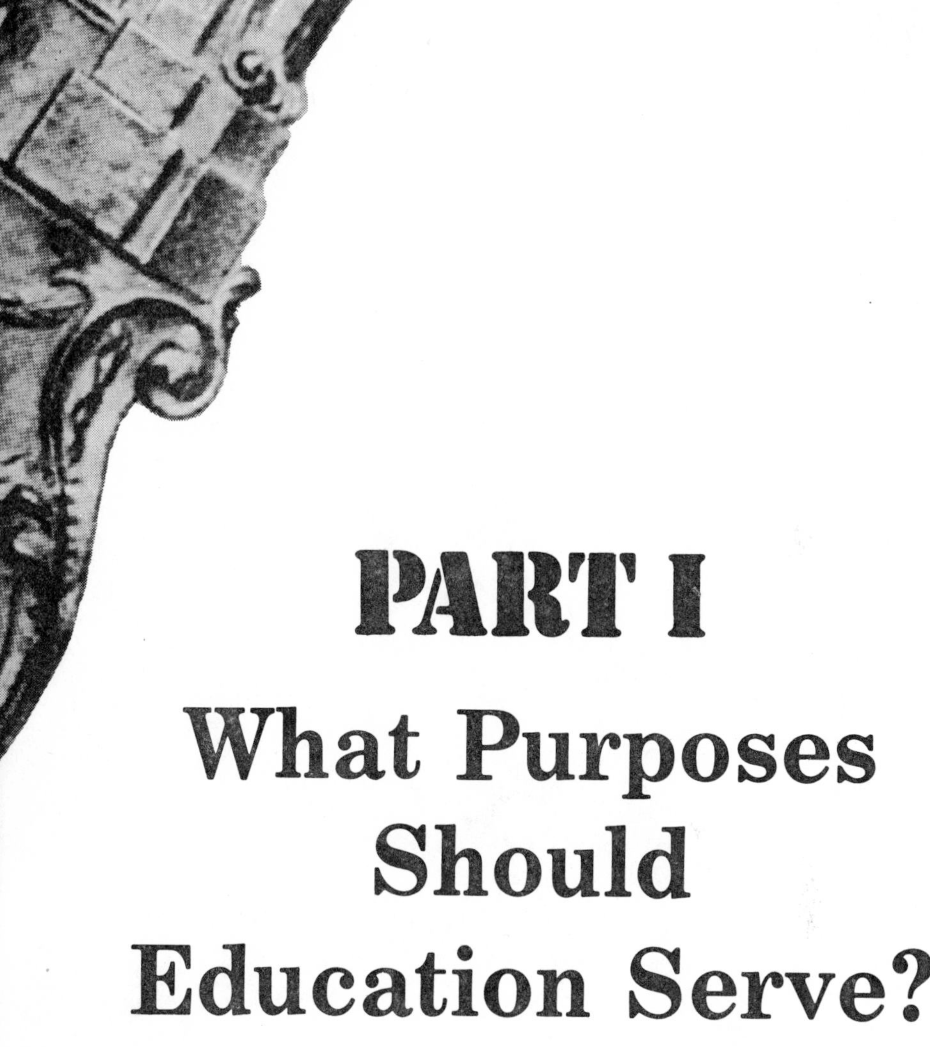

PART I

What Purposes Should Education Serve?

ISSUE 1

WHAT IS THE PRIMARY GOAL OF SCHOOLING?

Down through history organized educational experiences have served many purposes—the transmission of tradition, knowledge, and skills; the acculturation and socialization of the young; the building and preserving of political-economic systems; the provision of opportunity for social mobility; the enhancement of the quality of life; and the cultivation of individual potential, among others. At any given time, the schools pursue a number of such goals, but the elucidation of a primary or over-riding goal which gives focus to all others has been a source of continuous contention.

Particularly in the last hundred years, during which schooling in America has been expanded to vast numbers of young people, has the argument over aims gained momentum. By the turn of the century, John Dewey was raising serious questions about the efficacy of the prevailing approach to schooling. He believed that schooling was often arid and pedantic, detached from the real lives of children and youth. In establishing his laboratory school at the University of Chicago, Dewey hoped to demonstrate that experiences provided by schools could be meaningful extensions of the normal social activities of learners, having as their primary aim the full experiential growth of the individual.

In order to accomplish this, Dewey sought to bring the learner into an active and intimate relationship to the subject matter. The problem-solving or inquiry approach which he and his colleagues at Columbia University devised became the cornerstone of the "new education"—the progressive education movement.

By 1938, Dewey himself (as expressed in his article which follows) sounded a note of caution to progressive educators who may have abandoned too completely the traditional disciplines in their attempt to link schooling with the needs and interests of the learners. Having spawned an educational revolution, Dewey, in his later years, emerges as more of a compromiser.

In that same year of 1938, William C. Bagley, in "An Essentialists' Platform for the Advancement of American Education," harshly criticized what he felt were anti-intellectual excesses promulgated by progressivism. In the 1950s and 1960s this theme was elaborated on by others who demanded a return of intellectual discipline, higher standards, and moral guidance, among them Robert M. Hutchins, Adm. Hyman Rickover, Arthur Bestor, and Max Rafferty.

Rafferty's attack on Dewey and progressive education was perhaps the most pungent—as can be witnessed in the excerpt from his writings presented here. Rafferty and most other "essentialists" argue that the progressive influence diminished the effect of the school on the shaping of thinking skills and the instilling of behavioral habits. Some have expressed concern about the pragmatic emphasis on change and moral relativism and about the amount of attention given by progressives to psychological and social adjustment and to the use of schools as social reform instruments.

In the following selection, John Dewey charts the necessary shift from the abstractness and isolation of traditional schooling to the concreteness and connectedness of the newer conception, recognizing at the same time the problems and challenges which the shift itself poses. Max Rafferty dissects the assumptions on which Dewey based his theories and progressive education practices, illustrating what he feels are the resulting evils.

John Dewey

TOTAL EXPERIENTIAL GROWTH

Mankind likes to think in terms of extreme opposites. It is given to formulating its beliefs in terms of *Either-Ors,* between which it recognizes no intermediate possibilities. When forced to recognize that the extremes cannot be acted upon, it is still inclined to hold that they are all right in theory but that when it comes to practical matters circumstances compel us to compromise. Educational philosophy is no exception. The history of educational theory is marked by opposition between the idea that education is development from within and that it is formation from without; that it is based upon natural endowments and that education is a process of overcoming natural inclination and substituting in its place habits acquired under external pressure.

At present, the opposition, so far as practical affairs of the school are concerned, tends to take the form of contrast between traditional and progressive education. If the underlying ideas of the former are formulated broadly, without the qualifications required for accurate statement, they are found to be about as follows: The subject-matter of education consists of bodies of information and of skills that have been worked out in the past; therefore, the chief business of the school is to transmit them to the new generation. In the past, there have also been developed standards and rules of conduct; moral training consists in forming habits of action in conformity with these rules and standards. Finally, the general pattern of school organization (by which I mean the relations of pupils to one another and to the teachers) constitutes the school a kind of institution sharply marked off from other social institutions. Call up in imagination the ordinary schoolroom, its time-schedules, schemes of classification, of examination and promotion, of rules of order, and I think you will grasp what is meant by "pattern of organization." If then you contrast this scene with what goes on in the family, for example, you will appreciate what is meant by the school being a kind of institution sharply marked off from any other form of social organization.

The three characteristics just mentioned fix the aims and methods of instruction and discipline. The main purpose or objective is to prepare the

Continued on p. 6

From *Experience and Education* (1938). Reprinted by permission of Kappa Delta Pi, "Educational Forum."

Max Rafferty

ORGANIZED DISCIPLINED THINKING

Does Junior tell you that competition to get good grades is bad? A self-destructive pursuit of sterile status symbols? He learned this in school.

Does Susie believe that popularity with her peers and acceptance by her group are more important than learning how to spell properly? She learned this in school, I'm afraid.

Are both your children convinced that everything is relative—that what's good today may be bad tomorrow, and vice-versa—and that there are really no lasting values or eternal truths in this vale of tears? They learned this in school, too.

Oh, not in all schools, of course, nor from all teachers. But from entirely too many these days. For this is the tired old dogma of Progressive Education, with its bubble-headed jargon of "life-adjustment," "meeting felt needs," "relevance," "togetherness," and "on-going, forward-looking in-groupness." Since the mid-Thirties, it has clung to the body of American education like a barnacle to the bottom of a boat.

See the hairy Hell's Angel, unsavory, uncouth, a thrall to kicks. One reason he's this way is because his school taught him as a kid that rigid standards went out with high-button shoes, and that it's perfectly okay for each person to evolve his own moral code. So he did, God help him.

See the noisome hippie, diseased, debauched, degenerate. Down in the grades and with the same good intentions which pave Hell-road, his teachers let him get the idea that life is a ball where imposed toil is tyranny, where loafing on somebody else's money is everybody's right, and where happiness consists of doing your own thing. Sorry. It doesn't.

See the campus rioter, brandishing four-letter-word placards and Molotov cocktails with equal abandon. Some years back, his school told him a lot about individual freedom and nothing at all about individual responsibility. Now he exercises his own freedom at the expense of someone else's. Responsibility? That's Squaresville, man.

Good teachers the world over stress a moral code that places others' rights

Continued on p. 12

(Dewey, cont. from p. 4)
young for future responsibilities and for success in life, by means of acquisition of the organized bodies of information and prepared forms of skill which comprehend the material of instruction. Since the subject-matter as well as standards of proper conduct are handed down from the past, the attitude of pupils must, upon the whole, be one of docility, receptivity, and obedience. Books, especially textbooks, are the chief representatives of the lore and wisdom of the past, while teachers are the organs through which pupils are brought into effective connection with the material. Teachers are the agents through which knowledge and skills are communicated and rules of conduct enforced.

I have not made this brief summary for the purpose of criticizing the underlying philosophy. The rise of what is called new education and progressive schools is of itself a product of discontent with traditional education. In effect it is a criticism of the latter. When the implied criticism is made explicit it reads somewhat as follows: The traditional scheme is, in essence, one of imposition from above and from outside. It imposes adult standards, subject-matter, and methods upon those who are only growing slowly toward maturity. The gap is so great that the required subject-matter, the methods of learning and of behaving are foreign to the existing capacities of the young. They are beyond the reach of the experience the young learners already possess. Consequently, they must be imposed; even though good teachers will use devices of art to cover up the imposition so as to relieve it of obviously brutal features.

But the gulf between the mature or adult products and the experience and abilities of the young is so wide that the very situation forbids much active participation by pupils in the development of what is taught. Theirs is to do—and learn, as it was the part of the six hundred to do and die. Learning here means acquisition of what already is incorporated in books and in the heads of the elders. Moreover, that which is taught is thought of as essentially static. It is taught as a finished product, with little regard either to the ways in which it was originally built up or to changes that will surely occur in the future. It is to a large extent the cultural product of societies that assumed the future would be much like the past, and yet it is used as educational food in a society where change is the rule, not the exception.

If one attempts to formulate the philosophy of education implicit in the practices of the new education, we may, I think, discover certain common principles amid the variety of progressive schools now existing. To imposition from above is opposed expression and cultivation of individuality; to external discipline is opposed free activity; to learning from texts and teachers, learning through experience; to acquisition of isolated skills and techniques by drill, is opposed acquisition of them as means of attaining ends which make direct vital appeal; to preparation for a more or less remote future is opposed making the most of the opportunities of present life; to static aims and materials is opposed acquaintance with a changing world.

Now, all principles by themselves are abstract. They become concrete only in the consequences which result from their application. Just because the principles set forth are so fundamental and far-reaching, everything depends upon the interpretation given them as they are put into practice in the school and the home. It is at this point that the reference made earlier to *Either-Or* philosophies becomes peculiarly pertinent. The general philosophy of the new education may be sound, and yet the difference in abstract principles will not decide the way in which the moral and intellectual preference involved shall be worked out in practice. There is always the danger in a new movement that in rejecting the aims and methods of that which it would supplant, it may develop its principles negatively rather than positively and constructively. Then it takes its clew in practice from that which is rejected instead of from the constructive development of its own philosophy.

I take it that the fundamental unity of the newer philosophy is found in the idea that there is an intimate and necessary relation between the processes of actual experience and education. If this be true, then a positive and constructive development of its own basic idea depends upon having a correct idea of experience. Take, for example, the question of organized subject-matter. . . . The problem for progressive education is: What is the place and meaning of subject-matter and of organization *within* experience? How does subject-matter function? Is there anything inherent in experience which tends towards progressive organization of its contents? What results follow when the materials of experience are not progressively organized? A philosophy which proceeds on the basis of rejection, of sheer opposition, will neglect these questions. It will tend to suppose that because the old education was based on ready-made organization, therefore it suffices to reject the principle of organization *in toto,* instead of striving to discover what it means and how it is to be attained on the basis of experience. We might go through all the points of difference between the new and the old education and reach similar conclusions. When external control is rejected, the problem becomes that of finding the factors of control that are inherent within experience. When external authority is rejected, it does not follow that all authority should be rejected, but rather that there is need to search for a more effective source of authority. Because the older education imposed the knowledge, methods, and the rules of conduct of the mature person upon the young, it does not follow, except upon the basis of the extreme *Either-Or* philosophy, that the knowledge and skill of the mature person has no directive value for the experience of the immature. On the contrary, basing education upon personal experience may mean more multiplied and more intimate contacts between the mature and the immature than ever existed in the traditional school, and consequently more, rather than less, guidance by others. The problem, then, is: how these contacts can be established without violating the principle of learning through personal experience. The solution of this problem requires a well thought-out philosophy of the social factors that operate in the constitution of individual experience.

What is indicated in the foregoing remarks is that the general principles of the new education do not of themselves solve any of the problems of the actual or practical conduct and management of progressive schools. Rather, they set new problems which have to be worked out on the basis of a new philosophy of experience. The problems are not even recognized, to say nothing of being solved, when it is assumed that it suffices to reject the ideas and practices of the old education and then go to the opposite extreme. Yet I am sure that you will appreciate what is meant when I say that many of the newer schools tend to make little or nothing of organized subject-matter of study; to proceed as if any form of direction and guidance by adults were an invasion of individual freedom, and as if the idea that education should be concerned with the present and future meant that acquaintance with the past has little or no role to play in education. Without pressing these defects to the point of exaggeration, they at least illustrate what is meant by a theory and practice of education which proceeds negatively or by reaction against what has been current in education rather than by a positive and constructive development of purposes, methods, and subject-matter on the foundation of a theory of experience and its educational potentialities.

It is not too much to say that an educational philosophy which professes to be based on the idea of freedom may become as dogmatic as ever was the traditional education which is reacted against. For any theory and set of practices is dogmatic which is not based upon critical examination of its own underlying principles. Let us say that the new education emphasizes the freedom of the learner. Very well. A problem is now set. What does freedom mean and what are the conditions under which it is capable of realization? Let us say that the kind of external imposition which was so common in the traditional school limited rather than promoted the intellectual and moral development of the young. Again, very well. Recognition of this serious defect sets a problem. Just what is the role of the teacher and of books in promoting the educational development of the immature? Admit that traditional education employed as the subject-matter for study facts and ideas so bound up with the past as to give little help in dealing with the issues of the present and future. Very well. Now we have the problem of discovering the connection which actually exists *within* experience between the achievements of the past and the issues of the present. We have the problem of ascertaining how acquaintance with the past may be translated into a potent instrumentality for dealing effectively with the future. We may reject knowledge of the past as the *end* of education and thereby only emphasize its importance as a *means*. When we do that we have a problem that is new in the story of education: How shall the young become acquainted with the past in such a way that the acquaintance is a potent agent in appreciation of the living present? . . .

In short, the point I am making is that rejection of the philosophy and practice of traditional education sets a new type of difficult educational problem for those who believe in the new type of education. We shall operate blindly and in confusion until we recognize this fact; until we thoroughly appreciate that departure from the old solves no problems. What is said in the following pages is, accordingly, intended to indicate some of the main problems with which the newer education is confronted and to suggest the main lines along which their solution is to be sought. I assume that amid all uncertainties there is one permanent frame of reference: namely, the organic connection between education and personal experience; or, that the new philosophy of education is committed to some kind of empirical and experimental philosophy.

But experience and experiment are not self-explanatory ideas. Rather, their meaning is part of the problem to be explored. To know the meaning of empiricism we need to understand what experience is.

The belief that all genuine education comes about through experience does not mean that all experiences are genuinely or equally educative. Experience and education cannot be directly equated to each other. For some experiences are mis-educative. Any experience is mis-educative that has the effect of arresting or distorting the growth of further experience. An experience may be such as to engender callousness; it may produce lack of sensitivity and of responsiveness. Then the possibilities of having richer experience in the future are restricted. Again, a given experience may increase a person's automatic skill in a particular direction and yet tend to land him in a groove or rut; the effect again is to narrow the field of further experience. An experience may be immediately enjoyable and yet promote the formation of a slack and careless attitude; this attitude then operates to modify the quality of subsequent experiences so as to prevent a person from getting out of them what they have to give. Again, experiences may be so disconnected from one another that, while each is agreeable or even exciting in itself, they are not linked cumulatively to one another. Energy is then dissipated and a person becomes scatter-brained. Each experience may be lively, vivid, and "interesting," and yet their disconnectedness may artifically generate dispersive, disintegrated, centrifugal habits. The consequence of formation of such habits is inability to control future experiences. They are then taken, either by way of enjoyment or of discontent and revolt, just as they come. Under such circumstances, it is idle to talk of self-control.

Traditional education offers a plethora of examples of experiences of the kinds just mentioned. It is a great mistake to suppose, even tacitly, that the traditional schoolroom was not a place in which pupils had experiences. Yet this is tacitly assumed when progressive education as a plan of learning by experience is placed in sharp opposition to the old. The proper line of attack is that the experiences which were had, by pupils and teachers alike, were largely of a wrong kind. How many students, for example, were rendered callous to ideas, and how many lost the impetus to learn because of the way in which learning was experienced by them? How many acquired special skills by means of automatic drill so that their power of judgment and capacity to act intelligently in new situations was limited? How many came to associate the learning process with ennui and boredom? How many found what they did learn so foreign to the situations of life outside the school as to give them no power of control over the latter? How many came to associate books with dull drudgery, so that they were "conditioned" to all but flashy reading matter?

If I ask these questions, it is not for the sake of wholesale condemnation of the old education. It is for quite another purpose. It is to emphasize the fact, first, that young people in traditional schools do have experiences; and, secondly, that the trouble is not the absence of experiences, but their defective and wrong character—wrong and defective from the standpoint of connection with further experience. The positive side of this point is even more important in connection with progressive education. It is not enough to insist upon the necessity of experience, nor even of activity in experience. Everything depends upon the *quality* of the experience which is had. The quality of any experience has two aspects. There is an immediate aspect of agreeableness or disagreeableness, and there is its influence upon later experiences. The first is obvious and easy to judge. The *effect* of an experience is not borne on its face. It sets a problem to the educator. It is his business to arrange for the kind of experiences which, while they do not repel the student, but rather engage his activities are, nevertheless, more than immediately enjoyable since they promote having desirable future experiences. Just as no man lives or dies to himself, so no experience lives and dies to itself. Wholly independent of desire or intent, every experience lives on in further experiences. Hence the central problem of an education based upon experience is to select the kind of present experiences that live fruitfully and creatively in subsequent experiences.

Later, I shall discuss in more detail the principle of the continuity of experience or what may be called the experiential continuum. Here I wish simply to emphasize the importance of this principle for the philosophy of educative experience. A philosophy of education, like any theory, has to be stated in words, in symbols. But so far as it is more than verbal it is a plan for conducting education. Like any plan, it must be framed with reference to what is to be done and how it is to be done. The more definitely and sincerely it is held that education is a development within, by, and for experience, the more important it is that there shall be clear conceptions of what experience is. Unless experience is so conceived that the result is a plan for deciding upon subject-matter, upon methods of instruction and discipline, and upon material equipment and social organization of the school, it is wholly in the air. It is reduced to a form of words which may be emotionally stirring but for which any other set of words might equally well be substituted unless they indicate operations to be initiated and executed. Just because traditional education was a matter of routine in which the plans and programs were handed down from the past, it does not follow that progressive education is a matter of planless improvisation.

The traditional school could get along without any consistently developed philosophy of education. About all it required in that line was a set of abstract words like culture, discipline, our great cultural heritage, etc., actual guidance being derived not from them but from custom and established routines. Just because progressive schools cannot rely upon established traditions and institutional habits, they must either proceed more or less haphazardly or be directed by ideas which, when they are made articulate and coherent, form a philosophy of education. Revolt against the kind of organization characteristic of the traditional school constitutes a demand for a kind of organization based upon ideas. I think that only slight acquaintance with the history of education is needed to prove that educational reformers and innovators alone have felt the need for a philosophy of education. Those who adhered to the established system needed merely a few fine-sounding words to justify existing practices. The real work was done by habits which were so fixed as to be institutional. The lesson for progressive education is that it requires in an urgent degree, a degree more pressing than was incumbent upon former innovators, a philosophy of education based upon a philosophy of experience.

I remarked incidentally that the philosophy in question is, to paraphrase the saying of Lincoln about democracy, one of education of, by, and for experience. No one of these words, *of, by,* or *for,* names anything which is self-evident. Each of them is a challenge to discover and put into operation a principle of order and organization which follows from understanding what educative experience signifies.

It is, accordingly, a much more difficult task to work out the kinds of materials, of methods, and of social relationships that are appropriate to the new education than is the case with traditional education. I think many of the difficulties experienced in the conduct of progressive schools and many of the criticisms leveled against them arise from this source. The difficulties are aggravated and the criticisms are increased when it is supposed that the new education is somehow easier than the old. This belief is, I imagine, more or less current. Perhaps it illustrates again the *Either-Or* philosophy, springing from the idea that about all which is required is *not* to do what is done in traditional schools.

I admit gladly that the new education is *simpler* in principle than the old. It is in harmony with principles of growth, while there is very much which is artificial in the old selection and arrangement of subjects and methods, and artificiality always leads to unnecessary complexity. But the easy and the simple are not identical. To discover what is really simple and to act upon the discovery is an exceedingly difficult task. After the artificial and complex is once institutionally established and ingrained in custom and routine, it is easier to walk in the paths that have been beaten than it is, after taking a new point of view, to work out what is practically involved in the new point of view. The old Ptolemaic astronomical system was more complicated with its cycles and epicycles than the Copernican system. But until organization of actual astronomical phenomena on the ground of the latter principle had been effected the easiest course was to follow the line of least resistance provided by the old intellectual habit. So we come back to the idea that a coherent *theory* of experience, affording positive direction to selection and organization of appropriate educational methods and materials, is required by the attempt to give new direction to the work of the schools. The process is a slow and arduous one. It is a matter of growth, and there are many obstacles which tend to obstruct growth and to deflect it into wrong lines.

I shall have something to say later about organization. All that is needed, perhaps, at this point is to say that we must escape from the tendency to think of organization in terms of the *kind* of organization, whether of content (or subject-matter), or of methods and social relations, that mark traditional education. I think that a good deal of the current opposition to the idea of organization is due to the fact that it is so hard to get away from the picture of the studies of the old school. The moment "organization" is mentioned imagination goes almost automatically to the kind of organization that is familiar, and in revolting against that we are led to shrink from the very idea of any organization. On the other hand, educational reactionaries, who are now gathering force, use the absence of adequate intellectual and moral organization in the newer type of school as proof not only of the need of organization, but to identify any and every kind of organization with that instituted before the rise of experimental science. Failure to develop a conception of organization upon the empirical and experimental basis gives reactionaries a too easy victory. But the fact that the empirical sciences now offer the best type of intellectual organization which can be found in any field shows that there is no reason why we, who call ourselves empiricists, should be "push-overs" in the matter of order and organization.

(Rafferty, cont. from p. 5)

ahead of one's own, which emphasizes the duties of citizenship as well as its joys, and which condemns illegality and violence as ways to solve problems. Bad teachers say that morals are relative, that citizenship is all taking and no giving, and that violence is all right if you can't get your own way any other way.

Mind you, I've never known a teacher who came right out and said these things to children. But I've known too many of them who espoused and mouthed an educational philosophy that caused convictions like these to take root in the minds of their pupils as inevitably as the general amnesty that invariably follows the burning down of the university administration building nowadays.

How did all this get started?

It happened about three decades ago, when John Dewey's permissive pragmatism became the unofficial philosophy of the American educational establishment. Here's how it's affected the schools:

(1) *In regard to knowledge.* To Dewey, knowledge equals experience. There are no self-evident truths, no universals, no absolutes of any kind. Anything that satisfies a want is a "good." Otherwise the word has no meaning. Life is a stream of sensations to which the child must be taught to respond successfully, nothing more.

Understand now why so many of the kids live it up with raw sex and cooked pot?

(2) *In regard to the learning process.* Dewey taught that the child learns only what he lives. Education must therefore be an exercise in living. "Learning by doing" thus becomes one of the ritual responses in the litany of Progressive Education. The fundamentals of learning—the "Three R's"—are taught only as the child finds them necessary in helping him lead a "good" life.

Wonder any longer why the hippies stress the "back to nature" routine? And why so many of their protest placards are misspelled?

(3) *In regard to curriculum.* The Progressive Educationists term the curriculum the whole living experience of the child. So the school must interest itself in everything about the child and take the steps necessary to remedy any gaps in his experience that a foolish or shortsighted parent may refuse to fill up. The accumulation of knowledge for the mere sake of knowledge is not only unnecessary; it is probably actively harmful. Development of creativity is the important thing. The

child must feel completely unrepressed and free from inhibitions so that his natural creativity will blossom and flourish.

Help you figure out why some of our teen-agers go around looking like unmade beds and exuding an almost visible aura of unwashed disinhibition?

(4) *In regard to education's aims.* The two main goals of Progressive Education are to aid the child to live the life of the group and to enable him to "adjust" to a constantly changing environment. The child is constantly reminded that he is merely one member of the group and that his success is being measured by how well he is accepted by his companions.

Remind you of the S.D.S. zombies prior to their recent split, all salivating together on cue like Pavlov's dogs, all breathing the same obscenities, all mouthing the same party line, knowing no life as individuals, experiencing only what the group experiences?

Indeed the Progressive Educationists have much to answer for. Most dangerous when they are most dedicated, they war against your children in the firm belief that they are helping them. They treat parents as though they were retarded first-graders, glaciating all over them in a fine mixture of contemptuous kindness and smug superiority.

But isn't Progressive Education as dead as Moses? That's what you've been told, isn't it?

Judge for yourself. Visit your local school. Look around. Listen closely. Above all, ask questions. Questions like these:

Do the people running your school believe "life adjustment" is the main goal of the instructional program? If they do, this is Progressive Education.

Does your school place primary emphasis upon the happy, easy, comfortable acceptance of your child by his "peer group"? If it does, your school is "progressively" oriented.

Is subject matter in your school paid lip service but relegated to a back seat? Are things like "social studies" and "language arts" and "orientation" being taught instead of history and geography and English? If these things are being done, it doesn't much matter what they call it. What you've got is Progressivism.

Do your teachers and administrators tell you that report cards are old-fashioned? Do they refuse to assign more than token homework down in the grades because it is "meaningless drudgery"? Do they teach phonics only as an adjunct to the "look-say" method of reading that has wreaked such ruin on a whole generation of functional nonreaders? These are all manifestations and outcroppings of Progressive Education.

A big-city reporter, fellow Gael Terence O'Flaherty, recently invaded one of our teeming junior colleges, intent upon an intriguing experiment. He wanted to find out what the younger generation thought of that blood-stained old nut Adolf Hitler.

He came away muttering to himself. Here are some of the representative comments from the finely honed college minds of all races and both sexes:

"I think Hitler was great. He carried out his plans. He did what he said he was going to do."

"There are atrocities in every war."

"I don't have any feelings, really. I don't know much about him."

"It's not for me to say. He may have been off his rocker, but then again he may have had a good idea."

"You can't really judge. I mean, I'm not a person who can judge another person because I don't think anybody has a right to do that."

Exit for a breath of fresh air the enterprising Mr. O'Flaherty, disgustedly concluding, "Apparently the philosophy of the permissive society has not fallen on deaf ears."

But just what spawned the permissive society? The thirty-year-old mismatch between behavioristic psychology and John Dewey's progressive education, that's what. This charmingly prolific couple had some other offspring, too. Tolerance of immorality. Willingness to compromise with evil. Acceptance of treason. Sympathy for crime.

It's quite a family.

For almost three decades now, I've watched the high priests of progressivism innoculate children with the germs of relativism. And as the injection begins to take, certain symptoms invariably develop that have to be treated immediately.

Toxin: "Society shouldn't try to judge anyone. Every person is responsible only to himself."

Antitoxin: Society has to judge its dynamiters, or it will quickly cease to be a society. Every person is responsible to every other person, to say nothing of being responsible to God.

Toxin: "Who's to say what's good and what's bad? Is there any validity to these terms anymore?"

Antitoxin: Oh, for Heaven's sake, come off it. You could reduce any value system to absurdity by this kind of lame-brained questioning. Is there any validity to such terms as "honor," "virtue" or "decency," for example? Or even "life" and "death"? Of course the terms are valid. Otherwise we might as well abandon language altogether, and go back to monosyllabic grunts punctuated by blows from a stone club.

Toxin: "What's wrong with marijuana? Alcohol is even worse."

Antitoxin: You can't justify a new evil by comparing it favorably to an even older greater evil. This kind of logic went out with old Pharaoh, who probably justified his wickedness to the Children of Israel by claiming that the Assyrians treated them even worse. As for marijuana, one question only: "Who the devil needs it?" And if no one needs it and if it can do no good but only harm, why legalize it?

The Progressive Educationists over the years have labored diligently to produce the permissive society. They have succeeded beyond their wildest expectations.

So now at last you have it: a culture where Hitler is acceptable, where Bonnie and Clyde are their own judges, and where everybody is as good as everybody else because there really isn't any reality to the word "good" anyhow.

How do you like it?

The deep thinkers of my profession, who regard me with the same lasting love and heartfelt esteem that they customarily reserve for Admiral Rickover, have been needling me in their learned journals because I keep throwing rocks at Progressive Education.

"Why doesn't Rafferty wake up and shut up?" one of them inquired testily the other day. "Progressive Education has been dead for years. He's just exhuming it for use as a political punching bag."

All right. Why not try a little experiment? Let's try it first on the sixth-graders, because in most states they represent the end product of elementary school education.

Get sixth-grader Johnny in off the Little League diamond for a few minutes.

Stand him in front of you, with his soiled sneakers and torn T-shirt. Ask him to tell you something about Charlemagne. Get him to expound on Hannibal. Ask him what century Julius Caesar lived in, who knocked him off, and why.

Ask him who crossed the Delaware and what he did when he reached the other side. See if he ever heard of James Madison or Theodore Roosevelt or Henry Clay. You're going to be mighty, mighty interested in Johnny's answers.

Then get sixth-grader Mary in on the carpet. See what she can tell you about Evangeline or Silas Marner or the Lady of the Lake. Ask her to quote just the opening lines of "Paul Revere's Ride" or "The Charge of the Light Brigade" or "Old Ironsides." Get her to tell you something—anything—about "The Village Blacksmith" or "The Wreck of the Hesperus" or "Hiawatha." She'll probably think you've gone right off your rocker.

But don't stop here. Ask the same questions of the first eighth-grader you come across. See for yourself what "life adjustment" junior high schools are teaching.

Last of all, ask an average graduating senior in high school—not the college prep youngster but the average one. When you recover from the shock, don't blame the kids. Or their teachers. Blame yourself for permitting this sort of quasi-illiteracy to flourish unchecked in some of your own tax-supported schools.

And if you think Longfellow and Tennyson are old hat, try them on Browning or Dickens or even Homer—names that have stood the test of time and become part of the cultural heritage of mankind.

I've been looking through a moderately old textbook. It was written back in 1886 and adopted by my home state as a grade school reader. Here are some of its contributors, the men who wrote the material that the boys and girls were reading down in the grades in the days of Grover Cleveland: William Cullen Bryant, Lord Byron, William Shakespeare, Nathaniel Hawthorne, Sir Walter Scott, Edgar Allan Poe, Bret Harte, and a host of others.

These names have held up pretty well during the intervening decades, haven't they? The consensus among literary authorities would be that these writers have contributed significantly to literature. Great-Grandpa and Great-Grandma weren't so far wrong, were they, when they insisted through their state-adopted textbooks that their children be exposed to writing of such lasting value?

If you really want a shock, try these names on sixth graders today. Or ninth-graders. Or even the great majority of twelfth-graders.

But apparently Grandma and Grandpa learned to read this sort of beautiful, valuable, interesting material, didn't they? And don't let anybody tell you that Grandma and Grandpa weren't in school eighty years ago. They may have missed high school—a lot of them—but they were certainly in the grade schools.

The reading consultants and the curriculum experts and the education professors will tell you that today's children aren't "mature" enough to grasp such "advanced" material.

Well, why aren't they? Our grandparents were.

Whose fault is it that they're not? Are our children more stupid than the children of eighty years ago?

Or are they just not being asked to tackle tough material because of a philosophy that has decided unilaterally that a child's mind exists not to be stretched but to be adjusted? A philosophy that preaches that the easy, comfortable, happy acceptance of the child by his "peer group" is the be-all and the end-all of education?

Johnny daydreams and refuses to socialize with the group. So did Shelley and Beethoven and Michelangelo, and even Winston Churchill. But the day of the lone thinker is past, it seems. Today, Johnny must learn to practice togetherness and in-groupness and democratic socializing with his peers even if it means that Miss Smith must construct a class sociogram and call in the district psychologist.

Ignorance, inaccuracy, unenlightenment—all the immemorial enemies and targets of education must take a back seat now to the new and supreme offense: unpopularity. But the purpose of a school is not to make pupils popular or well-adjusted or universally approved. It is to make them learned. It is to teach them to use the tools that the race, over the centuries, has found to be indispensable in the pursuit of truth.

It is said by some that subject matter is secondary to the main goal of education, which is acceptance and adjustment and appreciation. But I say that the schools exist to teach organized, systematic, disciplined subject matter to the children. For this they were created; for this they are maintained by the millions of Americans who support and populate them. I say further that the schools are the only societal agencies specifically designed to perform this function. And I say finally that if the schools do not so teach subject matter, the children are never going to learn it.

"Life adjustment" is taught by the home, the church, and by society itself in a hundred forms. Only the school can forge for the child the wonderful, shining, sharp-edged sword of subject matter.

The Progressive Educationists have long held the only eternal verity to be that of constant change and flux. All values are relative. All truths are mutable. All standards are variable.

So the only thing worth teaching to youngsters is the ability to react to an ever-shifting environmental kaleidoscope. It is the philosophy of the man on the roller coaster.

It's a way of thinking and of teaching with which American democracy cannot coexist. Within it lie the seeds of the rumbles and the riots, the frantic search for "kicks," the newsstand filth and the cinematic garbage that mark the last descent into the cloying, clinging sickness of ultimate decay by every civilization that has ever permitted this infection to overcome its resistence.

Despite all this, my more turgid readers still take me to task for beating the dead horse of Progressive Education. The current party line on this, incidentally, is that (a) Progressive Education was always far more sinned against than sinning, poor thing, and (b) it's been completely extinct for years anyhow, so forget it.

For the devotees of party-line subsection (b) to mull over, I append the following recent statement by one of teacher Victor Harke's pupils in Hollywood, Florida, as reported by the faithful press:

> The first day of school was wild. Mr. Harke didn't say a thing. The lights went out and pictures started floating all over the room. On one wall was a movie about child molestation. On the same wall, superimposed on half of the first

movie, was a travelog on Switzerland.

On another wall, slides flashed pictures of famous paintings. Three tape recorders were going at once: one a Bible reading, another with music, and another with weird electronic sounds. To top it off, when the bell rang, Mr. Harke got up and left without saying a word.

Queried by a presumably ear-plugged reporter with equally presumable dark glasses, Mr. Harke defended his own private version of Bedlam as follows:

"I try to make my classroom a part of the outside world, to get ideas of what the kids are interested in. This year it's psychedelics."

And next year perhaps it will be Molotov cocktails, or homosexuality, or maybe Murder, Incorporated. The possibilities, in fact, are fascinating and well-nigh limitless. Children do swing through quite a kaleidoscopic spectrum of interests, don't they? It would certainly be interesting to see Mr. Harke's classroom if he keeps it faithful to the good old outside world, which more and more these days resembles a cross between a hippie pad and a shooting gallery.

The news story concluded with a glowing report on how much Harke's students "like his unorthodox methods." Quoth one breathless graduate: "When we complained about the dull classroom, he told us to go ahead and do what we liked. In his class we even made our own lesson plans."

It's hard to pinpoint the first educational quack. I suppose the line of frauds goes back well beyond Jean-Jacques Rousseau, but that heartless mountebank will serve as a starting point.

Jean-Jacques, with an irresponsibility characteristic of his entire philosophy, fathered several bastards and thoughtfully shunted them into foundling asylums for his more humdrum fellow-citizens to support. At various times he practiced voyeurism, exhibitionism, and masturbation with equally feverish enthusiasm, preserving himself from any legal unpleasantness by pleading softening of the brain. He fought viciously if verbally with every normal intellect in Europe, and died insane.

Rousseau spawned a frenetic theory of education that after two centuries of spasmodic laboring brought forth a byblow in the form of John Dewey's Progressive Education. According to the confused Frenchman, education was running, jumping, shouting, doing as one pleased. The first impulses of nature are always right. Keep the child's mind idle as long as you can. And suchlike rot.

This sort of piffle is as old as the human race. The child is a Noble Savage, needing only to be let alone in order to insure his intellectual salvation. Don't inhibit him. Never cross him, lest he develop horrid neuroses later on in life. The cave children of the Stone Age grew up happier, better-adjusted, and less frustrated than do ours today, simply because they were in a blissful state of nature. So just leave the kids alone. They'll educate themselves.

Twaddle. Schooling is not a natural process at all. It's highly artificial. No boy in his right mind ever wanted to study multiplication tables and historical dates when he could be out hunting rabbits or climbing trees. In the days when hunting and climbing contributed to the survival of *homo sapiens,* there was some sense in letting the kids do what comes naturally, but when man's future began to hang upon the systematic mastery of orderly subject matter, the primordial, happy-go-lucky, laissez-faire kind of learning had to go. Today it's part and parcel of whatever lost innocence we may ever have possessed. Long gone. A quaint anachronism.

Except in Hollywood, Florida, apparently, and a few thousand other places.

The story of mankind is the rise of specialization with its highly artificial concomitants. Over the years, natural medicine gave way to anesthesia, antiseptics, and antibiotics. In the field of transportation, hiking sturdily along dim forest trails took a back seat to freeways, air routes, and eventually lunar orbits. Old Stentor himself, brass lungs and all, couldn't compete today with radio and the telephone.

So it is with education. When writing was invented, "natural" education went down the drain of history. From then on, children were destined to learn artificially, just as men around the world were increasingly to live artificially. This is civilization—the name of the game. When Rousseau and his cave-dwelling modern imitators cry out against artificiality, they are in fact down on all fours, mopping and mowing, hurling twigs and dirt at civilization. For all civilization is artificial.

I don't doubt for one moment that Mr. Harke's class is very, very popular with the kids. So is a discotheque. So is a penny arcade. So is a three-ring circus. So was Rousseau's "back to Nature" approach to education.

What I *do* doubt is that the youngsters are becoming educated in his class, or indeed in any other "class" where the pupils write their own lesson plans, horse around with colored lights, and spend their time on niggling trivia when all the while the whole vast ocean of human learning lies around them for the dipping into.

A school is not intended and was never created to reflect like a dime-store mirror all the jimcrackery and tawdry fustian of our present-day society. It's intended rather to be a beacon, generating its own laserlike beam and constantly urging its captive audience on to something finer and better than the mess we see around us every day. We don't need schools to show us what's going on. We need schools to show us what *ought* to be going on.

The purpose of education is not to sensationalize, not to entertain children, not to dazzle them with colored lights, not to deafen them with orgiastic sounds, nor yet to titillate them with discreet pornography. The purpose of education is to make pupils learned. Period.

POSTSCRIPT

WHAT IS THE PRIMARY GOAL OF SCHOOLING?

Intellectual training vs. social-emotional-mental growth—the argument between Dewey and Rafferty reflects an historical debate which flows from the ideas of Plato and Aristotle and which continues today. The positions put forth by Paul Goodman and Clifton Fadiman in the next Issue, "How Should the Curriculum Be Organized?" reflect this continuing debate, as do some of the other selections in this volume. Psychologists, sociologists, curriculum and instruction specialists, and popular critics have joined philosophers in commenting on this central concern.

Followers of Dewey contend that the training of the mental powers cannot be isolated from other factors of development and, indeed, can be enhanced by attention to the concrete social situations in which learning occurs. Critics of Dewey worry that the expansion of effort into the social and emotional realm only detracts from the intellectual mission which is schooling's unique province.

Was the progressive education movement ruinous, or did it lay the foundation for the education of the future? A reasonably even-handed appraisal can be found in Lawrence Cremin's *The Transformation of the School* (1961). The free school movement of the 1960s, at least partly derived from progressivism, is analyzed in Allen Graubard's *Free the Children* (1973) and Jonathan Kozol's *Free Schools* (1972). A good review of more recent manifestations of the debate can be found in Neil Postman and Charles Weingartner's "A Careful Guide to the School Squabble" *(Psychology Today,* October 1973).

Other sources which widen the spectrum of views regarding primary goals for education include *The Educated Man,* edited by Paul Nash, Andreas M. Kazamias, and Henry J. Perkinson; R.S. Peters' "Must an Educator Have an Aim?" (*Authority, Responsibility, & Education,* [1959]); Jerome S. Bruner's "After John Dewey, What?" in his *On Knowing* (1962); Paulo Freire's *Pedagogy of the Oppressed* (1970); Arthur Pearl's *The Atrocity of Education* (1972); and Stephen K. Bailey's *The Purposes of Education* (1976).

Questions which must be addressed include: Can the "either/or" polarities of this basic argument be overcome? Is the articulation of over-arching general aims essential to the charting of a productive and worthwhile educational experience? How can the classroom teacher relate to general philosophical aims?

ISSUE 2

HOW SHOULD THE CURRICULUM BE ORGANIZED?

The curricular aspects of the fundamental controversy over the purpose of schooling have occupied center stage since the mid-1960s. Two ideological positions have dominated the discussion of what should be taught: the free school/open education movement, and the back-to-basics movement.

Paul Goodman, John Holt, Edgar Friedenberg, Herbert Kohl, and Charles Silberman, among others, have portrayed the typical public school as a mindless, indifferent social institution dedicated to producing fear, docility, and conformity. As a result, students are either alienated from a meaningless curriculum or learn to play the school "game" and achieve a phony success.

Taking cues from the ideas of John Dewey and A.S. Neill, these "radical reformers" gave rise to a flurry of alternatives to regular schooling in the late 1960s, some of which persist today. Among these alternatives were free schools following the Summerhill model of Neill; urban storefront schools which attempted to develop a true sense of "community"; schools without walls following Philadelphia's Parkway Program model; "commonwealth" schools in which students and teachers shared responsibility; and various "humanistic education" projects emphasizing student self-concept and choice-making ability.

The curricular emphasis in most of these alternatives, and in some of the "open classroom" variations within public schools, has been on the actual needs and desires of the learners. The utilitarian tradition descended from Benjamin Franklin, Horace Mann, and Herbert Spencer, coupled with Dewey's theory of active experience and Neill's insistence on free and natural development, undergird this curricular position. In order to make such an approach possible, it was felt that the usual structures and strictures of school organization must be abandoned. The free school ideology rejects the factory model of schooling, the rigidly set curriculum, the social engineering functioning of schools, and the formalism which such schools demand.

The drift toward informalism is precisely the point of attack by the other dominant ideology, currently symbolized by the "back-to-basics" movement. Taking their philosophical cues from Plato's belief that certain subject matters have universal qualities which prompt intellectual discipline and development toward wisdom, Clifton Fadiman, Jacques Barzun, Robert M. Hutchins, Arthur Bestor, James Koerner, and others make a case for a curriculum of basic studies. Their argument against incidental learning and for structured and standardized schooling is fueled by widespread parental concern about the teaching of fundamentals and the establishment of discipline and by ideological groups such as the Council for Basic Education. Barzun summarizes the viewpoint succinctly: "Nonsense is at the heart of those proposals that would replace definable subject matters with vague activities copied from 'life' or with courses organized around 'problems' or 'attitudes.' "

In the following selection, Paul Goodman reviews the progressive education movement and sees in it the seeds of a reformed approach to the school curriculum which would maximize flexibility and practicality. In turn, Clifton Fadiman establishes criteria for building a hierarchy of subject matters which assures that the learner will not be lost in the seas of uncertainty.

Paul Goodman

FLEXIBILITY AND INDIVIDUALIZATION

The program of progressive education always anticipates the crucial social problems that everybody will be concerned with a generation later, when it is too late for the paradisal solutions of progressive educators. This is in the nature of the case. Essentially, progressive education is nothing but the attempt to naturalize, to humanize, each new social and technical development that is making traditional education irrelevant. It is not a reform of education, but a reconstruction in terms of the new era. If society would *once* adopt this reconstruction, we could at last catch up with ourselves and grow naturally into the future. But equally in the nature of the case, society rejects, half-accepts, bastardizes the necessary changes; and so we are continually stuck with "unfinished revolutions," as I called them in *Growing Up Absurd.* Then occur the vast social problems that *could* have been avoided—that indeed the older progressive education had specifically addressed—but it is too late. And progressive educators stoically ask, What is the case *now?*

During the current incredible expansion of increasingly unnatural schooling, and increasing alienation of the young, it is useful to trace the course of progressive education in this century, from John Dewey to the American version of A.S. Neill.

The recent attacks on Deweyan progressive education, by the Rickovers and Max Raffertys, have really been outrageous—one gets impatient. Historically, the intent of Dewey was exactly the opposite of what the critics say. Progressive education appeared in this country in the intellectual, moral, and social crisis of the development of big centralized industrialism after the Civil War. It was the first thoroughgoing modern analysis of the crucial modern problem of every advanced country in the world: how to cope with high industrialism and scientific technology which are strange to people; how to restore competence to people who are becoming ignorant; how to live in the rapidly growing cities so that they will not be mere urban sprawl; how to have a free society in mass conditions; how to make the high industrial system good for something, rather than a machine running for its own sake.

Continued on p. 24

Clifton Fadiman

THE CASE FOR BASIC EDUCATION

The present educational controversy, like all crucial controversies, has its roots in philosophy. One's attitude toward the proposals advanced in this book depends on one's conception of man. It depends on one's view of his nature, his powers, and his reason for existence.

If, consciously or unconsciously, one takes the position that his nature is essentially animal; that his powers lie largely in the area of social and biological adaptation; and that his reason for existence is either unknowable or (should he advance one) a form of self-delusion—then the case for basic education, and consequently for education itself, falls to the ground. By the same token the case for physical, social, and vocational training becomes irrefutable.

On the other hand, if one takes the position that man's nature is both animal *and* rational; that his powers lie not only in the area of adaptation but also in that of creation; and that his reason for existence is somehow bound up with the fullest possible evolution of his mental and spiritual capacities—then the case for basic education, and consequently for education itself, is established; and further discussion becomes a matter, however interesting and important, of detail.

A crisis period is not necessarily marked by disaster or violence or even revolutionary change. It is marked by the absence of any general, tacit adherence to an agreed-upon system of values. It is in such a crisis period that we live. Of the two positions briefly outlined above, a minority adheres to the first. Another minority adheres to the second. But most of us waver between the two or have never reflected on either. Our present educational system quite properly mirrors this uncertainty of the majority. It mirrors our own mental chaos. There is nothing else it *can* do, for ours is a democratic society, and all our institutions are representative.

Now neither of the positions is logically demonstrable, though some have tried to bend them to logic, as well as to propaganda. They are faiths. The scholars whose essays comprise this book deal explicitly with questions of curriculum. Implicitly, however, they are proclaiming the faith by which they

Continued on p. 30

Reprinted by permission from James D. Koerner (ed.), *The Case for Basic Education* (1959), sponsored by the Council for Basic Education (Washington, D.C.).

(Goodman, cont. from p. 22)

That is, progressive education was the correct solution of a real problem that Rickover is concerned with, the backwardness of people in a scientific world. To put it more accurately, if progressive education had been generally adopted, we should not be so estranged and ignorant today.

The thought of John Dewey was part of a similar tendency in architecture, the functionalism of Louis Sullivan and Frank Lloyd Wright, that was trying to invent an urbanism and an esthetic suited to machine-production and yet human; and it went with the engineering orientation of the economic and moral theory of Veblen. These thinkers wanted to train, teach—perhaps accustom is the best word—the new generation to the actualities of industrial and technical life, working practically with the machinery, learning by doing. People could then be at home in the modern world, and possibly become free.

At-homeness had also a political aspect. Dewey was distressed by both the robber-baron plutocracy and the bossed mass-democracy; and he was too wise to espouse Veblen's technocracy, engineer's values. Dewey put a good deal of faith in industrial democracy, overestimating the labor movement—he did not foresee the bureaucratization of the unions. As a pragmatist he probably expected that the skilled would become initiators in management and production; he did not foresee that labor demands would diminish to wages and working conditions.

But the school, he felt, could combine all the necessary elements: practical learning of science and technology, democratic community, spontaneous feeling liberated by artistic appreciation, freedom to fantasize, and animal expression freed from the parson's morality and the schoolmaster's ruler. This constituted the whole of Deweyan progressive education. There would be spontaneous interest (including animal impulse), harmonized by art-working; this spontaneity would be controlled by the hard pragmatism of doing and making the doing acually work; and thus the young democratic community would learn the modern world and also have the will to change it. Progressive education was a theory of continual scientific experiment and orderly, nonviolent social revolution.

As was inevitable, this theory was entirely perverted when it began to be applied, either in private schools or in the public system. The conservatives and the businessmen cried out, and the program was toned down. The practical training and community democracy, whose purpose was to live scientifically and change society, was changed into "socially useful" subjects and a psychology of "belonging." In our schools, driver-training survives as the type of the "useful." (By now, I suspect, Dewey would have been urging us to curtail the number of cars.) Social-dancing was the type of the "belonging." The Americans had no intention of broadening the scientific base and taking technological expertness and control out of the hands of the top managers and their technicians. And democratic community became astoundingly interpreted as conformity, instead of being the matrix of social experiment and political change.

Curiously, just in the past few years, simultaneous with the attack on "Dewey," his ideas have been getting most prestigious official endorsement (though they are not attributed to Dewey). In the great post-Sputnik cry to increase the scientific and technical pool, the critics of "Dewey" call for strict lessons and draconian grading and weeding-out (plus bribes), to find the elite group. (Dr. Conant says that the "academically talented" are 15% and these, selected by national tests, will be at home *for* us in the modern technical world as its creative spirits.) However, there is an exactly contrary theory, propounded by the teachers of science, e.g. the consensus of the Woods Hole Conference of the National Science Foundation, reported in Professor Bruner's *The Processes of Education.* This theory counsels practical learning by doing, entirely rejects competition and grading, and encourages fantasy and guesswork. There is no point, it claims, in learning the "answers," for very soon there will be different answers. Rather, what must be taught are the underlying ideas of scientific thought, continuous with the substance of the youngster's feelings and experience. In short, the theory is Deweyan progressive education.

To be sure, Professor Bruner and his associates do not go on to espouse democratic community. But I am afraid they will eventually find that also this is essential, for it is impossible to do creative work of any kind when the goals are pre-determined by outsiders and cannot be criticized and altered by the minds that have to do the work, even if they are youngsters. (Dewey's principle is, simply, that good teaching is that which leads the student to want to learn something more.)

The compromise of the National Science Foundation on this point is rather comical. "Physical laws are not asserted; they are, it is hoped, discovered by the student"; "there is a desire to allow each student to experience some of the excitement that scientific pursuits afford"—I am quoting from the NSF's *Science Course Improvement Projects.* That is, the student is to make a leap of discovery to—what is already known, in a course precharted by the Ph.D.'s at M.I.T. Far from being elating, such a process must be profoundly disappointing; my guess is that the "discovery" will be greeted not by a cheer but by a razz. The excitement of discovery is reduced to the animation of puzzle-solving. I doubt that puzzle-solving is what creative thought is about, though it is certainly what many Ph.D.'s are about.

Authentic progressive education, meantime, has moved into new territory altogether, how to cope with the over-centralized organization and Organization Men of our society, including the top-down direction of science by the National Science Foundation. The new progressive theory is "Summerhill."

The American Summerhill movement is modeling itself on A.S. Neill's school in England, but with significant deviations—so that Neill does not want his name associated with some of the offshoots.

Like Dewey, Neill stressed free animal expression, learning by doing, and *very* democratic community processes (one person one vote, enfranchising small children!). But he also asserted a principle that to Dewey did not seem important, the freedom to choose to go to class or stay away altogether. A child at Summerhill can just hang around; he'll go to class when he damned well feels like it—and some children, coming from compulsory schools, don't damned well feel like it for eight or nine months. But after a while, as the curiosity in the soul revives—and since their friends go—they give it a try.

It is no accident, as I am trying to show in this book, that it is just *this* departure in progressive education that is catching on in America, whereas most of the surviving Deweyan schools are little better than the good suburban schools that imitated them. The advance-guard problem is that the compulsory school system, like the whole of our economy, politics, and standard of living, has become a lockstep. It is no longer designed for the maximum growth and future practical utility of the children into a changing world, but is inept social engineering for extrinsic goals, pitifully short-range. Even when it is benevolent, it is in the bureaucratic death-grip of a uniformity of conception, from the universities down, that cannot possibly suit the multitude of dispositions and conditions. Yet 100% of the children are supposed to remain for at least 12 years in one kind of box; and of course those who attend private Deweyan schools are being aimed for 4 to 8 years more. Thus, if we are going to experiment with real universal education that educates, we have to start by getting rid of compulsory schooling altogether.

One American variant of Summerhill has developed in a couple of years in an unforeseen direction. Like Summerhill this school is not urban, but, unlike Summerhill, it is not residential. Many of the children come from a nearby colony of artists, some of them of international fame. The artist parents, and other parents, come into the school as part-time teachers, of music, painting, building, dancing.

Being strong-minded, they, and the regular teachers, soon fell out with the headmaster, the founder, who had been a Summerhill teacher; they stripped him of important prerogatives and he resigned. Inevitably other parents had to join in the discussions and decisions, on real and difficult issues. The result seems to have been the formation of a peculiar kind of extended family, unified by educating the children, and incorporating a few professional teachers. But meantime, imitated from Neill, there is the democratic council, in which the children have a very loud voice and an equal vote, and this gives them an institutional means to communicate with, and get back at, their parents. It is stormy and factional. Some parents have pulled out and teachers have quit. Yet, inadvertently, there is developing a brilliant solution to crucial problems of American life: how can children grow up in live contact with many adults; how can those who do the work run the show; how to transcend a rigid professionalism that is wasteful of human resources. . . .

The future—if we survive and have a future, which is touch and go—will certainly be more leisurely. If that leisure is not to be completely inane and piggishly affluent, there must be a community and civic culture. There must be more employment in human services and less in the production of hardware gadgets; more citizenly initiative and less regimentation; and in many spheres, decentralization of control and administration. For these purposes, the top-down dictated national plans and educational methods that are now the fad are quite irrelevant. And on the contrary, it is precisely the society of free choice, lively engagement, and social action of Summerhill and American Summerhill that are relevant and practical.

Thus, just as with Dewey, the new advance of progressive education is a good index of what the real situation is. And no doubt society will again seek to abuse this program which it needs but is afraid of. . . .

By and large primary schooling is, and

should be, mainly baby-sitting. It has the great mission of democratic socialization—it certainly must not be segregated by race and income; apart from this, it should be happy, interesting, not damaging. The noise about stepping-up the primary curriculum is quite uncalled for; I have seen no convincing evidence—not by progressive educators either—that early schooling makes much academic difference in the long run. But in the secondary schools, after puberty, the tone of the babysitting must necessarily turn to regimentation and policing, and it is at peril that we require schooling; it fits some, it hurts others. A recent study by Edgar Friedenberg concludes that spirit-breaking is the *principal* function of typical lower middle-class schools. . . .

At present, in most states, for 10 to 13 years every young person is obliged to sit the better part of his day in a room almost always too crowded, facing front, doing lessons predetermined by a distant administration at the state capital and that have no relation to his own intellectual, social, or animal interests, and not much relation even to his economic interests. The overcrowding precludes individuality or spontaneity, reduces the young to ciphers, and the teacher to a martinet. If a youth tries to follow his own bent, he is interrupted and even jailed. If he does not perform, he is humiliated and threatened, but he is *not allowed to fail and get out*. . . .

If our present high schools, junior colleges, and colleges reflected the desire, freedom, and future of opportunity of the young, there would be no grading, no testing except as a teaching method, and no blackboard jungles. In fact, we are getting lockstep scheduling and grading to the point of torture. The senior year of high school is sacrificed to batteries of national tests, and policemen are going to stand in the corridors. Even an elite school such as Bronx Science—singled out by Dr. Conant as the best school in the country—is run as if for delinquents, with corridor passes and a ban on leaving the building. The conclusion is inevitable: The scholastically bright are not following their aspirations but are being pressured and bribed; the majority—those who are bright but not scholastic, and those who are not especially bright but have other kinds of vitality—are being subdued. . . .

In my opinion, the public buys this unexamined "education" because of the following contradiction: The Americans are guilty because these youth *are* useless in the present set-up, so they spend money on them (though they get oddly stingy at crucial moments); on the other hand, they insist that the youth work hard at something "useful"—namely useless training. One can't just let them play ball; they must compete and suffer.

I agree that we ought to spend more public money on education. And where jobs exist and there is need for technical training, the corporations ought to spend more money on apprenticeships. We are an affluent society and can afford it. And the conditions of modern life are far too complicated for independent young spirits to get going on their own. They need some preparation, though probably not as much as is supposed; but more important, they need various institutional frameworks in which they can try out and learn the ropes.

Nevertheless, I would not give a penny more to the present school administrators. The situation is this: to make the present school set-up even *tolerable,* not positively damaging—e.g. to cut the elementary class size to 20 or to provide colleges enough to diminish the frantic competition for places—will require at least *doubling* the present school budgets. I submit that this kind of money should be spent in other ways.

What, then, ought the education of these youth to be? We are back to our fundamental question: what are the alternatives?

Fundamentally, there is no right education except growing up into a worthwhile world. Indeed, our excessive concern with problems of education at present simply means that the grown-ups do not have such a world. The poor youth of America will *not* become equal by rising through the middle class, going to middle-class schools. By plain social justice, the Negroes and other minorities have the right to, and must get, equal opportunity for schooling with the rest, but the exaggerated expectation from the schooling is a chimera—and, I fear, will be shockingly disappointing. But also the middle-class youth will not escape their increasing exploitation and *anomie* in such schools. A decent education aims at, prepares for, a more worthwhile future, with a different community spirit, different occupations, and more real utility than attaining status and salary.

We are suffering from a bad style, perhaps a wrong religion. Although it is pretty certain, as I have said, that the automated future will see less employment in the manufacture of hardware and more employment in service occupations, as well as more leisure, yet astoundingly the mass-production and cash-accounting attitude toward the hardware is carried over unchanged into the thinking about the services and leisure! The lockstep regimentation and the petty-bourgeois credits and competitive grading in the schooling are typical of all the rest. (For a charming, and grim study of the spread of "business methods" to schooling, from 1900 to 1930, let me refer the reader to Callahan's *The Cult of Efficiency in American Education.*)

My bias is that we should maximize automation as quickly as possible, *where it is relevant*—taking care to cushion job dislocation and to provide adequate social insurance. But the spirit and method of automation, logistics, chain of command, and clerical work are *entirely irrelevant* to humane services, community service, communications, community culture, high culture, citizenly initiative, education, and recreation. To give a rather special but not trivial example of what I mean, TV sets should be maximum-mass-produced with maximum automation, in a good standard model, as cheaply as possible; but TV programming should, except for a few national services, be as much decentralized, tailor-made, and reliant on popular and free-artist initiative as possible.

The dangers of the highly technological and automated future are obvious: We might become a brain-washed society of idle and frivolous consumers. We might continue in a rat race of highly competitive, unnecessary busy-work with a meaninglessly expanding Gross National Product. In either case, there might still be an out-cast group that must be suppressed. To countervail these dangers and make active, competent, and initiating citizens who can produce a community culture and a noble recreation, we need a very different education than the schooling that we have been getting.

Large parts of it must be directly useful, rather than useless and merely aiming at status. Here we think of the spending in the public sector, advocated by Myrdal, Keyserling, Galbraith, and many others. E.g. the money spent on town improvement, community service, or rural rehabilitation can also provide educational occasions. (When these economists invariably list schooling as high—and often first—in the list of public expenditures, they fail to realize that such expense is probably wasted and perhaps even further dislocates the economy. I would say the same about Galbraith's pitch for new highways.)

On the whole, the education must be voluntary rather than compulsory, for no growth to freedom occurs except by intrinsic motivation. Therefore the educational opportunities must be various and variously administered. We must diminish rather than expand the present monolithic school system. I would suggest that, on the model of the GI-Bill, we experiment, giving the school money directly to the high-school age adolescents, for any plausible self-chosen educational proposals, such as purposeful travel or individual enterprise. This would also, of course, lead to the proliferation of experimental schools.

Unlike the present inflexible lockstep, our educational policy must allow for periodic quitting and easy return to the scholastic ladder, so that the young have time to find themselves and to study when they are themselves ready. This is Eric Erickson's valuable notion of the need for *moratoria* in the life-career; and the anthropological insistence of Stanley Diamond and others, that our society neglects the crises of growing up.

Education must foster independent thought and expression, rather than conformity. For example, to countervail the mass communications, we have an imperative social need, indeed a constitutional need to protect liberty, for many thousands of independent media: local newspapers, independent broadcasters, little magazines, little theaters; and these, under professional guidance, could provide remarkable occasions for the employment and education of adolescents of brains and talent. (I have elsewhere proposed a graduated tax on the audience-size of mass-media, to provide a Fund to underwrite such new independent ventures for a period, so that they can try to make their way.)

Finally, contemporary education must inevitably be heavily weighted toward the sciences. But this does not necessarily call for school-training of a relatively few technicians, or rare creative scientists (if such can indeed be trained in schools). Our aim must be to make a great number of citizens at home in a technological environment, not alienated from the machines we use, not ignorant as consumers, who can somewhat judge governmental scientific policy, who can enjoy the humanistic beauty of the sciences, and, above all, who can understand the morality of a scientific way of life. . . .

(Fadiman, cont. from p. 23)
live. Furthermore they are proclaiming that this is the faith by which Western civilization lives.

Because all faiths are attackable, everything they say can be attacked. Indeed everything they say may be wrong. But the attack can only be sustained by the proclamation of an opposing faith. And if they are wrong, they are wrong only in the sense that no faith can be "proved" right.

Thus the *Metaphysics* of Aristotle opens with the well-known statement: "All men by nature desire to know." This is not a statement of fact in the sense that "All men are born with lungs" is a statement of fact. It is not statistically checkable. It is not a self-evident truth. Cursory observation of many men seems to give it the lie. Depending on whether we prefer the language of logic or the language of emotion we may call it either an assumption or a declaration of faith. If the assumption is denied, or the declaration countered by an opposing declaration, this book, as well as education itself, becomes an irrelevancy. But in that case the cultural fruits of civilization also become an irrelevancy, because they would appear to flow, not from some blind process of unending adaptation, but from Aristotle's proposition. Any doubt cast on that proposition also casts doubt on the permanent value of culture.

It may be that the proposition *is* untenable. Perhaps all men do not by nature desire to know. We can then fall back on a second line of defense. We can say that at least men have acted *as if* they did so desire. Aristotle's dictum may be an illusion. But it looks like a creative illusion.

He has another dictum. He tells us that man is a social animal. Put the two statements together. Were man not a social animal but an anarchic animal, his desire to know would have both its origin and its terminus located in himself. But, as he is a social and not an anarchic animal, he socializes and finally systematizes his desire to know. This socialization and systematization are what we mean by education. The main, though not the only, instrument of education is an odd invention, only three thousand years old, called the school. The primary job of the school is the efficient transmission and continual reappraisal of what we call tradition. Tradition is the mechanism by which all past men teach all future men.

Now arises the question: If all men by nature desire to know, and if that desire is best gratified by education and the transmission of tradition, what should be the character of that education and the content of that tradition? At once a vast, teeming chaos faces us: apparently men desire to know and transmit all kinds of matters, from how to tie a four-in-hand to the attributes of the Godhead.

Obviously this chaos cannot be taught. Hence in the past men have imposed upon it form, order, and hierarchy. They have selected certain areas of knowledge as the ones that, to the exclusion of others, both *can* and *should* be taught.

The structure of this hierarchy is not a matter of accident. Nor is it a matter of preference. The teacher may not teach only what happens to interest him. Nor may the student choose to be taught only what happens to interest him. The criteria of choice are many and far from immutable. But there is an essential one. Basic education concerns itself with those matters which, once learned, enable the student to learn all the other matters, whether trivial or complex, that cannot properly be the subjects of elementary and secondary schooling. In other words, both logic and experience suggest that certain subjects have generative power and others do not have generative power. When we have learned to tie a four-in-hand, the subject is exhausted. It is self-terminating. Our knowledge is of no value for the acquisition of further knowledge. But once we have learned to read we can decipher instructions for the tieing of a four-in-hand. Once we have learned to listen and observe, we can learn from someone else how to tie a four-in-hand.

It has, up to our time, been the general experience of men that certain subjects and not others possess this generative power. Among these subjects are those that deal with language, whether or not one's own; forms, figures and numbers; the laws of nature; the past; and the shape and behavior of our common home, the earth. Apparently these master or generative subjects endow one with the ability to learn the minor or self-terminating subjects. They also endow one, of course, with the ability to learn the higher, more complex developments of the master subjects themselves.

To the question, "Just what are these master subjects?" the contributors to this book supply a specific answer. It happens to be a traditional answer. That is, these are, more or less, with modifications in each epoch, the subjects that Western civilization has up to very recent times considered basic. That they are traditional is not an argument in their favor. The contributors believe that they are sanctioned not only by use and wont but by their intrinsic value.

The word *intrinsic* is troublesome. Is it possible that, as the environment changes, the number and names of the basic subjects must also change? At a certain time, our own for example, is it possible that driver-education is more basic than history? Many of us think so, or act as if we thought so. Again I would suggest that if we do think so, or act as if we thought so, it is not because we wish to lower the accident rate (though that is what we say) but because we unconsciously conceive of man primarily as an adaptive animal and not as a rational soul. For if he is primarily the first, then at the present moment in our human career driver-education *is* basic; but if he is primarily the second it is, though desirable, not basic.

I think the authors of this book would concede that with environmental changes the relative importance of the basic subjects will also change. It is obvious that a post-Newtonian world must accord more attention to the mathematical and physical sciences than did the pre-Newtonian world. But *some* science has at all times been taught. Similarly in a hundred years the American high school student may be universally offered Russian rather than French or German. But this does not affect the principle that *some* systematic instruction in *some* leading foreign language will remain a basic necessity.

In other words, however their forms may be modified, a core of basic or generative subjects exists. This core is not lightly to be abandoned, for once it is abandoned we have lost the primary tools which enable us to make any kind of machine we wish. Other subjects may seem transiently attractive or of obvious utility. It is pleasant to square-dance, for instance, and it is useful to know how to cook. Yet we cannot afford to be seduced by such "subjects." Hard though it may be, we must jettison them in favor of the basic subject matters. And there is no time for an eclectic mixture: only a few years are available in which [to] educe, to educate the rational soul. We cannot afford bypaths. We cannot afford pleasure. All education, Aristotle tells us, is accompanied by pain. Basic education is inescapably so accompanied, as well as by that magnificent pleasure that comes of stretching, rather than tickling, the mind.

I have briefly outlined the standard case for basic education insofar as it rests on an unchanging philosophic faith or view of human nature. But there is a more urgent, though less fundamental, argument still to be advanced. In sum it is this: while basic education is *always* a necessity, it is peculiarly so in our own time. . . .

I am a very lucky man, for I believe that my generation was just about the last one to receive an undiluted basic education. As this is written, I am fifty-four years old. Thus I received my secondary school education from 1916 to 1920. Though I was not well educated by European standards, I was very well educated by present-day American ones. . . .

My high school was part of the New York City system. It had no amenities. Its playground was asphalt and about the size of two large drawing rooms. It looked like a barracks. It made no provision for dramatics or square dancing. It didn't even have a psychiatrist—perhaps because we didn't need one. The students were all from what is known as the "underprivileged"—or what we used to call poor—class. Today this class is depended on to provide the largest quota of juvenile delinquents. During my four years in high school there was one scandalous case in which a student stole a pair of rubbers.

Academically my school was neither very good nor very bad. The same was true of me. As the area of elective subjects was strictly limited, I received approximately the same education my fellows did. (Unfortunately Latin was not compulsory: I had to learn it—badly—by myself later on.) Here is what—in addition to the standard minors of drawing, music, art and gym—I was taught some forty years ago:

Four years of English, including rigorous drill in composition, formal grammar and public speaking.

Four years of German.

Three years of French.

Three or four years (I am not sure which) of history, including classical, European and American, plus a no-nonsense factual course in civics. . . .

One year of physics.

One year of biology.

Three years of mathematics, through trigonometry.

That, or its near equivalent, was the standard high school curriculum in New York forty years ago. That was all I learned, all any of us learned, all all of us learned. All these subjects can be, and often are, better taught today—when they are taught at all on this scale. However, I was taught French and German well enough so that in later years I made part of my living as a translator. I was taught rhetoric and composition well enough to make it possible for me to become a practicing journalist. I was taught public speaking well enough to enable me to replace my lower-class accent with at least a passable one; and I learned also the rudiments of enunciation, placing, pitch, and proper breathing so that in after years I found it not too difficult to get odd jobs as a public lecturer and radio-and-television handyman.

I adduce these practical arguments only to explode them. They may seem important to the life-adjuster. They are not important to me. One can make a living without French. One can even make a living without a knowledge of spelling. And it is perfectly possible to rise to high estate without any control whatsoever over the English language.

What *is* important about this old-fashioned basic education (itself merely a continuation and sophistication of the basic education then taught in the primary schools) is not that it prepared me for life or showed me how to get along with my fellow men. Its importance to me and, I believe, to most of my fellow students, irrespective of their later careers, is twofold:

(1) It furnished me with a foundation on which later on, within the limits of my abilities, I could erect any intellectual structure I fancied. It gave me the wherewithal for the self-education that should be every man's concern to the hour of his death.

(2) It precluded my ever becoming Lost.

In drawing the distinction between generative and self-terminating subjects we have already discussed (1).

I want now to explain (2) because the explanation should help to make clear why in our time basic education is needed not only in principle but as a kind of emergency measure. . . .

Considered as a well-rounded American I am an extremely inferior product. I am a poor mechanic. I play no games beyond a little poorish tennis and I haven't played that for five years. I swim, type, dance and drive raggedly, though, with respect to the last, I hope non-dangerously. I have had to learn about sex and marriage without benefit of classroom instruction. I would like to be well-rounded and I admire those who are. But it is too late. I take no pleasure in my inferiorities but I accept the fact that I must live with them.

I feel inferior. Well and good. It seems to hurt nobody. But, though I feel inferior, I do not feel Lost. I have not felt lost since being graduated from high school. I do not expect ever to feel lost. This is not because I am wise, for I am not. It is not because I am learned, for I am not. It is not because I have mastered the art of getting along with my peers, for I do not know the first thing about it. I am often terrified by the world I live in, often horrified, usually unequal to its challenges. But I am not lost in it.

I know how I came to be an American citizen in 1959; what large general movements of history produced me; what my capacities and limitations are; what truly interests me; and how valuable or valueless these interests are. My tastes are fallible but not so fallible that I am easily seduced by the vulgar and transitory—though often enough I am unequal to a proper appreciation of the noble and the permanent. In a word, like tens of millions of others in this regard, I feel at home in the world. I am at times scared but I can truthfully say that I am not bewildered.

I do not owe this to any superiority of nature. I owe it, I sincerely believe, to the conventional basic education I received beginning about a half century ago. It taught me how to read, write, speak, calculate, and listen. It taught me the elements of reasoning and it put me on to the necessary business of drawing abstract conclusions from particular instances. It taught me how to locate myself in time and space and to survey the present in the light of an imperfect but ever-functioning knowledge of the past. It provided me with great models by which to judge my own lesser performances. And it gave me the ability to investigate for myself anything that interested me, provided my mind was equal to it. . . .

The average high school graduate today is just as intelligent as my fellow students were. He is just as educable. But he is Lost, in greater or less degree.

By that I mean he feels little relation to the whole world in time and space, and only the most formal relation to his own country. He may "succeed," he may become a good, law-abiding citizen, he may produce other good, law-abiding citizens, and on the whole he may live a pleasant—that is, not painful—life. Yet during most of that life, and particularly after his fortieth year or so, he will feel vaguely disconnected, rootless, purposeless. Like the very plague he will shun any searching questions as to his own worth, his own identity. He will die after having lived a fractional life.

Is this what he really wants? Perhaps it is. It all comes round again to what was said at the opening of these remarks. Again it depends on one's particular vision of man. If we see our youngster as an animal whose main function is biological and social adaptation on virtually a day-to-day basis, then his fractional life is not fractional at all. It is total. But in that case our school curriculum should reflect our viewpoint. It should include the rudiments of reading so that our high school graduate may decipher highway markers, lavatory signs, and perhaps the headlines of some undemanding newspaper. It should include a large number of electives, changing every year, that may be of use to him in job hunting. And primarily it should include as much play and sport as possible, for these are the proper activities of animals, and our boy is an animal.

Yet the doubt persists. *Is* this really what he wants? And once again the answer depends on our faith. For example, the "Rockefeller Report" on Education (published in 1958 and called *The Pursuit of Excellence*) did not issue, except indirectly, from surveys, analyses, polls or statistical abstracts. It issued from faith. The following sentences do not comprise a scientific conclusion. They are an expression of faith, like the Lord's Prayer:

"What most people, young or old, want is not merely security or comfort or luxury—although they are glad enough to have these. They want meaning in their lives. If their era and their culture and their leaders do not or cannot offer them great meanings, great objectives, great convictions, then they will settle for shallow and trivial meanings."

There is no compulsion to believe this. If we do not believe it, and unqualifiedly, there is no case for basic education. Which means that, except for the superior intellect, there is no case for traditional education at all. In that event we should at once start to overhaul our school system in the light of a conception of man that sees him as a continually adjusting, pleasure-seeking, pain-avoiding animal.

But if we do believe it, and unqualifiedly, then the proposals contained [here] might at least be considered as guidelines, subject to discussion and modification.

The root of our trouble does not lie in an unbalanced curriculum, or in an inadequate emphasis on any one subject, or in poor teaching methods, or in insufficient facilities, or in underpaid instructors. It lies in the circumstance that somehow the average high school graduate does not know who he is, where he is, or how he got there. It lies in the fact that naturally enough he "will settle for shallow and trivial meanings."

POSTSCRIPT

HOW SHOULD THE CURRICULUM BE ORGANIZED?

The free/open school movement values small, personalized educational settings in which students engage in activities which have personal meaning. One of the movement's ideological assumptions, emanating from the philosophy of Jean-Jacques Rousseau, is that, given a reasonably unrestrictive atmosphere, the learner will pursue avenues of creative and intellectual self-development.

The "basics movement," on the other hand, runs the risk of inflexibility and inattention to the wide spectrum of individual needs and differential learning styles. Yet the note sounded by advocates of a basic curriculum responds to the widely perceived need for clarity and certainty. Most people believe that there *are* skills and knowledge which every person should have and which the schools should be responsible for teaching.

This position has dominated organized education and has influenced curriculum development. The rationale set forth by Ralph Tyler in his *Basic Principles of Curriculum and Instruction* (1949) detailed methodological suggestions which paved the way for the behavioral objectives movement which is currently highly influential. Competency-based education, designed to assure basic learnings, has gained great favor in the public schools. At the college level, a movement is afoot toward more explicitly stipulated liberal arts exposure. *The Philosophy of the Curriculum* (1975), edited by Sidney Hook, Paul Kurtz, and Miro Todorovich, provides a wide exploration of the search for an appropriate general education.

In the field of curriculum theory a movement fueled by humanistic psychology and the philosophical viewpoints of existential phenomenology has gained some momentum. Volumes of articles and essays enunciating this new direction include *Curriculum Theorizing: The Reconceptualists* (1975), edited by William Pinar, and *Curriculum and the Cultural Revolution* (1972), edited by David E. Purpel and Maurice Belanger, which offers specifications of a general view that stands for greater curricular emphasis on self-fulfillment, personal liberty, social justice, diversity, and pluralism. Some of the publications of the Association for Supervision and Curriculum Development, particularly *Schools in Search of Meaning* (1975), edited by James B. Macdonald and Esther Zaret, pursue similar ideological paths toward curricular reform. An even broader spectrum of curriculum approaches may be reviewed in *Conflicting Conceptions of Curriculum* (1974), edited by Elliot Eisner and Elizabeth Vallance.

ISSUE 3

WHAT PSYCHOLOGICAL ATMOSPHERE IS NEEDED?

Intimately enmeshed with considerations of aims and purposes and determination of curriculum elements is the psychological base that affects the total setting in which learning takes place and the basic means of motivating learners. Historically, the atmosphere of schooling has often been characterized by harsh discipline, regimentation, and restriction. The prison metaphor often used by critics in describing school conditions rings true all too often.

Calls to make schools pleasant places have been sounded frequently but seldom widely heeded. The Roman Quintilian advocated a constructive learning atmosphere. John Amos Comenius in the 17th century suggested a gardening metaphor in which learners were given kindly nurturance. Johann Heinrich Pestalozzi established a model school in the 19th century which replaced authoritarianism with love and respect.

Yet school as an institution retains the stigma of authoritarian control—attendance is compelled, social and psychological punishment is meted out, and the decision-making freedom of students is limited and often curtailed. These practices lead to rather obvious conclusions: either the prevailing belief is that young people are naturally evil and wild and therefore must be tamed in a restricting environment, or that schooling as such is so unpalatable that people must be forced and cajoled to reap its benefits—or both.

Certainly John Dewey was concerned about this circumstance, citing at one time the superintendent of his native Burlington, Vermont, school district as admitting that the schools were a source of "grief and mortification" and were "unworthy of patronage." Dewey rejected both the need for "taming" and the defeatist attitude that the school environment must remain unappealing. He hoped to create a motivational atmosphere which would engage learners in real problem-solving activities, thereby sustaining curiosity, creativity, and attachment. The rewards were to flow from the sense of accomplishment and freedom which was to be achieved through the disciplined actions necessary to solve the problem at hand.

More recent treatment of the allied issues of freedom, control, and motivation has come from the two major camps in the field of educational psychology, the behaviorists (rooted in the early 20th-century theories of Pavlov, Thorndike, and Watson) and the humanists (emating from the Gestalt and field theory psychologies developed in Europe and America earlier in this century).

B.F. Skinner has been the dominant force in translating behaviorism into recommendations for school practices. The humanistic viewpoint has been championed by Carl R. Rogers, Abraham Maslow, Fritz Perls, Rollo May, and Erich Fromm, most of whom ground their psychological theories in the philosophical assumptions of existentialism and phenomenology.

Skinner believes that "inner" states are merely convenient myths, that motives and behaviors are shaped by environmental factors. These shaping forces, however, need not be negative, nor must they operate in an uncontrolled manner. Our present understanding of human behavior allows us the freedom to shape the environmental forces which in turn shape us. With this power, Skinner contends, we can replace aversive controls in schooling with positive reinforcements which heighten the students' motivation level and make learning more efficient. Skinner deals with the problem of freedom and control in the selection which follows.

Carl R. Rogers, representing humanistic psychology, here offers a critique of Skinner's behaviorist approach and sets forth his argument supporting the reality of freedom as an inner human state which is the wellspring of responsibility, will, and commitment.

B.F. Skinner

FREEDOM THROUGH CONTROL

Almost all living things act to free themselves from harmful contacts. A kind of freedom is achieved by the relatively simple forms of behavior called reflexes. A person sneezes and frees his respiratory passages from irritating substances. He vomits and frees his stomach from indigestible or poisonous food. He pulls back his hand and frees it from a sharp or hot object. More elaborate forms of behavior have similar effects. When confined, people struggle ("in rage") and break free. When in danger they flee from or attack its source. Behavior of this kind presumably evolved because of its survival value; it is as much a part of what we call the human genetic endowment as breathing, sweating, or digesting food. And through conditioning similar behavior may be acquired with respect to novel objects which could have played no role in evolution. These are no doubt minor instances of the struggle to be free, but they are significant. We do not attribute them to any love of freedom; they are simply forms of behavior which have proved useful in reducing various threats to the individual and hence to the species in the course of evolution.

A much more important role is played by behavior which weakens harmful stimuli in another way. It is not acquired in the form of conditioned reflexes, but as the product of a different process called operant conditioning. When a bit of behavior is followed by a certain kind of consequence, it is more likely to occur again, and a consequence having this effect is called a reinforcer. Food, for example, is a reinforcer to a hungry organism; anything the organism does that is followed by the receipt of food is more likely to be done again whenever the organism is hungry. Some stimuli are called negative reinforcers; any response which reduces the intensity of such a stimulus—or ends it—is more likely to be emitted when the stimulus recurs. Thus, if a person escapes from a hot sun when he moves under cover, he is more likely to move under cover when the sun is again hot. The reduction in temperature reinforces the behavior it is "contingent upon"—that is, the behavior it follows. Operant conditioning also occurs when a person simply avoids a hot sun—when, roughly speaking, he escapes from the *threat* of a hot sun.

Continued on p. 40

Carl R. Rogers

INNER FREEDOM AND COMMITMENT

One of the deepest issues in modern life, in modern man, is the question as to whether the concept of personal freedom has any meaning whatsoever in our present day scientific world. The growing ability of the behavioral scientist to predict and to control behavior has brought the issue sharply to the fore. If we accept the logical positivism and strictly behavioristic emphases which are predominant in the American psychological scene, there is not even room for discussion. . . .

But if we step outside the narrowness of the behavioral sciences, this question is not only *an* issue, it is one of the primary issues which define modern man. Friedman in his book (1963, p. 251) makes his topic "the problematic of modern man—the alienation, the divided nature, the unresolved tension between personal freedom and psychological compulsion which follows on 'the death of God.' " The issues of personal freedom and personal commitment have become very sharp indeed in a world in which man feels unsupported by a supernatural religion, and experiences keenly the division between his awareness and those elements of his dynamic functioning of which he is unaware. If he is to wrest any meaning from a universe which for all he knows may be indifferent, he must arrive at some stance which he can hold in regard to these timeless uncertainties.

So, writing as both a behavioral scientist and as one profoundly concerned with the human, the personal, the phenomenological and the intangible, I should like to contribute what I can to this continuing dialogue regarding the meaning of and the possibility of freedom.

MAN IS UNFREE

. . . In the minds of most behavioral scientists, man is not free, nor can he as a free man commit himself to some purpose, since he is controlled by factors outside of himself. Therefore, neither freedom nor commitment is even a possible concept to modern behavioral science as it is usually understood.

To show that I am not exaggerating, let me quote a statement from Dr. B.F. Skinner of Harvard, who is one of the most consistent advocates of a strictly

Continued on p. 44

(Skinner, cont. from p. 38)

Negative reinforcers are called aversive in the sense that they are the things organisms "turn away from." The term suggests a spatial separation—moving or running away from something—but the essential relation is temporal. In a standard apparatus used to study the process in the laboratory, an arbitrary response simply weakens an aversive stimulus or brings it to an end. A great deal of physical technology is the result of this kind of struggle for freedom. Over the centuries, in erratic ways, men have constructed a world in which they are relatively free of many kinds of threatening or harmful stimuli—extremes of temperature, sources of infection, hard labor, danger, and even those minor aversive stimuli called discomfort.

Escape and avoidance play a much more important role in the struggle for freedom when the aversive conditions are generated by other people. Other people can be aversive without, so to speak, trying: they can be rude, dangerous, contagious, or annoying, and one escapes from them or avoids them accordingly. They may also be "intentionally" aversive—that is, they may treat other people aversively because of what follows. Thus, a slave driver induces a slave to work by whipping him when he stops; by resuming work the slave escapes from the whipping (and incidentally reinforces the slave driver's behavior in using the whip). A parent nags a child until the child performs a task; by performing the task the child escapes nagging (and reinforces the parent's behavior). The blackmailer threatens exposure unless the victim pays; by paying, the victim escapes from the threat (and reinforces the practice). A teacher threatens corporal punishment or failure until his students pay attention; by paying attention the students escape from the threat of punishment (and reinforce the teacher for threatening it). In one form or another intentional aversive control is the pattern of most social coordination—in ethics, religion, government, economics, education, psychotherapy, and family life.

A person escapes from or avoids aversive treatment by behaving in ways which reinforce those who treated him aversively until he did so, but he may escape in other ways. For example, he may simply move out of range. A person may escape from slavery, emigrate or defect from a government, desert from an army, become an apostate from a religion, play truant, leave home, or drop out of a culture as a hobo, hermit, or hippie. Such behavior is as much a product of the aversive conditions as the behavior the conditions were designed to evoke. The latter can be guaranteed only by sharpening the contingencies or by using stronger aversive stimuli.

Another anomalous mode of escape is to attack those who arrange aversive conditions and weaken or destroy their power. We may attack those who crowd us or annoy us, as we attack the weeds in our garden, but again the struggle for freedom is mainly directed toward intentional controllers—toward those who treat others aversively in order to induce them to behave in particular ways. Thus, a child may stand up to his parents, a citizen may overthrow a government, a communicant may reform a religion, a student may attack a teacher or vandalize a school, and a dropout may work to destroy a culture.

It is possible that man's genetic endowment supports this kind of struggle for freedom: when treated aversively people tend to act aggressively or to be reinforced by signs of having worked aggressive damage. Both tendencies should have had evolutional advantages, and they can easily be demonstrated. If two organisms which have been coexisting peacefully receive painful shocks, they immediately exhibit characteristic patterns of aggression toward each other. The aggressive behavior is not necessarily directed toward the actual source of stimulation; it may be "displaced" toward any convenient person or object. Vandalism and riots are often forms of undirected or misdirected aggression. An organism which has received a painful shock will also, if possible, act to gain access to another organism toward which it can act aggressively. The extent to which human aggression exemplifies innate tendencies is not clear, and many of the ways in which people attack and thus weaken or destroy the power of intentional controllers are quite obviously learned.

What we may call the "literature of freedom" has been designed to induce people to escape from or attack those who act to control them aversively. The content of the literature is the philosophy of freedom, but philosophies are among those inner causes which need to be scrutinized. We say that a person behaves in a given way because he possesses a philosophy, but we infer the philosophy from the behavior and therefore cannot use it in any satisfactory way as an explanation, at least until it is in turn explained. The literature of freedom, on the other hand, has a simple objective status. It consists of books, pamphlets, manifestoes, speeches, and other verbal products, designed to induce people to act to free themselves from various kinds of intentional control. It does not impart a philosophy of freedom; it induces people to act.

The literature often emphasizes the aversive conditions under which people live, perhaps by contrasting them with conditions in a freer world. It thus makes the conditions more aversive, "increasing the misery" of those it is trying to rescue. It also identifies those from whom one is to escape or those whose power is to be weakened through attack. Characteristic villains of the literature are tyrants, priests, generals, capitalists, martinet teachers, and domineering parents.

The literature also prescribes modes of action. It has not been much concerned with escape, possibly because advice has not been needed; instead, it has emphasized how controlling power may be weakened or destroyed. Tyrants are to be overthrown, ostracized, or assassinated. The legitimacy of a government is to be questioned. The ability of a religious agency to mediate supernatural sanctions is to be challenged. Strikes and boycotts are to be organized to weaken the economic power which supports aversive practices. The argument is strengthened by exhorting people to act, describing likely results, reviewing successful instances on the model of the advertising testimonial, and so on.

The would-be controllers do not, of course, remain inactive. Governments make escape impossible by banning travel or severely punishing or incarcerating defectors. They keep weapons and other sources of power out of the hands of revolutionaries. They destroy the written literature of freedom and imprison or kill those who carry it orally. If the struggle for freedom is to succeed, it must then be intensified.

The importance of the literature of freedom can scarcely be questioned. Without help or guidance people submit to aversive conditions in the most surprising way. This is true even when the aversive conditions are part of the natural environment. Darwin observed, for example, that the Fuegians seemed to make no effort to protect themselves from the cold; they wore only scant clothing and made little use of it against the weather. And one of the most striking things about the struggle for freedom from intentional control is how often it has been lacking. Many people have submitted to the most obvious religious, governmental, and economic controls for centuries, striking for freedom only sporadically, if at all. The literature of freedom has made an essential contribution to the elimination of many aversive practices in government, religion, education, family life, and the production of goods.

The contributions of the literature of freedom, however, are not usually described in these terms. Some traditional theories could conceivably be said to define freedom as the absence of aversive control, but the emphasis has been on how that condition *feels.* Other traditional theories could conceivably be said to define freedom as a person's condition when he is behaving under nonaversive control, but the emphasis has been upon a state of mind associated with doing what one wants. According to John Stuart Mill, "Liberty consists in doing what one desires." The literature of freedom has been important in changing practice (it has changed practices whenever it has had any effect whatsoever), but it has nevertheless defined its task as the changing of states of mind and feelings. Freedom is a "possession." A person escapes from or destroys the power of a controller in order to feel free, and once he feels free and can do what he desires, no further action is recommended and none is prescribed by the literature of freedom, except perhaps eternal vigilance lest control be resumed.

The feeling of freedom becomes an unreliable guide to action as soon as would-be controllers turn to nonaversive measures, as they are likely to do to avoid the problems raised when the controllee escapes or attacks. Nonaversive measures are not as conspicuous as aversive and are likely to be acquired more slowly, but they have obvious advantages which promote their use. Productive labor, for example, was once the result of punishment: the slave worked to avoid the consequences of not working. Wages exemplify a different principle; a person is paid when he behaves in a given way so that he will continue to behave in that way. Although it has long been recognized that rewards have useful effects, wage systems have evolved slowly. In the nineteenth century it was believed that an industrial society required a hungry labor force; wages would be effective only if the hungry worker could exchange them for food. By making labor less aversive—for instance, by shortening hours and improving conditions—it has been possible to get men to work for lesser rewards. Until recently teaching was almost entirely aversive: the student studied to escape the consequences of not studying, but nonaversive techniques are gradually being discovered and used. The skillful parent learns to reward a child for good behavior rather than punish him for bad. Religious agencies move from the threat of hellfire to an emphasis on God's love, and governments turn from aversive sanctions to various kinds of inducements, as we shall note again shortly. What the layman calls a reward is a "positive reinforcer," the effects of which have been exhaustively studied in the experimental analysis of operant behavior. The effects are not as easily recognized as those of aversive contingencies because they tend to be deferred, and applications have therefore been delayed, but techniques as powerful as the older aversive techniques are now available. . . .

The literature of freedom has never come to grips with techniques of control which do not generate escape or counterattack because it has dealt with the problem in terms of states of mind and feelings. In his book *Sovereignty,* Bertrand de Jouvenel quotes two important figures in that literature. According to Leibnitz, "Liberty consists in the power to do what one wants to do," and according to Voltaire, "When I can do what I want to do, there is my liberty for me." But both writers add a concluding phrase: Leibnitz, ". . . or in the power to want what can be got," and Voltaire, more candidly, ". . . but I can't help wanting what I do want." Jouvenel relegates these comments to a footnote, saying that the power to want is a matter of "interior liberty" (the freedom of the inner man!) which falls outside the "gambit of freedom."

A person wants something if he acts to get it when the occasion arises. A person who says "I want something to eat" will presumably eat when something becomes available. If he says "I want to get warm," he will presumably move into a warm place when he can. These acts have been reinforced in the past by whatever was wanted. What a person *feels* when he feels himself wanting something depends upon the circumstances. Food is reinforcing only in a state of deprivation, and a person who wants something to eat may feel parts of that state—for example, hunger pangs. A person who wants to get warm presumably feels cold. Conditions associated with a high probability of responding may also be felt, together with aspects of the present occasion which are similar to those of past occasions upon which behavior has been reinforced. Wanting is not, however, a feeling, nor is a feeling the reason a person acts to get what he wants. Certain contingencies have raised the probability of behavior and at the same time have created conditions which may be felt. Freedom is a matter of contingencies of reinforcement, not of the feelings the contingencies generate. The distinction is particularly important when the contingencies do not generate escape or counterattack. . . .

The literature of freedom has encouraged escape from or attack upon all controllers. It has done so by making any indication of control aversive. Those who manipulate human behavior are said to be evil men, necessarily bent on exploitation. Control is clearly the opposite of freedom, and if freedom is good, control must be bad. What is overlooked is control which does not have aversive consequences at any time. Many social practices essential to the welfare of the species involve the control of one person by another, and no one can suppress them who has any concern for human achievements. We shall see later that in order to maintain the position that all control is wrong, it has been necessary to disguise or conceal the nature of useful practices, to prefer weak practices just because they can be disguised or concealed, and—a most extraordinary result indeed!—to perpetuate punitive measures.

The problem is to free men, not from control, but from certain kinds of control, and it can be solved only if our analysis takes all consequences into account. How people feel about control, before or after the literature of freedom has worked on their feelings, does not lead to useful distinctions.

Were it not for the unwarranted generalization that all control is wrong, we should deal with the social environment as simply as we deal with the nonsocial. Although technology has freed men from certain aversive features of the environment, it has not freed them from the environment. We accept the fact that we depend upon the world around us, and we simply change the nature of the dependency. In the same way, to make the social environment as free as possible of aversive stimuli we do not need to destroy that environment or escape from it; we need to redesign it.

Man's struggle for freedom is not due to a will to be free, but to certain behavioral processes characteristic of the human organism, the chief effect of which is the avoidance of or escape from so-called "aversive" features of the environment. Physical and biological technologies have been mainly concerned with natural aversive stimuli; the struggle for freedom is concerned with stimuli intentionally arranged by other people. The literature of freedom has identified the other people and has proposed ways of escaping from them or weakening or destroying their power. It has been successful in reducing the aversive stimuli used in intentional control, but it has made the mistake of defining freedom in terms of states of mind or feelings, and it has therefore not been able to deal effectively with techniques of control which do not breed escape or revolt but nevertheless have aversive consequences. It has been forced to brand all control as wrong and to misrepresent many of the advantages to be gained from a social environment. It is unprepared for the next step, which is not to free men from control but to analyze and change the kinds of control to which they are exposed.

(Rogers, cont. from p. 39)

behavioristic psychology. He says,

> The hypothesis that man is not free is essential to the application of scientific method to the study of human behavior. The free inner man who is held responsible for his behavior is only a prescientific substitute for the kinds of causes which are discovered in the course of scientific analysis. All these alternative causes lie *outside* the individual (1953, p. 477).

This view is shared by many psychologists and others who feel, as does Dr. Skinner, that all the effective causes of behavior lie outside of the individual and that it is only through the external stimulus that behavior takes place. The scientific description of behavior avoids anything that partakes in any way of freedom. For example, Dr. Skinner (1964, pp. 90-91) describes an experiment in which a pigeon was conditioned to turn in a clockwise direction. The behavior of the pigeon was "shaped up" by rewarding any movement that approximated a clockwise turn until, increasingly, the bird was turning round and round in a steady movement. This is what is known as operant conditioning. Students who had watched the demonstration were asked to write an account of what they had seen. Their responses included the following ideas: that the pigeon was conditioned to *expect* reinforcement for the right kind of behavior; that the pigeon *hoped* that something would bring the food back again; that the pigeon *observed* that a certain behavior seemed to produce a particular result; that the pigeon *felt* that food would be given it because of its action; that the bird came to *associate* his action with the clock of the food dispenser. Skinner ridicules these statements because they all go beyond the observed behavior in using such words as *expect, hope, observe, feel,* and *associate*. The whole explanation from his point of view is that the bird was reinforced when it emitted a given kind of behavior; the pigeon walked around until the food container again appeared; a certain behavior produced a given result; food was given to the pigeon when it acted in a given way; and the click of the food dispenser was related in time to the bird's action. These statements describe the pigeon's behavior from a scientific point of view.

Skinner goes on to point out that the students were undoubtedly reporting what they would have expected, felt and hoped under similar circumstances. But he then makes the case that there is no more reality to such ideas in the human being than there is in the pigeon, that it is only because such words have been reinforced by the verbal community in which the individual has developed, that such terms are used. He discusses the fact that the verbal community which conditioned them to use such terms saw no more of their behavior than they had seen of the pigeon's. In other words the internal events, if they indeed exist, have no scientific significance.

As to the methods used for changing the behavior of the pigeon, many people besides Dr. Skinner feel that through such positive reinforcement human behavior as well as animal behavior can be "shaped up" and controlled. In his book, *Walden Two,* Skinner says,

> Now that we know how positive reinforcement works and how negative doesn't, we can be more deliberate and hence more successful in our cultural design. We can achieve a sort of control under which the controlled, though they are following a code much more scrupulously than was ever the case under the old system, nevertheless *feel free*. They are doing what they want to do, not what they are forced to do. That's the source of the tremendous power of positive reinforcement—there is no restraint and no revolt. By a careful cultural design we control not the final behavior but the *inclination* to behave—the motives, the desires, the wishes. The curious thing is that in that case *the question of freedom never arises* (1948, p. 218).

. . . I think it is clear from all of this that man is a machine—a complex machine, to be sure, but one which is increasingly subject to scientific control. Whether behavior will be managed through operant conditioning as in *Walden Two* or whether we will be "shaped up" by the unplanned forms of conditioning implied in social pressure, or whether we will be controlled by electrodes in the brain, it seems quite clear that science is making out of man an object and that the purpose of such science is not only understanding and prediction but control. Thus it would seem to be quite clear that there could be no concept so foreign to the facts as that man is free. Man is a machine, man is unfree, man cannot commit himself in any meaningful sense; he is simply controlled by planned or unplanned forces outside of himself.

MAN IS FREE

I am impressed by the scientific advances illustrated in the examples I have given. I regard them as a great tribute to the ingenuity, insight, and persistence of the individuals making the investigations. They have added enormously to our knowledge. Yet for me they leave something very important unsaid. Let me try to illustrate this, first from my experience in therapy.

I think of a young man classed as schizophrenic with whom I had been working for a long time in a state hospital. He was a very inarticulate man, and during one hour he made a few remarks about individuals who had recently left the hospital; then he remained silent for almost forty minutes. When he got up to go, he mumbled almost under his breath, "If some of *them* can do it, maybe I can too." That was all—not a dramatic statement, not uttered with force and vigor, yet a statement of choice by this young man to work toward his own improvement and eventual release from the hospital. It is not too surprising that about eight months after that statement he was out of the hospital. I believe this experience of responsible choice is one of the deepest aspects of psychotherapy and one of the elements which most solidly underlies personality change.

I think of another young person, this time a young woman graduate student, who was deeply disturbed and on the borderline of a psychotic break. Yet after a number of interviews in which she talked very critically about all of the people who had failed to give her what she needed, she finally concluded: "Well, with that sort of a foundation, it's really up to *me*. I mean it seems to be really apparent to me that I can't depend on someone else to *give* me an education." And then she added very softly: "I'll really have to get it myself." She goes on to explore this experience of important and responsible choice. She finds it a frightening experience, and yet one which gives her a feeling of strength. A force seems to surge up within her which is big and strong, and yet she also feels very much alone and sort of cut off from support. She adds: "I am going to begin to do more things that I know I should do." And she did.

I could add many other examples. One young fellow talking about the way in which his whole life had been distorted and spoiled by his parents finally comes to the conclusion that, "Maybe now that I *see* that, it's up to *me*."...

For those of you [who] have seen the film *David and Lisa*—and I hope that you have had that rich experience—I can illustrate exactly what I have been discussing. David, the adolescent schizophrenic, goes into a panic if he is touched by anyone. He feels that "touching kills," and he is deathly afraid of it, and afraid of the closeness in human relationships which touching implies. Yet toward the close of the film he makes a bold and positive choice of the kind I have been describing. He has been trying to be of help to Lisa, the girl who is out of touch with reality. He tries to help at first in an intellectually contemptuous way, then increasingly in a warmer and more personal way. Finally, in a highly dramatic moment, he says to her, "Lisa, take my hand." He *chooses,* with obvious conflict and fear, to leave behind the safety of his untouchableness, and to venture into the world of real human relationships where he is literally and figuratively in *touch* with another. You are an unusual person if the film does not grow a bit misty at this point.

Perhaps a behaviorist could try to account for the reaching out of his hand by saying that it was the result of intermittent reinforcement of partial movements. I find such an explanation both inaccurate and inadequate. It is the *meaning* of the *decision* which is essential to understanding the act.

What I am trying to suggest in all of this is that I would be at a loss to explain the positive change which can occur in psychotherapy if I had to omit the importance of the sense of free and responsible choice on the part of my clients. I believe that this experience of freedom to choose is one of the deepest elements underlying change.

THE MEANING OF FREEDOM

Considering the scientific advances which I have mentioned, how can we even speak of freedom? In what sense is a client free? In what sense are any of us free? What possible definition of freedom can there be in the modern world? Let me attempt such a definition.

In the first place, the freedom that I am talking about is essentially an inner thing, something which exists in the living person quite aside from any of the outward choices of alternatives which we so often think of as constituting freedom. I am speaking of the kind of freedom which Viktor Frankl vividly describes in his experience of the concentration camp, when everything—possessions, status, identity—was taken from the prisoners. But even months and years in such an environment showed only "that everything can be taken from a man but one thing: the last of the human freedoms—to choose one's own attitude in any given set of circumstances, to choose one's own way" (1959, p. 65). It is this inner, subjective, existential freedom which I have observed. It is the realization that "I can live myself, here and now, by my own choice." It is the quality of courage which enables a person to step into the uncertainty of the unknown as he chooses himself. It is the discovery of meaning from within oneself, meaning which comes from listening sensitively and openly to the complexities of what one is experiencing. It is the burden of being responsible for the self one chooses to be. It is the recognition of a person that he is an emerging process, not a static end product. The individual who is thus deeply and courageously thinking his own thoughts, becoming his own uniqueness, responsibly choosing himself, may be fortunate in having hundreds of objective outer alternatives from which to choose, or he may be unfortunate in having none. But his freedom exists regardless. So we are first of all speaking of something which exists within the individual, something phenomenological rather than external, but nonetheless to be prized.

The second point in defining this experience of freedom is that it exists not as a contradiction of the picture of the psychological universe as a sequence of cause and effect, but as a complement to such a universe. Freedom rightly understood is a fulfillment by the person of the ordered sequence of his life. The free man moves out voluntarily, freely, responsibly, to play his significant part in a world whose determined events move through him and through his spontaneous choice and will.

I see this freedom of which I am speaking, then, as existing in a different *dimension* than the determined sequence of cause and effect. I regard it as a freedom which exists in the subjective person, a freedom which he courageously uses to live his potentialities. The fact that this type of freedom seems completely irreconcilable with the behaviorist's picture of man is something which I will discuss a bit later. . . .

THE EMERGENCE OF COMMITMENT

I have spoken thus far primarily about freedom. What about commitment? Certainly the disease of our age is lack of purpose, lack of meaning, lack of commitment on the part of individuals. Is there anything which I can say in regard to this?

It is clear to me that in therapy, as indicated in the examples that I have given, commitment to purpose and to meaning in life is one of the significant elements of change. It is only when the person decides, "I am someone; I am someone worth being; I am committed to being myself," that change becomes possible.

At a very interesting symposium at Rice University recently, Dr. Sigmund Koch sketched the revolution which is taking place in science, literature and the arts, in which a sense of commitment is again becoming evident after a long period in which that emphasis has been absent.

Part of what he meant by that may be illustrated by talking about Dr. Michael Polanyi, the philosopher of science, formerly a physicist, who has been presenting his notions about what science basically is. In his book, *Personal Knowledge,* Polanyi makes it clear that even scientific knowledge is personal knowledge, committed knowledge. We cannot rest comfortably on the belief that scientific knowledge is impersonal and "out there," that it has nothing to do with the individual who has discovered it. Instead every aspect of science is pervaded by disciplined personal commitment, and Polanyi makes the case very persuasively that the whole attempt to divorce science from the person is a completely unrealistic one. I think I am stating his belief correctly when I say that in his judgment logical positivism and all the current structure of science cannot save us from the fact that all knowing is uncertain, involves risk, and is grasped and comprehended only through the deep, personal commitment of a disciplined search.

Perhaps a brief quotation will give something of the flavor of his thinking. Speaking of great scientists, he says:

> So we see that both Kepler and Einstein approached nature with intellectual passions and with beliefs inherent in these passions, which led them to their triumphs and misguided them to their errors. These passions and beliefs were theirs, personally, even universally. I believe that they were competent to follow these impulses, even though they risked being misled by them. And again, what I accept of their work today, I accept personally, guided by passions and beliefs similar to theirs, holding in my turn that my impulses are valid, universally, even though I must admit the possibility that they may be mistaken (1958, p. 145).

Thus we see that a modern philosopher of science believes that deep personal commitment is the only possible basis on which science can firmly stand. This is a far cry indeed from the logical positivism of twenty or thirty years ago, which placed knowledge far out in impersonal space.

Let me say a bit more about what I mean by commitment in the psychological sense. I think it is easy to give this word a much too shallow meaning, indicating that the individual has, simply by conscious choice, committed himself to one course of action or another. I think the meaning goes far deeper than that. Commitment is a total organismic direction involving not only the conscious mind but the whole direction of the organism as well.

In my judgment, commitment is something that one *discovers* within oneself. It is a trust of one's total reaction rather than of one's mind only. It has much to do with creativity. Einstein's explanation of how he moved toward his formulation of relativity without any clear knowledge of his goal is an excellent example of what I mean by the sense of commitment based on a total organismic reaction. He says:

> "During all those years there was a feeling of direction, of going straight toward something concrete. It is, of course, very hard to express that feeling in words but it was decidedly the case and clearly to be distinguished from later considerations about the rational form of the solution" (quoted in Wertheimer, 1945, p. 183–184).

Thus commitment is more than a decision. It is the functioning of an individual who is searching for the directions which are emerging within himself. Kierkegaard has said, "The truth exists only in the process of becoming, in the process of appropriation" (1941, p. 72). It is this individual creation of a tentative personal truth through action which is the essence of commitment.

Man is most successful in such a commitment when he is functioning as an integrated, whole, unified individual. The more that he is functioning in this total manner the more confidence he has in the directions which he unconsciously chooses. He feels a trust in his experiencing, of which, even if he is fortunate, he has only partial glimpses in his awareness.

Thought of in the sense in which I am describing it, it is clear that commitment is an achievement. It is the kind of purposeful and meaningful direction which is only gradually achieved by the individual who has come increasingly to live closely in relationship with his own experiencing—a relationship in which his unconscious tendencies are as much respected as are his conscious choices. This is the kind of commitment toward which I believe individuals can move. It is an important aspect of living in a fully functioning way.

THE IRRECONCILABLE CONTRADICTION

I trust it will be very clear that I have given two sharply divergent and irreconcilably contradictory points of view. On the one hand, modern psychological science and many other forces in modern life as well, hold the view that man is unfree, that he is controlled, that words such as purpose, choice, commitment have no significant meaning, that man is nothing but an object which we can more fully understand and more fully control. Enormous strides have been and are being made in implementing this perspective. It would seem heretical indeed to question this view.

Yet, as Polanyi has pointed out in another of his writings (1957), the dogmas of science can be in error. He says:

3. WHAT PSYCHOLOGICAL ATMOSPHERE IS NEEDED?

> In the days when an idea could be silenced by showing that it was contrary to religion, theology was the greatest single source of fallacies. Today, when any human thought can be discredited by branding it as unscientific, the power previously exercised by theology has passed over to science; hence science has become in its turn the greatest single source of error.

So I am emboldened to say that over against this view of man as unfree, as an object, is the evidence from therapy, from subjective living, and from objective research as well, that personal freedom and responsibility have a crucial significance, that one cannot live a complete life without such personal freedom and responsibility, and that self-understanding and responsible choice make a sharp and measurable difference in the behavior of the individual. In this context, commitment does have meaning. Commitment is the emerging and changing total direction of the individual, based on a close and acceptant relationship between the person and all of the trends in his life, conscious and unconscious. Unless, as individuals and as a society, we can make constructive use of this capacity for freedom and commitment, mankind, it seems to me, is set on a collision course with fate. . . .

A part of modern living is to face the paradox that, viewed from one perspective, man is a complex machine. We are every day moving toward a more precise understanding and a more precise control of this objective mechanism which we call man. On the other hand, in another significant dimension of his existence, man is subjectively free; his personal choice and responsibility account for the shape of his life; he is in fact the architect of himself. A truly crucial part of his existence is the discovery of his own meaningful commitment to life with all of his being.

POSTSCRIPT

WHAT PSYCHOLOGICAL ATMOSPHERE IS NEEDED?

The freedom-determinism or freedom-control argument has raged in philosophical, political, and psychological circles down through the ages. Is freedom of choice and action a central, perhaps *the* central, characteristic of being human? Or is freedom only an illusion, a refusal to acknowledge the external shaping of all human actions?

Moving the debate into the field of education, John Dewey depicts a developmental freedom which is acquired through increasing one's ability to cope with problems. A.S. Neill sees a more natural, inborn freedom in human beings which must be protected and allowed to flourish. B.F. Skinner refuses to recognize this "inner autonomous man," but sees freedom resulting from the scientific reshaping of the environment which influences us. Skinner ends *Beyond Freedom and Dignity* with the challenging statement, "We have not yet seen what man can make of man."

Just as Skinner has struggled to remove the stigma from the word "control," arguing that it is the true gateway to freedom, John Holt, in *Freedom and Beyond* (1972), points out that freedom and free activities are not "unstructured"—indeed, that the structure of an open classroom is vastly more complicated than the structure of a traditional classroom

If both of these views have validity, then we are in a position, as Dewey counselled, to go beyond either-or polemics on these matters and build a more constructive educational atmosphere. Jerome S. Bruner has consistently suggested ways in which free inquiry and subject matter structure can be effectively blended. Arthur W. Combs, in journal articles and in a report titled *Humanistic Education: Objectives and Assessment* (1978) has helped to bridge the ideological gap between humanists and behaviorists by demonstrating that subjective outcomes can be assessed by direct or modified behavioral techniques.

Other sources which offer different perspectives on the basic psychological environment in education include John D. Nolan's defense of a moderate behaviorism in "The True Humanist: The Behavior Modifier" (*Teachers College Record,* December 1974), Gerald Weinstein's and Mario Fantini's *Toward Humanistic Education—A Curriculum of Affect* (1970), William Glasser's "reality therapy" approach as described in his *Schools Without Failure* (1969), and Philip W. Jackson's *Life In Classrooms* (1968). Two popular treatments of the issue are *The Brain Changers* by Maya Pines (1973) and *The People Shapers* by Vance Packard (1977).

ISSUE 4

CAN MORAL DEVELOPMENT BE ASSURED?

Do the schools have a moral purpose? Can virtue be taught? Should the shaping of character take precedence over the training of the intellect? Is the person possessing a highly developed rationality automatically ethical? Are contemporary schools limited to teaching a secularized morality? Should the schools cease meddling in value-charged matters?

Much of the history of education is a chronicle of how philosophers, theorists, education officials, and the general public have responded to the questions above. In most all countries, and certainly in early America, the didactic teaching of moral values, often those of a particular religious interpretation, was central to the process of education.

Although the direct connection between religion and schooling has faded, the image of the teacher as a value model at least somewhat persists, and the ethical dimension of everyday activities and human relations intrudes itself into the school atmosphere regardless of any curricular ignoring of moral controversy. Normative discourse inundates the educational environment; school is a world of "rights" and "wrongs" and "oughts" and "don'ts."

We are faced, at present, with trying to define and delineate the moral intentions of public education. Storms of controversy rage over the instructional use of value-laden materials and over methodological approaches which seem to some to be value-destructive. Localized explosions regarding textbooks (as in Kanawha County, West Virginia), entire curricula (as with Man: A Course of Study), and films (as with Shirley Jackson's "The Lottery") bear witness to the volatility of the moral dimension of education.

Additional problems emerge in the attempt to delineate the school's role: can school efforts supplement the efforts of home and church; can the schools avoid representing a "middle-class morality" which disregards the cultural base of minority group values; should the schools do battle against the value-manipulation forces of the mass media and the popular culture?

Two fundamental courses through these difficulties have been charted in recent years. One is an approach developed primarily by Lawrence Kohlberg which links ethical growth to levels of cognitive maturity, tracing a range of moral stages from punishment avoidance to recognition of universal principles. The approach employs discussion of moral dilemmas which demand increasingly sophisticated types of moral reasoning.

The other approach, developed and refined by Louis Raths, Sidney Simon, Merrill Harmin, and Howard Kirschenbaum, is known as values clarification. The crux of this moral education strategy is assisting learners in understanding their own attitudes, preferences, and values and the values of others. In contrast to the basically rational approach of Kohlberg, this method emphasizes feelings, emotions, sensitivity, and shared perceptions.

If either or both of these strategies is found to be reasonably neutral and generally acceptable to parents and students, the question of implementation remains. Recent years have seen the marketing of a wide range of materials, activities, and games slanted toward this educational aim. Some seem totally superficial, while others border on the psychoanalytical. With or without such prepackaged aids, can teachers navigate the waters of moral education in an organized and effective manner?

Lawrence Kohlberg and Howard Kirschenbaum believe that it is essential that teachers develop such capability and explain why in the selections which follow. Kohlberg contends that the teacher will be on firm ground if his or her strategies are properly concentrated on rights and justice. Kirschenbaum sees promise if teachers are explicitly trained in awareness and communication.

Lawrence Kohlberg

MORAL GROWTH STAGES

The cognitive-developmental approach was fully stated for the first time by John Dewey. The approach is called *cognitive* because it recognizes that moral education, like intellectual education, has its basis in stimulating the *active thinking* of the child about moral issues and decisions. It is called developmental because it sees the aims of moral education as movement through moral stages. According to Dewey:

> The aim of education is growth or *development,* both intellectual and moral. Ethical and psychological principles can aid the school in the *greatest of all constructions—the building of a free and powerful character.* Only knowledge of the *order and connection of the stages in psychological development can insure this.* Education is the work of *supplying the conditions* which will enable the psychological functions to mature in the freest and fullest manner.

Dewey postulated three levels of moral development: 1) the *pre-moral* or *preconventional* level "of behavior motivated by biological and social impulses with results for morals," 2) the *conventional* level of behavior "in which the individual accepts with little critical reflection the standards of his group," and 3) the *autonomous* level of behavior in which "conduct is guided by the individual thinking and judging for himself whether a purpose is good, and does not accept the standard of his group without reflection."[1]

Dewey's thinking about moral stages was theoretical. Building upon his prior studies of cognitive stages, Jean Piaget made the first effort to define stages of moral reasoning in children through actual interviews and through observations of children (in games with rules). Using this interview material, Piaget defined the pre-moral, the conventional, and the autonomous levels as

1. These levels correspond roughly to our three major levels: the preconventional, the conventional, and the principled. Similar levels were propounded by William McDougall, Leonard Hobhouse, and James Mark Baldwin.

Continued on p. 56

From Lawrence Kohlberg, "The Cognitive-Developmental Approach to Moral Education," *Phi Delta Kappan,* June 1975.

Howard Kirschenbaum

VALUES CLARIFICATION

Since the publication of *Values and Teaching,*[1] in 1966, proponents of the values-clarification approach in education have continued to develop scores of new *techniques* and *applications* for their work.[2] There has, however, been little or no change in the *theoretical foundation* upon which the approach is built. This has been especially true of Louis Raths' seven criteria for a value—the Gibraltar upon which values clarification has rested for many years.

Like many other approaches in the humanistic education field, values clarification has grown up as a separate "movement" with its own terminology, concepts, and methods. Although I believe the approach, by itself, has a great deal to offer, over the last several years I have felt increasingly hamstrung by some of its theories and concepts. Many of my colleagues and students in this field have expressed similar misgivings. The problem seems to be that many of us have experienced several different branches of humanistic education and are not convinced that any one approach has all the answers or even the best answers. What many people are seeking is a wider view of our goals as humanistic educators—one that encompasses values clarification, but also integrates it with the other valuable approaches which exist. In this essay, I would like to describe my own evolution on this issue and my attempts, both theoretical and practical, to move beyond values clarification as a separate approach.

My first introduction to values-clarification theory was back in 1964 when one of Sid Simon's students told me about Louis Raths' seven criteria for a value. I learned that if a belief or behavior were to qualify as a value, according to Raths, it must be: (1) chosen from alternatives; (2) chosen after thoughtful

1. Louis E. Raths, Merrill Harmin, and Sidney B. Simon, *Values and Teaching* (Columbus, Ohio: Charles E. Merrill Publishing Co., 1966)

2. Sidney B. Simon, Leland W. Howe, and Howard Kirschenbaum, *Values Clarification: A Handbook of Practical Strategies for Teachers and Students* (New York: Hart Publishing Company, Inc., 1972), and Merrill Harmin, Howard Kirschenbaum, and Sidney B. Simon, *Clarifying Values Through Subject Matter: Applications for the Classroom* (Minneapolis: Winston Press, Inc., 1973).

Continued on p. 63

Reprinted by permission of the author. For a listing of materials available on the values clarification approach, write the National Humanistic Education Center, 110 Spring St., Saratoga Springs, N.Y. 12866.

(Kohlberg, cont. from p. 54)
follows: 1) the *pre-moral stage,* where there was no sense of obligation to rules; 2) the *heteronomous stage,* where the right was literal obedience to rules and an equation of obligation with submission to power and punishment (roughly ages 4-8); and 3) the *autonomous stage,* where the purpose and consequences of following rules are considered and obligation is based on reciprocity and exchange (roughly ages 8-12).[2]

In 1955 I started to redefine and validate (through longitudinal and cross-cultural study) the Dewey-Piaget levels and stages. The resulting stages are presented in Table 1.

We claim to have validated the stages defined in Table 1. The notion that stages can be *validated* by longitudinal study implies that stages have definite empirical characteristics. The concept of stages (as used by Piaget and myself) implies the following characteristics:

1. Stages are "structured wholes," or organized systems of thought. Individuals are *consistent* in level of moral judgment.
2. Stages form an *invariant sequence.* Under all conditions except extreme trauma, movement is always forward, never backward. Individuals never skip stages; movement is always to the next stage up.
3. Stages are "hierarchical integrations." Thinking at a higher stage includes or comprehends within it lower-stage thinking. There is a tendency to function at or prefer the highest stage available.

Each of these characteristics has been demonstrated for moral stages. Stages are defined by responses to a set of verbal moral dilemmas classified according to an elaborate scoring scheme. Validating studies include:

1. A 20-year study of 50 Chicago-area boys, middle- and working-class. Initially interviewed at ages 10-16, they have been reinterviewed at three-year intervals thereafter.
2. A small, six-year longitudinal study of Turkish village and city boys of the same age.
3. A variety of other cross-sectional studies in Canada, Britain, Israel, Taiwan, Yucatan, Honduras, and India.

With regard to the structured whole or consistency criterion, we have found that more than 50% of an individual's thinking is always at one stage, with the remainder at the next adjacent stage (which he is leaving or which he is moving into).

With regard to invariant sequence, our longitudinal results have been presented in the *American Journal of Orthopsychiatry,* and indicate that on every retest individuals were either at the same stage as three years earlier or had moved up. This was true in Turkey as well as in the United States.

With regard to the hierarchical integration criterion, it has been demonstrated that adolescents exposed to written statements at each of the six stages comprehend or correctly put in their own words all statements at or below their own stage but fail to comprehend any statements more than one stage above their own. Some individuals comprehend the next stage above their own; some do not. Adolescents prefer (or rank as best) the highest stage they can comprehend.

To understand moral stages, it is important to clarify their relations to stage of logic or intelligence, on the one hand, and to moral behavior on the other. Maturity of moral judgment is not highly

2. Piaget's stages correspond to our first three stages: Stage 0 (pre-moral), Stage 1 (heteronomous), and Stage 2 (instrumental reciprocity).

Table 1. Definition of Moral Stages

I. Preconventional level

At this level, the child is responsive to cultural rules and labels of good and bad, right or wrong, but interprets these labels either in terms of the physical or the hedonistic consequences of action (punishment, reward, exchange of favors) or in terms of the physical power of those who enunciate the rules and labels. The level is divided into the following two stages:

Stage 1: *The punishment-and-obedience orientation.* The physical consequences of action determine its goodness or badness, regardless of the human meaning or value of these consequences. Avoidance of punishment and unquestioning deference to power are valued in their own right, not in terms of respect for an underlying moral order supported by punishment and authority (the latter being Stage 4).

Stage 2: *The instrumental-relativist orientation.* Right action consists of that which instrumentally satisfies one's own needs and occasionally the needs of others. Human relations are viewed in terms like those of the marketplace. Elements of fairness, of reciprocity, and of equal sharing are present, but they are always interpreted in a physical, pragmatic way. Reciprocity is a matter of "you scratch my back and I'll scratch yours," not of loyalty, gratitude, or justice.

II. Conventional level

At this level, maintaining the expectations of the individual's family, group, or nation is perceived as valuable in its own right, regardless of immediate and obvious consequences. The attitude is not only one of *conformity* to personal expectations and social order, but of loyalty to it, of actively *maintaining,* supporting, and justifying the order, and of identifying with the persons or group involved in it. At this level, there are the following two stages:

Stage 3: *The interpersonal concordance or "good boy–nice girl" orientation.* Good behavior is that which pleases or helps others and is approved by them. There is much conformity to stereotypical images of what is majority or "natural" behavior. Behavior is frequently judged by intention—"he means well" becomes important for the first time. One earns approval by being "nice."

Stage 4: *The "law and order" orientation.* There is orientation toward authority, fixed rules, and the maintenance of the social order. Right behavior consists of doing one's duty, showing respect for authority, and maintaining the given social order for its own sake.

III. Postconventional, autonomous, or principled level

At this level, there is a clear effort to define moral values and principles that have validity and application apart from the authority of the groups or persons holding these principles and apart from the individual's own identification with these groups. This level also has two stages:

Stage 5: *The social-contract, legalistic orientation,* generally with utilitarian overtones. Right action tends to be defined in terms of general individual rights and standards which have been critically examined and agreed upon by the whole society. There is a clear awareness of the relativism of personal values and opinions and a corresponding emphasis upon procedural rules for reaching consensus. Aside from what is constitutionally and democratically agreed upon, the right is a matter of personal "values" and "opinion." The result is an emphasis upon the "legal point of view," but with an emphasis upon the possibility of changing law in terms of rational considerations of social utility (rather than freezing it in terms of Stage 4 "law and order"). Outside the legal realm, free agreement and contract is the binding element of obligation. This is the "official" morality of the American government and constitution.

Stage 6: *The universal-ethical-principle orientation.* Right is defined by the decision of conscience in accord with self-chosen *ethical principles* appealing to logical comprehensiveness, universality, and consistency. These principles are abstract and ethical (the Golden Rule, the categorical imperative); they are not concrete moral rules like the Ten Commandments. At heart, these are universal principles of *justice,* of the *reciprocity* and *equality* of human *rights,* and of respect for the dignity of human beings as *individual persons* ("From Is to Ought," pp. 164, 165).

—Reprinted from *The Journal of Philosophy,* October 25, 1973.

correlated with IQ or verbal intelligence (correlations are only in the 30s, accounting for 10% of the variance). Cognitive development, in the stage sense, however, is more important for moral development than such correlations suggest. Piaget has found that after the child learns to speak there are three major stages of reasoning: the intuitive, the concrete operational, and the formal operational. At around age 7, the child enters the stage of concrete logical thought: He can make logical inferences, classify, and handle quantitative relations about concrete things. In adolescence individuals usually enter the stage of formal operations. At this stage they can reason abstractly, i.e., consider all possibilities, form hypotheses, deduce implications from hypotheses, and test them against reality.[3]

Since moral reasoning clearly is reasoning, advanced moral reasoning depends upon advanced logical reasoning: a person's logical stage puts a certain ceiling on the moral stage he can attain. A person whose logical stage is only concrete operational is limited to the preconventional moral stages (Stages 1 and 2). A person whose logical stage is only partially formal operational is limited to the conventional moral stages (Stages 3 and 4). While logical development is necessary for moral development and sets limits to it, most individuals are higher in logical stage than they are in moral stage. As an example, over 50% of late adolescents and adults are capable of full formal reasoning, but only 10% of these adults (all formal operational) display principled (Stages 5 and 6) moral reasoning.

The moral stages are *structures of moral judgment* or *moral reasoning*. *Structures* of moral judgment must be distinguished from the *content* of moral judgment. As an example, we cite responses to a dilemma used in our various studies to identify moral stage. The dilemma raises the issue of stealing a drug to save a dying woman. The inventor of the drug is selling it for 10 times what it costs him to make it. The woman's husband cannot raise the money, and the seller refuses to lower the price or wait for payment. What should the husband do?

The choice endorsed by a subject (steal,don't steal) is called the *content* of his moral judgment in the situation. His reasoning about the choice defines the structure of his moral judgment. This reasoning centers on the following 10 universal moral values or issues of concern to persons in these moral dilemmas:

1. Punishment
2. Property
3. Roles and concerns of affection
4. Roles and concerns of authority
5. Law
6. Life
7. Liberty
8. Distributive justice
9. Truth
10. Sex

A moral choice involves choosing between two (or more) of these values as they *conflict* in concrete situations of choice.

The stage or structure of a person's moral judgment defines: 1) *what* he finds valuable in each of these moral issues (life, law), i.e., how he defines the value, and 2) *why* he finds it valuable, i.e., the reasons he gives for valuing it. As an example, at Stage 1 life is valued in terms

3. Many adolescents and adults only partially attain the stage of formal operations. They do consider all the actual relations of one thing to another at the same time, but they do not consider all possibilities and form abstract hypotheses. A few do not advance this far, remaining "concrete operational."

of the power or possessions of the person involved; at Stage 2, for its usefulness in satisfying the needs of the individual in question or others; at Stage 3, in terms of the individual's relations with others and their valuation of him; at Stage 4, in terms of social or religious law. Only at Stages 5 and 6 is each life seen as inherently worthwhile, aside from other considerations.

MORAL JUDGMENT VS. MORAL ACTION

Having clarified the nature of stages of moral *judgment,* we must consider the relation of moral judgment to moral *action.* If logical reasoning is a necessary but not sufficient condition for mature moral judgment, mature moral judgment is a necessary but not sufficient condition for mature moral action. One cannot follow moral principles if one does not understand (or believe in) moral principles. However, one can reason in terms of principles and not live up to these principles. As an example, Richard Krebs and I found that only 15% of students showing some principled thinking cheated as compared to 55% of conventional subjects and 70% of preconventional subjects. Nevertheless, 15% of the principled subjects did cheat, suggesting that factors additional to moral judgment are necessary for principled moral reasoning to be translated into "moral action." Partly, these factors include the situation and its pressures. Partly, what happens depends upon the individual's motives and emotions. Partly, what the individual does depends upon a general sense of will, purpose, or "ego strength." As an example of the role of will or ego strength in moral behavior, we may cite the study by Krebs: Slightly more than half of his conventional subjects cheated. These subjects were also divided by a measure of attention/will. Only 26% of the "strong-willed" conventional subjects cheated; however, 74% of the "weak-willed" subjects cheated.

If maturity of moral reasoning is only one factor in moral behavior, why does the cognitive-developmental approach to moral education focus so heavily upon moral reasoning? For the following reasons:

1. Moral judgment, while only one factor in moral behavior, is the single most important or influential factor yet discovered in moral behavior.

2. While other factors influence moral behavior, moral judgment is the only distinctively *moral* factor in moral behavior. To illustrate, we noted that the Krebs study indicated that "strong-willed" conventional stage subjects resisted cheating more than "weak-willed" subjects. For those at a preconventional level of moral reasoning, however, "will" had an opposite effect. "Strong-willed" Stages 1 and 2 subjects cheated more, not less, than "weak-willed" subjects, i.e., they had the "courage of their (amoral) convictions" that it was worthwhile to cheat. "Will," then, is an important factor in moral behavior, but it is not distinctively moral; it becomes moral only when informed by mature moral judgment.

3. Moral judgment change is long-range or irreversible; a higher stage is never lost. Moral behavior as such is largely situational and reversible or "loseable" in new situations.

AIMS OF MORAL AND CIVIC EDUCATION

Moral psychology describes what moral development is, as studied empirically. Moral education must also consider moral philosophy, which strives to tell us what moral development ideally *ought to be.* Psychology finds an invariant sequence of moral stages; moral philosophy must be invoked to answer whether a later stage is a better stage. The "stage" of senescence and death follows the "stage" of adulthood, but that does not mean that senesence and death are better. Our claim that the latest or principled stages of moral reasoning are morally better stages, then, must rest on considerations of moral philosophy.

The tradition of moral philosophy to which we appeal is the liberal or rational tradition, in particular the "formalistic" or "deontological" tradition running from Immanuel Kant to John Rawls. Central to this tradition is the claim that an adequate morality is *principled,* i.e., that it makes judgments in terms of *universal* principles applicable to all mankind. *Principles* are to be distinguished from *rules.* Conventional morality is grounded on rules, primarily "thou shalt nots" such as are represented by the Ten Commandments, prescriptions of kinds of actions. Principles are, rather, universal guides to making a moral decision. An example is Kant's "categorical imperative," formulated in two ways. The first is the maxim of respect for human personality, "Act always toward the other as an end, not as a means." The second is the maxim of universalization, "Choose only as you would be willing to have everyone choose in your situation." Principles like that of Kant's state the formal conditions of a moral choice or action. In the dilemma in which a woman is dying because a druggist refuses to release his drug for less than the stated price, the druggist is not acting morally, though he is not violating the ordinary moral rules (he is not actually stealing or murdering). But he is violating principles: He is treating the woman simply as a means to his ends of profit, and he is not choosing as he would wish anyone to choose (if the druggist were in the dying woman's place, he would not want a druggist to choose as he is choosing). Under most circumstances, choice in terms of conventional moral rules and choice in terms of principles coincide. Ordinarily, principles dictate not stealing (avoiding stealing is implied by acting in terms of a regard for others as ends and in terms of what one would want everyone to do). In a situation where stealing is the only means to save a life, however, principles contradict the ordinary rules and would dictate stealing. Unlike rules which are supported by social authority, principles are freely chosen by the individual because of their intrinsic moral validity.[4]

The conception that a moral choice is a choice made in terms of moral principles is related to the claim of liberal moral philosophy that moral principles are ultimately principles of justice. In essence, moral conflicts are conflicts between the claims of persons, and principles for resolving these claims are principles of justice, "for giving each his due." Central to justice are the demands of *liberty, equality,* and *reciprocity.* At every moral stage, there is a concern for justice. The most damning statement a school child can make about a teacher is that "he's not fair." At each higher stage, however, the conception of justice is reorganized. At Stage 1, justice is punishing the bad in terms of "an eye for an eye and a tooth for a tooth." At Stage 2, it is

4. Not all freely chosen values or rules are principles, however. Hitler chose the "rule," "exterminate the enemies of the Aryan race," but such a rule is not a universalizable principle.

exchanging favors and goods in an equal manner. At Stages 3 and 4, it is treating people as they desire in terms of the conventional rules. At Stage 5, it is recognized that all rules and laws flow from justice, from a social contract between the governors and the governed designed to protect the equal rights of all. At Stage 6, personally chosen moral principles are also principles of justice, the principles any member of a society would choose for that society if he did not know what his position was to be in the society and in which he might be the least advantaged. Principles chosen from this point of view are, first, the maximum liberty compatible with the like liberty of others and, second, no inequalities of goods and respect which are not to the benefit of all, including the least advantaged.

As an example of stage progression in the orientation to justice, we may take judgments about capital punishment. Capital punishment is only firmly rejected at the two principled stages, when the notion of justice as vengeance or retribution is abandoned. At the sixth stage, capital punishment is not condoned even if it may have some useful deterrent effect in promoting law and order. This is because it is not a punishment we would choose for a society if we assumed we had as much chance of being born into the position of a criminal or murderer as being born into the position of a law abider.

Why are decisions based on universal principles of justice better decisions? Because they are decisions on which all moral men could agree. When decisions are based on conventional moral rules, men will disagree, since they adhere to conflicting systems of rules dependent on culture and social position. Throughout history men have killed one another in the name of conflicting moral rules and values, most recently in Vietnam and the Middle East. Truly moral or just resolutions of conflicts require principles which are, or can be, universalizable.

ALTERNATIVE APPROACHES

We have given a philosophic rationale for stage advance as the aim of moral education. Given this rationale, the developmental approach to moral education can avoid the problems inherent in the other two major approaches to moral education. The first alternative approach is that of indoctrinative moral education, the preaching and imposition of the rules and values of the teacher and his culture on the child. In America, when this indoctrinative approach has been developed in a systematic manner, it has usually been termed "character education."

Moral values, in the character education approach, are preached or taught in terms of what may be called the "bag of virtues." In the classic studies of character by Hugh Hartshorne and Mark May, the virtues chosen were honesty, service, and self-control. It is easy to get superficial consensus on such a bag of virtues—until one examines in detail the list of virtues involved and the details of their definition. Is the Hartshorne and May bag more adequate than the Boy Scout bag (a Scout should be honest, loyal, reverent, clean, brave, etc.)? When one turns to the details of defining each virtue, one finds equal uncertainty or difficulty in reaching consensus. Does honesty mean one should not steal to save a life? Does it mean that a student should not help another student with his homework?

Character education and other forms of indoctrinative moral education have aimed at teaching universal values (it is assumed that honesty or service are desirable traits for all men in all societies), but the detailed definitions used are relative; they are defined by the opinions of the teacher and the conventional culture and rest on the authority of the teacher for their justification. In this sense character education is close to the unreflective valuings by teachers which constitute the hidden curriculum of the school.[5] Because of the current unpopularity of indoctrinative approaches to moral education, a family of approaches called "values clarification" has become appealing to teachers. Values clarification takes the first step implied by a rational approach to moral education: the eliciting of the child's own judgment or opinion about issues or situations in which values conflict, rather than imposing the teacher's opinion on him. Values clarification, however, does not attempt to go further than eliciting awareness of values; it is assumed that becoming more self-aware about one's values is an end in itself. Fundamentally, the definition of the end of values education as self-awareness derives from a belief in ethical relativity held by many value-clarifiers. As stated by Peter Engel, "One must contrast value clarification and value inculcation. Value clarification implies the principle that in the consideration of values there is no single correct answer." Within these premises of "no correct answer," children are to discuss moral dilemmas in such a way as to reveal different values and discuss their value differences with each other. The teacher is to stress that "our values are different," not that one value is more adequate than others. If this program is systematically followed, students will themselves become relativists, believing there is no "right" moral answer. For instance, a student caught cheating might argue that he did nothing wrong, since his own hierarchy of values, which may be different from that of the teacher, made it right for him to cheat.

Like values clarification, the cognitive-developmental approach to moral education stresses open or Socratic peer discussion of value dilemmas. Such discussion, however, has an aim: stimulation of movement to the next stage of moral reasoning. Like values clarification, the developmental approach opposes indoctrination. Stimulation of movement to the next stage of reasoning is not indoctrinative, for the following reasons:

1. Change is in the way of reasoning rather than in the particular beliefs involved.

2. Students in a class are at different stages; the aim is to aid movement of each to the next stage, not convergence on a common pattern.

3. The teacher's own opinion is neither stressed nor invoked as authoritative. It enters in only as one of many opinions, hopefully one of those at a next higher stage.

4. The notion that some judgments are more adequate than others is communicated. Fundamentally, however, this means that the student is encouraged to articulate a position which seems most adequate to him and to judge the adequacy of the reasoning of others.

In addition to having more definite aims than values clarification, the moral development approach restricts value education to that which is moral or, more specifically, to justice. This is for two

5. As an example of the "hidden curriculum," we may cite a second-grade classroom. My son came home from this classroom one day saying he did not want to be "one of the bad boys." Asked "Who are the bad boys?" he replied, "The ones who don't put their books back and get yelled at."

reasons. First, it is not clear that the whole realm of personal, political, and religious values is a realm which is nonrelative, i.e., in which there are universals and a direction of development. Second, it is not clear that the public school has a right or mandate to develop values in general.[6] In our view, value education in the public schools should be restricted to that which the school has the right and mandate to develop: an awareness of justice, or of the rights of others in our Constitutional system. While the Bill of Rights prohibits the teaching of religious beliefs, or of specific value systems, it does not prohibit the teaching of the awareness of rights and principles of justice fundamental to the Constitution itself.

When moral education is recognized as centered in justice and differentiated from value education or affective education, it becomes apparent that moral and civic education are much the same thing. This equation, taken for granted by the classic philosophers of education from Plato and Aristotle to Dewey, is basic to our claim that a concern for moral education is central to the educational objectives of social studies.

6. Restriction of deliberate value education to the moral may be clarified by our example of the second-grade teacher who made tidying up of books a matter of moral indoctrination. Tidiness is a value, but it is not a moral value. Cheating is a moral issue, intrinsically one of fairness. It involves issues of violation of trust and taking advantage. Failing to tidy the room may under certain conditions be an issue of fairness, when it puts an undue burden on others. If it is handled by the teacher as a matter of cooperation among the group in this sense, it is a legitimate focus of deliberate moral education. If it is not, it simply represents the arbitrary imposition of the teacher's values on the child.

(Kirschenbaum, cont. from p. 55)

consideration of consequences; (3) chosen freely; (4) prized and cherished; (5) publicly affirmed; (6) acted upon; and (7) acted upon with some pattern and repetition.

I was very impressed. My friends and I had grown up in an educational system which did little but moralize and indoctrinate. Rarely were we given a chance to get in touch with what we thought was important, what we prized and cherished. Nor did we have much of a chance to explore alternatives or make free choices as a part of our education. And schooling certainly didn't involve action for us; it had little to do with our lives in the real world. Moreover, I had just been very involved with the civil-rights movement in Mississippi. I saw in values-clarification—in the methods and approaches that fostered Raths' seven criteria—the educational implementation of my political and social views. If young people could only be encouraged to see more alternatives, to question their values, to act on their ideals, I felt certain they could play an integral role in changing and improving our society and world.

So when I began teaching in 1966, values clarification was one important part of my repertoire. I believed then (and do now) that few educational goals are more important than helping young people determine who they are, what they stand for, and where they want to go. I was also very impressed with the by-products of the approach when used in a group setting—the greater tolerance of others' points of view, the realization that we are not so unique and that others share our problems and concerns, the sense of trust and community the activities foster. . . .

But I soon became aware that values clarification wasn't all that was important in education. In 1968 I took a group dynamics course at Temple University and a Human Relations Work-shop at the National Training Laboratories in Bethel, Maine. In these powerful educational experiences, I realized how the goals of more effective *communication* and the ability to deal with one's *feelings* were as important as the choosing, prizing, and acting goals of values clarification. Simultaneously, Sid Simon and Merrill Harmin also were experiencing the power of verbal and nonverbal communication exercises in their work.

In the summers of 1968 and 1969, we began to introduce these communication and awareness exercises into our week-long values workshops. We made two big charts, headed "Values-Clarification Strategies" and "Feeling Strategies" (or "Emotional-Awareness Exercises"), and after the group had participated in or observed a particular strategy, we would write the name of the technique on the appropriate chart. The implication was that "values" was the primarily cognitive area and "feelings" was, of course, the affective area. We even set aside the first hour of every morning for nonverbal activities, which were usually very powerful, emotion-laden experiences for those who participated. At the end of the workshop, we would offer a theory I had developed, based on an essay by Carl Rogers, for how the feeling area and the values area fit together.

Not everyone, however, appreciated the affective component in these workshops. It often produced some threat and resistance for many of the participants who had come for values clarification and were not interested in these "touchy-feely" exercises. We wanted to respect their rights, too. It was something of a dilemma. In the long run, we decided we had little enough time in a weekend or a week to do all we wanted with values clarification, let alone introduce these deeper communication and feeling-awareness exercises. So we abandoned most of these in our values workshops and saved them for separate human relations and personal growth workshops which we began to conduct at about that time.

Perhaps we had been close to something important—an integration of values clarification with other areas of humanistic education. At any rate, we backed off from that and went back to thinking of values clarification as including only those exercises that could be seen to stem directly from Rath's seven criteria. Over the years, we continued to introduce, from time to time, different types of activities into our workshops—listening exercises, reevaluation counseling methods, Gestalt approaches. But we did this mostly in an intuitive way, making little attempt to consciously or explicitly integrate them with values clarification. . . .

Meanwhile, I was becoming increasingly dissatisfied with Raths' seven criteria—for two reasons. First, I didn't like the notion of "criteria." Secondly, I had a lot of problems with several of the seven criteria.

In *Values and Teaching,* the authors had written:

> We therefore cannot be certain what values, what style of life, would be most suitable for any person. We do, however, have some ideas about

> what *processes* might be most effective for obtaining values. These ideas grow from the assumption that whatever values one obtains should work as effectively as possible to relate one to his world in a satisfying and intelligent way.
>
> From this assumption comes what we call the *process of valuing.* A look at this process may make clear how we define a value. Unless something satisfies *all* seven of the criteria noted below, we do not call it a value. In other words, for a value to result, all of the following seven requirements must apply. Collectively, they describe the process of valuing.

I have never heard anyone dispute that Raths did identify seven ways that our beliefs or behaviors take on added value for us—seven processes of valuing. But when the authors extended these processes to also serve as "criteria," they created a problem.

For the word "criterion" to have some meaning, other than theoretical, it must be usable. By definition, a criterion is a standard. It is used to determine whether whatever is being evaluated measures up to the standard. Whether the criterion is an objective one (New York City policemen must be at least 5' 8" tall) or a subjective one (my house site must be secluded and quiet) the principle is the same: if we know all the criteria and we know all the facts of the situation, we should be able to tell whether the criteria are met or not.

In the case of Raths' seven criteria for a value, this principle does not apply.

How proud must someone be of his belief or behavior in order to meet the prizing criteria? Very proud? Just a little proud? What about pleased? When does pleased turn into proud?

How many times must someone publicly affirm something in order to satisfy the fifth criteria? Is once enough? If I publicly affirmed my views on pollution six years ago, have I satisfied that criteria?

How many alternatives does one have to choose from before whoever is doing the judging tells me I have met the third criteria?

How many consequences must I thoughtfully consider? If I spend one minute thoughtfully considering one consequence, have I satisfied the criteria? How much consideration is involved in being thoughtful?

And how free does my choice have to be? And how many times must I act before I've "actualized" my value? And how many inconsistencies am I allowed before I flunk the test of its being a pattern in my life?

The argument becomes almost absurd. Of course, no one can answer these questions. Ultimately each individual must decide for himself how many alternatives to consider, how many times to act, or how proud he must feel about something before wanting to do it or repeat it. By using the word and the concept "criteria," we suggest that it is possible for someone (perhaps I, the workshop leader) to judge whether or not a particular belief or behavior of someone else is a value. Time and again, I have seen this implicit suggestion produce resistance among workshop participants. Understandably, they resent having someone else define for them what their values are or aren't. As a consequence, they often deny the importance of some of the valuing processes, rather than accept that certain values they thought they held are not values after all (they're only "value indicators," we say). Ironically, we become another type of moralizer, making people feel guilty because they haven't met this or that criterion on a given issue.

Therefore, I prefer to talk only of the *processes* of valuing, to emphasize that here are seven ways we develop and enrich the values in our lives—by getting in touch with what we prize and cherish, by considering alternatives, by acting on our beliefs and goals, by examining our patterns, and so on. My goal is not for people to be able to say, "Look here, I've got five values which meet all seven criteria," but to help people, including myself, learn to use skillfully the seven processes in our lives. Then, as a matter of course, we will continue to examine what we prize and cherish, make thoughtful choices from alternatives, act on our beliefs and goals—*but only when we feel the need to do so and not just to meet someone else's criteria.* It seems to me that one of the overall goals of values clarification is to return the locus of evaluation to the person, so that he is the controller of his own valuing process. The seven criteria imply an external frame of reference which seems inimical to values clarification. I want to use the seven valuing processes in my life because they help my inner needs find expression and fulfillment. I do not want to use them because they are criteria.

This differentiation between "processes" and "criteria" may seem like only a semantic distinction, important only in its possibility for producing less resistance when explaining the seven processes of values-clarification workshops. On the contrary, I think that once one firmly shifts his focus to the valuing *process* the very nature of the seven processes begins to change.

Consider the fourth process or criteria—that of prizing and cherishing. To hold beliefs and engage in behaviors that one prizes and cherishes is clearly one of the goals of values clarification. In this sense, the prized beliefs or behaviors are a *product* of values clarification; the "criterion" of prizing and cherishing has been met. But, in reality, we know two things: first, that one does not quickly or easily arrive at fully developed beliefs and behaviors that are prized and cherished; second, what one prizes and cherishes continually changes, from moment to moment or from year to year. Again, we see that prizing and cherishing is not so much an attained state as it is an ongoing process.

What, then, is this ongoing process by which one continually discovers what he prizes and cherishes? Here we return to the problem we experienced several years ago when we abandoned the use of the emotional-awareness exercises in the values-clarification workshops. Whether we know how to integrate it in workshops or not, it seems clear that the affective realm, the feeling area, is one of the crucial ingredients in values clarification, and that the process by which one discovers what he prizes and cherishes is, in part, a deepening awareness of one's own feelings. In Carl Rogers' terminology, it would be an "openness to our inner experience." And this includes not only the positive experience; it involves the full gamut of human emotion.

One needs only to recall the most recent, extremely important decision in his life—perhaps involving a love relationship, a choice or change of job, a move to another locality, or the like. It was probably necessary to process numerous emotions—fear, hope, anxiety, excitement, dependence, love, hate, loneliness, competence, incompetence—before coming to a better understanding of which choices one would prize or cherish the most.

What all this implies is that if we are describing the valuing process, instead of the criterion, we shall have to adopt new terminology. For the fourth process, we might move from "prizing and cherishing," which is the by-product, to talk about *discovering* what one prizes and cherishes. Yet even this is perhaps a misnomer for the task, placing too much emphasis on the results. I prefer "being open to one's inner experience," as this connotes an ongoing process of identifying and sorting through one's feelings in order to keep arriving at choices which one can prize and cherish. But the terminology is far less important than the process described and the implication of such a shift in emphasis. What is implied is that values clarification, which has been treated as primarily a cognitive process even by the leaders in the approach, must be much more fully recognized as also an in-depth affective process. If this is so, then we can no longer exclude the learnings and techniques from psychotherapy, human relations training, Gestalt therapy, bioenergetics, and many other areas from our concepts or from our practices in values clarification. These latter methods may focus more on discovering all of one's feelings in the present moment (the "here and now"), and values-clarification strategies may focus more on discovering our prizing and cherishing feelings as evident in our beliefs and behavior patterns: but both are needed and complementary. All the methods by which people become aware of all their feelings and learn to deal with and understand them are crucial for developing one's own values and making difficult values decisions. The "criteria" of beliefs and behaviors which are prized and cherished are reached only through an ongoing awareness of one's inner, feeling world. . . .

The door is open. Once we change the emphasis from *criteria* for a value to the *processes* of valuing, we are forced to ask: What are all the processes by which individuals achieve an identity, develop values, and decide what they stand for and what they wish to live for? The older "choosing, prizing, and acting" areas of values clarification are no longer enough to encompass the answer.

In my own thinking, I would expand the three major areas of valuing into these five major processes:

1. Feeling
2. Thinking
3. Communicating
4. Choosing
5. Acting

It seems to me that each of these areas is an essential part of the valuing process. Individually, each area is comprised of several sub-processes of valuing which I will discuss briefly below. Collectively, these five valuing processes describe an effective human being, utilizing most of his or her faculties for living fully and satisfyingly in our society. Moreover, these five areas seem necessary for living fully and satisfyingly in any society. True, different societies have different norms; for example, one society might have standards for self-disclosure that would be entirely inappropriate in another society. But to live effectively in either society, one has to learn the *skills* for knowing when and how to reveal himself. Therefore, each of the areas is not only a major valuing process; each is also a set of *life skills* that can be learned, practiced, and improved in time.

Feeling

This is the area that schools have

studiously avoided throughout history, believing that wisdom resided in the mind and the solution to most of life's problems lay in the rational processes. Today, there is a significant movement to bring *affective* education into the schools.

The primary process in the feeling area of valuing, as discussed at length above, is to be "open to one's inner experience." Others have described this process, or parts of it, in various terms: "Know thyself." "Be in touch with your feelings." "Know what you prize and cherish." All these things are part of the bigger process. To be open implies an acceptance of one's feelings. The person who distrusts himself, who is guilty about certain feelings, who is fearful of certain of his emotions, cannot be open to all portions of his inner experience. To the extent that he denies these feelings (or thoughts) or distorts them in his awareness, he will deprive himself of important data in making values decisions. His thinking, communicating, choosing, and acting processes will all suffer as a result. Therefore, all the approaches which have been or are being developed to help people learn the skills for becoming aware of and sorting through or "processing" their feelings are extremely important for the values-clarification process to operate effectively.

Thinking

Most of us would assume that thinking skills are necessary to develop clear values; but this has rarely been made explicit by humanistic educators. Probably the reason for this is that it is widely assumed that schools are being effective in the cognitive realm (a questionable assumption). Therefore, humanistic educators have spent most of their time focusing on the affective realm. But, both in theory and in practice, the thinking area should not be slighted.

People have thought of thinking skills in a variety of ways, and it seems to me that all are important. Benjamin Bloom and Norris Sanders have emphasized the levels of thinking—memory, translation, interpretation, application, analysis, synthesis, and evaluation, for example, and have encouraged teachers to help students learn the higher levels of thinking, not only memory. Others have taught "critical thinking," distinguishing fact from opinion, analyzing propaganda, etc. Logic is another thinking skill that is taught in many schools, often through the math department. Creative thinking is yet another.

Clearly, the choosing and communicating processes of valuing, especially, are dependent on the thinking process. In my own high school teaching experience, I have been guilty at times of emphasizing the other four major valuing processes to the detriment of the cognitive, without which no person can be an effective human being. We sometimes assume that people learn to think by themselves. Piaget and Kohlberg, however, have demonstrated, both in the areas of pure cognition and in moral reasoning, that by manipulating the environment, we can help people advance to higher, more flexible levels of thinking. The dichotomy between "traditional" and "humanistic" education is often misleading in this respect. Thinking always has been—and should continue to be—a major concern for the humanist.

Communicating

As discussed earlier, the process of communicating can be both verbal and nonverbal. In either case, some of the major subprocesses or separate skills are: sending clear messages, empathic listening, and giving and receiving feedback. Drawing another person out and asking clarifying questions could also be listed. Conflict resolution might be mentioned as another valuing process, for whenever conflicts arise, this skill is necessary to resolve the conflict in a way that best realizes the values of all the parties involved.

Choosing

The discussion of this area will also be short, because I would list the three standbys in Raths' seven processes as subprocesses in the choosing area—choosing from alternatives, choosing after thoughtful consideration of consequences, and choosing freely. Perhaps different types of planning and problem-solving processes could also be included here; for example, the type of achievement-planning strategy advocated and taught by Alfred Alschuler and his colleagues. Clearly, choosing is a process that is dependent on both feeling and thinking skills and enhanced by good communication skills.

Acting

Here again, Raths' subprocesses would apply. One way we value is to act upon something with repetition. The more we act on it, the more our behavior shows that we value it. Quantity is the issue. Second, the *quality* of our actions also shows what we value. As I build patterns into my life, as I eliminate the inconsistencies, my actions take on a harmonious and cumulative momentum which has that much more chance of actualizing what I prize and cherish. This emphasis is consistent with those existentialists who say that we define ourselves through our actions.

Thus, the school program that wishes to encourage the action aspect of valuing provides opportunities for students to examine the patterns of action and inaction in their lives and, moreover, provides them with the opportunity to act on the choices they make. This may mean that they actually control some aspects of their education (choice of classes, choice of reading, choice of how they spend their time during the day, etc.), or it may mean that they get out into the world and involve themselves in action projects where they can put some of their beliefs and ideals into real practice.

The school which is interested in building skills in this action area not only allows students to act on their choices, it helps them learn to act more effectively. This may be done in two ways. One is to help the student learn the other four major valuing processes. Simply by being more skillful as a feeler, thinker, communicator, and chooser, it follows that a person's chosen actions will work out that much more successfully. Whether the student chooses to write, work with automobiles, or engage in social change, the school can provide the settings or resources whereby he can learn to do those chosen actions more effectively. Not only schools, but parents, group leaders, peers, or anyone else can help foster this and the other valuing processes.

The discussion of each of the five major processes of valuing is intentionally short and suggestive. The more I think about the valuing process, the more it seems to encompass. The present enlarged view of the valuing process could be outlined in the following form. Each major process (for example, thinking) and each sub-

3. It is interesting that, while some existentialists and others say that our actions reveal our values, there are others who equate our beliefs and opinions with our values. Still others see values as synonymous with attitudes and preferences. Values clarification is unique in that it sees the valuing process as involving feelings, thoughts, and actions, not one to the exclusion of the others.

process (for example, critical thinking) is considered a valuing process, because if an individual can and does utilize the process effectively, he is more likely to guide his life in a satisfying and continually growing direction.

The Valuing Process

I. Feeling

1. Begin open to one's inner experience.
   a. awareness of one's inner experience
   b. acceptance of one's inner experience

II. Thinking

1. Thinking on all seven levels.
   a. memory
   b. translation
   c. application
   d. interpretation
   e. analysis
   f. synthesis
   g. evaluation
2. Critical thinking.
   a. distinguishing fact from opinion
   b. distinguishing supported from unsupported arguments
   c. analyzing propaganda, stereotypes, etc.
3. Logical thinking (logic).
4. Creative thinking.
5. Fundamental cognitive skills.
   a. language use
   b. mathematical skills
   c. research skills

III. Communicating—Verbally and Nonverbally

1. Sending clear messages.
2. Empathic listening.
3. Drawing out.
4. Asking clarifying questions.
5. Giving and receiving feedback.
6. Conflict resolution.

IV. Choosing

1. Generating and considering alternatives.
2. Thoughtfully considering consequences, pros and cons.
3. Choosing strategically.
   a. goal setting
   b. data gathering
   c. problem solving
   d. planning
4. Choosing freely.

V. Acting

1. Acting with repetition.
2. Acting with a pattern and consistency.
3. Acting skillfully, competently. . . .

Even in a short presentation on values clarification, should we try to explain the much fuller conception of the valuing process and risk overloading the listeners with too much detail? Or do we stick with the shorter, safer version of the seven processes which have worked well for many years? What are some other alternatives? If, in a workshop, we have decided to emphasize only some of the major valuing processes, how do we set our priorities? Is feeling more important than acting? Which is more likely to result in consistent actions that are in harmony with what people say they prize and cherish—the values-clarification choosing strategies, the Hilda Taba critical thinking strategies, the Gestalt feeling exercises, or the Kohlberg-derived moral reasoning activities?

We don't really know the answers to these and many other questions. And, although they offer rich possibilities for research, it will probably be some time before answers begin to emerge. Meanwhile, undoubtedly, we will continue to insert all kinds of feeling-oriented and communication-oriented exercises into our workshops and our writings. Intuitively, we'll know we have to go beyond the original confines of values-clarification theory. I ask that those of us who are interested in this work admit that we are going beyond values clarification, that we expand our conception of what values clarification is, that we encourage dialogues with other branches of humanistic education, and that, together, we build new theoretical models and practical designs which mutually enhance what we all are seeking—the more effective, more fulfilled, more self-actualizing human being.

POSTSCRIPT

CAN MORAL DEVELOPMENT BE ASSURED?

The two approaches to the moral growth function of education described here—the cognitive-developmental and the values clarification—have been tested in classroom situations and have been found to be generally effective. Neither, however, is the be-all and end-all of the values dimension of schooling. And neither answers the range of problems cited in the introduction of this issue.

For a full view of the educational problems and alternatives bearing on the values domain, one must sample widely. Amid a deluge of books and articles devoted to this topic, the following are particularly illuminating: Abraham Maslow's *New Knowledge in Human Values* (1959), R.S. Peters' *Ethics and Education* (1966), Milton Rokeach's *The Nature of Human Values* (1973), the June 1975 Moral Education issue of *Phi Delta Kappan, Moral Education—It Comes With the Territory* (1976) edited by David Purpel and Kevin Ryan, and *Religion and Public Education* by Lawrence Byrnes.

Other sources which might help clarify this difficult area are the Association for Supervision and Curriculum Development's booklet, *The School's Role as Moral Authority* (1977), Elizabeth Monroe Drew's and Leslie Lipson's *Values and Humanity* (1971), Philip Phenix's "The Moral Imperative in Contemporary American Education" in *Perspectives on Education,* (Winter 1969), the report of the NEA's Educational Policies Commission on *Moral and Spiritual Values in the Public Schools* (1951), and John Dewey's *Moral Principles in Education* (1911).

Jacob W. Getzels offers a summation of the central problem for teachers in "Schools and Values" (*The Center Magazine,* May-June 1976). Getzels finds that contemporary young people often lack visible and consistent models for identification, a situation that causes extraordinary difficulties in social adaptation. He contends that it is not sufficient to teach values or to clarify values; teachers and other adults must also act as models with whom the young can identify. Educators often lecture students about the importance of their acquisition of "appropriate" values without demonstrating by their own actions what those values are.

ISSUE 5

HOW CAN INSTRUCTION BE MADE EFFECTIVE?

The best aims, the best curriculum design, and the best psychological atmosphere float in limbo without effective instructional theories and teaching strategies. A theory of instruction, while concentrating on modes and methods, is intimately connected with and often directly derived from a theory of growth and development.

In the 19th century, for example, Johann Friedrich Herbart's associationist theory of mental development led him to formulate an instructional methodology consisting of articulated steps which prompted and solidified the associative patterns which the learning theory hypothesized. In the present century, the careful study of the stages of human growth—by Erik Erikson, Jean Piaget, Robert Havighurst, and Jerome Bruner, among others—has expanded the realm of instructional concerns. Piaget's close descriptions of cognitive structures and of the growth periods of sensorimotor intelligence, concrete operations, and formal operations, for instance, have given instructional methodologists a base for precision.

Given impetus by the increasing study of human behavior, the effort to devise a science of teaching during the past fifty years has produced mixed results. Technological devices aimed at greater precision and efficiency have often suffered from a thinness of quality in the content materials handled. The latest advances in electronic media, however, hold promise of blending the *science* of teaching with a rekindled awareness of the *art* of teaching.

The linking of principles of learning to instructional strategies and the blending of art and science in the teaching act have occupied the attention of Jerome S. Bruner and Robert M. Gagné. Their experiments and resulting recommendations have substantially influenced educational practices. While their concerns for instructional effectiveness are similar, their points of departure for achieving such effectiveness are at variance, as the accompanying excerpts from their work point out.

Bruner's *The Process of Education* (1960) and his *Toward a Theory of Instruction* (1966) dominated discussions of teaching and learning for over a decade. Rejuvenating and validating Dewey's insights regarding the disciplinary structures of knowledge and the cruciality of the learner's active engagement in knowledge-seeking, Bruner turned educators' attention toward understanding basic principles and concepts as the primary instructional goal, and pointed to the inquiry process as the main access route.

Such ideas led to the reconstruction of approaches to various fields of knowledge and the emergence of new curricula in mathematics, physics, chemistry, and social studies based on the inquiry method. It was Bruner's contention that the emphasis on structure, basic concepts, and problem-solving skills makes subject matter more comprehensible, assists memory, makes the acquired knowledge and skills more transferable, and provides a greater sense of attachment between "advanced" knowledge and "elementary" knowledge.

Robert M. Gagné places himself among learning theorists who hold to an "information-processing" conception which views learning as a complex of processes within the learner's nervous system. His primary focus is on the "enabling conditions," both internal and external, which make learning possible. This conception leads him to the construction of systems and sequences of instructional activities geared to stimulating the present capabilities of the individual learner. This approach and Bruner's inquiry approach are detailed in the selections which follow.

Jerome S. Bruner

THE ACT OF DISCOVERY

The immediate occasion for my concern with discovery is the work of the various new curriculum projects that have grown up in America during the last few years. Whether one speaks to mathematicians or physicists or historians, one encounters repeatedly an expression of faith in the powerful effects that come from permitting the student to put things together for himself, to be his own discoverer.

First, I should be clear about what the act of discovery entails. It is rarely, on the frontier of knowledge or elsewhere, that new facts are "discovered" in the sense of being encountered, as Newton suggested, in the form of islands of truth in an uncharted sea of ignorance. Or if they appear to be discovered in this way, it is almost always thanks to some happy hypothesis about where to navigate. Discovery, like surprise, favors the well-prepared mind. In playing bridge, one is surprised by a hand with no honors in it and also by one that is all in one suit. Yet all particular hands in bridge are equiprobable: to be surprised one must know something about the laws of probability. So too in discovery. The history of science is studded with examples of men "finding out" something and not knowing it. I shall operate on the assumption that discovery, whether by a schoolboy going it on his own or by a scientist cultivating the growing edge of his field, is in its essence a matter of rearranging or transforming evidence in such a way that one is enabled to go beyond the evidence so reassembled to new insights. It may well be that an additional fact or shred of evidence makes this larger transformation possible. But it is often not even dependent on new information.

Very generally, and at the risk of oversimplification, it is useful to distinguish two kinds of teaching: that which takes place in the *expository mode* and that in the *hypothetical mode*. In the former, the decisions concerning the mode and pace and style of exposition are principally determined by the teacher as expositor; the student is the listener. The speaker has a quite different set of decisions to make: he has a wide choice of alternatives; he is anticipating paragraph content while the listener is still intent on the words; he

Continued on p. 76

Excerpted by permission of the publisher from *On Knowing: Essays For The Left Hand* by Jerome S. Bruner, Cambridge, Mass.: The Belknap Press of Harvard University Press, Copyright © 1962 by the President and Fellows of Harvard College.

Robert M. Gagné

THE CONDITIONS OF LEARNING

The occurrence of learning is inferred from a difference in a human being's performance as exhibited before and after being placed in a "learning situation." One may, for example, think of designing some conditions of learning to teach a child how to form the plurals of nouns. The child could then be placed in the learning situation, and following this, his performance in making plural nouns could be observed. But it would be embarrassing to discover that his performance in making plurals was no better than that of a child of equivalent age and ability who had *not* been placed in the same learning situation. The presence of the performance does not make it possible to conclude that learning has occurred. It is necessary to show that there has been a *change in performance.* The incapability for exhibiting the performance *before* learning must be taken into account as well as the capability that exists after learning.

It is in fact the existence of prior capabilities that is slighted or even ignored by most of the traditional learning prototypes. And it is these prior capabilities that are of crucial importance in drawing distinctions among the varieties of conditions needed for learning. . . . The child who is learning to tie his shoelaces does not begin this learning "from scratch"; he already knows how to hold the laces, how to loop one over the other, how to tighten a loop, and so on. The child who learns to call the mailman "Mr. Wells" also does not begin without some prior capabilities: he already knows how to imitate the words "mister" and "Wells," among other things. The theme is the same with more complex learning. The student who learns to multiply natural numbers has already acquired many capabilities, including adding and counting and recognizing numerals and drawing them with a pencil. The student who is learning how to write clear descriptive paragraphs already knows how to write sentences and to choose words.

The initial capabilities of the learner play an important part in determining the conditions required for subsequent learning. If one has determined that a child does not have the capability of saying the words "mister" and "Wells,"

Continued on p. 82

(Bruner, cont. from p. 74)
is manipulating the content of the material by various transformations while the listener is quite unaware of these internal options. But in the hypothetical mode the teacher and the student are in a more cooperative position with respect to what in linguistics would be called "speaker's decisions." The student is not a bench-bound listener, but is taking a part in the formulation and at times may play the principal role in it. He will be aware of alternatives and may even have an "as if" attitude toward these, and he may evaluate information as it comes. One cannot describe the process in either mode with great precision of detail, but I think it is largely the hypothetical mode which characterizes the teaching that encourages discovery.

Consider now what benefits might be derived from the experience of learning through discoveries that one makes oneself. I shall discuss these under four headings: (1) the increase in intellectual potency, (2) the shift from extrinsic to intrinsic rewards, (3) the learning of the heuristics of discovering, and (4) the aid to conserving memory.

Intellectual potency. I should like to consider the differences among students in a highly constrained psychological experiment involving a two-choice machine. In order to win chips, they must depress a key either on the right or the left side of the apparatus. A pattern of payoff is designed so that, say, they will be paid off on the right side 70 percent of the time, on the left 30 percent, but this detail is not important. What is important is that the payoff sequence is arranged at random, that there is no pattern. There is a marked contrast in the behavior of subjects who think that there is some pattern to be found in the sequence—who think that regularities are discoverable—and the performance of subjects who think that things are happening quite by chance. The first group adopts what is called an "event-matching" strategy in which the number of responses given to each side is roughly commensurate to the proportion of times that it pays off: in the present case, 70 on the right to 30 on the left. The group that believes there is no pattern very soon settles for a much more primitive strategy allocating *all* responses to the side that has the greater payoff. A little arithmetic will show that the lazy all-and-none strategy pays off more if the environment is truly random: they win 70 percent of the time. The event-matching subjects win about 70 percent on the 70-percent payoff side (or 49 percent of the time there) and 30 percent of the time on the side that pays off 30 percent of the time (another 9 percent for a total take-home wage of 58 percent in return for their labors of decision).

But the world is not always or not even frequently random, and if one analyzes carefully what the event matchers are doing, one sees that they are trying out hypotheses one after the other, all of them containing a term that leads to a distribution of bets on the two sides with a frequency to match the actual occurrence of events. If it should turn out that there is a pattern to be discovered, their payoff could become 100 percent. The other group would go on at the middling rate of 70 percent.

What has this to do with the subject at hand? For the person to search out and find regularities and relationships in his environment, he must either come armed with an expectancy that there will be something to find or be aroused to such an expectancy so that he may devise ways of searching and finding. One of the chief enemies of search is the assumption that there is nothing one can find in the environment by way of regularity or relationship. In the experiment just cited, subjects often fall into one of two habitual attitudes: either that there is nothing to be found or that a pattern can be discovered by looking. There is an important sequel in behavior to the two attitudes.

We have conducted a series of experimental studies on a group of some seventy schoolchildren over a four-year period. The studies have led us to distinguish an interesting dimension of cognitive activity that can be described as ranging from *episodic empiricism* at one end to *cumulative constructionism* at the other. The two attitudes in the above experiments on choice illustrate the extremes of the dimension. One of the experiments employs the game of Twenty Questions. A child—in this case he is between ten and twelve—is told that a car has gone off the road and hit a tree. He is to ask questions that can be answered by "yes" or "no" to discover the cause of the accident. After completing the problem, the same task is given him, though this time he is told that the accident has a different cause. In all, the procedure is repeated four times. Children enjoy playing the game. They also differ quite markedly in the approach or strategy they bring to the task. In the first place, we can distinguish clearly between two types of questions asked: one is intended to locate constraints in the problem, constraints that will eventually give shape to an hypothesis; the other is the hypothesis as question. It is the difference between, "Was there anything wrong with the driver?" and "Was the driver rushing to the doctor's office for an appointment and the car got out of control?" There are children who precede hypotheses with efforts to locate constraint and there are those who are "potshotters," who string out hypotheses noncumulatively one after the other. A second element of strategy lies in the connectivity of information gathering: the extent to which questions asked utilize or ignore or violate information previously obtained. The questions asked by children tend to be organized in cycles, each cycle usually given over to the pursuit of some particular notion. Both within cycles and between cycles one can discern marked differences in the connectivity of the children's performances. Needless to say, children who employ constraint location as a technique preliminary to the formulation of hypotheses tend to be far more organized in their harvesting of information. Persistence is another feature of strategy, a characteristic compounded of what appear to be two factors: sheer doggedness and a persistence that stems from the sequential organization that a child brings to the task. Doggedness is probably just animal spirits or the need to achieve. Organized persistence is a maneuver for protecting the fragile cognitive apparatus from overload. The child who has flooded himself with disorganized information from unconnected hypotheses will become discouraged and confused sooner than the child who has shown a certain cunning in his strategy of getting information—a child who senses that the value of information is not simply in getting it but in being able to carry it. The persistence of the organized child stems from his knowledge of how to organize questions in cycles and how to summarize things to himself.

Episodic empiricism is illustrated by information gathering that is unbound by prior constraints, that is deficient in organizational persistence. The opposite extreme, what we have called cumulative constructionism, is characterized by sensitivity to constraint, by connective maneuvers, and by organized persistence. Brute persistence seems to be one of those gifts from the gods that make people more exaggeratedly what they are.

Before returning to the issue of discovery and its role in the development of thinking, there is a word more to say about the ways in which the problem solver may transform information he has dealt with actively. The point arises from the pragmatic question: what does it take to get information processed into a form best designed to fit some future use? An experiment by R.B. Zajonc in 1957 suggests an answer. He gave groups of students information of a controlled kind, some groups being told that they were to transmit the information later on, others that they were merely to keep it in mind. In general, he found more differentiation of the information intended for transmittal than of information received passively. An active attitude leads to a transformation related to a task to be performed. There is a risk, to be sure, in the possible overspecialization of information processing. It can lead to such a high degree of specific organization that information is lost for general use, although this can be guarded against.

Let me convert the foregoing into an hypothesis. Emphasis on discovery in learning has precisely the effect on the learner of leading him to be a constructionist, to organize what he is encountering in a manner not only designed to discover regularity and relatedness, but also to avoid the kind of information drift that fails to keep account of the uses to which information might have to be put. Emphasis on discovery, indeed, helps the child to learn the varieties of problem solving, of transforming information for better use, helps him to learn how to go about the very task of learning. So goes the hypothesis; it is still in need of testing. But it is an hypothesis of such important human implications that we cannot afford not to test it—and the testing will have to be in the schools.

Intrinsic and extrinsic motives. Much of the problem in leading a child to effective cognitive activity is to free him from the immediate control of environmental rewards and punishments. Learning that starts in response to the rewards of parental or teacher approval or to the avoidance of failure can too readily develop a pattern in which the child is seeking cues as to how to conform to what is expected of him. We know from studies of children who tend to be early overachievers in school that they are likely to be seekers after the "right way to do it" and that their capacity for transforming learning into viable thought structures tends to be lower than that of children achieving at levels predicted by intelligence tests. Our tests on such children show them to be lower in analytic ability than those who are not conspicuous in overachievement. As we shall see later, they develop rote abilities and depend on being able to "give back" what is expected rather than to make it into something that relates to the rest of their cognitive life. As Maimonides would say, their learning is not their own.

The hypothesis I would propose here is that to the degree that one is able to approach learning as a task of discovering something rather than "learning about" it, to that degree there will be a tendency for the child to work with the autonomy of self-reward or, more properly, be rewarded by discovery itself.

To readers familiar with the battles of

the last half-century in the field of motivation, this hypothesis will be recognized as controversial. For the traditional view of motivation in learning has been, until very recently, couched in terms of a theory of drives and reinforcements: learning occurs because a response produced by a stimulus is followed by the reduction in a primary drive. The doctrine is greatly but thinly extended by the idea of secondary reinforcement: anything that has been "associated" with such a reduction in drive or need can also serve to reinforce the connection between a stimulus and the response that it evokes. Finding a steak will do for getting a food-search act connected with a certain stimulus, but so will the sight of a nice restaurant.

In 1959 there appeared a most searching and important criticism of this ancient hedonistic position, written by Robert White, reviewing the evidence of recently published animal studies, of work in the field of psychoanalysis, and of research on the development of cognitive processes in children. Professor White comes to the conclusion, quite rightly I think, that the drive-reduction model of learning runs counter to too many important phenomena of learning and development to be either regarded as general in its applicability or even correct in its general approach. Let me quote some of his principal conclusions and explore their applicability to the hypothesis stated above.

> I now propose that we gather the various kinds of behavior just mentioned, all of which have to do with effective interaction with the environment, under the general heading of competence. According to Webster, competence means fitness of ability, and the suggested synonyms include capability, capacity, efficiency, proficiency, and skill. It is therefore a suitable word to describe such things as grasping and exploring, crawling and walking, attention and perception, language and thinking, manipulating and changing the surroundings, all of which promote an effective—a competent—interaction with the environment. It is true, of course, that maturation plays a part in all these developments, but this part is heavily overshadowed by learning in all the more complex accomplishments like speech or skilled manipulation. I shall argue that it is necessary to make competence a motivational concept; there is *competence motivation* as well as competence in its more familiar sense of achieved capacity. The behavior that leads to the building up of effective grasping, handling, and letting go of objects, to take one example, is not random behavior that is produced by an overflow of energy. It is directed, selective, and persistent, and it continues not because it serves primary drives, which indeed it cannot serve until it is almost perfected, but because it satisfies an intrinsic need to deal with the environment.

I am suggesting that there are forms of activity that serve to enlist and develop the competence motive, that serve to make it the driving force behind behavior. I should like to add to White's general premise that the *exercise* of competence motives has the effect of strengthening the degree to which they gain control over behavior and thereby reduce the effects of extrinsic rewards or drive gratification. . . .

In this matter of the control of learning, then, my conclusion is that the degree to which the desire for competence comes to control behavior, to that degree the role of reinforcement or "outside rewards" wanes in shaping behavior. The child comes to manipulate his environment more actively and achieves his gratification from coping with problems. As he finds symbolic modes of representing and transforming the environment, there is an accompanying decline in the importance of stimulus-response-reward sequences. To use the metaphor that David Riesman developed in a quite different context, mental life moves from a state of outer-directedness, in which the fortuity of stimuli and reinforcement are crucial, to a state of inner-directedness in which the growth and maintenance of mastery become central and dominant.

The heuristics of discovery. Lincoln Steffens, reflecting in his *Autobiography* on his undergraduate education at Berkeley, comments that his schooling paid too much attention to learning what was known and too little to finding out about what was not known. But how does one train a student in the techniques of discovery? Again there are some hypotheses to offer. There are many ways of coming to the arts of inquiry. One of them is by careful study of its formalization in logic, statistics, mathematics, and the like. If one is going to pursue inquiry as a way of life, particularly in the sciences, certainly such study is essential. Yet whoever has taught kindergarten and the early primary grades or has had graduate students working with him on their theses—I choose the two extremes for they are both periods of intense inquiry--knows that an understanding of the formal aspect of inquiry is not sufficient. Rather, several activities and attitudes, some directly related to a particular subject and some fairly generalized, appear to go with inquiry and research. These have to do with the *process* of trying to find out something and, though their presence is no guarantee that the *product* will be a great discovery, their absence is likely to lead to awkwardness or aridity or confusion. How difficult it is to describe these matters—the heuristics of inquiry. There is one set of attitudes or methods that has to do with sensing the relevance of variables—avoiding immersion in edge effects and getting instead to the big sources of variance. This gift partly comes from intuitive familiarity with a range of phenomena, sheer "knowing the stuff." But it also comes out of a sense of what things among many "smell right," what things are of the right order of magnitude or scope or severity.

Weldon, the English philosopher, describes problem solving in an interesting and picturesque way. He distinguishes among difficulties, puzzles, and problems. We solve a problem or make a discovery when we impose a puzzle form on a difficulty to convert it into a problem that can be solved in such a way that it gets us where we want to be. That is to say, we recast the difficulty into a form that we know how to work with—then we work it. Much of what we speak of as discovery consists of knowing how to impose a workable kind of form on various kinds of difficulties. A small but crucial part of discovery of the highest order is to invent and develop effective models or "puzzle forms." It is in this area that the truly powerful mind shines. But it is surprising to what degree perfectly ordinary people can, given the benefit of instruction, construct quite interesting and what, a century ago, would have been considered greatly original models.

Now to the hypothesis. It is my hunch that it is only through the exercise of problem solving and the effort of discovery that one learns the working heuristics of discovery; the more one has practice, the more likely one is to generalize what one has learned into a style of problem solving or inquiry that serves for any kind of task encountered—or almost any kind of task. I think the matter is self-evident, but what is unclear is the kinds of training and teaching that produce the best effects. How, for instance, do we teach a child to cut his losses but at the same time be persistent in trying out an idea; to risk forming an early hunch without at the same time formulating one so early and with so little evidence that he is stuck with it while he waits for appropriate evidence to materialize; to pose good testable guesses that are neither too brittle nor too sinuously incorrigible? And so on and on. Practice in inquiry, in trying to figure out things for oneself is indeed what is needed—but in what form? Of only one thing am I convinced: I have never seen anybody improve in the art and technique of inquiry by any means other than engaging in inquiry.

Conservation of memory. I have come to take what some psychologists might consider a rather drastic view of the memory process. It is a view that in large measure derives from the work of my colleague, George Miller. Its first premise is that the principal problem of human memory is not storage but retrieval. In spite of the biological unlikeliness of it, we seem to be able to store a huge quantity of information—perhaps not a full tape recording, though at times it seems we even do that, but a great sufficiency of impressions. We may infer this from the fact that recognition, the ability to recall with maximum promptings, is so extraordinarily good in human beings and that spontaneous recall, with no promptings, is so extraordinarily bad. The key to retrieval is organization or, in even simpler terms, knowing where to find information that has been put into memory.

Let me illustrate with a simple experiment. We present pairs of words to twelve-year-olds. The children of one group are told only to remember the pairs and that they will be asked to repeat them later. Others are told to remember the pairs by producing a word or idea that will tie them together in a way that will make sense. The word pairs include such juxtapositions as "chair-forest," "sidewalk-square," and the like. One can distinguish three styles of mediators, and children can be scaled in terms of their relative preference for each: generic mediation, in which a pair is tied together by a superordinate idea: "chair and forest are both made of wood"; thematic mediation, in which the two terms are imbedded in a theme or a little story: "The lost child sat on a chair in the middle of the forest"; and part-whole mediation, in which "chairs are made from trees in the forest" is typical. Now the chief result, as you would predict, is that children who provide their own mediators do best—indeed, one time through a set of thirty pairs, they recover up to 95 percent of the second words when presented with the first ones of the pairs, whereas the uninstructed children reach a maximum of less than 50 percent recovered. Also, children do best in recovering materials tied together by the form of mediator they most often use.

One can cite a myriad of findings to indicate that any organization of information that reduces the aggregate complexity of material by imbedding it into a cognitive process a person has constructed for himself will make that material more accessible for retrieval. We may say that the process of memory, looked at from the retrieval side, is also a process of problem solving: how can material be "placed" in memory so that it can be obtained on demand?

We can take as a point of departure the example of the children who developed their own technique for relating each word pair. The children with the self-made mediators did better than the children who were given ready-made ones. Another group of children were given the mediators developed by this group to aid them in memorizing—a set of "ready-made" memory aids. In general, material that is organized in terms of a person's own interests and cognitive structures is material that has the best chance of being accessible in memory. It is more likely to be placed along routes that are connected to one's own ways of intellectual travel. Thus, the very attitudes and activities that characterize figuring out or discovering things for oneself also seem to have the effect of conserving memory.

(Gagné, cont. from p. 75)

obviously the conditions of learning represented by a parent saying, "That's Mr. Wells" will not succeed in teaching the child the mailman's name. One must, instead, begin this learning with quite a different set of conditions. For an individual who has one kind of prior capability, the printed sentence, "When glucose sugar ferments, alcohol is formed, and carbon dioxide is given off" may serve to bring about in that individual the learning of a principle, at least as readily as the child learns to name the mailman. But for another individual without the prerequisite capabilities such a printed statement is likely to accomplish nothing at all.

The set of initial capabilities possessed by the learner may be spoken of as conditions *internal* to the learner. But there is also a second category of learning conditions that are *external* to the learner, and that are independent in their action. Let us suppose an individual possesses all the prerequisite capabilities needed for learning the English equivalents of ten foreign words. Another individual possesses all the prior capabilities for learning how to multiply two negative numbers. Ignoring the differences in content, there is no particular reason to suppose that the external conditions needed for learning in one case are the same as the external conditions needed for learning in the other. In the first case, common observation would lead us to expect that the pairs of words would need to be repeated a number of times in order for learning to occur. But in the second case it is not at all apparent that similar amounts of repetition would work very well. . . . At this point, the important thing to note is that the conditions are not the same. Two different kinds of capabilities are being learned. They require not only different prior capabilities, but also different external conditions for learning.

The point of view to be expanded on in this book will probably be apparent from previous paragraphs. In brief, it is this: there are as many varieties of learning as there are distinguishable conditions for learning. These varieties may be differentiated by means of descriptions of the factors that comprise the learning conditions in each case. In searching for and identifying these, one must look, first, at the capabilities internal to the learner, and second, at the stimulus situation outside the learner. Each type of learning starts from a different "point" of internal capability, and is likely also to demand a different external situation in order to take place effectively. The useful prototypes of learning are those delineated by these descriptions of learning conditions.

EDUCATIONAL IMPLICATIONS

The identification of varieties of learning in terms of the conditions that produce them obviously has some definite implications for education and educational practices. Some of these may be immediately evident to the reader as he becomes acquainted with the conditions of learning for each variety. Others, however, need to be separately specified and more extensively discussed, since they are so fundamentally related to educational procedure.

It will be apparent from the discussion of educational problems in later chapters that the fewest possible assumptions are made about the mechanics (or "logistics") of education. None of these logistic elements is assumed as a "given." Quite to the contrary, the point of view is presented that these features of the educational process should be determined by the requirements of getting students to learn efficiently. In discussing implications, therefore, it is not assumed that a school building is necessarily needed, nor a set of books, nor desks, nor chalkboards, nor even a teacher. Insofar as these components of the educational system are shown to be necessary because of the requirements of learning, well and good. The only thing that must be assumed is the existence of a student who is capable of learning. This is the starting point.

Limitations of Learning Implications. The reader needs to be made aware, also, that there are some problems of great importance to education which *cannot* be solved by applying a knowledge of the principles of learning as they are here described. For example, there are many aspects of the personal interaction between a teacher and his students that do not pertain, in a strict sense, to the acquisition of skills and knowledges that typically form the content of a curriculum. These varieties of interaction include those of motivating, persuading, and the establishment of attitudes and values. The development of such human dispositions as these is of tremendous importance to education as a system of modern society. In the most comprehensive sense of the word "learning," motivations and attitudes must surely be considered to be learned. But the present treatment does not attempt to deal with such learnings, except in a tangential sense. Its scope is restricted to what may be termed the intellectual, or subject matter content that leads to improvement in human performances having ultimate usefulness in the pursuit of the individual's vocation or profession.

Another kind of limitation needs to be mentioned. Regardless of how much may be known about how to *begin* the process of establishing competence through learning, it is clear that no one knows very much at present about how to *continue* the process to its highest levels. It does not seem possible at present to specify all the conditions necessary to attain the highest and most complex varieties of human performance such as those displayed in invention or esthetic creativity. How does one produce an Albert Einstein or a Leonardo da Vinci? Certainly there are distinct limits to currently available knowledge bearing on such questions. The most that can be said here is that the production of genius is not based on "tricks," but on the learning of a great variety of specific capabilities.

To understand how learning operates in everyday situations of the school is a most valuable kind of understanding. But it does not unlock all the mysteries of education. What it can do is to illuminate some of the activities of the curriculum planner, the course designer, and the instructor. Specifically, an understanding of the conditions of learning is of value in the kinds of activities mentioned in the following paragraphs. . . .

Planning for Learning. One important implication of the identification of learning conditions is that these conditions must be carefully planned *before* the learning situation itself is entered into by the student. In particular, there needs to be planning in terms of the student's capabilities both before and after any learning enterprise. From where does the student begin; and where is he going? What are the specific prerequisites for learning, and what will he be able to learn next? The needed specificity of such planning is suggested by the following: What is meant by "prerequisite" is not that fourth-grade social studies must precede fifth-grade social studies. Rather, the meaning is that learning to pronounce foreign words must precede learning to use them in sentences; or that learning to count numerically must precede learning to add numbers.

The planning that precedes effective design for learning is a matter of specifying with some care what may be called the *learning structure* of any subject to be acquired. In order to determine what comes before what, the subject must be analyzed in terms of the types of learning involved in it. The acquisition of knowledge is a process in which every new capability builds on a foundation established by previously learned capabilities. The convenient escape mechanism that the student is not "mature" enough to learn any particular content needs to be studiously avoided, since it is valid for only the very earliest years of life. A student is ready to learn something new when he has mastered the prerequisites; that is, when he has acquired the necessary capabilities through preceding learning. Planning for learning is a matter of specifying and ordering the prerequisite capabilities within a topic to be learned, and later perhaps among the topics that make up a "subject."

Managing Learning. The learning conditions to be described also have implications for the management of learning. How can the student be motivated to begin and to continue learning? How should the direction of his interest and effort be guided? What can be done to assess the outcomes of learning? These are questions that pertain to the *management* of learning and the learning situation. They are questions which are general, in the sense that their answers are independent of both the content to be learned and the particular conditions of learning required for that content.

Clearly, these functions are among the most important that a teacher performs. A student cannot ordinarily do these things by himself (although, to be sure, he tends to improve constantly as he gains experience in taking over these functions). Getting the student interested in what he is doing, in the capabilities he is going to acquire, is a task that takes great skill and persuasiveness by a person, usually a teacher, who represents the adult world of experience and wisdom. Determining and advising on the branches of knowledge, the directions of further learning, the possibilities of additional topics and areas to be explored are important activities of learning management that again demand a great deal of knowledge and broad experience of the sort that may be possessed by a good teacher. Finally, the outcomes of learning, the achievements of the learner, need to be assessed by an agent "external" to the student, in order to ensure that they are objective and unbiased. Such assessment needs to be undertaken for the primary purpose of informing the student of what he has been able to achieve through learning, and is therefore likely to be intimately connected with his motivation.

The needs for these various functions of learning management are clearly implied for any system whose purpose it is to accomplish learning in an effective manner. They are required regardless of what particular conditions of learning may be appropriate at any given time. The proper exercise of these functions in an educational setting by a teacher requires that he understand the conditions of learning. Knowing these conditions makes it possible for the teacher to reach the proper decisions about what achievements the student is being motivated for, and to give suitable guidance concerning the possible directions of future learning that may be available to the student. In addition, the teacher must know the conditions of learning that have entered into any new attainment of the student in order to assess such achievement realistically.

Instructing. The function of *instructing* derives in a specific sense from a description of the required conditions of learning. Instructing means arranging the conditions of learning that are external to the learner. These conditions need to be constructed in a stage-by-stage fashion, taking due account at each stage of the just previously acquired capabilities of the learner, the requirements for retention of these capabilities, and the specific stimulus situation needed for the next stage of learning. As a consequence, instruction is seen to be a very intricate and demanding activity.

Sometimes instruction is predesigned, as in the case of a well-constructed textbook or workbook, or, more typically, in the programmed instruction of teaching machines. Sometimes it is extemporaneously designed by a teacher. In any case, instruction very often involves communicating verbally with the student for the purposes of informing him of what he is going to achieve, reminding him of what he already knows, directing his attention and actions, and guiding his thinking along certain lines. All these events are instituted for the purpose of establishing the proper external conditions for learning. Assuming that the necessary internal capabilities have been previously learned, a suitable arrangement of instructional events will bring about efficient learning.

Instructing is an activity that is at the heart of the educational process. It is extremely difficult to do well with a group of students. It is easier to accomplish under the rare conditions in which a single teacher communicates with a single student. Alternatively, it can be largely if not wholly predesigned and used in programs of self-instruction. There is reason to suppose that an instructional mode which requires self-instruction may be very efficient, when properly designed, and may also help to establish valuable habits of independent study on the part of the student. Obviously, the mature student (for example, the university graduate student) is a person who has developed his own very efficient habits of self-instruction.

One aspect of instructing, however, deserves special mention because it takes a special form. This pertains to the function of *knowledge generalization* (or *knowledge transfer*), which is to be contrasted to the initial learning of knowledge. Knowledge transfer is frequently emphasized as a purpose of education. It is said that education should be concerned not simply with the acquisition of knowledge, but more importantly with the use and generalization of knowledge in novel situations. First of all, it is evident that knowledge transfer cannot occur if the knowledge itself has not been initially mastered. But beyond this, there is an important question of what conditions of instruction are required to encourage generalization of knowledge. For a number of reasons, the instructional mode of organized *group discussion* is one that appears to be well designed to accomplish this function. When properly led, such discussion not only stimulates the production of new extensions of knowledge by students but also provides a convenient means of critical evaluation and discrimination of these ideas.

Selecting Media for Instruction. Still another implication that derives from a specification of the conditions of learning concerns the choice of media for instruction. Media are here to be considered in a broad and inclusive sense, including such traditional instructional media as *oral* and *printed verbal communication,* and such relative newcomers as *motion pictures* and *television receivers.*

The required conditions for learning can be put into effect in different ways and to differing degrees by each medium. Some media are much more broadly adaptable for instructional purposes than are others. For example, the concrete objects that may be needed to convey the distinctions among a solid, a liquid, and a gas can obviously not be successfully supplanted by a mere verbal description in print. Conversely, though, examples of a solid, a liquid, and a gas, or even pictures of them, have extremely limited functions in instruction when compared with verbal communication. By themselves, the objects or pictures cannot instruct in the varieties of solids, liquids, and gases, nor in the principles that relate them to each other. There are, then, some positive characteristics and some limitations of each instructional medium that become evident when they are examined in the light of their learning functions.

As has often been said, instructional media constitute the valuable "resources for learning" that an educational system has to draw on. When these resources are put to use, they are usually placed in some particular arrangement called a *mode of instruction.* Some of these, like the lecture, are very widely and frequently used, but others, like the tutoring session, are employed rather infrequently (at least in this country). The various modes of instruction are employed for the purpose of getting the greatest instructional usefulness from media and combinations of media. Thus the choice of modes is also a matter of aiming for optimal functioning in generating the proper conditions for learning.

POSTSCRIPT

HOW CAN INSTRUCTION BE MADE EFFECTIVE?

There is much left to be learned about the science of teaching and the art of teaching. Education as a profession is incomplete. We test out the latest devices and techniques, we board bandwagons with abandon, and we fall back on models from the distant past. And as new electronic media force us to retool, our perplexity often increases.

Sources of possible rescue abound but are often ignored. John Dewey's *How We Think* (1910), Gilbert Highet's *The Art of Teaching* (1950), Jean Piaget's *The Psychology of Intelligence* (1950) and *The Child and Reality* (1973), J.P. Guilford's *The Nature of Human Intelligence* (1967), Benjamin S. Bloom's *Stability and Change in Human Characteristics* (1964) and *Human Characteristics and School Learning* (1976), Robert E. Ornstein's *The Psychology of Consciousness* (1972), and Marc Belth's *The Process of Thinking* (1977) are all worthy of attention.

To round out the portrayal of the modes and intricacies of instruction one could consult the following: *Exemplars of Teaching Method* (1965) by Harry S. Broudy and John R. Palmer, which describes various instructional models from the Sophists and Socrates to Dewey and Kilpatrick; *Ways of Teaching* (2nd ed., 1974) by Ronald T. Hyman, which provides a thorough delineation of a wide range of methods and techniques; and *The Activities of Teaching* (1971) by Thomas F. Green, which offers a close analysis of the multiple aspects of instruction.

Finally, an emerging mode of inquiry, existential phenomenology, is finding its way into areas of educational concern. This viewpoint holds that in order to obtain the most concrete description of learning as a human activity you must put the abstractions of scientific theories aside and attempt, through self-exploration, to uncover the experience of learning as you have lived it. This may be accomplished by reliving specific learning experiences, and sharing them with fellow self-explorers who participate in a dialogue that develops a portrayal of experiential commonalities. The identification, through this process, of elements commonly associated with the phenomenon of learning can serve as a base for instructional alteration and eventual theory-building—from the inside out.

David Attie

PART II

How Should Schooling Be Controlled?

ISSUE 6

HAVE THE SCHOOLS MET THEIR SOCIAL GOALS?

What are the social purposes of organized schooling? What forces are most influential in shaping those goals? Are the stated or assumed purposes being met? In the past two decades these questions have set off an explosion of controversy among historians, sociologists, and educators.

Have the schools met the promise stated by Horace Mann at the inception of the public system that they would become the equalizers of opportunity for all? Have the schools, by design or by practice, been a primary agency of social control, serving to bar certain groups from gaining access to oppportunities in the socio-economic realm? Does the school remain a basically conservative and stabilizing institution in the social order? Can it be employed effectively as a vehicle of social criticism and reform?

Have we developed a system of education which provides services with reasonable equality and effectiveness to each young citizen? Some recent figures and observations prompt a basically negative conclusion. *Barred from School—2 Million Children* (1976) by Thomas J. Cottle catalogues the recent history of exclusion from opportunity on the basis of cultural factors such as linguistic difficulties, curricular tracking, physical handicaps and illnesses, pregnancy, and poverty. *The Twelve-Year Sentence* (1974), edited by William F. Rickenbacker, raises serious questions about a compulsory school system that does disservice to some people and yet demands ever-increasing levels of tax support. Data summarized in *U.S. News & World Report* (May 14, 1979) show that while the educational gap between black and white young people has diminished over the last twenty years, overall family income of blacks is still only 57% of white-family income and has been declining since 1975.

This and the two issues that follow offer appraisals of the relationship between schools and the larger society. Special attention is devoted to the historical record and the current scene regarding the equalization of opportunity in a culturally diverse nation. The record is, of course, clear: large numbers of people, as members of nondominant cultural groups—blacks, women, Jews, Hispanics, American Indians, and most other ethnic minorities—have been disadvantaged in this society and continue to be deprived of full opportunity.

This condition of being disadvantaged involves two intertwining levels: cultural and social. Cultural disadvantage is the result of centuries of exclusionary practices which have become engrained in the prevailing attitudes and values. Historical patterns of racism and sexism shape the developmental environment as well as the victims' consciousness of discrimination. The psychological effects of such patterns—feelings of inferiority, limited aspiration, and suppression of self-assertion, for example—often control personal development. Social disadvantage, on the other hand, is a product of laws, current practices, and other social arrangements which restrict some people's opportunities. A person suffers social disadvantage when he or she is deprived of civil rights generally granted to other members of the same society; when he or she is excluded from educational and training opportunities or separated, singled-out, or stereotyped on the basis of group membership; and when he or she is deprived of access to occupational and other economic opportunities.

Governmental action, through the courts, through legislation, and through alterations in social institutions (such as schools), can reverse or at least modify the effects of social disadvantage. But, because social disadvantage reflects the more deep-seated cultural disadvantage, quick and easy redress is never possible.

The following selections by Peter Schrag and Patricia Graham examine the role of school as a social institution. Schrag feels that the hope that the schools could reform themselves and play a central role in social reform has proved an impossible dream and will remain so as long as the schools are entrapped by their own structure and by outside social and political pressures. Graham's historical review covers some of the same tribulations cited by Schrag but also points to some definite triumphs which may lead to broader successes in the future.

Peter Schrag

END OF THE IMPOSSIBLE DREAM

It is ten years later, and the great dream has come to an end. We thought we had solutions to everything—poverty, racism, injustice, ignorance; it was supposed to be only a matter of time, of money, of proper programs, of massive assaults. Perhaps nothing was ever tried without restraint or dilution, perhaps we were never willing to exert enough effort or spend enough money, but it is now clear that the confidence is gone, that many of the things we *knew* no longer seem sure or even probable. What we believed about schools and society and the possibilities of socially manageable perfection has been reduced to belying statistics and to open conflict in the street and the classroom.

Twenty years ago we took as fact the idea that American public schools—that *the school system*—could be reformed, first to make the education enterprise more intellectually rigorous and selective; and then to make it more democratic. Thus, we had our decade with the Rickovers, the Bestors, the Conants, and the Zachariases; men who believed that students did not know enough physics or French or English, and that through new programs, or a return to "the fundamentals," or through adjustments in teacher training, students could become superior academic operators and, above all, better qualified candidates for the university. And then, beginning in about 1960, we had our decade with the democrats, the integrationists, and the apostles of universal opportunity: Kenneth B. Clark, Thomas Pettigrew, Francis Keppel, and John Gardner, who believed that by changing teacher attitudes, or through busing, or through fiscal and geographical rezoning, all children could have equal educational opportunities.

In the first instance the reformers represented the aspirations of the enfranchised, the suburban parents of affluence who once sent their children to Harvard by right of birth and now had to do it by right of achievement. In the second, the reformers demanded for the deprived what they thought the advantaged were getting, believing in the magic of the good school and accepting the rhetoric of individual accomplishment. Now, suddenly, the

Continued on p. 94

Patricia Albjerg Graham

AMERICA'S UNSYSTEMATIC EDUCATION SYSTEM

The American "system of education" is an organizational nightmare but a functional triumph. It nearly defies explanation as a coherent enterprise, but persons regularly emerge from their encounters with it more knowledgeable than when they entered it. If it is to be judged on the educational attainments of the entire American public, then its success is real. However, few American institutions have suffered as much criticism, particularly in the last 24 years, as have those concerned with education.

The paradox of functional success but massive criticism raises perplexing questions about this enigmatic enterprise. Apparently it is successfully accomplishing one task while being expected to do another. Six questions seem helpful in approaching some understanding of the American educational system: What is it? What is expected of it? What does it do? Who uses it? Who runs it? and Who pays for it?

What is it? The essential unit of the American educational system (and of any educational system today) is the school—the physical plant and the organization it symbolizes. Thus, not until the latter part of the 19th century could the United States really be said to have an "educational system" as such, because until that time education had been acquired through a variety of rather haphazard methods. Children studied at home with their parents or with a tutor, or perhaps at the home of a nearby spinster or widow in a "dame school" with a few other neighborhood children, and only rarely at a building formally designated "school" and subsidized by the local community, the church, the children's tuition, private beneficence, or some combination of these. Such formal work often was supplemented by individual study, by perusal of books and local newspapers and journals, by instructional messages embedded in sermons and Sunday school programs, and through apprenticeships both formal and informal to persons who had achieved some degree of mastery of a particular field.

These various ways of learning were by no means mutually exclusive. Generally a young person encountered several of them en route to adulthood,

Continued on p. 101

Reprinted from American Education, July 1974.

(Schrag, cont. from p. 92)

optimism is gone, and the declining faith in educational institutions is threatening the idea of education itself.

If we want to understand why the schools have "failed," we have only to state the criteria of success. The schools achieved their reputation when they did not have to succeed, when there were educational alternatives—the farm, the shop, the apprenticeship—and when there were other routes to economic and social advancement. Every poor little boy who became a doctor represented a victory. Poor little boys who became ditch diggers disappeared from the record. As soon as we demanded success for everyone—once there were no alternatives—failure was inevitable, not only because the demands were too great, but because they were repressive and contradictory. No other nation, wrote Henry Steele Commager in a representative flight of self-congratulation, "ever demanded so much of schools and of education . . . none other was ever so well served by its schools and its educators." We expected the schools to teach order, discipline, and democracy, the virtues of thrift, cleanliness, and hard work, the evils of alcohol, tobacco, and later of sex and communism; we wanted them to acculturate the immigrants, to provide vocational skills, to foster patriotism and tolerance, and, above all, to produce a high standard of literacy throughout the population. All this they sometimes did and still do.

The impossible demand was enshrined in the mythology of the American dream itself: that the schools constitute the ultimate promise of equality and opportunity; that they enable American society to remain somehow immune from the economic inequities and social afflictions that plague the rest of mankind; that they, in short, guarantee an open society. In 1848, Horace Mann, in one of his annual reports as secretary of the Massachusetts Board of Education, described his vision of the common school—the school for children of all classes and backgrounds—as "a great equalizer of the conditions of men, the balance wheel of the social machinery. . . . It does better than disarm the poor of their hostility toward the rich: It prevents being poor. . . ." The school is our answer to Karl Marx—and to everything else. With the closing of the frontier, which once was regarded as a safety valve and from which the schools inherited many of their mythological functions (if you're not born rich you can go west, can, that is, go to school), and with the rise of a certificated, schooled meritocracy, the educational system has become the central institution of the American dream. Education, it has often been said, is the American religion. Thus, if the school system fails, so does the promise of equality, so does the dream of the classless society, so does our security against the inequalities of society. The school system has failed.

Evidence? Is it necessary again to cite statistics, dropout rates, figures on black and white children who go to college (or finish high school), comparisons of academic success between rich and poor kids, college attendance figures for slums and suburbs? The most comprehensive data on hand indicate that, in the final analysis, nothing in school makes as much difference as the economic background of the student and the social and economic backgrounds of his peers. There is no evidence that increasing educational expenditures in a particular district will produce greater achievement, and a fair amount of evidence that it will not. But this sort of argument is still misleading and, in the final analysis, rather useless, because it presumes that we agree on what constitutes success. Failure to complete high school is regarded as some sort of cosmic failure, a form of personal and social death. Dropout becomes synonymous with delinquent. Yet the evidence indicates that in some school systems the smart ones drop out and the dumb ones continue. Self-educated men used to be heroes; now they are prejudged unfit, or more likely, they just don't appear in the social telescope at all.

Then why have the schools failed? Why boycotts and strikes, why the high school SDS, why the battles over long hair, underground newspapers, and expressions of independent student opinion? Why are there cops in the corridors and marijuana in the gym lockers? Why is it that most students panic when they're invited to work on their own, to study independently? Why is it that most students are more interested in what the teacher wants or what's going to be on the test than they are in understanding the subject that's ostensibly under study? Why bells, monitors, grades, credits, and requirements? Why do most students learn to cheat long before they learn how to learn? Yes, there are exceptions—there are teachers who ask real questions and schools that honor real intellectual distinction and practice real democracy. But a system that requires all children (except the very rich who can buy their way out) to attend a particular school for a specified period—that, in other words, sentences everyone to twelve years of schooling—such a system can and must be judged by its failures.

Everything that we could not, or would not, do somewhere else we expected to be done in the schools. And in the process we thought we saw what in fact does not exist. The greatest failure of American educational journalism in the last decade is that its practitioners refused to believe what they saw, and reported instead what they were supposed to see. Thus we have been inundated with millions of words about the new math, the new physics, the compensatory this and advanced that, about BSCS and PSSC, about IPI and SMSG, about individual progress and head start, upward bound, and forward march. And thus also we have read, with increasing incomprehension, about student uprisings, protests and boycotts and strikes. But few of us ever described the boredom, the emptiness, the brutality, the stupidity, the sheer waste of the average classroom.

What choices does a fifteen-year-old have in the average high school? Choices as to courses, teacher, or physical presence? What does he do most of the day? He sits—and maybe listens. Follow him, not for a few minutes, but for six hours a day, 180 days a year. What goes on in the class? What is it about, what questions are asked? Is it about the real world? Is it about an intellectually honest discipline? Is it about the feelings, passions, interests, hopes, and fears of those who are present? No. It is a world all of its own. It is mostly about nothing.

It worked as long as the promise of schooling itself appeared credible, that is, as long as the proffered reward looked more like a rainbow and less like a mirage, before the end of the road was crowded with people reporting back that the trip wasn't worth it. It is not necessary again to describe the travesties of the average classroom or the average school. But it is important to point out the nothingness of schooling because nothingness (or conformity and repression and boredom) is necessary to the system. Which is not to suggest an Establishment conspiracy to keep children docile so they will become satisfactory candidates for the military-industrial complex. No one planned schools this way, nor have teachers and principals betrayed them: The schools do what they do out of a structural necessity, because we don't know enough about learning and because social mythology permits very little else.

Any single, universal public institution—and especially one as sensitive as the public school—is the product of a social quotient verdict. It elevates the lowest common denominator of desires, pressures, and demands into the highest public virtue. It cannot afford to offend any sizable community group, be it the American Legion, the B'nai B'rith, or the NAACP. Nor can it become a subversive enterprise that is designed to encourage children to ask real questions about race or sex or social justice or the emptiness and joys of life. Occasionally, of course, it does do these things, but rarely in a significant and consistent manner. Students who ask real questions tend to be threatening to teachers, parents, and the system. They destroy the orderliness of the management procedure, upset routines, and question prejudices. The textbook, the syllabus, the lesson plan are required not only because most teachers are lost without them, but because they represent an inventory for the community, can be inspected to ascertain the purity of the goods delivered. Open-ended programs, responsive to the choices and interests of students, are dangerous not only because all real questions are dangerous, but because they cannot be preinspected or certified for safety. The schools are not unresponsive to the immediate demands of the society. They are doing precisely what most Americans expect.

Earlier, I spoke about contradictory objectives. One is the objective of "equality of educational opportunity"; the other is to reinforce and legitimize distinctions. For many years, these objectives were, in fact, consistent. They share certain behavioral values that are honored and enforced in the average classroom: discipline, order, certain kinds of manners, style of speech and dress, punctuality, cleanliness, and so on. Kids who do not meet these standards are ridiculed, punished, and demeaned. The two sets of values also share a declared commitment to certain skills: reading, writing, the skills of the average intelligence test—and a disdain for other attributes: originality, curiosity, diversity. They share, in other words, a linear standard of success and failure. Slow and bright, average and retarded, all fall on one scale, one straight line that runs from zero to one hundred, from A to F. Any teacher in any school can tell any other teacher in any other school about his good, average, and slow students, about his difficult students, and about his cooperative ones, and both will know precisely who and what is being described. (Occasionally, of course, some school or teacher honors a "difficult" child, or a genuinely curious one, or one who has skills—in music or dance, for example—which are outside the normal scale of classroom success. But those are rare instances.)

About a decade ago, something began to change. Until then "equality of educational opportunity" was understood in simple (and misleading) terms. It was the equality inherited from social Darwinism: Everyone in the jungle (or in society, or in school) was to be treated equally: one standard, one set of books, one fiscal formula for children everywhere, regardless of race, creed, or color. Success went to the resourceful, the ambitious, the bright, the strong. Those who failed were stupid or shiftless, but whatever the reason, failure was the responsibility of the individual (or perhaps of his parents, poor fellow), but certainly not that of the school or the society. It was this premise that fired the drive for school integration. Negro schools, we believed, were older, more poorly equipped, badly financed. By equalizing resources, and perhaps throwing in a little compensation to offset differences deriving from "cultural disadvantage," everybody would be competing in the same race. Thus Head Start and "counterpoise" and "early enrichment." Every program launched in the past decade assumed a linear standard of success; each took for granted that schooling was a competitive enterprise and that life was a jungle where only the fit survive. Integration was, more than anything else, a political attempt to win white hostages to black education: Where white kids went to school with black there would be better resources and teachers. Apparently it never occurred to anyone that as long as we operated by a linear standard (bright, average, slow, or whatever) the system would, by definition, have to fail at least some kids. Every race has a loser. Failure is structured into the American system of public education. Losers are essential to the success of the winners.

In the process of compensating and adjusting, of head starting, and upward bounding, the burden of responsibility shifted subtly from the individual to the school and the society. Failure used to be the kid's fault; now, increasingly, it seems, at least in part, to be the fault of the system. And thus all was thrown into confusion. Do we measure equality by what goes in or what comes out? That is, do we measure it in terms of resources provided, efforts made, or by achievement? Assuming some form of cultural pluralism (not yet proved or even argued)—assuming, for example that certain groups in the society are not merely "disadvantaged" but culturally distinct, and that those distinctions are valuable—assuming these things, what does equality mean when it comes to education? Equality before the law, yes; equality in medical treatment, yes; equality in the hiring of plumbers and mechanics, yes. But equality in education? James Coleman, who directed the huge federal study called "Equality of Educational Opportunity," subsequently wrestled with the question (in an article in *Public Interest*) and concluded that "equality of educational opportunity implies not merely 'equal' schools but equally effective schools, whose influences will overcome the differences in starting point of children from different social groups." This is the statement of a homogenizer, hardly different from that of the DAR lady who, sixty years ago, gave the schools a similar mission. "What kind of American consciousness can grow," she asked, "in the atmosphere of sauerkraut and limburger cheese?" The differences, in these views, should be equalized away: All comers should be transformed into mainstream, middle-class competitors (or consumers?) who are equally able to run the race.

There was nothing insidious or sinister about these things; they are as American as the flag. Our dream, as a society, was in the possibilities of transformation: frogs into princes, immigrants into Americans, poor children into affluent adults. And now, with other options closed, the schools, which always have received a major share of the credit for such accomplishments, are expected to do it all. But the schools never did what they were praised for doing; many immigrant groups, for example, did not achieve economic and social success through the public school, but through an open market for unskilled and semi-skilled labor, through sweatshops and factories, through political organizations and civil service jobs. There are more poor whites in America than poor blacks, and if the schools can be credited with the success of those who made it, they also have to be blamed for the failure of those who did not. But to say all this is not to say very much, because in the definition of making it, in a competitive race with one set of criteria, one man's success is defined by another's failure.

Then what do the schools actually do? More than anything else they certify and legitimize success and failure. "Equality of educational opportunity," even if it has no meaning, is necessary because it says to the loser, "You had your chance." Therefore equality remains a significant political and moral imperative, a tune that has to be sung by politicians, guidance counselors, and other apologists of the status quo. (Increasingly it also becomes a rallying cry of liberal intellectuals, who now ascribe their personal triumphs in the brain business to the same ego-flattering virtues as the self-made entrepreneurs of another age: opportunity, hard work, ingenuity. I have made it, son, and so can you.) But there is, as Mr. Conant once said in another context, social dynamite in this propaganda.

The common school, quite simply, no longer exists, except as public rhetoric. With the large-scale movement to the suburbs after World War II, much of the American middle class seceded from the common school by physically removing its children to what it regarded as a more salubrious educational environment. For the successful in the suburbs the schools became contractual partners in a bargain that trades economic support (higher taxes, teacher salaries, bond issues) for academic credentials and some guarantee of advancement in the form of college admission. They went there seeking not equality but advantage, a head start for the rich. And who can blame them? We all "want the best for our children." Education, and especially higher education, is regarded as the sine qua non of position and power in this society. The "new class" of managers and technicians, as David Bazelon has said, is not based on birth or social standing but on educational skills (or at least on credentials). Cash and power, in other words, can be converted into degrees, then reconverted into more cash and power. The suburban school, the current demands for community control, and the concomitant failure of integration are all massive testimonials to the end of the common school.

What is being ignored is that the suburban schools don't actually do anything for most kids, other than bore them. Their prime function (aside from baby sitting) is to certify skills and reinforce characteristics and attitudes that are produced somewhere else. The money, in other words, did not buy much learning. But it did buy exclusiveness. They come in at this end, bright and shiny, and come out at that one, ready for Harvard or Cornell. The schools are, in brief, selective mechanisms,and through their selections they appear to justify (and are, in turn, justified by) the distinctions the society wants to make.

This is why we are fighting about schools and why we are in such serious trouble. Part of the fight—in the cities at least—is over a share of political power, over jobs and patronage and control. But the ideology that gives that battle energy, the ideas that help rally the troops, is the belief in the schools and in what remains of the dream of opportunity. But if *the* school system is the only mode of access to social and economic salvation (house in the suburbs, job at IBM, life insurance, and a certain set of manners), and if the school excludes any sizable minority from such salvation, then we have obviously defined ourselves into a choice between revolution and repression. The great dream of universal opportunity originated in an era of social alternatives, when schooling was one of several options for advancement; the school therefore could demand certain kinds of conformity. Individuality and pluralism could take refuge and sustenance elsewhere. But for the moment all advancement (we are told, are indeed required, to believe) begins in school, and we are, for this reason if for no other, no longer an open society. By definition, no society with but one avenue of approved entry into the mainstream of dignity can be fully open. When that single instrument of entry is charged with selecting people out, and when there are no honorable alternatives for those who are selected out, we are promising to all men things that we cannot deliver.

Inevitably, there are questions about the demands of a technological society and the necessity for universal literacy. Haven't many schools succeeded; don't we have one of the highest standards of literacy in the world? Don't schools make selections according to the demands that the technology and the culture impose? The answer is complicated, but there is nothing in it that makes the existing system of schooling imperative or even desirable except—as always—the maintenance of the status quo. Which is to say that the system is necessary if the system is to be preserved.

Obviously, the society, as organized, makes certain demands—sometimes irrelevant, but often not—for employment and acceptability. Computers impose a rigid discipline on programmers, and heart transplants are better performed by people who have learned what they are doing. A dishwasher with the soul of a poet (or even the skills of a poet) may be more valuable than one without, but he is still a dishwasher. But for every flight of romantic nonsense there are a hundred statements about the rigors and demands of technology and about the complexities of this world. We have hitched the deities of complexity and technology to the rhetoric of success. Technology is not the curriculum (nor, needless to say, is complexity); it is the liturgy of motivation.

Even if the school system were proficient in training people to deal with a world defined as technological (which it is not), it would still be guilty of the worst sort of parochialism and idolatry. Part of the significance of technology, we are told, is to free men from all those boring, menial tasks, maybe even to free him from the necessity of working at all. To prepare for this, the school system imposes boring, menial tasks. The very propaganda of technology would suggest other worlds, other options, time for other concerns. It suggests more, not less, pluralism, more leisure time, more lonely moments, and the necessity for more personal resources for recreation, satisfaction, and human encounter. But what actually happens is that by deifying technology, or by joining the rest of us in so doing, the schools are reinforcing the existing linear standards of judgment and selection—are, in other words, employing the rhetoric of the brave new world to coerce kids and parents rather than to free them.

What the technology argument does is to lock the schools into one definition of complexity, one version of education, and hence only one honorable way of becoming a full human being. It perpetuates and updates an essentially vocational view of schooling. Technological complexity, yes; inner, human complexity, no. We are always—all of us—asked to understand the world by studying the transistor and the laser. All arguments to the contrary notwithstanding, the message comes out backwards: Technology is given; people are dependent variables who must be trained to use and control it.

Mathematics and history and literature thus becomes tokens of acquiescence rather than instruments of liberation. They are used by teachers to maintain order, reinforce distinctions, and intimidate or embarrass students. Complexity becomes a club and technology a prison. We are training a generation of people who regard the disciplines of the intellect as instruments of oppression.

One of the things we learned in the past decade is that we don't know very much. We don't know much about kids, about learning, or about motivation. One of the more fundamental assumptions of ten years ago was that curriculum planners sitting in some university, a foundation, or a central school office could invent programs (for teachers and students) and thereby engineer pedagogical success. What we discovered is that most of the time it couldn't be done, which may well be a good thing. If our pedagogical instruments were really powerful, we would have in hand one of the most totalitarian instruments imaginable. It is by now patently clear that not only history and politics but the very way that people think can be loaded with cultural and social presumptions, and that "reason" itself is often, if not always, political. Teaching inevitably assumes a form of control; it may be directed toward independence, but there is no assurance of it: The more centralized our school systems and our social agencies become, the greater the danger of creating pressures for the production of socially and technologically acceptable people. Fortunately, we don't yet know how to do these things.

What we do know is that children are different, and that different people learn different things in different ways, that some people think better in numbers than in words, that certain groups perceive and understand mathematical relationships more easily than verbal relationships, and that still others are particularly skillful in manipulating spatial problems but relatively incompetent with literature. Most of all, we know that personalities, backgrounds, and interests differ. It may be well that certain levels of literacy and ability in arithmetic constitute "fundamentals" for survival in America or anywhere in the Western world. But it does not follow that learning these things can be achieved by a single set of techniques, or that any teacher can be trained to them. More defensible is the assumption that, while drill, order, and right discipline may be suitable for some students and teachers, they may be destructive for others; that "permissive" classes or Deweyan practices may work well with certain personalities but not with everyone. It is even possible to assume that the "fundamentals" should not always precede music or auto mechanics, but may, in many cases, grow naturally from other activities and from curiosity stimulated in other ways. We know that illiterate adults, properly motivated, have learned to read and write in a few months, and that recruits who almost failed Selective Service intelligence tests can be trained to operate computers and maintain radar equipment.

Most important, we should have learned in the last decade that there is no magic in the single school system or in any set of curricular prescriptions, and that the most successful motivating device may simply be the sense that one has chosen what one wants to learn and under what conditions. In urban areas there is no reason why children in one neighborhood should be forced to attend one particular school for a specified period of time; why there should not be choice as to place, subject, style of teaching, and hours; why, for all children, French and history and algebra should have absolutely equal value; why, for some, art or dance or music should not be given more time than history; why reading a book is more of a humanistic activity than making a film or playing an instrument; why children should not be allowed to choose between permissive and highly structured situations (many would choose the latter); why parents and children should not have the economic power to punish unsuccessful schools (by leaving them) and reward effective ones; or why single, self-serving bureaucracies should continue to hold monopoly power in what is probably the most crucial, and certainly the most universal, public enterprise in America.

(Graham, cont. from p. 93)

after which, it was hoped, learning did not stop but was even less likely to be institutionalized than it was in youth. Undoubtedly the most universal form of instruction was apprenticeship, although most apprenticeships were not of the formal variety on the English model that prescribed certain numbers of years of service to the master. Much more common was the informal variety in which a youngster learned one specific skill or a few general ones simply by helping someone who had these skills. For half the population (the female half) this was the basic mode of learning household management. Girls helped their mothers and thereby acquired the necessary cooking techniques, simple sewing skills, and some notion of how to keep a house functioning. Later generations would be taught these topics in junior high school home economics classes.

By the end of the 19th century fundamental changes had occurred in America. Prior to that time an "educated man" in America would undoubtedly have been characterized as one with knowledge of the classics, however that knowledge was gained. Around the turn of the century the popular definition changed so that an "educated man" was one who had been to college. This shift in the public conviction about what constituted education was a crucial one, for it illustrated the belief that education had become a commodity which one got at an educational institution. The era of multiple educational possibilities had faded, and the narrower definition of education as what one learned in school had arrived. This acceptance of the schools as the pre-eminent educational enterprise laid the foundation for the American educational system, for the schools were nearly the only elements within that system until well into the 20th century.

Whether the schools were public, private, or parochial probably made little difference in terms of what the students learned. The different auspices under which the schools functioned did, however, complicate the pattern of American education. Numerically the public schools have dominated the enrollments. For most of this century about 85 percent of American school children have attended public schools. Now the figure is over 90 percent, principally as a result of declining enrollments in Roman Catholic schools, which account for 80 percent of the nonpublic school students. The remaining 20 percent of nonpublic school students are either at other religious schools (13 percent) or schools without religious affiliation (seven percent).

Some educators' fascination with the organizational differences between public and private school systems has obscured the essential similarities between them. Both cover a very broad range of schools serving the top, middle, and bottom of the socioeconomic groups in America. Both tend to serve the residential community near them, thus making individual schools relatively homogeneous ethnically and economically. Both use the same curriculum materials and teach courses in similar sequences. These similarities have been true throughout the history of American education. For example, in the early 20th century the differences between a public school located in an immigrant neighborhood with predominantly Jewish families and a Roman Catholic parochial school attached to an ethnic parish composed primarily of Italian immigrant families were not enormous, except, of course, for the addition of Christian doctrine in the parochial school. In both schools a premium was placed upon literacy and upon Americanization, and in neither was there much opportunity to mix with children of other economic or ethnic backgrounds. Today the public schools of Great Neck, Long Island, are probably more similar in curriculum and clientele to such private schools as Dalton and Fieldston, 20 miles away in New York City, than they are to public ones in Wyandanch or Roosevelt, 20 miles in the opposite direction.

Schools, then, whether they be public or private, are the essential element in the network that makes up the American educational system. In recent years they have been supplemented by a variety of other educational enterprises, particularly television, which is likely to become even more important in coming years. The anticipated revolution wrought by audiotapes and videotapes has not yet occurred but it is certainly a technical possibility, although not yet clearly a psychic one. Nonschool institutions still are the chief remaining element in the educational system. Most important among these are libraries, which in this century have become publicly supported and nearly universal throughout the Nation instead of being concentrated among the wealthy and in urban areas. No longer novelties as they were at the turn of the century, social settlements still provide important educational services, as do such other pioneers as county and home demonstration agents. The list could go on, but further additions would not modify the essential picture of the American educational system as a conglomerate of local schools assisted by other local institutions.

What is expected of it? Undoubtedly the most serious problem the American educational system has ever faced is the gap between public expectations of it and its performance. A recent book on the history of American education in the late 19th and early 20th century is titled *The Imperfect Panacea,* and that is a superbly succinct account of the fate of the American educational system.

From Puritan times to the present, education has been asked to solve all kinds of religious, national, social, economic, and even intellectual problems. In the 17th century, education was intimately tied to religious salvation: Puritans believed salvation and ignorance were contradictory. By the late 18th century, Thomas Jefferson, more concerned with the problems of this life than the next, looked to education to provide the informed citizenry upon which his notions of the democratic republic rested. "If a nation expects to be ignorant and free in a state of civilization," he wrote, "it expects what never was and never will be." Concern with the republic and with the citizenry's commitment to it prompted Noah Webster to write his "Grammatical Institute of the English Language, Part I" (less ostentatiously known as the Blue-Backed Speller). There Webster tried to insure that through the widespread use of these materials, the American child would grow up with a body of patriotic allusions common to his fellows. "Let the first words he lisps be Washington," he urged. Later in the 19th century, Horace Mann preached the gospel of the possibilities of the public schools for moral uplift to a predominantly Protestant Massachusetts population beginning to face large Catholic immigration. By the beginning of the 20th century, faced with the immense numbers of immigrants, with the rapidly urbanizing and industrializing nation, and with the tremendous decline in need for unskilled labor, education had a new mission. Via the schools the nascent American educational system was supposed to "Americanize" the immigrants and to make everyone literate in English. Furthermore, it was to provide extended educational opportunities at the high school level to large numbers of children whose parents had never ventured beyond the rudiments of literacy.

Although much has been expected of education in the past, the failure of the schools or other educational agencies to meet these goals, though regrettable, was not as serious as it became in the 20th century. For the first time, literacy—and literacy at a reasonably high level—was crucial. It became very difficult to make a living without it and therefore very obvious when persons could not get or hold jobs because they did not have the necessary skills. The blame was placed on the schools for failing to educate such people properly. Accepting the Mann dogma that the public (or "common") schools brought all the children together, the public asked the school to undertake those difficult social tasks that the society had been unable to deal with itself. For example, when automobile accidents began to be a serious national problem, the solution was to mandate driver training in the schools. A more direct method of coping with the problem would have been to forbid automobile manufacturers to produce automobiles that would go faster than 55 miles an hour, or to enforce a rigid prohibition against driving after any drinking of alcoholic beverages. Only recently has any serious attention been given by manufacturers to improving the safety of their vehicles. Despite widespread acceptance of driver education in schools, auto accidents have not declined.

A far more serious example of expecting the schools to do what the rest of the society either did not want to do or found itself unable to do has been the racial integration issue. Since the *Brown v. Board of Education* decision in 1954, schools throughout the United States have been wrestling with the question of bringing together in classrooms children whose parents have never associated at work, at church, or at play. Since the schools not only were supposed to make the children literate but also to "socialize" them, it is not surprising that many parents expressed extreme reluctance to see their offspring associate with children whose parents they did not see. Again the schools were asked to assume an impossible burden. If Americans had really wanted integration in the Fifties (and there is little evidence they did, although many *said* they did), the areas to have moved on were real estate and job recruitments.

In short, the principal expectations for the educational system have been both academic and social. Too often the social problems the school was supposed to solve have overwhelmed it so that it was unable to resolve the academic. Probably the period of most intense criticism of the American educational system came in the early Fifties at the height of the "life adjustment movement" when the critics sought more rigorous academic programs. Few today would maintain that schools are the sole place to learn how to adjust to life: that complicated task is not likely to be accomplished between the ages of six and 16. That such a program could even be inaugurated, however, is indicative of the unwieldly obligations the schools had become accustomed to accepting. In that case unlike many of the others, they were told to lay the burden down.

What does it do? Despite the fact that the educational system has not brought justice, affluence, and personal fulfillment to all Americans, it has some remarkable achievements. To an important degree it is responsible for America's international intellectual leadership. Obviously many other nations have well-trained scholars, but none is the academic mecca that the United States is today. This has not always been true. Until early in the 20th century the United States suffered an unfavorable academic balance of trade: more American scholars studied abroad than foreigners did here. The shift came primarily as a result of the emphasis upon research at American universities in the years immediately surrounding World War I, a time that sapped the economic, spiritual, and human energies of the previous leaders: Germany, England, and France. American scholarship was also augmented considerably by the arrival of political refugees, particularly from Russia (both as a result of the pogroms and later from the Bolshevik revolution) and later from fascist Germany, Italy, and Spain. Many of these émigrés greatly enhanced the intellectual and cultural life of America, and it is to the credit of the much-maligned educational institutions that they (the universities, in particular) included many of these distinguished scholars on their faculties and enrolled many of their children as students, often with scholarships.

In addition to the substantial intellectual contribution made by these émigrés was their social impact. Until their arrival college and university faculties, except for the Catholic institutions, had been composed typically of persons of multigeneration American lingeage of Protestant background. Many of the refugees from Hitler, of course, were Jewish, and when they joined American faculties, they were often the first Jews ever to have been appointed to permanent positions. This generation of émigré Jewish intellectuals in turn helped to open the barriers for American Jews to widespread participation in American academic life. Discrimination against Catholics, always less systematic than against Jews, also diminished, but moves to bring blacks and women into the mainstream of American academic life remained for later decades.

There is ample evidence that the American educational system has done well at the top. Comparative studies with other nations show that the academically superior graduates of American secondary schools rate favorably with the top students of more selective secondary programs in other countries. What of the great mass that America attempts to educate? On the whole the degree of success with them is considerable, even though never as great as hoped. Despite the immense diversity of the U.S. population, nearly all are literate, and 87 percent of the age group five to 17 are enrolled in public elementary and secondary schools, an increase of 30 percentage points between 1870 and 1970. At the present time over half the high school graduates are continuing their formal educations. Most impressive is the fact that "streaming" (requiring students to make an educational choice, such as a technical institute, which will later limit their vocational choice) is much less characteristic of the U.S. educational system than that of any other industrialized nation.

In addition to educating masses of young people (and large numbers of older ones as well, in community colleges and continuing education programs), the American educational system has specialized in enlarging and broadening curriculum. One can study nearly anything in the United States today and receive academic credit for it. From the constricted offerings of the elementary school at the turn of the century, which typically provided an unpalatable mix of reading, arithmetic, penmanship, Bible study, history, occasionally science, and always "rote work" (memorization), elementary children today look at newts under microscopes, write their own stories, learn arithmetic with a computer, and replace history with economics based on experiences in the local stores. Even more dramatic changes have occurred in the curriculum of the colleges, where a century ago most colleges gave their students little if any choice (electives) in their entire four-year program. Today it is a rare college that requires more than freshman English, possibly some science and foreign language, and a major to be included among the 120 odd credits that make up the Bachelor's degree. At the turn of the century such languages as French or German were new additions to the curriculum and considered barely respectable academically. Today they have faded, as Greek and Latin before them, to be replaced in student interest by majors in urban studies, ecology, or psychology.

Even more dramatic curricular changes

have occurred outside the liberal arts framework in the development during this century of professional schools, especially schools focusing on agriculture, education, library science, home economics, and journalism. Formerly each of these skills was learned on an informal apprenticeship basis, but now they are degree-granting programs. All these courses make up the "system."

Who uses it? The simple answer to "Who uses the American educational system? is "Practically all children and a great many adults as well." The rate of growth of educational attendance has zoomed in this century, especially for the post-elementary group. Estimates vary, but a reasonable one is that less that five percent of the college age children were in school in America in 1900. Today over 40 percent are. Secondary school enrollments practically doubled every decade from 1890 to 1920, when they began to level off. Although much of this increase was of course due to growth in the population, more of it could be attributed to the increasing tendency for children to remain in school beyond the eighth grade.

Currently, for the first time in the Nation's history, school attendance is not growing. Segments of the educational system have experienced periods of contraction or no growth in the past, notably the elementary schools in the Thirties and Forties, which were reflecting the low birth rate of the Thirties, and the colleges in the late 19th century, which were reflecting a general disenchantment with higher education and an economic depression. At present, however, neither the elementary nor the secondary school population is expected to increase but rather to shrink, a result of the drop in the birth rate, the absence of significant immigration, and the already established pattern of full participation in the elementary and secondary schools. College enrollment predictions—which are subject to much more fluctuation, since such institutions can enroll students of all ages and since considerably less than half the eligible population has ever attended them—call for only modest gains, and these gains probably will be chiefly in the public institutions.

Statistically children from middle class homes are over-represented in the college population in the United States and this is particularly true of male children from middle class homes. Thus whereas women currently constitute more than 50 percent of the Nation's population, they represent only a little more than 44 percent of the undergraduate enrollment. Bright girls from economically depressed circumstances form the largest category of persons who might be expected to profit from college but who do not do so. The male-female discrepancy is even greater at the doctorate level, where women currently receive only about 18 percent of the doctorates awarded annually. Until recently blacks did not attend college in anything like their proportion in the population, but in the last few years their undergraduate enrollment proportion has come closer to approximating their proportion of the population. They are still far behind at the doctorate level, however, receiving less than one percent of the doctorates awarded annually, although they constitute over 11 percent of the population.

If one assumes that intellectual capacity is distributed evenly throughout the population, then it is clear that the school performance is affected by factors other than sheer intellect. Such basic characteristics as race, class, and sex, as well as such less tangible influences as motivation and teacher expectation, remain important variables affecting academic success and intellectual growth. Over 30 years ago George S. Counts asked, "Dare the schools build a new social order?" He had hoped for an affirmative answer, but the reply then and now is negative.

Despite the disclaimer that the schools are not primarily avenues of social mobility in this country, a recent incident involving the U.S.S.R., a nation that has made a genuine effort to eliminate class distinctions in its society, is illustrative. In 1973 a group of six American professors and one journalist met in the Soviet Union with a counterpart group there to discuss domestic problems of mutual concern. At the opening session each participant—they ranged in age from early 30s to mid 50s—was asked to introduce himself or herself and to say a bit about family background. The Americans, all of whom had been educated at Harvard, Yale, or Columbia, represented a more diverse group in terms of family background than the Soviets. Over half of the Americans were the second generation of their family in this country, and less than half came from families who were professionals. The Soviets, on the other hand, almost unanimously came from families in which the parents had been professionals and had attended college. This was all the more unusual since the proportion of Russians attending college of their parents' generation was very small indeed. Although our educational system clearly has serious limitations as a vehicle for social mobility, it is noteworthy that the most prestigious universities in this country have not limited their enrollments, particularly at the graduate level, to children of the upper middle class.

Who runs it? Two of the most distinctive features of the American educational system are related to its organization. One is the extraordinary degree of lay control that still exists in school systems in this country, and the other is the system's highly decentralized structure. Lay control through school boards and boards of trustees made up typically of community leaders dates from the time when the number of educated persons in a community was very small, and the one or two schoolmasters (or more rarely, schoolmistresses) were not regarded as among the most enlightened citizens. Until the 20th century the school teacher commonly was a young, single person (no one could support a family on a teacher's wage) either en route to a career or marriage, or when the teacher was older, a misfit for either. Such persons were not likely to inspire the confidence of the statesmen of the community, who therefore undertook responsibility for the schools themselves.

A county in central Indiana exemplifies the school board model: When the first public school system was organized in the community of Franklin in 1866, it was supplanting miscellaneous educational endeavors that had been carried on by the local Baptist, Methodist, and Presbyterian churches, each of which had operated its own school at one time or another. The town fathers accommodated to the history of rivalry among the faiths by naming the pastors of the three churches as the first Franklin school board. Two years later they were succeeded by the county judge, the local doctor, and the leading Franklin merchant, a trio that looked after the schools for many years, hiring and firing superintendents of schools at two and three year intervals.

6. HAVE THE SCHOOLS MET THEIR SOCIAL GOALS?

Tension between the lay boards of control and the professional educators has tended to increase during the 20th century with the growth of the professional educator group. In many large systems the professional educators making up the established, continuing bureaucracy of the school system have become the effective determinants of educational policy. Although they are nominally responsible to the superintendent of schools, this official occupies such an exposed and vulnerable position in the community that his (one can say "his" advisedly, since over 99 percent of school superintendents in this country are male) incumbency is likely to be no more than three or four years. The professional educators making up the staff of the system, on the other hand, usually are protected by tenure, and their position is therefore much more secure and their influence more sustained. Functionally that is where the power lies in a school system. Lay school boards and superintendents can enunciate all the reforms they want, but unless the teachers change their ways, nothing will happen. It is often difficult to change an experienced teacher's view about pedagogical method or children's abilities.

One of the most persistent tensions in school systems has been that between parents of school children and the policy-makers of the schools, whoever they have been. Generally parents have played a rather small role in setting priorities for the schools, and when the schools did not seem to be educating their children satisfactorily, they have complained. Such parental dissatisfaction was evident during the 1950s in the denunciation of progressive education by the Council for Basic Education, a group that included many parents who were not educators. More recently the school decentralization controversy in New York City has been marked by vivid complaints from some parents that the centrally controlled schools were not responsive to the needs of their children.

Who pays for it? The question of control of the American educational system is inevitably closely linked with the question of finance. There is very little nationalized central authority over education in the United States, and proportionately there is also relatively little Federal expenditure for elementary and secondary education. Funding for higher education, particularly for research carried on in colleges and universities, is much more likely to come from Federal sources than is support for the schools, though the latter has grown. Forty years ago nearly 83 percent of the funds allocated to public schools came from local governments, with 17 percent coming from State government and 0.3 percent from the Federal Government. Currently approximately 52 percent comes from local sources, 40 percent from the State, and about eight percent from the Federal Government. Over 80 percent of the local funds come from property taxes. As many critics have pointed out, given this structure of support, wealthy communities with high property values are able to provide better-financed schools than are poor communities. Such differences in educational opportunity have been held in recent court suits to violate the equal protection clause of the Fourteenth amendment to the Constitution, most notably in 1971 in the California case of *Serrano v. Priest.*

As the Serrano case illustrates, one of the striking features of the financing of the American educational system is the difference in support to be found in differing regions, a variation that has characterized the financing of public education throughout the Nation's history. Robert D. Reischauer and Robert W. Hartman have pointed out in *Reforming School Finance,* for example, that school districts in New York spend on the average more than twice as much as the average district in nine other States. Throughout the country the districts with the highest levels of expenditure are usually those found in the most prosperous suburban areas, a shift from the pre-World War I era when the city districts were typically the leaders in educational expenditures. Rural areas—particularly those in the South—have always spent the least on public education. The estimated range there for the 1972-73 school year was from $590 in Alabama, $651 in Arkansas, and $689 in Mississippi, in contrast to the figures for the three highest States: $1,584 for New York, $1,473 for Alaska, and $1,307 for Vermont.

Since the end of the 19th century, there has been considerable willingness by taxpayers to finance the schools, at least in part because of widespread faith of many Americans in the ability of the schools to provide children with helpful and necessary skills. In the last half-dozen years, however, voters have been rejecting school bond issues and budgets with alacrity. Explanations differ on the reasons for these rejections, but two issues are clearly significant. One is a demand for a more diverse financial base for public education than the present heavy reliance on local property taxes. The second and more subtle hypothesis involves citizens' loss of faith in the capacity of the schools to accomplish the many tasks assigned to them, a reaction compounded not only of a tradition of overexpectation but of certain noteworthy recent developments.

One of these arises from the fact that for the first time in American history we have reached a point where children no longer regularly receive more formal education than their parents did and where opportunities for children to do better than their parents economically do not abound. Many college-educated parents today are aghast at the lack of concern displayed by their teenage or young adult children for college or for entering the economic mainstream. Others who were unable to attend college themselves but who have worked hard so that their children could do so are similarly disturbed. Both groups may attribute their offsprings' disinterest in these opportunities to what they see as permissiveness in the schools. Such parents cannot vote against the changed culture that has in fact produced their children's attitudes, but they can vote against school budgets.

Dissatisfaction with the schools is endemic. Ever since there have been schools there has been criticism of them. It comes from parents who blame the schools for the inadequacies they find in their own children. It comes from employers who find their employees ill prepared (somehow young people were always better prepared a generation ago when the employer was young). It comes from teachers who find their students uncooperative (again, a generation ago when the teachers were young the students were better). And it comes from the students, who find the schools dull (as students always have.)

With the American educational system—as with most systems—the halcyon days always seem to be in the past. Its contemporary triumphs are often obscure, particularly to persons currently struggling with it. Since education has become so widespread in America today—and that, of course, is one of its principal accomplishments—higher proportions of Americans are directly concerned with how it fares. Many of them believe the past to be preferable to the present; what survives from the past tends to be the successes of the past, not the failures. What troubles us in the present are our difficulties, not our achievements. It is to our credit that we are dissatisfied with the present, for then our future may be even better.

POSTSCRIPT

HAVE THE SCHOOLS MET THEIR SOCIAL GOALS?

Both Peter Schrag and Patricia Graham view the development of education into a "commodity" which can only be obtained through a specified institution as one of the most debilitating factors in contemporary schooling. This view of education may be altered or broken by widespread disillusionment with the school as an institution, by already emerging competition from other agencies of education, and by improved instructional technology which would demand vast changes in the traditional expectations of the schooling process. Both authors counsel a reconsideration of the schools' social reform role in light of evidence that such a role overwhelms academic development aims.

This raises problems of educational structure and organization, of school-society relations, of control and financing of educational institutions, and of the power and rights of education professionals, parents, and students. Such problems are discussed in the various issues comprising the remainder of Part II of this book.

The following sources offer perspectives on the historical development of these and related problems: *The Social Ideas of American Educators* (1961) by Merle Curti; *Popular Education and Democratic Thought in America* (1962) by Rush Welter; David Tyack's *Turning Points in American Educational History* (1967); *The Educating of Americans: A Documentary History* (1969) edited by Daniel Calhoun; *The Public School Movement: A Critical Study* (1973) by Richard Pratte; and Lawrence Cremin's *Public Education* (1976).

Among sources which deal more specifically with the school as a social reform vehicle are Henry J. Perkinson's *The Imperfect Panacea* (1968), Michael B. Katz's *Class, Bureaucracy, and Schools* (1971), and Colin Greer's *The Great School Legend* (1972). The intention of these and similar recent works is to further elevate consciousness about the myths and the realities of American schooling.

The wave of professional self-criticism exemplified by the works cited above was perhaps influenced by the provocative exploration of the school-society relationship by Solon T. Kimball and James E. McClellan, Jr. in *Education and the New America* (1962). The search by these authors for a revitalized commitment to the improvement of education within the changing social context provides a keynote for many of the ideas included in this volume.

ISSUE 7

SHOULD MULTICULTURALISM DOMINATE SCHOOL POLICY?

The argument persists over the public school's historical function of increasing social and economic opportunities for all its constituents. The "melting pot" ideology associated with 19th-century justifications of public schooling is now seen by many as a convenient myth. The assimilation of diverse cultural groups into a true "melting pot" society would entail a diminution of the power and prestige of the dominant group, a general withering of cultural roots, and the emergence of a less-differentiated societal mass. This has not occurred.

Two factors have worked against the achievement of the assimilation ideal (or myth): the institutional dominance of Anglo-Saxon Protestants who viewed themselves as either the controllers or the transformers of minority groups, and the members of those racial and ethnic minorities who were unwilling or unable to reject their cultural heritage in order to accomplish the transformation. These phenomena have been extensively described and analyzed in such works as *Cultural Pluralism and the American Idea* (1956) by Horace M. Kallen; *Beyond the Melting Pot* (2nd edition, 1970) by Nathan Glazer and Daniel P. Moynihan; *The Rise of the Unmeltable Ethnics* (1971) by Michael Novak; *Ethnicity in the United States* (1974) by Andrew M. Greeley; and *Divided Society: The Ethnic Experience in America* (1974) edited by Colin Greer.

Greer, in *The Great School Legend* (1972), examines more specifically the school's role in the assimilation (or transformation) of minority-group members. His analysis shows that public school rhetoric promised common experiences that would equip diverse groups for economic prosperity, but that the reality was much to the contrary. The "Americanization" implied in the schooling experience, demanding conformity to avoid "failure," was always narrowly defined by the dominating elite. Greer further contends that, despite the absence of an overt status system, "issues of ethnicity, race, and culture have been superimposed on economic and occupational differences to provide a basis for discrimination, prejudice, and social inequality."

Michael B. Katz provides another look at school-society relationships in dealing with opportunities for diverse groups of citizens in the expanded edition of *Class, Bureaucracy, and Schools* (1975). Katz feels that the inequities of American education are the inequities of the larger society, and that, contrary to the heretofore-prevalent national myth, the schools are not the place to begin the task of changing society. The immediate focus, according to Katz, must be on the redistribution of power and resources within the total social system, for without this the emergence of democratic pluralism is impossible.

While agreeing that the schools cannot lead the way to vast social reform and cultural change, in *Cultural Pluralism and American Education* (1969), Seymour W. Itzkoff calls upon the schools to nurture rather than extinguish pluralism. This stance seems to be gaining wide and official acceptance as a basis for educational policy. Recent publications by the Association for Supervision and Curriculum Development (ASCD) and the American Association of Colleges for Teacher Education (AACTE) have made a case for a major thrust in policy and curriculum reform in the direction of multicultural education. The AACTE statement, "No One Model American," rejects both assimilation and separatism as social goals, calls for an educational effort supporting cultural diversity and individual uniqueness, and encourages explorations in alternative life styles.

James A. Banks and Orlando Patterson examine in the following brief selections the meaning of cultural pluralism in the context of schooling and arrive at quite different appraisals.

James A. Banks

MAXIMIZE CULTURAL OPTIONS

During the Colonial period, many different ethnic and nationality groups immigrated to North America to practice freely their religious and political beliefs and to improve their economic status. These groups were provincial, ethnocentric, and intolerant of ethnic differences. Each nationality group tried desperately to establish European institutions on American soil and to remake North America in the image of its native land.

Very early in Colonial history the English became the dominant ethnic group, and controlled entry to most social, economic, and political institutions. The English did not allow immigrants from other nations to participate fully in the social system. Thus, the French Huguenots, the Irish, the Scotch-Irish, and the Germans were victims of overt discrimination in Colonial America. The attainment of Anglo characteristics became a requisite for full societal participation. Immigrants who remained distinctly "ethnic" were punished and ridiculed.

THE MELTING POT IDEOLOGY

The public schools, like other social institutions, were dominated by Anglo-Americans. One of their major functions was to rid children of ethnic characteristics and to make them culturally Anglo-Saxon. The schools taught the children of immigrants contempt for their cultures and forced them to experience self-alienation and self-rejection. The melting pot ideology, which was popularized by the English Jewish author, Israel Zangwill, became the philosophical justification for the cultural and ethnic destruction which the schools promoted. All European cultures, it was argued, were to be blended and from them a novel and superior culture would emerge. Most immigrants, however, abandoned their cultures and attained Anglo cultural characteristics. One dominant culture emerged rather than a synthesis of diverse cultures. Most of the non-English cultures stuck to the bottom of the mythical melting pot.

In many significant ways, the Anglo-dominated society, and the schools which helped to perpetuate it, succeeded both in acculturating European-

Continued on p. 116

James A. Banks, "Cultural Pluralism and the Schools," *Educational Leadership*, December 1974, pp. 163–66. Reprinted with permission of the Association for Supervision and Curriculum Development and James A. Banks.

Orlando Patterson

BEWARE GROUPISM AND CONFORMITY

In one of his most penetrating essays, David Riesman, writing in the early fifties, contrasts the virtues and problems of individualism with what he called "groupism": "There has developed today a great preoccupation, less with specific needs, than with group mood—a feeling on the part of individuals that they wanted or felt they had to spend their energies, first, in making a group, and second, in attending to and improving its morale."

It is remarkable that Riesman should have written this in 1950. The specific concerns that prompted his elegant defense of individualism (which I prefer to call individuality, as distinct from the laissez-faire individualism of the late nineteenth and early twentieth centuries, which actually assumed strong group loyalties) were the threats to personal freedom from both the Stalinist left and the jingositic right, on both the domestic and international fronts. What is striking about Riesman's observations is the fact that they are as relevant today as they were in the late forties and early fifties.

The dangers of "groupism" and conformism, in fact, are as great today as they were in the fifties. In view of its wholly internal origins and its strong support by the very group of people who should be most opposed to it—the liberal intelligentsia—its dangers may even be greater today. At least America survived these dangers in the early fifties. The view from my window, which lies only a few miles across the river from Boston, "the cradle of liberty" with its warring ethnic groups, leaves me in great doubt about the possibility that individuality will survive the forces now stacked against it.

Ethnicity, and the spurious social philosophy of pluralism that rationalizes it, are the new dangers to individuality and personal autonomy. The revival of ethnicity was, to some extent, a necessary evil: even with hindsight, I can think of no alternative way in which blacks and other nonEuropean ethnic groups could have achieved the political and social gains they did in the sixties. But what was an unfortunate by-product of a necessary development has become an end in itself. The vulgar extremes to which ethnicity has been taken and the unscrupulous uses to which it has been put create a classic situation in which

Continued on p. 119

(Banks, cont. from p. 114)
Americans and in helping them to attain inclusion into mainstream American life. Once they attained Anglo-American characteristics, most European-Americans were able to participate fully in the social, economic, and political life of American society. We should, however, not underestimate the psychological pain which this process of self-alienation and re-socialization caused European immigrants and their descendants. Today, most American children of European descent find the school culture highly consistent with their culture, although a few, such as Amish and Appalachian youths, do not. However, this is not the case for most minority youths.

THE ALIEN SCHOOL CULTURE

Many ethnic minority youths find the school culture alien, hostile, and self-defeating. Because of institutional racism, poverty, and other complex factors, most ethnic minority communities are characterized by numerous values, institutions, behavior patterns, and linguistic traits which differ in significant ways from the dominant society. The youths who are socialized within these ethnic communities enter the school with cultural characteristics which the school rejects and demeans. These youths are also dehumanized in the school because they are non-White. Because of the negative ways in which their cultural and racial traits are viewed by the school, educators fail to help most minority youths to acquire the skills which they need to function effectively within the two cultural worlds in which they must survive. Consequently, many of them drop out of school, psychologically and physically.

THE SCHOOL'S ROLE IN A PLURALISTIC SOCIETY

What should be the role of the school within a society which has a dominant culture and many other cultures which, according to the democratic ideology that we extol, have a right to thrive? The school in this type of society has a difficult task, especially when those who make most of the major public decisions do not value, and often disdain, the minority cultures. This harsh reality must be seriously considered when we talk about the role of the school in a pluralistic society. Although cultural pluralism exists within American society, most major decisions in government and in industry are made by Anglo-Americans, many of whom are ethnocentric and intolerant of cultural, ethnic, and racial differences.

The school must help Anglo-Americans to break out of their ethnic encapsulations and to learn that there are other viable cultures in the United States, aspects of which can help to redeem and to revivify the dominant culture. The school should also help all students to develop *ethnic literacy,* since most Americans are very ignorant about cultures in the United States other than their own. Americans are socialized within ethnic enclaves where they acquire the belief that their ethnic cultures are the only valid and functional ones. To attain social and economic mobility, minorities are required to function in the dominant culture and are thus forced out of their ethnic encapsulations. However, Anglo-Americans are able to remain within their ethnic enclaves. Most minorities, nevertheless, are very ignorant about other minorities. Most Mexican-Americans know little about the cultures and problems of Afro-

Americans. Most Afro-Americans know as little about the diverse and complex cultures of Mexican-Americans.

THE NEED FOR BROADLY CONCEPTUALIZED ETHNIC STUDIES PROGRAMS

Broadly conceptualized ethnic heritage programs should be devised and implemented in all schools. Such programs should teach about the experiences of all American ethnic groups, including Jewish-Americans, Polish-Americans, and Puerto Rican-Americans. Most ethnic studies programs now in the schools deal only with the history and culture of the ethnic minority group which is present or dominant within the local school population.

Thus, it is rare to find an ethnic heritage program within a predominantly Black school which teaches about the experiences of Asian-Americans, Mexican-Americans, and Puerto Rican-Americans. Such narrowly conceptualized ethnic studies programs are parochial in scope and do not help students to develop the global view of ethnicity in the United States which they need to become effective change agents in contemporary society. We have reached a point in our history in which multiethnic approaches to the teaching of ethnic studies are not only appropriate but essential.

MAXIMIZING CULTURAL OPTIONS

The school within a pluralistic society should maximize the cultural and economic options of students from all income and ethnic groups. Minority students should be helped to attain the skills needed to function effectively both within their ethnic cultures and within the dominant culture. Black children who speak "Black English" should leave the school sensitive to the utility of their native dialect but proficient in Standard English. If Black high school graduates are unable to speak and to write Standard English, their careers and social options will be severely limited.

By arguing that the school must help minority youths to attain the skills needed to function effectively within the dominant culture, I do not mean to suggest that the school should conduct business as usual, and continue to demean the languages and cultures of minority students. Rather, educators should respect the cultural and linguistic characteristics of minority youths, and change the curriculum so that it will reflect their learning and cultural styles and greatly enhance their achievement. Minority students should not be taught contempt for their cultures. Teachers should use elements of their cultures to help them to attain the skills which they need to live alternative life styles.

Anglo-American students should also be taught that they have cultural options. We severely limit the potentiality of students when we merely teach them aspects of their own cultures. Anglo-American students should realize that using Black English is one effective way to communicate, that Native Americans have values, beliefs, and life styles which may be functional for them, and that there are alternative ways of behaving and of viewing the universe which are practiced within the United States that they can freely embrace. By helping Anglo-American students to view the world beyond their cultural perspectives, we will enrich them as human beings and enable them to live more productive and fulfilling lives.

TEACHING FOR SOCIAL REFORM

It is necessary but not sufficient for the school to help minority children to acquire the skills which they need to attain economic and social mobility. It must also help equip them with the skills, attitudes, and abilities needed to attain *power* so that they can effectively participate in the reformation of the social system. We will perpetuate the status quo if we merely acculturate students so that they will fit into the Anglo-Saxon mold. They must acquire both the skills and the commitment to engage in *radical social change* if we are ever going to create a society in which individuals and groups can freely participate without regard to their ethnicity, sex, and social class. If the school acculturates as well as politicizes students so that they become committed to radical reform, we should realize that it will be contradicting its historic mission of perpetuating the status quo and will be engaging in a subversive task.

CULTURAL PLURALISM: A CAVEAT

While the school should reflect and perpetuate cultural diversity, it has a responsibility to teach a commitment to and respect for the core values, such as justice, equality, and human dignity, which are expressed in our major historical documents. If carried to its logical extreme, the *cultural pluralism* argument can be used to justify racism, cultural genocide, and other cultural practices which are antithetical to a democratic society. There is also a danger that *cultural pluralism* may become the new myth, replacing the *melting pot.* This concept must be rigorously examined for all of its social and philosophical ramifications. The works of earlier advocates of cultural pluralism, such as Horace M. Kallen, who originated the concept, and of Julius Drachsler, merit serious study.

We should not exaggerate the extent of cultural pluralism in the United States, and should realize that widespread cultural assimilation has taken place in America. To try to perceive cultural differences where none exist may be as detrimental as ignoring those which are real. The school should foster those cultural differences which maximize opportunities for democratic living, but vigorously oppose those which do not. We should realize that racism, sexism, and dehumanization are also aspects of human cultures which can be justified with the cultural pluralism argument. Emerging concepts and unexamined ideas must not be used to divert attention from the humanistic goals that we have too long deferred, or from the major cause of our social ills—*institutional racism.*

(Patterson, cont. from p. 115)
the remedy many thought would cure the ills of the body politic now threatens the entire system. Most tragic of all is the horrible prospect that ethnicity, like a viper biting its tail, may well turn against the very groups whose condition required its revival.

This is not the place to specify the reactionary potentialities of ethnicity. I merely wish to point out a basic flaw in the thinking of those liberal intellectuals who continue to support it. Ethnic pluralism is often defended by liberals on two grounds. One is that diversity is good as an end in itself; it is better to have a society with a varied population since this adds to the vitality, interest, and possible range of human interaction. How much better it is, we are told, to live in a city such as Boston in which, within a few blocks, it is possible to move from the lively Mediterranean clutter of the Italian North End to the throbbing vitality of Roxbury and, not much further on, the impish charm of old Southie. The suicidal nature of such a promenade, whatever its sociological delights, should be obvious to anyone who has had anything to do with Boston lately or, for that matter, any of America's pluralist cities. But even if there were no risks to life and limb involved in this naive defense of pluralism, it can be questioned whether diversity of this kind is intrinsically good.

The second, more sophisticated defense of pluralism is the argument that it protects the rights of individuals to be different. A respect for the values and customs of other peoples is certainly more desirable than bigotry and ethnocentrism.

In response to these two defenses of pluralism, let me say first that I, too, strongly believe that diversity is good, and that tolerance is one of, if not the greatest of, all virtues. The problem is this: Diversity of what kind? And tolerance of what?

Once we ask these fundamental questions, we immediately come to the heart of the contradiction in the liberal defense of pluralism. For it turns out that this defense centers wholly on social groups rather than on individuals. When liberals today talk about a diverse society, they mean a diversity of ethnic groups; and when tolerance is mentioned, it refers to tolerance not of other individuals but of the groups to which they belong.

This defense of pluralism not only neglects individuality; much worse, an emphasis on group diversity and group tolerance works against a respect for individuality. This is what I call the pluralist fallacy, which originates in the failure to recognize a basic paradox in human interaction: the greater the diversity and cohesiveness of groups in a society, the smaller the diversity and personal autonomy of individuals in that society.

This follows logically from certain basic principles of social life. First, it is a commonplace of sociology that in those groups which are of the informal, communal type (as opposed to formal organizations, such as bureaucracies), group strength is a function of the degree to which individual members share a common set of values, live by a common set of norms, and aspire to a common set of ideals. People feel "together" because they feel alike. Thus South Boston is a strong ethnic community because "we in Southie all think alike; we are one." And every "conscious" black person now believes that the strength of the group requires that all blacks become "brothers." The strength and cohesiveness of an ethnic group, then, is bought at the expense of the individuality of members of that group.

Second, the greater the number of ethnic groups in a society, the greater the tendency toward cohesiveness within each group. The reasons for this are not hard to find. The legitimation of ethnicity in a society reinforces the tendency for ethnic groups to become interest groups. The more ethnic groups there are, the greater the number of groups competing for the scarce resources of society's power and wealth. It is the strength and cohesiveness of the ethnic group—the degree to which it can act "as one"—which determines its success in the competition for such resources. Therefore as the competition becomes keener, as more and more ethnic groups enter the system, the tendency will be for greater cohesiveness in each ethnic group.

The depressing conclusion to be derived from these two basic propositions should now be clear. Increasing ethnic cohesiveness implies increasing individual conformity, "groupism," or declining individuality. Increasing ethnic diversity implies increasing group cohesiveness. Therefore, increasing ethnic diversity implies declining individuality. Group diversity, in short, is antagonistic to individual diversity and autonomy.

Some may contend that the loss of individuality is the price to be paid for ethnic diversity and group mobility. I have two responses to this. First, the gains claimed for pluralism are seriously open to question. Many social scientists have convincingly argued that pluralism is essentially conservative in its social and political implications since, at best, it freezes the relative position of the various competing groups: it allows each to veto legislation against its special interests but, by the same token, prevents the deprived groups from making any gains relative to those groups which are better off. And, worse, it encourages unscrupulous political leaders to play off one group against the other, or one collection of groups against another. The vicious and divisive "law and order" rhetoric of the Nixon-Agnew years had nothing to do with law and order, but was an appeal to the worst fears of the white working-class ethnics with respect to blacks and other third-world minorities.

Second, even if there are some gains to be made from the legitimation of ethnic diversity, it is doubtful whether it is worth the price of individuality. A relatively homogeneous society, with a high degree of individual variation and disdain for conformity, is a far more desirable social order than one with many competing ethnic groups made up of gray, group-stricken conformists. It is also a more exciting and stimulating society in which to live. We do not relate to groups but to other individuals. It is not groups we love, or hate, or respect, or go to bed with. It is other individuals. It is astonishing that, in their retreat from individuality (which, once again, is not be confused with Hooverian, laissez-faire individualism), American liberals seem to have forgotten this simple fact.

But perhaps my sense of astonishment merely betrays my naiveté. Could it be that the liberals were never really liberal? Is this why it has been so easy for them to embrace the vulgar and insidious pluralist creed?

POSTSCRIPT

SHOULD MULTICULTURALISM DOMINATE SCHOOL POLICY?

In official education circles the concept of multicultural education has become firmly engrained. Efforts have been increased to improve sensitivity to cultural differences, to institute bilingual instruction, and to develop specific teaching aids aimed at the needs of disadvantaged children. With the exception of a few pockets of concern, such as that expressed by Patterson, the movement is meeting little resistance.

Some feel that the present level of acceptance is due to the fact that there is no widely accepted, explicit definition of multiculturalism and no full understanding of cultural pluralism and its consequent demands on human behavior. This is the note sounded by Carl J. Dolce in "Multicultural Education—Some Issues" (*The Journal of Teacher Education,* Winter 1973). Dolce claims that multiculturalism cannot be simply grafted onto an educational program, for it is based upon a different view of society than that which presently appears to exist. He further asks, "How can unity be fostered while simultaneously preserving and fostering cultural diversity?"

Indeed, the unity-within-diversity objective requires social reconceptualization. In *American Pluralism: A Study of Minority Groups and Social Theory* (1973), William M. Newman says that contemporary American society contains processes that pull toward assimilation and pluralism at the same time. The educational system must continue efforts to better prepare members of diverse minority groups to function effectively in the present cultural mainstream. At the same time, however, the schools can honestly portray the various values and lifestyles which emanate from different quarters of our national life, and treat these variations with due respect and understanding.

Reducing exclusionary practices and opening avenues of opportunity and choice are reasonable expectations of schools in a democratic society. Whether or not such goals need to be attached to wider social aims is the topic addressed in the next issue.

ISSUE 8

HOW CAN OPPORTUNITY BE EQUALIZED?

An emphasis on cultural pluralism, with its attendant focus on differential backgrounds, on dialect variation and linguistic difficulties, and on improving the quality of human relations, may at least establish a context for positive movement toward wide equalization of opportunity. The quality of human experience for people as individuals and as members of cultural groups must be the predominant criterion in charting courses of action.

Individual experience is shaped by cultural group membership and by existing social arrangements. If those social arrangements unjustly discriminate against certain groups, the affected individuals feel excluded, persecuted, humiliated, and powerless. Historically, many who have suffered from such discrimination have difficulty adjusting to the norms of the dominant group, have developed only the lowest levels of personal aspiration, and have often been condemned to lifelong poverty.

Governmental action to modify this situation has often been motivated by a meritocratic vision of a society in which all citizens, regardless of birth or circumstances, obtain equal opportunities to develop their abilities and gain access to "success." Actions emanating from this sentiment have ranged from removal of exclusionary restraints to programs and strategies aimed at integration, collective compensation, and preferential treatment through affirmative action.

Social science research such as that contained in the 1966 Coleman Report was prompted by the desire of the federal government to improve the life chances of the disadvantaged. This research showed that the relative achievement of disadvantaged students declined as they moved through the school system. It was found that the students' socio-economic background and the direct influence of their age-mates far outweighed any school-related factors in determining their skill development and occupational aspirations. Some felt that busing, for the purpose of integrating across socio-economic and racial lines, held promise of changing the existing patterns. Programs such as Head Start and Follow Through were intended to compensate for environmental deprivation by intervening at the early stages of development. Affirmative-action programs like Upward Bound and preferential college admissions were initiated in order to open doors to white-collar jobs and the professions.

There are those who feel that such efforts have been successful enough to warrant their continuation and possible expansion. Others claim that the vast expenditures and governmental manipulation involved have created as many negative social results as positive, and that the principle of compensation for past injustices is a dangerous policy to follow. Still others, following the social justice theory of John Rawls (*A Theory of Justice,* 1972), challenge the meritocratic principle because it still leaves the less fortunate behind in a condition of low self-esteem and diminished self-respect. Rawls' basic principle is that social and economic inequalities are just only if the least advantaged members of society benefit somehow from the situation.

In the following selections, Christopher Jencks summarizes his interpretations of the Coleman Report data, charting a course which redefines the school's role in social reform goals and suggesting political action on a far wider plane. Nathan Glazer attacks the trend in social policy toward differential treatment on the basis of racial and ethnic categories.

Christopher Jencks

FOCUS ON DIVERSITY AND CHOICE

We have seen that educational opportunities, cognitive skills, educational credentials, occupational status, income, and job satisfaction are all unequally distributed. We have not, however, been very successful in explaining most of these inequalities. The association between one variety of inequality and another is usually quite weak, which means that equalizing one thing is unlikely to have much effect on the degree of inequality in other areas. We must therefore ask whether attempts to produce equality by more direct methods would be more effective, or whether the status quo is essentially unalterable. Before trying to answer this question, however, a recapitulation of our findings may be helpful.

We began by looking at the distribution of educational opportunity. We found that access to school resources was quite unequal. Schools in some districts and neighborhoods spend far more than schools in other districts and neighborhoods. We also found that utilization of school resources was even more unequal than access to them, at least after the age of 16. Middle-class students have access to slightly more than their share of the nation's educational resources, and they utilize substantially more than their share. Access to white middle-class classmates is also quite unequal, in the sense that schools are somewhat segregated by class and quite segregated by race. It is hard to tell how much of this segregation would disappear if everyone had a chance to attend the school of his choice. Within schools, we found that most students were in the curriculum of their choice, but that a significant minority was not.

We next turned to the distribution of the cognitive skills measured by standardized tests. We found that both genetic and environmental inequality played a major role in producing cognitive inequality. We also found that those who started life with genetic advantages tended to get environmental advantages as well, and that this exacerbated inequality. We argued that genes influenced test scores both by influencing the way children were treated and by influencing how much children learned when they were treated in exactly

Continued on p. 126

Nathan Glazer

AFFIRMATIVE ACTION IS NOT THE KEY

A new course in dealing with the issues of equality that arise in the American multiethnic society has been set aside since the early 1970s. It is demonstrated that there is discrimination or at least some condition of inequality through the comparison of statistical patterns, and then racial and ethnic quotas and statistical requirements for employment and school assignment are imposed. This course is not demanded by legislation—indeed, it is specifically forbidden by national legislation—or by any reasonable interpretation of the Constitution. Nor is it justified, I have argued, by any presumed failure of the policies of nondiscrimination and of affirmative action that prevailed until the early 1970s. Until then, affirmative action meant to seek out and prepare members of minority groups for better jobs and educational opportunities. It still means only this much in the field of residential distribution. But in the early 1970s affirmative action came to mean much more than advertising opportunities actively, seeking out those who might not know of them, and preparing those who might not yet be qualified. It came to mean the setting of statistical requirements based on race, color, and national origin for employers and educational institutions. This new course threatens the abandonment of our concern for individual claims to consideration on the basis of justice and equity, now to be replaced with a concern for rights for publicly determined and delimited racial and ethnic groups.

The supporters of the new policy generally argue that it is a temporary one. They argue (or some do) that consideration of race, color, and national origin in determining employment and education is repugnant, but it is required for a brief time to overcome a heritage of discrimination. I have argued that the heritage of discrimination, as we could see from the occupational developments of the later 1960s, could be overcome by simply attacking discrimination. The statistical-pattern approach was instituted *after,* not before, the remarkably rapid improvement in the black economic and occupational position in the 1960s. I have argued that the claim that school assignment on the basis of race and ethnicity is only temporary is false,

Continued on p. 131

(Jencks, cont. from p. 124)
the same way, but we could not assess the relative importance of these two processes. We found no evidence that differences between schools contributed significantly to cognitive inequality, nor were we very successful in identifying other specific genetic or environmental determinants of test performance.

We then examined the distribution of educational credentials. We found that family background had much more influence than IQ genotype on an individual's educational attainment. The family's influence depended partly on its socio-economic status and partly on cultural and psychological characteristics that were independent of socio-economic level. The effect of cognitive skill on educational attainment proved difficult to estimate, but it was clearly significant. We found no evidence that the role of family background was declining or that the role of cognitive skill was increasing. Qualitative differences between schools played a very minor role in determining how much schooling people eventually got.

Men's occupational statuses turned out to be quite closely tied to their educational attainment. Yet there was a great deal of variation in the status of men with exactly the same amount of education, and this variation did not seem to be explained by any other readily identified characteristic. Both family background and cognitive skill influenced occupational status, but they did this largely by influencing the amount of schooling men got, not by influencing the status of men who had completed their education. Since educational attainment is only partly determined by family background, and since occupational status is only partly determined by educational attainment, family background ends up exerting a moderate influence on a man's eventual occupation. We confirmed this judgment by comparing the statuses of brothers raised in the same family, which often differed substantially.

Variation in men's incomes proved even harder to explain than variation in their occupational statuses. Educational credentials influence the occupations men enter, but credentials do not have much effect on earnings within any given occupation, so their overall effect on income is moderate. Family background and cognitive skills have some effect on a man's occupation, and some effect on his income even after he has entered a given occupation, but their overall influence is also moderate. The genes that influence IQ scores appear to have relatively little influence on income. As a result, we estimate that there is nearly as much income variation among men who come from similar families, have similar credentials, and have similar test scores, as among men in general. This suggests that competence does not depend primarily on family background, schooling, and test scores, or else that income does not depend on competence.

Job satisfaction proved even less explicable than other things. It is only marginally related to educational attainment, occupational status, or earnings.

These findings have important implications for both educators and social reformers. We will take up their implications for educators first.

None of the evidence we have reviewed suggests that school reform can be expected to bring about significant social changes outside the schools. More specifically, the evidence suggests that equalizing educational opportunity would do very little to make adults more equal. If all elementary schools were equally effective, cognitive inequality among twelfth graders would hardly decline at all, and disparities in their eventual attainment would decline less than 1 percent. Eliminating all economic and academic obstacles to college attendance might somewhat reduce disparities in educational attainment, but the change would not be large. Furthermore, the experience of the past 25 years suggests that even fairly substantial reductions in the range of educational attainments do not appreciably reduce economic inequality among adults.

The schools, of course, could move beyond equal opportunity, establishing a system of compensatory opportunity in which the best schooling was reserved for those who were disadvantaged in other respects. The evidence suggests, however, that educational compensation is usually of marginal value to the recipients. Neither the overall level of educational resources nor any specific, easily identifiable school policy has much effect on the test scores or educational attainment of students who start out at a disadvantage. Thus even if we reorganized the schools so their primary concern was for the students who most needed help, there is no reason to suppose that adults would end up appreciably more equal as a result.

There seem to be three reasons why school reform cannot make adults more equal. First, children seem to be far more influenced by what happens at home than by what happens in school. They may also be more influenced by what happens on the streets and by what they see on television. Second, reformers have very little control over those aspects of school life that affect children. Reallocating resources, reassigning pupils, and rewriting the curriculum seldom change the way teachers and students actually treat each other minute by minute. Third, even when a school exerts an unusual influence on children, the resulting changes are not likely to persist into adulthood. It takes a huge change in elementary school test scores, for example, to alter adult income by a significant amount. . . .

Instead of evaluating schools in terms of long-term effects on their alumni, which appear to be relatively uniform, we think it wiser to evaluate schools in terms of their immediate effects on teachers and students, which appear much more variable. Some schools are dull, depressing, even terrifying places, while others are lively, comfortable, and reassuring. If we think of school life as an end in itself rather than a means to some other end, such differences are enormously important. Eliminating these differences would not do much to make adults more equal, but it would do a great deal to make the quality of children's (and teachers') lives more equal. Since children are in school for a fifth of their lives, this would be a significant accomplishment.

Looking at schooling as an end in itself rather than a means to some other end suggests that we ought to describe schools in a language appropriate to a family rather than to a factory. This implies that we will have to accept diverse standards for judging schools, just as we do for judging families. Indeed, we can even say that diversity should be an explicit objective of schools and school systems. No single-home-away-from-home can be ideal for all children. A school system that provides only one variety of schooling, no matter how good, must almost invariably seem unsatisfactory to many parents and children. The ideal system is one that provides as many varieties of schooling as its children and parents want and finds ways of matching children to schools that suit them. Since the character of an individual's schooling appears to have relatively little long-term effect on his development, society as a whole rarely has a compelling interest in limiting the range of educational choices open to parents and students. Likewise, since professional educators do not seem to understand the long-term effects of schooling any better than parents do, there is no compelling reason why the profession should be empowered to rule out alternatives that appeal to parents, even if they seem educationally "unsound."

The argument that school life is largely an end in itself rather than a means to some other end does not mean we believe schools should be run like mediocre summer camps, where children are merely kept out of trouble. We doubt that a school can be enjoyable for either adults or children unless the children feel they are doing something purposeful. One good way to give children a sense of purpose is to give them activities that contribute to their becoming more like grownups. Our findings suggest that a school's choice of objectives has rather little long-term effect on what kinds of grownups the children become. That is determined by outside influences. But since we value ideas and the life of the mind, we favor schools that value these things too. Others, who favor discipline and competitive excellence, may prefer schools that value high reading and math scores. Still others, more concerned with teaching children to behave properly, will prefer schools that try to do this. The list of competing objectives is nearly endless, which is why we favor diversity and choice.

But even if school systems do not try to diversify their educational programs, parents and children will usually assume that some schools are better than others. Most parents will assume, for example, that a school in a white upper-middle-class neighborhood is better than one in a poor black neighborhood, even if the formal curriculums are identical. Under these circumstances equity seems to require that every family have a free choice as to which schools its children attend. . . . The basic principle is simply that every child in a district should have the same claim on every school, regardless of where he happens to live. This means, for example, that if a poor black mother wants her children in a predominantly white school, and if such a school exists in her district, she should be free to enroll them, and the district should transport them there. It does not mean that if she wants white children in her neighborhood school, the district must compel white students to enroll there.

Even if everyone had equal access to all the schools in their district, the problem of disparities between districts would remain. In principle, we can see no reason why students should not be free to attend schools outside their district, but this is not likely to become widespread unless the Supreme Court upholds busing across district lines to achieve racial balance. The Court may, however, require states to eliminate, or at least drastically reduce, expenditure differentials between districts. Even if it does not, legislatures can perhaps be pushed in this direction. In addition, the federal government could easily do more to reduce expenditure differences between states.

Many conservatives have opposed such changes, on the grounds that equalizing resources would mean more central financing, and that more central financing would mean more central control. Central control is, in turn, often said to make schools less responsive to local needs. Experience suggests, however, that while central control may make the schools less responsive to the local establishment, whatever that may be, it often makes schools more responsive to other local groups. (Blacks in the South are an obvious case in point.) We therefore tend to favor central financing, both as a means of equalizing expenditures and as a way of making local schools somewhat more responsive to groups they have traditionally ignored.

Finally, there is the problem of equalizing access to higher education. It would be relatively simple to design a system in which access to higher education no longer depended on getting money from home. Indeed, the Higher Education Act of 1972 contains the outlines of such a system, even though it will not fully achieve this objective. It is somewhat more difficult to design a system in which access no longer depends on test scores or other imperfect predictors of academic success. Open admission is a step in this direction, since it makes continued access depend on actual performance in college rather than performance in high school or on an aptitude test. Open admission does not, however, solve the problem of the student who persists in trying to learn subjects for which he has relatively little aptitude. That would require not only open admission, but open readmission.

The foregoing reforms are all aimed at equalizing people's claims on a public resource, namely schooling. If we try to move beyond equal access and ensure equal use of educational resources, the problem becomes far more complex. It is relatively simple, for example, to guarantee working-class families the same opportunity as middle-class families to send their children to schools in middle-class neighborhoods. But it is not easy to make them use this opportunity. They may think such schools inconvenient, or they may fear their children will be out of place and unhappy with classmates more affluent than themselves.

The same is also true of blacks, who can and should be guaranteed the right to attend predominantly white schools, but cannot always be persuaded to exercise this right. The problem is particularly difficult in the rural South, where the white community has often put enormous pressure on black families who tried to send their children to previously white schools. In such settings, judicial coercion and mandatory busing may be the only way to break the tradition of segregation. Once the tradition of complete segregation has been broken, however, mandatory busing makes less sense. If attending a desegregated school had significant long-term benefits for students, one could make a case against allowing parents to send their children to segregated schools even if they wanted to do so. The evidence we have reviewed suggests, however, that the long-term effects of segregation on individual students are quite small. This makes us favor a system in which black parents are free to decide for themselves whether they want their children in segregated or desegregated schools. For this to be a genuine choice, the school system must provide transportation, must give blacks access to nearby white schools, even if this makes them overcrowded, and must make sure that every parent is aware of having a choice. If this were done, experience with programs like Project Concern in Hartford suggests that most black parents would choose a desegregated school. But that should be their option, not a decision imposed by others for their alleged benefit.

Just as giving everyone access to every school may not lead to complete desegregation, so too giving everyone access to higher education will not persuade everyone to earn a doctorate, or even a B.A. We have already eliminated virtually all economic and academic obstacles to earning a high school diploma, and one student in five still drops out. This percentage is likely to keep falling. But the same considerations that lead students to quit high school will continue to operate in college, even if colleges are open to everyone and money is available to cover the costs.

We are not enthusiastic about coercion as a device for keeping reluctant students in school. Experience suggests that students who do not want to be in school rarely learn a great deal while they are there and that they often make schools extremely unpleasant for everyone else. Since keeping people in school the same length of time is not likely to make them significantly more equal in any other respect, we can see nothing to be said for it.

If we assume that higher education, like concerts and football games, will be used unequally, we must decide how to finance it. A system that makes students dependent on money from home, which many cannot get, is clearly unacceptable. But a system which finances higher education out of general tax revenues and then allows individual students to use their education for private gain also seems unacceptable. It is hard to see why, for example, an auto worker should pay taxes to send his cousin to law school and should then have to pay his cousin fat fees to obtain legal services. One alternative would be to equalize adult incomes. If the educated and the uneducated ended up with equal incomes, we could assume that the economic benefits of higher education were being more or less equally distributed. It would then seem reasonable that the costs also be equally distributed, coming out of general tax revenues.

In a society where individuals are free to retain most of the economic benefits of their education for themselves, it seems reasonable to ask them to pay most of the costs. The most equitable way to do this, in our judgment, would be to provide every student with free tuition and a living stipend, and then impose an income tax surcharge on those who had had these benefits. These surcharges should be large enough so that the average student repaid the cost of his schooling. Those who earned high incomes would repay more than their share, while those who earned low incomes would repay relatively little. Those who did not attend would pay nothing at all toward the cost of higher education. . . .

A successful campaign for reducing economic inequality probably requires two things. First, those with low incomes must cease to accept their condition as inevitable and just. Instead of assuming, like unsuccessful gamblers, that their numbers will eventually come up or that their children's numbers will, they must demand changes in the rules of the game. Second, some of those with high incomes, and especially the children of those with high incomes, must begin to feel ashamed of economic inequality. If these things were to happen, significant institutional changes in the machinery of income distribution would become politically feasible.

The long-term direction of such progress seems clear. In America, as elsewhere, the general trend over the past 200 years has been toward equality. In the economic realm, however, the contribution of public policy to this drift has been slight. As long as egalitarians assume that public policy cannot contribute to economic equality directly but must proceed by ingenious manipulations of marginal institutions like the schools, progress will remain glacial. If we want to move beyond this tradition, we will have to establish political control over the economic institutions that shape our society. This is what other countries usually call socialism. Anything else will end in the same disappointment as the reforms of the 1960s.

(Glazer, cont. from p. 125)

because the supporters of such an approach now demand it whatever the circumstances, and the Constitution is now so interpreted that it can be required permanently.

We have created two racial and ethnic classes in this country to replace the disgraceful pattern of the past in which some groups were subjected to an official and open discrimination. The two new classes are those groups that are entitled to statistical parity in certain key areas on the basis of race, color, and national origin, and those groups that are not. The consequences of such a development can be foreseen: They are already, in some measure, upon us. Those groups that are not considered eligible for special benefits become resentful. If one could draw a neat line between those who have suffered from discrimination and those who have not, the matter would be simpler. Most immigrant groups have had periods in which they were discriminated against. For the Irish and the Jews, for example, these periods lasted a long time. Nor is it the case that all the groups that are now recorded as deserving official protection have suffered discrimination, or in the same way.

The Spanish-surnamed category is particularly confused. It is not at all clear which groups it covers, although presumably it was designed to cover the Mexican Americans and Puerto Ricans. But in San Francisco, Nicaraguans from Central America, who were neither conquered by the United States nor subjected to special legislation and who very likely have suffered only from the problems that all immigrants do, given their occupational and educational background, their economic situation, and their linguistic facility were willy-nilly swept up into one of the categories that had to be distributed evenly through the school system. The Cuban immigrants have done well and already have received special government aid owing to their status as refugees: Are they now to receive, too, the special benefit of being considered Spanish-surnamed, a group listed in the goals required in affirmative action programs?

The protected groups include variously the descendants of free immigrants, conquered peoples, and slaves, and a single group may include the descendants of all three categories (e.g., the Puerto Ricans). Do free immigrants who have come to this country voluntarily deserve the same protected treatment as the descendants of conquered people and slaves? The point is that racial and ethnic groups make poor categories for the design of public policy. They include a range of individuals who have different legal bases for claims for redress and remedy of grievances. If the categories are designed to correct the injustices of the past, they do not work.

They do not work to correct the injustices of the present either, for some groups defined by race and ethnicity do not seem to need redress on the basis of their economic, occupational, and educational position. The Asian Americans have indeed been subjected to discrimination, legal and unofficial alike. But Chinese and Japanese Americans rank high in economic status, occupational status, educational status. (This does not prevent members of these groups from claiming the benefits that now accrue to them because they form a specially protected category under affirmative action programs.) If they were included in the protected category because they have faced discrimination, then groups in the unprotected categories also deserve inclusion. If they were included because they suffer from a poor economic, occupational and educational position, they were included in error. So if these ethnic and racial categories have been designed to group individuals with some especially deprived current condition, they do not work either. Just as the Chinese and Japanese and Indians (from India) do not need the protection of the Spanish-surnamed category, and middle-class blacks the protection of the Negro category in order to get equal treatment today in education and employment. The inequalities created by the use of these categories became sharply evident in 1975 when many private colleges and universities tried to cut back on special aid for racially defined groups, who did indeed include many in need, but also included many in no greater need than "white" or "other" students. But the creation of a special benefit, whether needed or not, is not to be given up easily: Black students occupied school buildings and demanded that the privileges given on the basis of race be retained. This is part of the evil of the creation of especially benefited ethnic and racial categories.

The racial and ethnic categories neither properly group individuals who deserve redress on the basis of past discriminatory treatment, nor properly group individuals who deserve redress on the basis of a present deprived condition. The creation of such specially benefited categories also has inevitable and unfortunate political consequences. Groups not included wonder whether it would not be to their benefit to be included. In India, whose history and circumstances are entirely different from ours, the scheduled castes, and then tribals, were given special rights in employment and education. Very likely one can make an excellent case for these "reservations," as the Indian quotas are called. But other groups have tried to qualify for these rights, to the point where an Indian state court had to rule that no more than 50 percent of the population could be so included—presumably, at that point a new minority was created that was being discriminated against. There are already cases of individuals who redefine themselves in this country for some benefit—the part American Indian who becomes Indian for some public purpose, the person with a Spanish-surnamed mother who now finds it advantageous to change his or her name; conceivably the black who has passed as white and who may reclaim black status for an educational or employment benefit. We have not yet reached the degraded condition of the Nuremberg laws, but undoubtedly we will have to create a new law of personal ethnic and racial status to define just who is eligible for these benefits, to replace the laws we have banned to determine who should be subject to discrimination.

The gravest political consequence is undoubtedly the increasing resentment and hostility between groups that is fueled by special benefits for some. The statistical basis for redress makes one great error: All "whites" are consigned to the same category, deserving of no special consideration. That is not the way "whites" see themselves, or indeed are, in social reality. Some may be "whites," pure and simple. But almost all have some specific ethnic or religious identification, which, to the individual involved, may mean a distinctive history of past—and perhaps some present—discrimination. We have analyzed the position and attitudes of the ethnic groups formed from the post-1880 immigrants from Europe. These groups were not particularly involved in the enslavement of the Negro or the creation of the Jim Crow pattern in the South, the conquest of part of Mexico, or the near-extermination of the American Indian. Indeed, they settled in parts of the country where there were few blacks and almost no Mexican Americans and American Indians. They came to a country which provided them with less benefits than it now provides the protected groups. There is little reason for them to feel they should bear the burden of the redress of a past in which they had no or little part, or to assist those who presently receive more assistance than they did. We are indeed a nation of minorities; to enshrine some minorities as deserving special benefits means not to defend minority rights against a discriminating majority but to favor some of these minorities over others.

Compensation for the past is a dangerous principle. It can be extended indefinitely and make for endless trouble. Who is to determine what is proper compensation for the American Indian, the black, the Mexican American, the Chinese or Japanese American? When it is established that the full status of equality is extended to every individual, regardless of race, color, or national origin, and that special opportunity is also available to any individual on the basis of individual need, again regardless of race, color, or national origin, one has done all that justice and equity call for and that is consistent with a harmonious multigroup society.

Each of the policies we have discussed of course raises special problems. Inclusion in employment goals and quotas is clearly a positive benefit for individuals in the benefited groups, an actual loss for the others. As a result, these benefits will be defended most fiercely. It is less clear what the benefit is in school desegregation. It is obviously considered no benefit at all but an actual loss by some of the populations involved, white and Asian American, may well be seen as a loss by many of the Spanish-surnamed groups involved, and is even seen as a loss by many of the blacks. Residential distribution is an even more ambiguous case. It is a clear gain if it means access to better housing and communities with better services. But it may imply only the dubious benefit of housing in a project or low-income section of the suburbs, rather than a project or a low-income section in the central city; and if we consider this concrete reality, many for whom such a policy is designed may well see it as a disadvantage, too.

These policies are based on two equally inadequate views of the nature of racial and ethnic groups in the United States. First, they assume that these groups are so easily bounded and defined, and so uniform in the condition of those included in them, that a policy designed for the group can be applied equitably and may be assumed to provide benefits for those eligible. The fact is that, for many of the groups involved, the boundaries of membership are uncertain, and the condition of those included in the groups are diverse. Furthermore, it clearly does not serve the creation of an integrated nation for government to intervene in creating sharper and more meaningful ethnic boundaries, to subdivide the population more precisely than people in general recognize and act on. The fact is, a good deal of integration—taken in the fullest sense of the term—has gone on in this country. The process will not be aided by trying to fix categories for division and identification and then make them significant for people's fates by law. We are not a nation such as Belgium, which can draw a geographical line across the country and pronounce one side Flemish and the other French (and even Belgium has a serious problem in considering what to do about mixed—that is, "integrated"—Brussels). Nor do we want to become such a nation, in which our people live within ironclad ethnic and racial divisions defined by law.

These policies make a second and opposite error, and that is to ignore the reality that some degree of community and fellow-feeling courses through these groups and makes them more than mere assemblages of individuals. We have seen how school desegregation policies have taken a positively hostile attitude toward any expression of such a group reality, how residential distribution policies assume that any community is a "ghetto," imposed from without rather than chosen from within. Even statistically oriented employment policies also ignore certain realities of community. Racial and ethnic communities have expressed themselves in occupations and work groups. Distinctive histories have channeled ethnic and racial groups into one kind of work or another, and this is the origin of many of the "unrepresentative" work distributions we see. These distributions have been maintained by an occupational tradition linked to an ethnic community, which makes it easier for the Irish to become policemen, the Italians fruit dealers, Jews businessmen, and so on. None of us would want these varied occupational patterns maintained by discrimination. Nor, however, should we want to see its strengths provided by an ethnic-occupational link—strengths for the group itself, and for the work it contributes to society—dissipated by policies which assumed all such concentrations were signs of discrimination and had to be broken up. A rigorous adherence to requirements of no discrimination on grounds of race, color, and national origin would weaken these concentrations and offer opportunities to many of other groups. A policy of statistical representation in each area of employment would eliminate them—but that would go beyond the demands of justice and equity.

Thus policies of statistical representation in employment, education, and residence insist that it is possible to divide the racial and ethnic groups with precision and assign them on the basis of past discrimination and present circumstance to a class for which a strict statistical parity must be required, and a class which does not warrant this protection (if protection it is—as we saw, in some cases, even the protected groups look dubiously on what is proposed for their putative benefit). But on the other hand, these policies insist that despite the precision with which these groups may be defined and discriminated, none of them may exist in any group or corporate form even if this is a matter of their own choosing. In contrast, the emergent American ethnic consensus we described in the first chapter of this book insisted that the group characteristics of an individual were of no concern to government, that it must take no account of an individual's race, color, or national origin. And on the other side the consensus insisted that any individual could participate in the maintenance of a distinctive ethnic group voluntarily, and that government could not intervene to break up and destroy these voluntary communal formations. Finally, . . . the American ethnic consensus would not accept these voluntary racial and ethnic formations as component parts of the American polity. There were to be no group political rights added to the rights of every individual and of the component states. This element, too, of the consensus is in process of being subverted by the emergence of a required statistical representation of some racial and ethnic groups in key areas of life, because to ascribe rights on the basis of ethnic group membership inevitably *strengthens* such groups and gives them a greater political role. . . .

We have a complex of education, culture, administration, and political institutions which has deflected us into a course in which we publicly establish ethnic and racial categories for differential treatment, and believe that by so doing we are establishing a just and good society. Behind it all stands, to my mind, a radical misunderstanding of how we in the United States have attempted to deal with the problems of a multiracial and multiethnic society. The pattern we have developed is not easily summed up in slogans—which is perhaps its defect—for we have decided against both the forcible assimilation of all groups into one mold and the legal recognition of each group for the establishment of a formal parity between them. It is a pattern that has emerged from the complex interplay of constitutional principles, political institutions, American culture, and that has had, at times, to be reestablished through force and violence.

For ten years now, we have drifted in another direction, certainly in some ways an easier one to understand, and in some ways even easier to institute. Let us number and divide up (some of) the people into their appropriate racial and ethnic groups, and let equality prevail between them and the "others." But this has meant that we abandon the first principle of a liberal society, that the individual and the individual's interests and good and welfare are the test of a good society, for we now attach benefits and penalties to individuals simply on the basis of their race, color, and national origin. The implications of the new course are an increasing consciousness of the significance of group membership, an increasing divisiveness on the basis of race, color, and national origin, and a spreading resentment among the disfavored groups against the favored groups. If the individual is the measure, however, our public concern is with the individual's capacity to work out an individual fate by means of education, work, and self-realization in the various spheres of life. Then how the figures add up on the basis of whatever measures of group we use may be interesting, but should be no concern of public policy.

This, I believe, is what was intended by the Constitution and the Civil Rights Act, and what most of the American people—in all the various ethnic and racial groups that make it up—believe to be the measure of a good society. It is now our task to work with the intellectual, judicial, and political institutions of the country to reestablish this simple and clear understanding, that rights attach to the individual, not the group, and that public policy must be exercised without distinction of race, color, or national origin.

POSTSCRIPT

HOW CAN OPPORTUNITY BE EQUALIZED?

One of the major arguments against busing to achieve expanded opportunities for the disadvantaged has been the contention that the practice continues the outlawed policy of assignment to schools on the basis of race or some other single attribute. Daniel Bell, examining quota systems in *The Coming of Post-Industrial Society* (1973), states, "we now find that a person is to be given preference by virtue of a role, his group membership"—once again using one overriding attribute in placing a person in society.

This attitude, coupled with recent U.S. Supreme Court decisions involving busing, equalization of school financing, and the quota system of preferential treatment, seems to be slowing down governmental action that concentrates on educational institutions for the redress of social ills. At the same time, some examples of "bootstrap" operations in inner-city areas show that, through community cooperation, schools can be established or improved to truly serve the needs of the underprivileged. The arguments over decentralized control of schooling are examined in the following issue.

For a more comprehensive view of the complex issue of equalization, these works may be helpful: Peter Schrag's *Out of Place in America* (1970); *Education for Whom?* (1974), compiled by Charles A. Tesconi, Jr. and Emanuel Hurwitz, Jr.; *Social Justice and Preferential Treatment* (1977), edited by William T. Blackstone and Robert D. Heslep; *More Equality* (1974) by Herbert J. Gans; *Discriminating Against Discrimination* (1975) by Robert M. O'Neil; and *Discrimination in Reverse: Is Turnabout Fair Play?* (1978) by Barry R. Gross.

Other sources which provide a backdrop for the current scene are Kenneth B. Clark's *Dark Ghetto* (1965); Michael Harrington's *The Other America: Poverty in the U.S.* (1962); *Schools and Inequality* (1971) by James W. Guthrie *et.al.;* Thomas J. Cottle's *Busing* (1976); Arthur R. Jensen's *Genetics and Education* (1972); and Ray C. Rist's *The Urban School: A Factory for Failure* (1973); Frank Riessman's *The Inner-City Child* (1976); and *Equality and Social Policy* (1978), edited by Walter Feinberg.

ISSUE 9

WHAT SHOULD BE THE LOCUS OF CONTROL?

Philosophical and sociological arguments about the purposes of education, the need for certain structures or reforms, and the utilization of the schools as agencies of conservation or radical change must eventually be resolved by political debate and action. Historically, in this country most of such debates have been carried out in local or perhaps state school boards. But recently state and federal courts and legislative bodies, teachers' unions and associations, citizens' action groups, powerful national lobbying organizations, and a myriad of other influence-wielding groups have addressed these concerns.

Changes in the financing of public education—from a reliance primarily upon local property taxes to increasing aid from the state and federal levels—has eroded the power of lay boards of education and local school officials. The distribution and threat of withholding of federal support has proved an increasingly potent political tool. Along with this shift of power has come an increase in the influence of national professional educators' organizations.

Many share the views of such writers as James Bryant Conant and Myron Lieberman that the movement away from local control is a victory against provincialism and authoritarianism and for consistency and elevated standards. Concern for the equalization of opportunity, however, has prompted a campaign for decentralization, for control of the local schools by those whom the schools serve. Mario Fantini, one of the major proponents of this view, claims that centralized control, even within the boundaries of a single large city, has been proven ineffective in meeting the needs of students. Fantini simply does not have confidence in highly bureaucratized and highly professionalized policy-making in dealing with the neighborhood realities of the contemporary urban environment.

Another scholar interested in political arrangements, Amitai Etzioni, agrees that a truly decentralized participatory system tends to be more responsive to local needs and fosters a citizenry that is informed and in control. However, in

"The Fallacy of Decentralization" (*The Nation,* August 25, 1969), he sounds a cautionary note. Decentralization, he contends, will tend to neglect interlocal, interregional, and national needs. He further insists that in the case of education the system is already decentralized and only weakly coordinated. He feels that the main avenue for citizen participation in educational policy development lies in national social movements.

Two recent volumes assembled by the National Society for the Study of Education focus on the issue of power and control in education. The 1977 yearbook, *The Politics of Education,* edited by Jay D. Scribner, provides a diverse selection of articles on such topics as political power in education; participation, representation, and control; intergovernmental and national policy influences; state decentralization; education and politics in large cities; and communication and decision-making in public education. The 1978 yearbook, *The Courts and Education,* edited by Clifford P. Hooker, examines, among other topics, the courts as educational policy-makers, the balance between lay and professional control, litigation concerning educational finance, and control of the curriculum.

These and many other recent works attempt to analyze and evaluate the tug-of-war between centralization and decentralization of control. Federal legislation involving the educational rights of women and of people with physical and mental handicaps, as well as the recent formation of a separate Department of Education with a cabinet-level secretary, clearly demonstrate the growth of federal centrality. Yet the argument for direct participation at the local level remains compelling and in keeping with the generally personalized slant of school reform campaigns.

James B. Conant, in the article which follows, does not envision a federal educational system but does argue for interstate cooperation in standardizing the quality of schooling. Mario Fantini and his associate, Marilyn Gittell, press the case for community control in urban areas.

James Bryant Conant

NATIONWIDE POLICY IS NEEDED

. . . Educational policy in the United States has been determined in the past by the more or less haphazard interaction of (1) the leaders of public school teachers, administrators and professors of education, (2) state educational authorities, (3) a multitude of state colleges and universities, (4) private colleges and universities, and (5) the variety of agencies of the Federal government, through which vast sums of money . . . have flowed to individual institutions and the states.

It is my thesis that such a jumble of influential private and public bodies does not correspond to the needs of the nation in the 1960s. Some degree of order needs to be brought out of this chaos, primarily for the benefit of the oncoming generations, but also, to achieve a more effective use of public and private moneys.

At the high school level and below, policy should not be determined solely by either "public school people" or state officials, but wise decisions cannot be made if either is excluded. At the level beyond the high school, plans cannot be made by the state alone, nor by private institutions alone, nor by Washington alone. But no nationwide policy can be successfully formulated if any one of the three is excluded. A single state . . . can develop a master plan for higher education; any single state can . . . keep its schools well up-to-date with the educational revolution. Congress can help meet the problems presented by the revolution by grants for specific purposes and a handsome assist to institutions of higher education. But all this does not add up to a nationwide educational policy, let alone a national educational policy which would be the equivalent of the national policy in Great Britain or France.

The fact is, of course, that without a drastic Constitutional amendment nobody is in a position to establish an educational policy in the United States. It is my contention that some form of cooperative exploration of educational problems between the states and the Federal government is imperative. We cannot have a national educational policy, but we might be able to evolve a *nationwide policy.* The concluding pages of this chapter give my suggestions as

Continued on p. 142

From James Bryant Conant, *Shaping Educational Policy,* McGraw-Hill Book Company, 1964. Reprinted with permission of Conant Studies of American Education, Educational Testing Service, Princeton, N.J.

Mario Fantini
and
Marilyn Gittell

POWER SHOULD BE DECENTRALIZED

Demands for urban decentralization and community control are indices of the inaccessibility, irresponsibility, and unresponsiveness of the institutions of urban government in the 1970's. How and why these institutions have become the focus of such widespread dissatisfaction can be understood only in the total context of urban politics in America and, particularly, from the historical perspective of developments over the last several decades.

Since the turn of the century, American political institutions and processes of government have been significantly reshaped in directions first set forth by the civic reformers and muckrakers of the early 1900's. Corruption in political parties had led to control of governmental structures and public services by seemingly incompetent politicians. And so, with economy and efficiency as their watchwords, the "Progressives" concentrated their efforts on getting politics out of the system. They placed their confidence in increased professionalism and centralization of governmental policy-making, encouraged by the technological revolution of the first half of the twentieth century and the emergence of scientific management as a panacea for government ills.

Centralization of services on all levels was promoted to resolve the problems of corruption, incompetence and lack of responsibility. During an era of vast growth of government services, the effort to remove the administration or implementation of policy (defined as nonpolitical) from the development of policy (defined as political) was manifested in a concentration on the expansion of executive and administrative autonomy. Local governments, it was rationalized, should be viewed as engaged in largely administrative functions; there should be no need for them to become entangled in "politics." The separation of politics and administration, reformers assumed, could be easily accomplished. Public authorities organized as business corporations could conduct their affairs independently of elected governments, and unencumbered by the constraints of public accountability.

Continued on p. 146

(Conant, cont. from p. 140)
to how this might be accomplished without an amendment to the Constitution of the United States. Before presenting my radical proposal, however, I must devote some pages to an analysis of the present situation.

Let me start with an examination of the powers of the Federal government to establish a national educational policy through the formation of a commission or committee appointed by the Congress or the President. Until one examines the Constitutional and political realities, such proposals seem quite persuasive. And it is true, of course, that for more than 100 years Congress, by its granting of land or its appropriation of money for the individual states, has enormously influenced the development of our educational system. But Congress has not the power, without an amendment to the Federal Constitution, to determine a total national educational policy. Why not? Because in government, as in business, authority to establish a policy requires full power (1) to establish a structure and to alter it as conditions change; (2) to appoint personnel; (3) to issue directions to the personnel; (4) to provide for the financing of the entire operation. It is the essence of our system of government, with its checks and balances and division of powers, that neither a single state nor the Federal government has the power to establish, maintain, and operate a system of education in the way a free nation without a federalized structure can establish educational policy.

The educational powers of each of the single states in practice is far greater than that of the Federal government. There are, however, three limitations on these powers. The first derives from the Federal Constitution as interpreted by the Supreme Court; the second is the power of Congress to pass laws affecting individuals as citizens of the United States, as for example the power to draft men into military service; the third is the practical limitations of a state's ability to raise money. There are a number of recent examples of Supreme Court decisions that limit the power of a state to determine its educational policy. These decisions, which have attracted widespread interest, involve the Court's interpretation of the First and Fourteenth Amendments of the Federal Constitution. The questions they raise concern state and local provisions as to the use of school time for ceremonies or instruction considered to be religious. It is interesting to note that no one now argues that a state would be free to establish a state-supported system of schools which were frankly connected with a religious denomination. Yet before the Fourteenth Amendment was passed after the Civil War, such a possibility existed, since the First Amendment originally was only a limitation on the power of the Federal government.

The decisions of the Supreme Court on racial segregation in the schools are clearly a limitation on a state's power to establish and maintain completely separate Negro schools, colleges, and universities. One of the earliest decisions in which the Court reversed a state educational policy held that the Fourteenth Amendment guaranteed to a parent a right to send his children to a private school of his own choice, notwithstanding any state law. The attempt of a state legislature (Oregon) to outlaw private schools was thus thwarted. The same issue had arisen in a less dramatic form in Nebraska, where the state legislature had by law regulated the teaching of foreign languages. The Court held that the legislature could not prevent a private school from offering instruction in German, since to do so would be to deprive a parent of a right to have his child so instructed. The power of the state to regulate the curriculum of the public schools was not contested.

The impact of Federal legislation for purposes of defense on schools and colleges was clearly evident during the two World Wars. The drafting of young men into the armed services does, in a sense, place a restriction on the power of the state to plan the education of its young people. To a certain extent the same may be said of Federal laws affecting the employment of youth in industries engaged in interstate commerce.

The greatest limitation on the ability of the state to provide for education of its youth at public expense comes from the limitations on the ability of the state to raise funds. (One need not dwell on the restraints imposed by the Federal Constitution, such as the prohibition of post-facto laws and the requiring of due process; these stand as a guard against arbitrary confiscation of personal property.) The practical limitations of the Federal income tax are most often in the minds of educators when they discuss the impact of the Federal power on state power. A generation ago conservative school people, deeply committed to the principle of local control of the public schools, openly deplored the amendment which authorized the Federal income tax. This amendment, it was said, would destroy the basic structure of our public schools.

There can be no doubt that the Federal taxing power, broadened by the Sixteenth Amendment, does mean that a state is not as independent a sovereign power as it once was insofar as supporting state activities is concerned. Not only does the Federal government absorb a large portion of the income available for taxation, but the methods by which some of this money is sent back to the states affects indirectly the way the state spends what money it collects. I refer to such measures as the Federal road-building program. The basis for this program is such that state funds are drawn into this type of expenditure because Federal money comes to the state only if the state itself provides money for the same purpose. The advocates of general Federal aid for public education have made much of the implication of such arrangements, and this argument has never been adequately answered by the opponents of Federal aid.

In writing of the limitations of the power of a state to establish an educational policy, I have made no reference to the state constitutional limitations on the power of the state legislature and the organs of government created by the legislature, such as the local school boards. In theory, the people of a state can change their constitution; therefore, in contrasting state with Federal power, it is unnecessary to consider the state constitution. This is fortunate as I doubt if the provisions of any two of the fifty state constitutions are alike, even on such basic matters as schools and colleges.

Because of the Federal Constitution and certain rights of the Federal government connected with defense and interstate commerce, it is evident that a state is not completely free to provide and regulate education. On the other hand, let it be noted that the Federal government is powerless to interfere with many aspects of state-supported schools, colleges, and universities. It has been pointed out more than once that a state need not provide any public instruction at all. Some states have no compulsory attendance laws. Therefore one might say that it is a happy accident that in all states, at present, there are free public schools and at least one state university and several state colleges. It is further a happy accident that in all but a few states children must attend school (public or private) from approximately six years of age until at least sixteen (in some states until eighteen). . . .

The states that have entered into . . . interstate compacts have certainly taken important steps in the direction of a rational approach to our educational problems. But one is still bound to ask: Are these regional pacts enough? They are excellent in principle and could be most effective in operation, but why only regional agreements? Why not a new venture in cooperative federalism? Why not a compact among *all* the states?

To be quite specific, let me be bold and make a suggestion for a possible way by which the road to the development of a nationwide educational policy might be opened up. *Let the fifty states, or at least fifteen to twenty of the more populous states, enter into a compact for the creation of an "Interstate Commission for Planning a Nationwide Educational Policy."* The compact would have to be drawn up by the states and approved by Congress. The document would provide for the membership of the commission and provide the guidelines for its operation. Each state would be represented, though a group of less populous states might decide to be represented by one person. Each state would be ready to listen to any conclusions of the commission but, of course, would not be bound to follow its recommendations.

Since such an interstate commission would be concerned with the drawing up of plans, *not* with administration, I see no constitutional or legal reason against a state legislature authorizing one or more persons to participate in it. Nor do I see any obstacles to a legislature expressing its willingness to examine any reports coming from such a group. The matter of finances might raise issues. It might be difficult to get any considerable number of state legislatures to appropriate the money; but I hope not, for if it were proposed that the Congress of the United States do so, certainly the cry of states' rights might be raised. Yet I would hope the commission would invite the chief United States school officer, the Commissioner of Education, as well as other Federal officials to attend each conference. . . .

Therefore I suggest that Congress appoint a National Advisory Committee to explore the workings of the present interstate compacts and to list the problems to be met. I am frank to say that I believe the report of such a preliminary survey would lead to the formation of the type of commission I have recommended based on an interstate compact.

I must admit that the record of national committees on education, however authorized and however appointed, is not such as to lead one to be optimistic about the results to be accomplished by still another committee. Yet the creation of a national commission which would be an interstate educational planning commission whose existence was the result of a compact between the states would be something quite new. It differs from schemes for appointing a Presidential or Congressional advisory commission in several respects. In the first place, because the commission would be an interstate commission, the reports of the working parties would be automatically concerned with state-by-state variations and would recognize the realities of the conditions in each state. In the second place, the recommendations would be directed to the state legislatures or state boards of education and would be considered by the state authorities because each state had been involved in the creation of the undertaking. In the third place, the magnitude and detailed nature of the financial demands required would be spelled out in such a way that Congress (through its own committees) and the Office of Education (through its own staff) could explore the significance of each item in terms of the function of the Federal governmental agencies.

Each working party would have to start with certain premises agreed upon by the commission. Within the framework thus established, the working party would be required first to make an exhaustive factual study of the structure state by state, second to come up with specific recommendations to the state authorities (the chief state school officer, the state school board, or the legislature). There might well be dissenting opinions on many points. The right to public dissent would be inherent in accepting an appointment on the working party. The more controversial the area, the more necessary would be such a provision.

Admittedly, in setting up any working party, the most difficult task for the interstate commission would be an agreement on what I have called the framework. And to let a working party loose in any controversial area without some guidelines would be to insure catastrophic failure at the onset. Certain premises could be agreed on without much difficulty. These would constitute part of the framework for all of the working parties. In my opinion, these premises might be formulated somewhat as follows:

1. It is assumed that our present form of government should be perpetuated; to that end all future citizens of the nation should receive an education that will prepare them to function as responsible members of a free society, as intelligent voters and, if appointed or elected to public office, as honest reliable servants of the nation, state, or locality.

2. It is assumed that each state is committed to the proposition of providing free schooling to all the children in the state through twelve grades. (Though the Federal government has no power to proclaim the doctrine of free schools, practically the action of all the states during the last 100 years enables the interstate commission to declare that providing free public schooling is a nationwide policy of the United States.)

3. It is assumed that in every state the parents have a right to send their children to private schools, colleges, and universities instead of to the publicly supported institutions. This assumption follows from the interpretation of the Federal Constitution by the Supreme Court on more than one occasion.

4. It is assumed that each state *desires* to have all normal children in the state attend school at least five hours a day, 150 days a year, at least until they reach the age of 18, but that the states differ and will continue to differ in regard to the laws requiring school attendance

and the way special provisions are provided for physically and mentally handicapped children.

5. It is assumed that each state accepts the responsibility of providing for the education of at least some of its youth beyond high school; the organization and financing of such education, however, differs and will continue to differ state by state; in each state opportunities for education beyond high school now include at least one university chartered by the state and largely supported by public funds; the continuation of such universities as centers of research, advanced study, and above all, fearless free inquiry is essential to the welfare of the state and the nation.

6. It is assumed that the education provided in high school and beyond by public institutions is designed to develop the potentialities of all the youth to fit them for employment in a highly industrialized society.

7. The financing of education, including research and scholarly work in the universities, is a concern of private universities, the states, and the Federal government.

The declaration of some such set of premises by an interstate commission would be the first step in shaping a nationwide educational policy. If each state legislature would pass a resolution accepting such a declaration, we should for the first time as a nation be officially committed to certain basic principles of educational policy. We now assume these principles to be valid, but in fact they have never been promulgated by representative assemblies and could not be promulgated by the Congress.

(Fantini and Gittell, cont. from p. 141)

Urban legislative bodies were undermined as the bureaucracies expanded their roles and powers. Professionalization of the bureaucracy was to guarantee "objective" responsibility as experts took over the operation of the government. Expert government, in contrast with the haphazard recruitment under a party patronage system, would minimize corruption and maximize efficiency. Decision-making would be based on more objective criteria, allowing little room for waste and assuring economy. Responsiveness to public needs and demands, it was reasoned, would be automatic, because professionals had no vested interest in power but were motivated to do what was "right."

City *managers,* for example, would be selected for their "professional" competence to run the city, unfettered by the normal political pressures of local community interests. Professional bureaucrats would run city departments on the same basis. They would be selected by a "merit" system of examination, so that patronage, the food of the party machine, would be destroyed. Intricate civil-service regulations would guarantee competence as a basis for hiring and would close off political patronage as the source of employment. Nonpartisan elections—another goal of the reformers—were instituted to undermine the role of the party and to assure "objectivity" in the selection of officials. "Good government" organizations in cities throughout the country became an army of watchdogs to oversee and encourage the transition of city governments.

Some social scientists have interpreted this reform movement as a middle-class attack on working-class government. The vote-seeking party machine was, after all, the mainstay of the immigrant class in the large cities. It was the welfare agency, housing authority, and employment agency of that era all rolled into one neighborhood government. The local party clubhouse saw its role as service to the community and responded to the needs and interests of an immigrant poor. The reforms of the first half of the twentieth century replaced this highly personalized structure with a depersonalized bureaucratic structure that lacked the incentive to serve those most in need in the large cities.

Whatever the original motives for these reforms, their consequences are clear: Unprecedented social changes in our cities during the last three decades suggest that these early reforms have had a shattering impact on life in the city, and that some of the assumptions on which they were based must be reevaluated. The institutions molded in terms of these concepts have been clearly insensitive to the demands of the urban community in the second half of the twentieth century.

The machinery set up by the reform movement gained added momentum after World War II, when the country turned to its neglected internal needs. Centralization took hold and public bureaucracies expanded beyond all expectations. The burden of urban development and a vastly increased role for government contributed significantly to that growth. At the same time, professionalism became an integral part of the bureaucratic system, in effect internalizing much of the public-policy process.

Post–World War II studies of decision-making in American cities generally agree that power has become concentrated in urban bureaucratic structures. The political party, elected officials, business and labor groups, and civic associations have consequently had a declining role in the development of public policy in the larger cities. As city functions have increased, the mayor's powers have declined; as greater responsibility has been placed on the mayor, he has been less able to cope with the demands. This is so, in part, because the public—particularly the more educated middle- and upper-class segments—has wholly accepted the validity and sanctity of the professionals' control of the decision-making process. The growth of professionalism and the unionization of city employees have narrowed the range of mayoral discretion in public-policy-making. Latter-day reformers continue to be pleased with the translation of their goals for removing government from politics, and many social scientists seem unconcerned with some of the repercussions of bureaucratic power or with the impact of public policy in terms of who benefits.

In addition to the physical expansion of urban communities and their enlarged governmental functions, the most obvious change in the nation's cities has been that in the character of their population. Nonwhite population has increased; the white, middle-class population has left the cities for the suburbs in large numbers. By 1970, more than half of the nonwhites in America were living in cities. Several of the largest cities in the country now have a nonwhite population that represents 25–50 per cent of their total population. This new population, composed largely of lower-class, rural blacks who are recent migrants from the South, is particularly hard pressed to cope with the institutions that have evolved to serve them. Those who contrast earlier waves of immigrant migrations and their adjustment to city life with the current situation ignore the vast changes in the environment of the city—changes in technology and changes in the structure of government and public welfare. Not to be ignored, either, are the differences in these groups' subculture characteristics. Also significant is the fact that local neighborhood agents, like the party clubhouse that served the welfare function for many earlier immigrant groups, can no longer function in that capacity. The intimacy of neighborhood government has been replaced by the remoteness of a highly bureaucratized government. It is ironic that the reform movement has provided the ideology and demand for removing government from the neighborhood as it has, at the same time, removed government from public influence.

Efforts for new reform through decentralization have emerged in recent years from the failure of the American political structure to adjust itself to the changing needs of society. Expansion of the bureaucracy and narrowing of the policy process limit the channels for the exercise of power, which particularly affects new, upwardly striving groups. Earlier, immigrants to the cities had means of mobility available to them; the unskilled labor force, the local political party, and government service were major routes for entering the system. Today, however, America's economic and political institutions no longer provide such ready means of access for new groups. Demands for decentralization and community control are a reflection of that general political circumstance. The movement represents an effort by powerless groups to become a part of the system and, at the same time, to make the system responsive to their needs. They seek a means of shared responsibility in the allocation of the resources of the society.

In dealing with the issue of political reform in American cities, one cannot ignore the issue of racism. The Kerner Commission Report documented much of what has happened in American cities and demonstrated the key role racism plays in what is defined as the urban crisis. Urban institutions reflect a basic racist attitude in their composition and attitude, and attempts to achieve change will have to appraise this circumstance realistically. Because the decentralization movement was spurred by the black community, it is often viewed only as a spearhead for black control. The political manifestation of racism seems to have shifted from the anti-integration movement to an anti-community power movement. This cannot be underestimated, in terms of its importance, as a part of the opposition strategy in challenging movement toward decentralization and community control. Many professionals who favor reform and admit to the shortcomings of urban institutions nonetheless look to the bureaucratic system and the professional for internal reform rather than risk a black power takeover.

Particularly because of this fear, it is difficult to convince many who recognize the need for change that only through the infusion of new energy from outside the present system can reform become meaningful or even possible. The major emphasis in the decentralization movement up until now has been to revise the system from within; to force a redistribution of power from within the system itself, that is, to foster state legislation or a city plan that shifts power from the central city to a neighborhood agency. Federal programs all embody provisions for some community role in the program. But, we have often seen, the more extreme the opposition to such reforms of the system, the more extreme the demands for community control. As the pressures mount and the opposing stands become more solidified and polarized, inaction and frustration may increase demands for destruction of existing institutions and their replacement by alternate systems.

Some of the more traditional liberal approaches ignore the fact that the powerless see community control as a way not only to make institutions more responsive to their needs but also to exercise their share of power within the society. When we talk about community control or decentralization as being a question of political power, and about achieving a balance of power between professional and public interests, we are dealing with fundamental issues in the society. One need only consider a local neighborhood government that could control the recruitment and selection of personnel and determine priorities in expenditures; this is the essence of power. What distinguishes this decentralization reform movement from earlier efforts is that it calls for the control of basic resources of power within the local community. At the present time, the local black and minority-group communities have only their ethnic solidarity as a base of power. Providing for control of local institutions can given them a stronger base and a direct role within the society. Obviously, the people who hold that power now are not likely to relinquish it without considerable struggle. Their conflict is further intensified by terminology: Those who seek community control tend to talk about tearing down institutions; those who want to protect the institutions are particularly frightened by that rhetoric. One must look very carefully at the content and substance of a decentralization plan in terms of division of powers and responsibility between a central and local agency and bypass the rhetoric; otherwise, battle may be waged unnecessarily on both sides.

Particularly relevant to our understanding of the character of urban government and the chances for change is the question of power. Political scientists looking at the question of local power have generally concluded, in a series of studies of community power, that in most cities there is to be found what is defined as a "multiple elite structure." This multiple elite structure suggests—contrary to the view that there is a single economic elite in the city that makes decisions of all kinds—that, in reality, various specialized elites both in and outside the bureaucracy appear to control functional areas of city government. For example, Robert Dahl found, in his study of New Haven, that school professionals controlled decision-making in the educational arena, political party professionals controlled the nominating process, and the business leadership and housing professionals—specifically, the redevelopment administrator—controlled the decisions in housing and urban redevelopment. This and other, similar studies led some political scientists to conclude that the pluralist system was working; there was no single elite structure, no overlapping of elite groups from one function to another.

Another group of political scientists challenged these conclusions, questioning whether this was truly a democratic or a pluralist system. That is, if a small, elite group held power in functional areas of policy—e.g., education, health, and so forth—while the vast majority of the public had no way at all of demanding accountability or participating in the decision-making process, was there not really a great deficiency in terms of the democratic process under this procedure? The latter group rejected the multiple-elite theory and stressed the need to develop a more participatory system in American government. These critics have reinforced the public cry for more intimate and responsive local government and for movement toward decentralization. Their combined efforts have raised a whole new challenge to the institutional structure of the American polity. These neoreformers stress that it is the degree to which lay citizens can choose to participate in government that has always been the essence of the democratic system, as distinguished from a society that is admittedly more closed. They argue that developments over the last several decades indicate a closing of access to the political system, as well as a lack of accountability and a lack of visibility of decision-making. The goal of the new reform is a redistribution of power to provide wider access to public-policy-making.

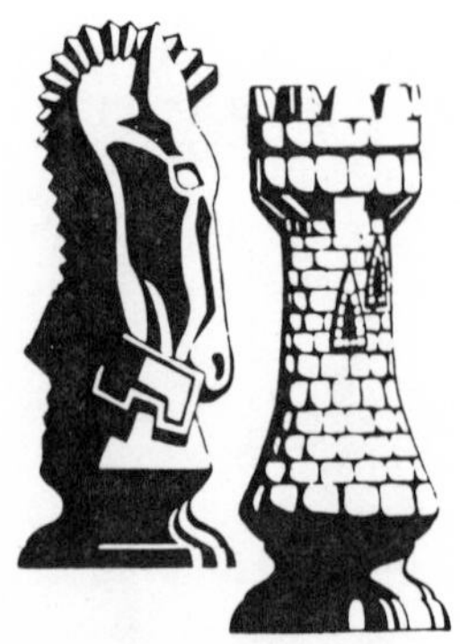

POSTSCRIPT

WHAT SHOULD BE THE LOCUS OF CONTROL?

Evidence regarding the effects of centralized or decentralized control on the quality of learning in schools is sparse and inconclusive. Some people contend that the decentralization campaign in urban areas is merely a power grab on the part of blacks and other minorities. Others hold the opinion that the new federal education department solidifies the power of the professional education establishment.

If the federal and state bureaucracies are too far removed from local problems and needs and are indeed controlled by the profession, and if local control mechanisms run the risk of serving narrow and political aims, suggestions for educational voucher systems represent another avenue leading toward more responsive educational services. Voucher plans, which have been experimented with on only a very limited basis, involve the return of tax monies to the parents of school-age children in the form of vouchers to be used to obtain a wider variety of sanctioned educational experiences. Some version of this approach to shared control may well be the wave of the future.

In any event, concern for the multiple influences which shape educational policy has become a major aspect of the professional literature. Early examinations of the political realm of educational decision-making can be found in Sidney W. Tiedt's *The Role of the Federal Government in Education* (1966); *Governing Education: A Reader on Politics, Power, and Public School Policy* (1969), edited by Alan Rosenthal; Stanley E. Ballinger's *The Nature and Function of Educational Policy* (1965); and *Education and the Political System* (1969) by Byron G. Massialas.

More recent analyses include *The Political Web of American Schools* by Frederick M. Wirt and Michael W. Kirst, a basic source book published in 1972; John Martin Rich's *New Directions in Educational Policy* (1974); *Education in National Politics* (1975), an analysis of the 90th Congress by Norman C. Thomas; *State Policy Making for the Public Schools* (1976) by Roald F. Campbell and Tim L. Mazzoni, Jr.; *The Limits of Educational Reform* (1976) by Martin Carnoy and Henry M. Levin; Donna H. Kerr's *Educational Policy: Analysis, Structure, and Justification* (1976); *History, Education, and Public Policy* (1978), edited by Donald R. Warren; and *Educational Handicap, Public Policy, and Social History* (1979) by Seymour B. Sarason and John Doris.

These many sources address the problems of what considerations should guide educational decisions, where ultimate responsibility must lie, and what balance of power best serves educational purposes. These problems also form the basis of the following three issues.

ISSUE 10

CAN SCHOOLS BE HELD ACCOUNTABLE FOR RESULTS?

As educational costs have soared and student achievement has languished or declined, the public, through its state legislators and local school boards, has pressed for increased quality controls in the public schools. Most of the responses to this call for greater efficiency are linked to a general "educational engineering" approach which includes emphases on behavioral objectives, systems analysis, competency-based education, and teacher accountability. This movement is dominating current educational policy and practices much as the business-industrial management model (described in 1962 by Raymond Callahan in *Education and the Cult of Efficiency*) dominated the schools in the early decades of the century.

The current movement focuses on criteria based on observable results in determining the allocation of resources. Many grant the short-term efficiency of the approach but express grave concern for the depersonalization entailed in many of its procedural requirements. The bureaucratic jargon, technical bias, and mechanistic interpretation of behavior which prevail have proven repulsive to educators in the humanistic camp.

The issue treated here, teacher accountability, is presented as an example of the types of argument involved in the implementation of the movement. Leon Lessinger has been a staunch supporter of accountability, taking the optimistic view that it will bring about a better level of educational organization and management, will not damage professional integrity, and will increase teacher commitment and use of effective technology to replace present primitive methods of instruction. His hope is that the increased sophistication which permeates the "engineering" approach will be instrumental in eliminating archaic budget procedures, poor utilization of resources, inadequate professional development, and uninspired instruction.

Robert Bundy is a representative of those who are concerned about the narrow scope of many aspects of this movement. While recognizing the reality of current educational inefficiencies, Bundy does not share Lessinger's optimism regarding the systematic evaluation of teacher performance which accountability dictates. Bundy feels that the emphasis on teacher accountability masks deeper problems which are basically not the fault of teachers—compulsoriness, dehumanization, bureaucratization, the building of a self-perpetuating monopoly, the decline of real services to students, etc. The movement, in fact, contributes to the maintenance of these deeper problems, according to Bundy.

In a rebuttal of Bundy's position ("Comments on Mr. Bundy's Own Dreamworld," *Phi Delta Kappan,* November 1974) Maureen Webster and Miriam Clasby argue that Bundy overlooks the dynamic potential of accountability for dealing in an integrated way with goals, values, and decisions. If viewed as a contemporary social action movement, accountability can rise above the "technicist" obsession with matters of instrumentality. Accountability can give impetus to a thorough reconsideration of educational goals, the nature of learning and instruction, and the development of reasonable and effective methods of evaluation. Accountability, they contend, means accepting the challenge to evoke the kind of learning that will contribute to the creation of "a human future for *all* people."

Support for Bundy's critique of educational engineering may be found in a 1975 volume, *Regaining Educational Leadership: Critical Essays on PBTE/CBTE, Behavorial Objectives and Accountability,* edited by Ralph A. Smith. Harry S. Broudy, Maxine Greene, Paul Nash, Michael W. Apple, Elliot Eisner, and other scholars critically treat all aspects of the movement and present much food for further thought.

In the following articles, Leon Lessinger presents his full argument for accountability and outlines the substantial changes he thinks it will induce, while Robert Bundy explains the context of his concerns.

Leon N. Lessinger

ACCOUNTABILILTY ASSURES IMPROVEMENT

Accountability is a policy declaration adopted by a legal body such as a board of education or a state legislation requiring regular outside reports of dollars spent to achieve results. The concept rests on three fundamental bases: *student accomplishment, independent review* of student accomplishment and a *public report,* relating dollars spent to student accomplishment. The grand jury, the congressional hearing, the fiscal audit are powerful and well-tested examples of means for achieving accountability. The absolute requirement of independent replication and commmunication in establishing scientific phenomena is another example of accountability. Accountability in education shares substance from all these examples. By focusing upon results, on student achievement, it can be a most powerful catalyst in achieving that basic reform and renewal so sorely needed in the school system.

A growing number of influential people are becoming convinced that it is possible to hold the schools—as other important agencies in the public and private sector are held—to account for the results of their activity. In his March 3rd Education Message, President Nixon stated, "From these considerations we derive another new concept: *Accountability.* School Administrators and school teachers alike are responsible for their performance, and it is in their interest as well as in the interest of their pupils that they be held accountable."

The preamble to the agreement between the Board of Education of the City of New York and the United Federation of Teachers for the period September 8, 1969–September 8, 1972, under the title Accountability says,

> The Board of Education and the Union recognize that the major problem of our school system is the failure to educate *all* our students and the massive academic retardation which exists especially among minority group students. The Board of the Union therefore agree to join in an effort, in cooperation with universities, community school boards and parent organizations, to seek solutions to this major problem and to develop objective criteria of professional accountability.

Continued on p. 156

From Leon N. Lessinger, "The Powerful Notion of Accountability in Education," *Journal of Secondary Education,* December 1970. Permission to reprint this article granted by the Association of California School Administrators, publisher.

Robert F. Bundy

ACCOUNTABILITY IS SELF-DEFEATING

Educational accountability is a classic example of myopic thinking and narrow vision. Parents, professional educators, boards of education, legislators, and the general public are justifiably questioning the monies spent on education, school efficiency, what schools are actually accomplishing, and who controls the results of schooling. But accountability, as envisioned by its major supporters, will address none of these problems in any fundamental way. In fact, if accountability is carried out along the lines proposed, there will be deeper entrenchment, increased homogeneity, and decreased innovation in formal education.

Accountability, in short, is industrial consciousness applied to nonindustrial problems. It is the misplaced response of frustrated consumers who have little place else to focus their anger. And it is rapidly becoming the articulated response of professional elites who fear public recrimination and must at all costs protect their position and power. Accountability promises, as Daniel Callahan might phrase it, false satisfactions for real needs. To strip away all its pretensions, accountability is a contrived smokescreen to confuse the public and distract attention from the real issues facing American schools today.

THE CURRENT CONDITION

American schools, in Ivan Illich's terms, have passed their second watershed and have become a major social threat. We can now identify quite clearly the characteristics of this second watershed, why schools occupy such a dangerous position in American society, and why our schools are such a disastrous model for the industrializing nations.

1. *The institution of compulsory schools has become deeply bureaucratized and dehumanized.* A central figure of modern society is what Herbert Marcuse calls the materialization of values. Human values areconstantly translated into mere technical tasks. Notions of human freedom, dignity, and self-determination increasingly become nostalgic carryovers from the prehistory of a mature technology of human behavior. To borrow from Manfred Stanley's description of technicism, we are experiencing a dehumanized notion of objectivity, an

Continued on p. 163

From Robert F. Bundy, "Accountability: A New Disneyland Fantasy," *Phi Delta Kappan,* November 1974.

(Lessinger, cont. from p. 154)

Many more pronouncements, program developments, and policy decisions of a similar sort could be described. A few examples follow:

1. The Oregon State Department of Education has employed a Director of Education Audits and is using an institute of educational engineering to promote its research and development activities.

2. The Virginia State Board of Education has encouraged and authorized the use of Title 1 E.S.E.A. funds (with U.S.O.E. stimulation) for performance contracting with private enterprise to eliminate deficits in reading and other academic skills among disadvantaged children in Virginia.

3. The guidelines for the federal bilingual and drop-out prevention program require an independent educational accomplishment audit.

4. The Louisville, Kentucky school system has an assistant superintendent for accountability.

5. The Colorado Legislature is considering the adoption of an accountability program.

6. The Office of Economic Opportunity is funding twenty-one school centers to experiment with performance contracts and incentives to achieve accountability.

7. The Dallas, Texas school system is developing a "second generation" Texarkana project to eliminate basic school failure among its disadvantaged children through performance contracts to be checked by an outside audit.

8. The Florida State Legislature has appropriated 1.2 million dollars to establish accountability through development of a variety of student output measures and other programs.

9. The Commission of the States has declared that its central theme along with National Assessment for the 70's is accountability.

10. The President of the National School Boards Association has made accountability the theme of his administration.

The list could be extended to fill the entire presentation. Clearly a new educational movement is under way. The school systems of America are entering what the Washington Post has termed "An Age of Accountability."

Many of the early school laws in America called for accountability. The concept has been rediscovered and elaborated to meet serious conditions in the schools especially those conditions relating to galloping costs, poor student achievement, and the erosion of public authority and confidence in the schools.

Accountability's pointed thrust for a regular public report of an outside review of demonstrated student achievement promise for the allocation of resources will fundamentally alter public education. Some of the more important changes are now discussed.

In the first place, successful implementation of an accountability policy will shift the principal focus in the school system from input to output, from teaching to learning. A growing research literature points up the independence of teaching and learning. There can be teaching without learning and learning without teaching. There can, of course, be learning as a result of teaching. So independent is this relationship, that some have called the phenomenon the "teaching/learning paradox." This suggests that the present and traditional methods of requesting resources as well as the principal bases for judging the quality of schools will undergo drastic change. In place of equating quality in terms of resources allocated in the form of inputs e.g., teachers, space, equipment, etc., the important criterion will be results—student learning. This will lead to a second by-product of accountability, a revised educational commitment for the nation.

In principle the American educational commitment has been that every child should have access to an adequate education—this is the familiar, but still unattained, principle of equal educational opportunity. This commitment has been translated into the dollar allocations for the people and the "things" of education. When a child has failed to learn, school personnel have often assigned him a label —"slow," or "unmotivated," or "retarded." Accountability triggers a revised commitment—that every child *shall* learn. Such a revision demands a "Can Do" spirit of enterprise, a willingness to change a system which does not work and find one which does; a seeking of causes of failure as often in the system, its personnel, its organization, its technology, and its knowledge base as is now spent in seeking it solely in students. This revised commitment may come to be called the principle of equity of results. The call for everyman's "Right to Read" clearly foreshadows this tradition.

A third major effect of accountability on schools centers on the technology of instruction and the notion of better standard practice in America's schoolrooms. Without accountability for results the spread of good practice and the adoption of better technology has moved at a snail's pace. In this connection, it should be remembered that technology is more than equipment, though equipment may be a part of technology. Technology refers to validated practice—the use of tested means to secure demonstrated results. It is the essence of the meaning in the phrase, "what works."

From an organizational, managerial and technological point of view, education is a cottage industry. It is in a backward state, passed by in a time of striking and exciting development in other significant areas of societal activity. As many educators can testify, educational technology is primitive. Teachers and students barely understand the breadth of use to which the household telephone can be used to gather knowledge. And while the telephone is being redesigned to operate in milliseconds under automated commands for slave efforts, education is just beginning to cope with the manual dial.

The example of the equipment portion of technology is not unique. The important part in validated practice played by professional competence in interpersonal behavior, is not used in many classrooms. There is a wealth of evidence acquired over the last 30 years about the ways in which people interact, learn from each other, intervene, aid, support, or undermine the work of each other. Yet, there are few teachers who have progressed beyond the classroom methods of several generations ago. In few other fields of any consequence are there patterns of behavior so predictable, so unchanged, so inefficient in terms of the contemporary human organism and how it learns as are commonly found in the classroom.

Accountability is the "hair-shirt" of formal education. It is the response at budget time to the question, "What did you do with that other money?" It is contained in the cry of the outraged parent "If you don't teach my child, I'm going to have you fired."

There is little to be gained by defensiveness or protestation on the part of educators. Nor is a ringing statement of the truly magnificent achievements of the public schools an effective antidote. Handwringing or defensiveness is not the same as problem-solving. Public institutions cannot run on the record of more of the same when conditions and public expectancies have changed. Accountability represents an attractive path for improving support and strengthening the schools. The process of implementing an accountability directive contains elements which can bring new capability and new insights to personnel. These elements are now discussed. The major elements treated here are: developmental capital, modes of proof and education engineering. Built on these foundations, accountability can be welcomed by teachers and administrators—the evidence is accumulating that this is happening. Without them, the concept can be disruptive and even dangerous. There is a history of danger in movements that center on efficiency and effectiveness so ably discussed, for example, in Callahan's *Cult of Efficiency.*

DEVELOPMENTAL CAPITAL AND ACCOUNTABILITY

Money available in a predictable and secure manner for responsible investment via grants management in both school personnel and private enterprise to produce results is the energy of accountability. This is a fourth major aspect of accountability. Developmental capital is the money set aside for investment by school leaders in promising activities, suggested by teachers, students or whomever, which produce results. Added to a good base of solid support plus equalization such monies can act as the "steering" mechanism and the "propeller" to move the "ship" ahead in the desired directions.

Business typically budgets amounts varying from 3 to 15 per cent for improved products, service, sales or capability. Until the passage of the Vocational Education Act of 1963 and the Elementary and Secondary Act of 1965 there was virtually no comparable money in education. With the passage of these acts and subsequent amendments, it is estimated that there is now approximately 1/3 of 1 per cent available as developmental capital.

School people need funds around which to bid for the opportunity to show results. The investment of small amounts of venture capital, administered in ways that call out the maximum involvement by staff, together with an outside audit of delivery on the promises to perform has been shown to be very effective. Such an approach needs widespread adoption by states and local education agencies in addition to the federal partner.

School systems today are characterized by archaic budgeting systems; poor use of buildings, staff and equipment; salaries unrelated to performance; inadequate personnel development programs; poorly developed promotion systems; outmoded organization and often repetitious and uninspired instruction. Developmental capital can serve as the incentive to cause movement toward change. It can be the necessary energy to cause the adaption, adoption, installation and successful long-term utilization of better practice and systemwide reform. The experience of the author as a superintendent of schools managing a 1 per cent fiscal set-aside in conjunction with teacher hearings as the quality control is an instructive example.

MODES OF PROOF AND ACCOUNTABILITY

The "eye" of accountability lies in the phrase, "modes of proof." Recognition of an expanded notion of assessment of results is a fifth major effect of accountability on school reform. For too long many have confused measurement of results in education with standardized achievement testing of the paper and pencil, normal curve-based variety. Not everything in education can be (or ought to be) quantified in such a manner. But accountability in education, like accountability in other governmental enterprise, can make use of "evidence" from a variety of modes of attaining evidence. The use of hearings, of experts, of certified auditors, of simulations of work situations together with such means of acquiring evidence as video-tape and demonstrated pupil performance selected using small sample statistics come easily to mind. To argue that scientific measurement is limited to narrow so-called objective tests is to display both ignorance of the rich field of assessment, limited experience with science and inability to foresee the rapid development of creative output instruments and strategies which money and attention can promote. The Eight-Year Study and the O.S.S. Assessment of Men activities certainly give cause for optimism in this regard.

The outside review component of accountability is the most vital mode of proof. Science relies for its very existence on qualified, independent review and replication. Nothing is established in science unless and until it can be demonstrated by someone other than he who claims discovery or invention. Scientists are neither better people nor better scholars than educators; they do not pursue more scientifically or intrinsically "better" problems than teachers. They are simply subject to better monitoring by a system that both encourages and mobilizes the criticism of competent peers throughout their lives. Education, on the other hand, substitutes the gaining of a credential or license at a single point in a career for a continuing process of independent review and mandated accomplishment replication.

The accountability process addresses this lack by insisting upon techniques and strategies which promote objectivity, feed back knowledge of results and permit outside replication of demonstrated good practice. The recent inclusion of independent education accomplishment auditors in 86 school systems to verify locally derived objectives in Title VII and VIII, the bilingual and dropout prevention programs of E.S.E.A., is a practical manifestation of this aspect of accountability.

Outside review tied to a public report probably explains the popularity of the emerging concept of accountability to the public at large. Schools in America serve and are accountable to the citizenry, not the professionals. Since the public served is in reality many "publics," each of whom have legitimate needs for information, accountability can lead to an opening up of the system to bring in new energy and new support.

EDUCATIONAL ENGINEERING AND ACCOUNTABILITY

The process of change in education starts with the design or location of good practice and ends with the installation of that good practice in the classroom and learning centers of the nation where it becomes standard practice. It is known that the change process involves adaptation of good practice and adoption. Educational engineering is the rapidly emerging field designed to produce personnel with competence in this change process. The development of this coherent body of knowledge and procedure represents a sixth powerful concomitant of accountability.

Since World War II several fields have been developed to enable leaders of very complex enterprises to operate effectively and efficiently. These emerging fields include: system design and analysis, management by objectives, contract engineering (including warrantees, performance contracts and incentives), logistics, quality assurance, value engineering and the like. The coordination of these fields around educational concerns for an improved technology of instruction may be conveniently called education engineering. Engineering has traditionally been a problem-solving activity, a profession dedicated to harnessing and creating technology to the accomplishment of desired ends, the resolution of difficulties and the promotion of opportunities.

The heart of the education engineering process is the performance contract. Performance contracts are not new to education. But the concept of holding an educational agency accountable for results is. When a student is able to demonstrate in concrete terms what he has or has not learned, educators will be in a better position to judge where or why a program succeeds or fails and make the necessary changes to achieve success.

In the main, educators have not developed performance criteria for measuring the effectiveness of instructional programs, and many programs are now under way which do not describe what students are expected to gain from their educational experiences.

Instead of vague promises to provide students with an "appreciation of reading," instructional program objectives should be stated as is done in the national assessment program in terms as specific as these in the following example:

> Given his state's written driving laws manual, a sample test and sufficient time, the student will be able to correctly answer 90 per cent of the questions.

There are and should be larger objectives in education that are difficult to define and impossible to measure as the consequence of any given program. The "training" components of education, illustrated in the basic skills of reading, arithmetic, vocational training, and the like are amenable to performance contracts.

But the fact that many results of education are subjective and not measurable in the "hard" scientific sense should not deter personnel from dealing precisely with those aspects of education that lend themselves to precise definition and assessment. Rather, it demands that maximum use be made of those individual parts that tell what the change in the whole has been.

Pursuit of accountability can be expected to cause substantive changes in the schools. A few of the probable changes are listed below. Since it is doubtful that results will be attained without some movement in the listed direction, commitment to accountability in education can be viewed as commitment to better instructional practice. This is the final major powerful aspect of accountability that can be explored in this presentation.

Here are some of the expected changes in schools as a result of the call for accountability:

1. The teaching role will finally change from information-giving to directing learning. In many classrooms, the person who is active more than a fraction of the

time is the teacher, who is generally doing the following:

(a) Preparing and delivering lectures or talks to students whose motivation for paying attention or whose interest in what is being covered may be insufficient.

(b) Preparing, administering, grading and reviewing tests, assignments and homework, and covering the textbook, which, because of the methods applied and the materials generally available have little value in helping the students to learn or the teachers to judge their own effectiveness.

2. The schools' facilities will become more open, more flexible and less group-oriented.

Students can learn as individuals or as members of a group. There are no alternatives in any specific learning situation. Group instruction has its values for motivation, for general direction, etc., but is contra-indicated for individual learning. The misuse of time and effort in attempting individual growth through sole or major reliance on group methods is monumental. Facilities encouraging individual instruction are essential in producing results.

3. The curriculum will become more relevant. When the emphasis moves from process to results, the whole environment becomes a source for schooling. "School" can then be held in businesses, homes or through "bull" sessions. Teachers can be assisted by students and adults. Since the criterion is results, the process becomes open to a variety of input. Variety is the essence of motivation and can provide the realism so deeply desired by all who seek revelance in their schooling.

4. Outmoded myths and an incomplete educational tradition can be exposed and perhaps eliminated from the schools.

Too much of the behavior towards children in school seems to reflect a "Can't Do" philosophy. Too many seem intent on proving that the bell-shaped curve, with its built-in reflection of failure, ought to be the symbol of education. Accountability for results will prime personnel toward a "Can Do" philosphy. They will be energized to try alternate ways if something isn't working. This change of attitude could be *the* major benefit of the concept of accountability.

Accountability in education may have substantive effects on two of the most pressing educational problems today: student unrest and boredom. Too often today the curriculum is a function of the materials and time. School personnel have the well-established use of textbooks as the chief teaching material and the idea that children have to go to school for approximately eight hours every weekday for roughly ten months a year. For too many, the chief characteristic of school can be listed as time serving, course taking, and credit getting.

Time serving is a basic cause of boredom. For, if time is standardized, one has to fill it up. There is unfortunately, a basic rhythm to time serving—the teacher introduces a topic, "teaches" it, gives an assignment, prepares for the test, gives the test, reviews the test, and then repeats the process until the course is *covered*—even if there is little mastery or great forgetting.

Many people with children in elementary schools, for example, have had their children out of school for extended periods of time for reasons of illness, moving, or vacations. It is not unusual for them to report that their children can miss half of the school year or even skip a year or more and still do the whole program without any difficulty. When time has to be filled, there is a tendency for incredible redundancy and repetition to appear. With over 20 per cent mobility in the population, this insight is spreading to many of the patrons of the school system.

Results, criterion performances, striving toward valued and clearly communicated ends can change the climate and place time as a function of outcome. Accountability is not a panacea; it is a change in attitude and perspective. It is precisely the kind of change which many have been seeking.

SUMMARY

The striking picture of the earth itself as a space vehicle, a counterpart of the space capsule from which the television cameras held in the hands of the astronaut beamed the pictures to televison sets, gave an enormous segment of the population the lesson that those who live on the earth are stewards of the glorious home God has given. It is clear that we all are managers of precious and limited resources: a planet stocked with life and beauty and opportunity beyond telling; a heritage of freedom as Americans bought so dearly in the sacrifice and work and enterprise of those who went before. In the 1970's we all shall account for that stewardship.

It does not take prophetic vision to know that many of us will discover the very real connection between the lives we lead, the careers we pursue, the institutions we support, the thoughts we think, the values we hold, the priorities we attack, and our future as a people.

The first exercise in accountability must center on the care and nurture of our children. We are stewards of their education and training and the education system we have created consists of more than the schools. Over the years we have gradually dispatched more and more of our personal responsibilities for the young to para-professional and professional strangers. The good and bad results of our stewardship are coming home for all to see and feel and experience.

Accountability runs counter to Larry Peter's principle. It jerks us up by the scruff of the neck to answer for our performance.

Perhaps the most fitting summary of the power and potential of accountability in American education can be gotten by considering its relationship to the unsettling change of which we are all so painfully aware.

We live in an age of massive, even shocking change. When men and women are bewildered by such change our efforts *must* speak to then urgent problems—developing and improving an educational system to enable people to cope with and to captain a society in the throes of intelllectual, technological and social revolutions far advanced is just such a problem.

Our time is marked as Robert Oppenheimer once said in a Columbia University speech by, "the dissolution of authority in belief, in ritual and in temporal order." It should not surprise us then that the school is not what it was, that there is great student unrest and patron dissatisfaction and that the issue of relevance is a central issue in our professional life.

Professor Houston Smith, philosopher and teacher at M.I.T. has posed the issue of social change at its most poignant in his recent powerful and wise little book called *Condemned To Meaning.* Let me quote some of his insights.

> "We live in a time when history appears to be rushing toward some sort of climax. New knowledge breaks over us with a force and

constancy that sweeps us off our feet and keeps us from regaining them. Life's tempo quickens as if to the beat of a conductor crying, 'Faster, faster.' " With moon travel we're prepared to make a pass at the infinite. With DNA we are thinking of retooling our offspring. What have we not done? What may we yet not do? . . . the future looks dazzling. Or rather, it would were it not for one thing: a growing question as to whether there's any point to the whole affair. For we are witness to one of the great ironies of history. The century which in the West has conquered disease, erased starvation, dispersed affuence, elongated life and education everybody has generated in aggregate and average the gloomiest depiction of the human condition ever rendered. An occasional Greek wondered whether it might not have been better never to have been born, but an ingrowing pessimism seems to characterize most of our writers. Almost unvaryingly they depict a world that is meaningless or absurd. Open nearly any book, enter almost any theater, and "Life is a lie, my sweet. It builds green trees that ease your eyes and draw you under them. Then when you're here in the shade, and you breathe in and say, 'Oh God, how beautiful,' that's when the bird on the branch lets go his droppings and hits you on the head. Never have men known so much while doubting whether it adds up to anything. Never has life been covertly so empty while overtly so full."

In the face of this void of meaning in our time, in this sustained crises of authority in our time, education must take on different dimensions. Accountability is the public policy declaration that speaks to those different dimensions. Engineering that policy into practical, vital programs is a matter of due urgency. Dr. Peter, bureaucrats, citizens, parents, board members, educators and fellow Americans, take heed!

(Bundy, cont. from p. 155)

elevation of the expert to exclusive definer of reality, a loss of mastery of our own language as machine and factory metaphors dominate our consciousness and conceal the unique dimensions of human experience, and a displacement of personal agency to the technicians. (Eric Gill: "Good Lord! The thing was a mystery and we measured it.")

Since schools are a reflection of the larger society, they too have become deeply affected by technicism. Everywhere in schools there is increasing emphasis on rational, efficient management; hierarchical, specialized, impersonal division of labor; assembly line production; and institutionalization of values. (Reading the accountability literature is often like studying a manual prepared by the American Management Association for Exxon executives.)

2. *The original purposes of schools have shifted to two new goals: survival and growth.* To paraphrase Jacques Ellul, the

institution of schools has become an end in itself with a life and direction of its own. Its central purposes are indefinite expansion and unlimited creation of new but unrealizable needs. The system is so resilient that, as participation and attainment rates approach saturation in K-12, the growth ethic shifts to post-secondary and continuing education. Thus, to the professional, the welfare of consumers of schools is secondary to loyalty to the profession and the perpetuation of the institution at all costs.

3. *Schools now exert a radical monopoly over learning* by being the primary sorting, selecting, and certifying instrument of society; by taking over what was once shared with other institutions; and by excluding altogether certain attitudes, questions, expressive modes, and intellectual content. Despite different brands of schools, all perform the same function: to legitimize a particular kind of socially acceptable learning endorsed by the larger industrial-military organizations. Schools train people 1) to value school; 2) to believe education is an institutional process; 3) to be "good" consumers; 4) to accept meekly compulsory change; 5) to believe that newer and bigger are better; 6) to define intellectual excellence, creativity, and modes of knowing in industrial terms; 7) to be properly submissive, passive, and loyal to organizational authority; and 8) to know what attitudes should be held toward professional subcultures, occupations, and life-styles.

Though not in earlier times, the formal educational ladder is today the only route by which most young people can enter the polity and the economy—and thus attain dignified adult social roles. Yet everywhere in this country schools are the same: in function, in administration and finance, in how success is defined, in how knowledge is organized around subject matter and disciplines, in expectations of students and teachers, in reward structures, control mechanisms, and curriculum design. There are differences in resources and organization, and differences in emphasis, efficiency, and quality in these factors from school to school (and of course higher-income groups are most highly advantaged), but the basic tasks and the underlying managerial values are the same.

Schools therefore exert a radical monopoly over learning; they are decisive in young people's lives. Acceptable alternatives are not widely available, hence schools promote severe conformity in behavior and thinking. The few exceptions to the managerial values of schools, as Thomas Green points out, don't have any significant influence on the overall system nor are they likely to in the foreseeable future.

4. *The monopoly exerted by schools is maintained by self-certifying elites.* At issue is not just that the institution of schools certifies its own products before they can assume leadership within the institution. More significant is the primary function of the controlling elites: to define what needs to be learned *in terms professionals can meet.* And what needs to be learned must fit the logic of large-scale production, be organized by professionals, transmitted by certified personnel, and judged on the basis of standards pre-established by the profession. Admittance into elite ranks of the controllers is jealously guarded, and widespread access by the general public to the tools for learning is skillfully denied.

5. *The services provided by schools are legally and psychologically compulsory.* In addition to compulsory attendance, the

services offered by schools are "sold" as basic necessities which can only be provided by schools (professionals). Any shift of management control from the profession to the community (as accountability seems to promise) would not, therefore, alter the function of schools but merely change who executes some of the tasks of schools.

Moreover, young people do not need to be physically in school all the time to be considered "still in school." This means professional educators can cut down drastically on the amount of school time without relinquishing their influence and control over what needs to be learned.

Accountability in the hands of professional educators is not a problem of how to reduce costs, fix responsibility for results, or improve basic skill acquisition, but how to accomplish these things without loss of their control. Professionals are prepared to make many concessions to maintain control.

6. *People who have internalized the values defined by schools have become dangerously addicted to the services provided by the schools.* Alternative ways to learn and alternative kinds of learning are pushed out of the social imagination of the community. The fact that abundant technology exists to facilitate a great deal of learning without mediation by certified teachers is not perceived as a critical contradiction in our society. So skillful is the professional educator's influence on public attitudes that education can only be visualized in terms of teachers, schools, and curricula controlled by the profession.

Thus, at a time when widespread access to the tools for learning is possible and young people need knowledge which is radically different from what schools now provide if Western civilization and planet Earth are to survive, these issues cannot even be seriously discussed.

And as is true with any addiction, people cannot think of simpler ways of doing things. They may dislike the institution, but they see no alternative other than returning to it to satisfy their needs. Society classifies people by their level of consumption of all types of institutional products. Schools are the prime supporters of this system, for young people learn early that the important social rewards go to those who have consumed more school curricula than others.

7. *The real services provided by schools are declining at an increasing rate,* due primarily to a deliberate scarcity created by professionals themselves. Multiplication of new areas of expertise, each with its own special training program and professional standards, coupled with an increasing number of newly discovered learning deficiencies needing treatment, has been standard practice for many years in education. (The genuine search for new knowledge should not be confused here with professional devices to mystify their disciplines, restrict access to knowledge and position, and increase addiction to the ready-made professional service rather than what people can do for themselves.)

Actual services, however, have generally decreased. The cost of schooling spirals upward. Test scores on certain national examinations have declined continuously over the past decade. In schools, less individual attention occurs. Large physical plants encourage impersonal processing. Teachers and administrators spend more time in negotiations, strikes, grievance meetings, record keeping, plant management, and security planning. Lower-income groups increasingly make it in the system, only to discover the educational target for entry into the more prestigious jobs has shifted yet higher up into the postsecondary system. People therefore get less at greater cost, except for the wealthy, who get the best that is offered.

8. *The natural competencies and privileges of young people are increasingly restricted.* Young people are taught that they cannot contribute in any meaningful way to truth and knowledge. Even more destructively, they are taught that the discovery of knowledge and truth are the work of institutions rather than personal endeavors individuals engage in.

Opportunities for young people to teach one another are also skillfully prevented. Children learn early the need to be taught by professionals, in contrast to self-defined, self-initiated learning (not to be confused with the pitiful programs called "individualized instruction"). Young people are thus prepared for a life of institutional processing and consumption through progressive consumption of curricula. They are instructed to give up their native abilities for things that can be done and made for them by institutions, and to rely on experts for definitions of reality. They are kept chronically dependent on professional treatment during their early years, with only one prime responsibility: *to be a learner in school.* In this poverty of action they are no longer permitted to have genuine responsibilities for the welfare of others. As James Coleman says, having kept young people so dependent, why should we be surprised when they are not productive? Having given them no responsibility, why we be surprised when they are irresponsible?

9. *The institution of schools has now entered a period of unstable escalation.* The rising gap between consumer expectations and actual services provided reveals the inadequacies of schools. People are angry as they pay more and get increasingly less. The profession, of course, does the predictable thing: It announces that a crisis has arrived. But the elites have only one response to problem solving: more of what is currently being offered. Bad management can be cured by more managment. Illiteracy can be cured by more teachers, books, and instructional technology, all whipped into effectiveness by the competitive market place and new venture-management teams. Rising costs can be corrected by training new systems specialists (at more cost) under the control of the guild. . . .

10. *Finally, the institution of compulsory schools has become a major social threat.* It has become repressive and unstable, and will need extensive legal and police protection to maintain its autonomy.

American schools, of course, also accomplish some positive things; they are a significant social invention one does not brush aside lightly. Nevertheless, the overall conclusions are inescapable: The institution of compulsory schools has passed its second watershed. Schools have become a major threat to learning. Professional educators have become a major threat to education. And young people now need to be protected from compulsory schools.

These are the real issues facing American schools today.

ACCOUNTABILITY AND EDUCATIONAL CHANGE

How then does accountablity, as defined by its supporters, deal with these issues? By avoiding them. Nowhere in the literature do I see a recognition of the issues discussed above. Instead, there is implicit agreement that current school functions should remain intact (or if certain functions move outside the schools, professional educators should still retain control), and the thrust should be to make schools more efficient in their current operations.

The late James Allen said that accountability was the top priority for education and that government and the profession have to provide it. But as long as professionals retain control over schools and curricula, accountability will serve only to enhance the profession's power and prevent widespread access to the tools for learning. The emphases will shift to those few skill areas where there is some history of measurement. It will be used as a political tool. Attention will focus on how to tie in learning increments with professional promotion, pay, and funding, and the public will be forced to rely on professionals to explain what accountability programs are accomplishing.

Accountability, therefore, despite the humanistic jargon about community and minority involvement, does not alter the professionals' deciding what needs to be learned in terms that professionals can meet (e.g., Michigan's experience, June, 1974, *Kappan*). The radical alternative, as Illich says, would be to ask not what do people need to learn, but what do people need if they want to learn, and then provide the necessary tools. Accountability doesn't speak to this premise.

But these matters aside, accountability can never lower the cost of formal education as it is presently organized. A few savings might result, but overall costs can only increase.

Economists like Daniel Bell tell us that today roughly two-thirds of our labor force is employed in the service-producing industries and one-third is employed in the goods-producing industries. Increases in productivity are higher in the goods sector, since human services are naturally more resistant to automation. As the labor force continues to shift into services there is a drag on productivity and the costs of services go up sharply. As Bell points out, if we were only a manufacturing economy the situation would be different. The labor costs in goods manufacturing are about 30% of total costs, and normal increases in wages can be offset by normal increases in productivity. In the service sector, however, because it is labor intensive, the wage proportion may run 70% or more of total costs. Wage increases therefore add a much higher percentage to the cost of services than can be made up by normal increases in productivity. Rising wages in the service sector thus cannot be offset by its small increases in productivity. In short, there is an inflationary spiral built into our economic system which no Western society knows how to control satisfactorily.

Applying these economic facts to education, it is clear that as long as we believe only professionals can create, organize, and disseminate accredited instruction for young people, the cost of curriculum materials and the schooling process will always be too expensive. (Full compensatory education is completely impossible.) With the current growth ethic and professional control there is no way to bring down costs other than by a state or federally imposed and relatively unchanging curriculum, or by the creation of an accounting fiction (having other institutions take on various child-care and educational responsibilities under professional surveillance).

Outside contractors have the same

problems, particularly if they attempt curriculum development. To be accepted by national funding agencies, state education departments, local school people, and the public, outside contractors must use people who have received an expensive education and employ the same generally accepted (and expensive) learning/administrative techniques. So the spiral continues. People are promised more and they get increasingly less at greater cost.

Accountability, therefore, is based on a Disneyland dream. It says that if we can get the capitalist system working properly and the market rightly attuned, we can lower the costs of education (or even prevent them from rising), fix responsibility for results, shift the onus of results from child to institution, involve the community, and increase public control over education. Not so. But even if these were all true, the main problem remains: Self-certifying elites would still be in the principal controlling position, setting the standards, jealously guarding the tools for learning, and keeping people addicted to schools and institutional treatment. This issue will remain until the professionals' death grip on prescribed learning is broken.

SOME ANSWERS

The issues described above are broader than just schools or professional educators. The same issues could be raised with every one of our major institutions today. Professional medicine has become a major threat to health, professional law a threat to justice, and professional government a threat to our continued existence.

The problems of schools are not the result of lazy, incompetent, or evil people. (There may be many of these, but there are also many loving, caring people in our schools.) More to the point, professionals have unwittingly lost their perspective and sense of mission. As Dr. Spock recently pointed out about doctors, professional educators have unintentionally created a chronic dependency relationship between themselves and their clients which must now be reversed. Such a reversal must start, however, not with a redefinition of schools but with our industrial, technicist consciousness.

To invent a more humanisitic future we must change the suicidal distortion between us and our social/technical tools. We must bury the industrial dream and the image of superindustrial splendor formed out of this dream. The industrial dream is dead. Moreover, the superindustrial society cannot happen at all, because of the finiteness of our biosphere and the Earth's resources (except perhaps temporarily for an affluent minority of Earth). But even if the superindustrial society were realizable for all, it would only deepen the current suicidal distortion between people and their tools. In short, we must now see with the poet Geoffrey Squires that the technological experiment has reached its limits. This does not mean that technology is wrong or evil, but that the particular experiment we have engaged in with technology has become humanly destructive. There are many dimensions to this destructiveness, but one of the most important is that we have tried to replace central, enduring human functions by technology—to our great loss.

We must, then, de-addict ourselves from the belief that institutional products provide happiness and can satisfy all our needs, that personal responsibility can be replaced by institutional process, that what is made for us is always superior to what we ourselves can make. As Illich says, we must restore a balance between the readymade and what people can make for themselves. We must break our meek acceptance of compulsory change. We must demystify our tools, exclude those tools which by their very nature are destructive, and restore abundant access to the tools which can enhance opportunities for people to come together, care for, learn from, and depend on each other; which can release the enormous personal energy and imagination of people; and which people need to express their meaning in action and engage in self-defined work. To accomplish this, institutions must stop asking, What should we professionals do for people? and begin to ask, What can people do for themselves? "People need new tools to work with rather than tools that 'work' for them," Illich says. "They need technologies to make the most of the energy and imagination each has, rather than more well-programmed energy slaves."

I believe radical alternatives to the current model of school are essential. Four critical functions of new schools should be: 1) *To deprofessionalize the tools for learning.* Ask what people need if they want to learn, then make the tools widely available to all who wish to use them. In short, teach people how to use the tools which open up access to the stored memories of the community in terms of persons, places, and things, and then bet on people's natural curiosity and imagination. The burden of proof, therefore, would always be on the professionals. They would have to demonstrate why a learning tool should not be made widely available to those who wish to use it responsibly. 2) *To help match those who want to share what they know with those who want to learn*—regardless of age, credentials, or training. The school becomes a broker to bring together responsible people who want to share mutual interests, enthusiasms, and ignorance. 3) *To provide opportunities for self-defined and self-initiated learning*—which break the tyranny of the expert, addiction to institutions, and the mystification of tools; which facilitate opportunities for people to learn from, care for, and depend on each other. 4) *To enhance the integration of learning with the life of the community* rather than chronic dependence on professional and institutional treatment. Schools would become, in James Coleman's terms, an action space for young people to engage in and be an integral part of real community problems, work, and festivity.

These four functions do not discredit specialized knowledge, scholarship, intellectual rigor, or even routine drill and practice learning. We have so narrowly defined excellence that it is hard to conceive of the alternative possibilities for learning styles, questioning, knowledge structures, personal and interpersonal awareness, and new social inventions which could emerge from widespread implementation of these functions. Different kinds of schools inculcating distinctly different value sets would inevitably develop, and choice in education could finally become a reality. Within this context it would then make sense to talk about facilitative learning organizations, competency exams for positions involving public trust, voucher systems, and even educational cost analysis.

But is this whole approach feasible? Would it reduce class bias and privileged position and create equal educational opportunities? Would it encourage what Vine Deloria calls the need for a coming together to discover a new sense of what it means to be an American? Yes, but only if the basic beliefs underlying the four proposed functions were widely shared by the larger society, i.e., there was a firm belief in limits to growth, a scaled-down society, use of low-energy tools, and alternative modes of economic production, a radical change in the notion of participatory politics, a resistance to compulsory change, a rejection of the cancerous belief that science is the only mode of knowing, and a commitment to exclude destructive tools whether social or technical. In short, a rejection of the superindustrial dream.

By design, these four functions are open-ended (and transitional in the sense that they should eventually not be associated just with schools). They open up the future to exciting possibilities for human growth and celebration which will be defined in the process of trying to achieve them. Thus these functions are goals from which many educational models can grow. Much thought will be needed to define the kinds of knowledge, attitudes, and skills which are consistent with these goals. A tentative listing would surely include: an expanded social imagination; deep sensitivity to tools in human relationships; a learned immunity to technicist goals; new organizing ideas such as "planetary citizenship" and Illich's notion of "conviviality"; a deep understanding of play, leisure, self-defined work, and personal agency; an understanding of global interdependencies; belief in the just sharing of the planet's resources; an outrage at racism in all its insidious forms; sophisticated organizational skills to make current institutions serve human ends; knowledge of living patterns using low-energy tools and alternative modes of production; and a sensitivity to the "dialectic authority" of history.

If we were to explore seriously the above four functions of schools and pursue the critical survival skills which our historical period calls for, then it would be highly rewarding to talk of accountability in the efficient and effective use of resources. In short, accountability placed in the narrow context of current schools becomes another oppressive instrument and a dangerous smokescreen. Change the context (or in Thomas Kuhn's language, the paradigm), however, and accountability addresses itself to another whole host of questions and problems which are really central to human welfare, survival, and progress.

CONCLUSION

Some people forecast that accountability will be the major issue in education during this decade. If true, I believe the major issue of the eighties will be how to restore any sense of confidence in formal education or any hope in basic reform of schools after the broken promises made about accountability in the seventies have been exposed. But perhaps by that time the professional elites will have conjured up yet another fantasy to protect their vested power and privilege. I sincerely hope not, for as William Thompson says, the future trembles with the possibility of apocalypse as we move to the very edge of history itself. We had better use our time, energy, and imagination wisely during the coming years, because the race H. G. Wells spoke of between education and catastrophe will have been decided before the twenty-first century becomes the present.

POSTSCRIPT

CAN SCHOOLS BE HELD ACCOUNTABLE FOR RESULTS?

Obviously, the schools must be held at least partly responsible for the achievement of their clients. Because of the myriad factors involved in personal motivation and accomplishment, it is just as obvious that the schools cannot be held totally responsible for successes and failures. The problems are to define reasonable limits of responsibility and to delineate appropriate means of assessing the fulfillment of the defined obligations.

John Goodlad concludes that the science-engineering model of accountability is simply inappropriate for use in an unscientific enterprise such as education. In "A Perspective on Accountability" (*Phi Delta Kappan*, October 1975), Goodlad identifies what he believes to be the central question: "What evidence do we have that any 10 or 50 behaviorally-stated objectives, if attained, add up to some larger human traits of the kind implied in educational aims?"

Arthur W. Combs, in *Educational Accountability: Beyond Behavioral Objectives* (1972), analyzes professional responsibility and concludes that it does not demand a prescribed way of behaving but does require that whatever methods are used have the presumption of being good for the client. In this view the emphasis is on the defensible character of what is done rather than on a set of guaranteed outcomes. In "Educational Accountability From a Humanistic Perspective" (*Educational Researcher*, September 1973), Combs deals with the problem that humanistic educational goals do not readily lend themselves to exacting modes of assessment. Because of this, humanistic aims centered in the development of personal meaning are often ignored in the behaviorist orientation. Combs offers a compromise position which rejects the dichotomization of behaviorism and humanism. He calls for a search for valid ways to assess the accomplishment of humanistic objectives which function alongside behavioral objectives.

Other views of this issue are offered in Henry Dyer's *How To Achieve Accountability in the Public Schools* (1973); *The Teacher You Choose To Be* (1975) by William A. Proefriedt; *The Making of a Teacher: A Plan for Professional Self-Development* (1975); and *Accountability in American Education* (1976) by Don T. Martin, George E. Overholt, and Wayne J. Urban.

ISSUE 11

WHAT POWER SHOULD TEACHERS HAVE?

The accountability movement has put the spotlight on teacher performance and has raised some serious questions regarding the professional status of educators. Jonathon Kozol, in *The Night is Dark and I am Far from Home* (1975), observes that "power knows where its own interest lies; so too do those machineries that serve and strengthen power." In public education power has resided in the hands of local school boards, school superintendents and their staffs, and local, state, and, lately, federal politicians and bureaucrats.

The prevailing situation has left the classroom teacher with only a modicum of autonomy, few opportunities for participation in the decision-making process, and, as AFT union president Albert Shanker points out, no right to bargain on policy matters. The growing strength of the two major organizations representing the interests of teachers, the National Education Association (NEA) and the American Federation of Teachers (AFT), has modified the tradition of paternalism which has controlled teachers' professional lives and, in many cases, their private lives as well.

A new sense of professionalism seems to be emerging from the growing power and increasing militancy of teachers. If, however, educators are ever to approach the level of professionalism attained by doctors and lawyers, they will have to have the opportunity for self-governance and prove themselves worthy of such trust.

Shanker contends that the present power structure has often blocked movement toward better schools and that teachers, if given wider opportunity to participate in policy-level decisions, could exert a major reform influence. Another educator, Herbert Kohl, feels that teacher organizations must have as primary objectives the protection of teacher rights and the humanization of their professional work.

Three recent source books have, primarily through the analysis of court cases and legislation, contributed much to the clarification of teacher rights and responsibilities. They are: a 1972 American Civil Liberties Union (ACLU) handbook, *The Rights of Teachers,* by David Rubin; *The Civil Rights of Teachers* (1973) by Louis Fischer and David Schimmel; and *Avoiding Teacher Malpractice: A Practical Legal Handbook for the Teaching Professional* (1976) by Rennard Strickland, Janet Frasier Phillips, and William R. Phillips.

The ACLU handbook deals mainly with the constitutional rights of teachers, concentrating on such school board actions as dismissal of tenured and nontenured teachers, punishment for insubordination, forced resignation, refusal to hire, and forbidding teachers' engagement in certain activities. The Fischer and Schimmel book illustrates a wide range of legal and professional issues, many of which deal with teacher activities outside the school, such as writing letters to the editor, participating in controversial community organizations, and acting in a way considered by school officials to be unexemplary. The "malpractice" handbook alerts teachers to the many accusations which they may encounter in their professional activities and offers practical suggestions for dealing with such situations.

The "teacher as model" aspect of the professional tradition has often served to justify school board and community control over the in-school and out-of-school actions of educators. Albert Shanker, in the article presented here, examines the paternalistic relationship between governing officials and classroom teachers and calls for greater professional unity. Herb Kohl, in his article, analyzes the struggle for power in education and, while sharing Shanker's solidarity goals, raises some questions about unthinking militancy.

Albert Shanker

UNIFIED ACTION IS NEEDED

If school boards are not merely curious about why teachers are angry, but genuinely want to re-establish good relations with teachers, they will need first to eliminate all vestiges of paternalism from their dealings with teachers and the unions of which teachers are members.

School boards also will need to give strong direction to their agents—both district-level and building-level administrators—to behave as educational managers and statesmen, rather than as guardians of a collection of unmanageable child-adults (which is how teachers sometimes are treated by school administrators).

Such paternalism is not new. Copies of *Rules for Teachers, 1872* hang on the walls of teacher union offices throughout the country. Promulgated by some anonymous school district, the *Rules* provide that:

> Men teachers may take one evening each week for courting purposes, or two evenings a week if they go to church regularly.
>
> Women teachers who marry or engage in unseemly conduct will be dismissed.
>
> Any teacher who smokes, uses liquor in any form, frequents pool or public halls, or gets shaved in a barber shop will give good reason to suspect his worth, intention, integrity and honesty.
>
> The teacher who performs his labor faithfully and without fault for five years will be given an increase of twenty-five cents per week in his pay, providing the Board of Education approves.

The oppressive paternalism of those *Rules* long survived the 1870s. Even today school boards in many rural areas regulate strictly the out-of-school lives of teachers. And while the Broward County board may have approved one of its teachers entering the Miss Nude Florida contest this year—and winning it—the Apple Valley, Calif., school board is probably more typical. It initiated dismissal proceedings this fall against a male physical education teacher for baring his all in a Playgirl centerfold last June.

Continued on p. 176

From Albert Shanker, "Why Teachers Are Angry." Reprinted, with permission, from *The American School Board Journal,* January 1975.

Herbert R. Kohl

ARE TEACHER STRIKES CONSTRUCTIVE?

There are two major teachers' organizations represented in most school districts. One of the organizations, usually called a Teachers Association, is affiliated with the National Education Association (NEA). The other, which is usually called a Teachers Federation, is affiliated with the American Federation of Teachers (AFT) and through it with the AFL-CIO.

Teachers Associations tend to be stronger in rural or small city communities. They have traditionally considered themselves "professional" organizations modeled somewhat after the American Medical Association. The American Federation of Teachers considers itself a union and not a professional association. It is most dominant in urban areas like New York and Chicago.

For many years the Teachers Associations were rather conservative educationally. More recently, it is becoming difficult to tell the organizations apart in terms of educational philosophy. Both the Teachers Federations and the Teachers Associations are dominated by traditional teachers and have within them smaller caucuses of individuals who advocate open education. There also are small groups within each organization that are politically radical. However, it is important to realize that even within the group of politically left teachers there are many disagreements on educational philosophy.

The NEA and the AFT are struggling for power these days. In states like California, where a collective bargaining law exists, they face each other in local elections to determine which group will be the sole bargaining agent for the district. In these organizational struggles the main issues are teacher salaries and benefits, and job protection. In order to win as large a following as possible the organizations avoid taking any bold educational positions. This is especially true on a state and national level within the organizations. Locals in different cities can develop different priorities, and some often find themselves at odds with the local and national organizations. It is crucial to understand, if you get involved in teachers' organization politics, that if you

Continued on p. 180

(Shanker, cont. from p. 174)

Although their personal lives now may be much freer of monitoring by school boards and administrators (much freer than they were even just a decade ago), teachers in most of the United States still are treated with a great deal of paternalism. The difference is that today the paternalism mostly affects their *professional* lives.

No group of professionals in American society—other than teachers—has so little to say about how its members discharge their responsibilities.

Between them, state agencies and local authorities leave teachers with almost no voice in defining the curriculum they must teach. The basic materials teachers use in their classrooms—from textbooks to chalk—are selected and rationed by others. Teachers rarely are consulted in discussions of the optimum school year, school day, or even class period. Streams of innovations—each one heralded as the century's greatest breakthrough—are *imposed* on teachers, often with no advance notice whatever, and usually with no chance for teachers either to evaluate them conceptually or even to examine their practicability.

When teachers rise up to demand "a voice in the educational decision-making process," they often meet stares of wonder and words of condescension from school board members and school administrators alike. "What can a mere classroom teacher possibly know about the truly big problems?" seems to be the attitude. And it is all but universal.

When then-Gov. Nelson Rockefeller appointed a commission, late in 1969, to study and evaluate the whole of public education in New York state, he consulted administrators in the state education department and even on the local school district level, as well as school board members and a variety of politicians.

He did not consult either of the organizations that then represented classroom teachers; and not a single teacher served on the governor's commission for evaluation.

What is true at the highest levels of state and national government is just as true on the local level.

The collective bargaining relationship between the New York City Board of Education and the United Federation of Teachers (Local 2, American Federation of Teachers, AFL-CIO) is a mature one. Since 1969 it has produced two excellent contracts without even the threat of a strike. But nearly every demand the union submitted in 1972 that related to the improvement of instruction was summarily rejected by the school board. The board's typical response to a demand: "That's educational policy, a management prerogative." And: "You have no right to bargain policy. The union's sphere is exclusively the salaries, benefits and working conditions of its members."

The result, of course, was that the teacher union returned to its members with spectacular gains in those areas (salaries, benefits and working conditions), but the children missed out on the many improvements we had sought in their learning conditions. And in a town as union-oriented as New York, the school board's refusal to permit us to negotiate *educational* gains could only have been a vestige of paternalism.

Over-all, of course, collective bargaining has sharply restricted the areas in which school boards can exercise their penchant for paternalism. Wherever teachers have won the right to negotiate, school boards can no longer set salaries and fringe benefits unilaterally, or deny teachers adequate job-security protections, or ignore working conditions. In such areas as class size—which *can* be defined, at least in part, as a *working* condition—teachers also have won *educational* improvements through collective bargaining channels.

Boards of education are not, however, the sole paternalists in any school system. Administrators are probably guilty of the worst excesses. Coming from classrooms themselves, they often see their faculties as classes of young children: and schools abound with unnecessary and demeaning rules, regulations and restrictions on teacher conduct. Faculty meetings at which principals prate endlessly about matters that could have been better summarized in one-paragraph memorandums grate teachers simply because of the time they consume.

But frequently the *substance* of those meetings is even more offensive. A high school teacher in California's San Joaquin Valley wrote to me recently to describe such a meeting. "The principal harangued us for several minutes because we allowed our sixth period classes to escape without picking up enough of the day's litter from classroom floors. At the end of his harangue, the principal picked up a wastebasket, said heatedly, 'I filled this entire wastebasket with the garbage left on just one of your floors today,' and proceeded to empty the basket in front of the podium. 'You people have got to do better,' he insisted. The more progressive teachers at [our] high school wouldn't even speak to their students that way, much less try to provide an object lesson in such a sophomoric way."

Paternalism is not, of course, the sole objection of teachers to the management of education by school boards and administrators. Inept supervision and criticism, unfair dismissals, the summary rejection of negotiating demands all exacerbate the attitudes of teachers, boards, and administrators toward one another.

Ultimately, mature collective bargaining relationships and sophisticated contractual agreements will resolve many of these more common labor-management conflicts.

But the paternalism with which teachers were so long treated is a problem that is unique, among professionals, to relations between teachers and their employers. Neither the changes in American society that have produced such radical changes in the schools generally, and in the rights and responsibilities of teachers in particular, nor the advent of collective bargaining—the most dramatic of those changes—has succeeded in completely eradicating that paternalism. It continues to be a major source of irritation for teachers, as any school board member who has attended a teacher union meeting during any period of conflict can testify.

Teachers also are angry, as are most other Americans, at inflation and recession—both of which have robbed them of many of the gains they won in the past decade and have threatened cutbacks in educational programs.

With teachers, moreover, the state of the economy is an even more special cause of resentment. From the launching of the first Sputnik to the first dose of Nixonomics—from, that is, the mid-1950s through the late 1960s—politicians from ward boss to President spoke of the need for better schools, and vowed their energies to improving education. Many gains were made, though less because of the politicians' commitment than because teachers began to organize and to achieve some of the latent power they had always possessed. Through collective bargaining and greater involvement in the political process, teacher organizations won significant salary increases (pay scales in New York City, for example, more than doubled between 1962 and 1972) and numerous other improvements in the terms and conditions of their employment in schools.

Like the emerging nations, teachers—the emerging professionals—developed a "revolution of rising expectations." They expected politicians to follow through on their pledges to place education among the nation's highest priorities. But the product of the politicians' promises was penury.

Outside of some very real gains during the Johnson Administration—gains emulated and supplemented by some state governments—the money simply has not been forthcoming to do what everyone agreed the schools must do: give more individual attention to children by lowering class size, develop better remedial programs, help the intellectually gifted, provide more effective ancillary services, such as guidance counseling.

Then the economy faltered; and education—which actually never was placed among the nation's highest priorities—seemed to teachers to become, once again, an afterthought in the minds of most state and national legislators.

Little wonder that the National Education Association entered the 1974 congressional elections with the campaign theme, "Get mad: it matters." However injudicious and petulant its theme may have appeared, the N.E.A.'s slogan fairly accurately reflected the general feeling of teachers that the people who govern America had reneged on a solemn promise—not only to the teaching profession, but especially to the children whom teachers teach.

To an extent, school boards are the targets of the anger generated in teachers by the failure of politicians generally. That may be unfair —just as it's unfair for voters to vent their resentments at rising taxes by voting against school bonds and levies, the one tax they can reject directly.

In another sense, nevertheless, teachers are justified in feeling that school boards have not exerted sufficient leadership in educating the public and lobbying the politicians to live up to their responsibilities.

Cooperative ventures between local school boards and teacher unions, and between their state and national organizations, on matters of mutual concern—including, especially, school finance—could have the effect not merely of helping to win needed legislation, but also of improving relations between the two groups. In addressing the New York State School Boards Association a year ago, I urged exactly that course, proposing further that we cement our alliance with an agreement to work with our less tractable local units to avoid unnecessry conflict in collective bargaining. I now urge a similar course on the national level.

For still another cause of teacher anger, school boards *are* more directly responsible.

The polemics of a gaggle of New Left critics—people like Jonathon Kozol, John Holt and James Herndon—produced severe disaffection with public education among the intelligentsia and, particularly, in the news media.

The message that the schools were failing was one that the general public never bought, as the Gallup Poll's annual surveys of public attitudes have demonstrated repeatedly. Teachers, too, knew full well that the schools were not the disaster areas they were described as being by these critics, nearly every one of whom was fired from the public schools.

Nevertheless, many school boards *did* believe — and were deeply influenced by the criticisms. Where reading scores had dropped *relatively*—even though they had risen *absolutely* almost everywhere—school boards panicked. They looked for and embraced a whole series of cure-alls. Other boards (in school districts where standardized results had given no cause for alarm whatever), not wishing to be left behind, did likewise. Panacea followed panacea—differentiated staffing, year-round school, performance contracting, merit pay, vouchers—until innovation became its own justification.

Not only were teachers rarely consulted about the adoption and implementation of these cure-alls; but their complaints about the disruption and ineffectiveness of each new panacea were generally brushed aside.

Moreover, when these grandiose reforms failed, as inevitably they did, teachers too often were made the scapegoats—alike by the superintendent, whose pet projects they had been, and by the school board that had endorsed the innovation and did not want to accept its own responsibility for initiating the reforms.

Recent evidence that the year-round school in Virginia Beach, Va., and the voucher plan in Alum Rock, Calif., have been total washouts—as performance contracting was earlier proved to be in Texarkana, Ark.—should give pause to the frenetic search for educational panaceas. School boards would do well to give more careful consideration to proposed innovations and to involve teachers in any plan to adopt and implement them.

School boards also would do well to take stock of the good job that the public schools are doing with their regular, everyday practices—and to let teachers and the public, and the news media as well, know that the job being done is a good one.

There is one last, major reason teachers are angry. They are also angry at *other teachers*—or, at least, at the rival organizations that represent them. There are nearly three million teachers in public and private elementary, secondary and higher education; but just more than half of them belong to the N.E.A. and the A.F.T. combined. The great bulk of non-joiners ignore both organizations because they see no worthwhile purpose in paying dues that will be used merely to fight other teachers. In New York before the statewide N.E.A.-A..F.T. merger in 1972, for example, the two competing organizations claimed, together, just 75 percent of their combined potential; the merged organization today enrolls more than 93 percent of the state's teachers.

United, the nation's three million teachers would be the largest and strongest union in the country. With articulate, well-informed members in every election district in all 50 states, that teacher union would have an enormous impact on local, state and national government. Teachers would have, in fact, the political power to achieve the goals that both the N.E.A. and the A.F.T. long have sought: from the governance of their own profession to smaller classes to a one-third contribution from the federal government toward the total cost of public education.

With a single, nationwide union, teachers also would enjoy greater leverage at the negotiating table. School boards would know that the teachers' state and national organizations had abundant resources to sustain a strike almost indefinitely—and also that they had sufficient political clout to win legislative and even judicial relief. Never again would teachers face the mass firings executed last year by school boards in Hortonville, Wis., and Timberlane, N.H.

In these and many other respects, "it's all sitting there" — unprecedented power to improve the schools and to win all the most important objectives that teachers have worked for over the past decade and more. It's even "there" to protect teachers during the current recession and the likely depression that is coming.

While the two national organizations did sit down briefly in late 1973 and early 1974, the N.E.A. precipitately broke off the talks (releasing a lengthy attack on the A.F.T. to the news services just moments after walking out of the final negotiating session); the prospects for an N.E.A.-A.F.T. merger in the immediate future are not bright.

The chances are, then, that—of all the angers that teachers feel—anger toward other teachers is likely to become increasingly prominent, as the two rival organizations gear up for bitter jurisdictional wars all across the country, and as teachers see all the good they might have done, united, sacrificed instead to narrow, partisan interests. The anger of teachers will mount the more as they see that organizational warfare playing into the hands of those school boards, administrators and politicians that would prefer teachers divided and weak, rather than united and strong.

Long after the present causes of teacher unrest have vanished, there will still be *some* discontent shared by teachers generally. A due measure of conflict is inevitable in labor-management relations. But much of the current anger reflects the fact that teachers have so recently been powerless, and only now are organized in such a way—in parts of the country—that they are beginning to set matters straight.

As they move closer to the goals they seek—adequate remuneration, professional dignity, and educational conditions that will permit them to do the kind of job they were trained to do, know they are able to do, and want to do—teachers will become less angry. To move faster toward that more happy time should be an objective equally of teacher unions, of administrator groups, and of school boards everywhere.

(Kohl, cont. from p. 175)

try to make too many changes or upset too many people, you will get pressure from the state and national organizations.

Over the past fifteen years I've been in and out of the teachers' union a number of times. In 1961, I joined the United Federation of Teachers in New York City. At that time there were about 5,000 members in the organization. At my school there were four teachers in the chapter. The rest of the staff either belonged to an NEA affiliate or didn't believe in teachers organizing at all. At union meetings we spent most of our time talking about educational issues—about reading programs, reorganizing the school, sharing materials and teaching ideas, and so forth. That year we went out on strike. I believe that was the first teachers' strike in New York City, and the union won the strike quickly. Teachers got across-the-board raises of $1,000, extra money for college credits beyond the B.A., and increased benefits. Educationally nothing was won or even fought for by the union leadership. However, the union got a dues check-off, which meant that union dues could simply be taken out of one's salary. Nobody had to go around urging teachers to pay their dues as we had to do before the dues check-off. The staff at our school, grateful for the raise that was won by the strike, all signed up for membership. The meeting after the strike the whole leadership of our chapter changed. We four original union members were the radicals who initiated a good thing but were no longer necessary and got voted out as delegates. The same thing happened throughout the city. Union membership went from around 5,000 to around 35,000, and many of the more radical delegates as well as those concerned primarily with educational issues were voted out.

I kept my union membership for several years despite those changes. However, in 1966, I quit in disgust over the union's position against community control of schools in Harlem and the Ocean Hill-Brownsville area of Brooklyn. I knew the schools and parents involved in the struggle in Harlem. The students in the schools couldn't read or write. Most of the teachers hated their work and couldn't stand being around the students. Parents at the school moved to take over the schools out of despair. The union's whole response was to protect any teacher, no matter how incompetent, and to discredit the parents. There were rumors, for example, that the parents were anti-Semitic. But a number of Jewish teachers, myself included, believed that the parents were right and crossed the picket lines and worked as hard as we could to develop community control of the schools.

I do not believe in being blindly loyal to organizations or in supporting any strike no matter what the reason for it. Working people should and must organize to protect their rights and to humanize their work. But if people strike for racist reasons, or to cover up their own incompetence, or to take power away from poorer people, I believe these strikes should be opposed.

There are times, however, when there are just reasons to go on strike, and one has to be prepared to take the risks involved in opposing public institutions like the school systems.

The day before school began last year the teachers in Berkeley voted overwhelmingly for a strike. There is no single bargaining agent for Berkeley teachers, yet about 40 percent belong to the union, 40 percent to an NEA affiliate, and 20 percent are independent. Together with a representative of the school counselors and psychologists, they form a Certificated Employees Council, which conducts negotiations with the administration and school board. This was the first time that all groups had agreed on a strike, and on the first day of school over 95 percent of the district's certificate staff stayed out.

The background to the strike was as

follows: on April 15, 1975, an agreement was reached for the next school year after four months of negotiations. There was to be no raise. Salaries and benefits were to be maintained, as well as limits on classroom size and grievance procedures that had been worked out with the administration over the past few years. However, on June 28, the school board, declaring a fiscal emergency, unilaterally rescinded the agreement, which is possible under California state law. They announced a 2.5 percent salary cut and over a 2 percent cut in benefits. In addition, they eliminated class-size maximums and instituted a policy of transferring teachers from school to school without prior notice or hearings. This last policy was implemented over the summer so that a number of teachers returned from vacation to find themselves at new schools.

Many of the teachers I spoke to did not believe in strikes. They never imagined themselves on picket lines, and it was not money that brought so many out. They felt they had been treated arrogantly and inconsiderately and that their dignity had been damaged.

All the teachers at Hillside School, where I have worked and where my three children go to school, went on strike. None had ever been on a picket line before, and for some the decision to strike was not made until the night before the strike began. I, with many parents and former teachers, came out that first day of the strike to help and to let the picketers know they were not alone in their struggle.

It was awkward that morning. People didn't know whether to carry signs or not. They were uncertain about how to act toward the principal, who is popular with the staff, and the school secretary and custodian, both of whom are liked and respected. Fortunately, the principal arrived early that day and had a chance to talk to the picket captains and a few of the other teachers. He had to cross the line or lose his job, and none of the teachers wanted him forced out. It was decided to support him in crossing the line for the sake of the school after the strike. At other schools, where the principal was not as popular or the teachers were angrier, it was more difficult for the administrators.

The same consideration was shown to the custodian, bus driver, and school secretary, all of whom expressed overt sympathy with the strike for one day, as did the custodian. The bus driver, along with her colleagues, published a letter of support in our local newspaper. They had all done as much as they felt they could to help the teachers since their organizations did not vote to strike.

A major problem was deciding how to respond to substitutes from outside the district who had been offered fifty dollars a day to cross the picket line. The teachers felt they could not afford to be lenient about this, and eventually a number of strategies were used. Some subs were talked into leaving. Others were either given a silent treatment or informed that they would be denied future work in Berkeley and other districts. A list of their names was posted outside the school. There was no violence, but the extreme anger that the teachers felt came out in various ways. In response, the district began to rotate subs from school to school.

When parents came to school, it was important to meet them and to discuss the issues. We chose to have teachers talk to those parents they knew best and could reach most easily. For people with day-care needs alternatives were provided by other parents as well as some of the teachers.

During the second week of the strike, it became apparent that though they refused to give in, some teachers did not feel comfortable on the picket line. The picketers talked to each other, supported each other, and tried to keep anxieties down.

The teachers had to find ways to keep their time occupied. Several decided to devote their nonpicketing time to child care centers in different parts of the community or to support strikers at schools that weren't as unified as Hillside. One teacher, Dan Peletz, composed songs for the strike and took his guitar from school to school, singing them. In all the years I have been with Hillside I have never seen the staff so warm and supportive toward each other.

There were continually a number of anxieties lurking in the teachers' minds. Would someone try to cross the line? How could you deal with a member of your own staff who tried to break the strike? There were schools in the district where some teachers did go in, and there were feelings of bitterness. Old friendships were wrecked; there was harassment, shouts of "scab."

Of course, there was also the financial anxiety and the fear of being fired. The school board tried to play on all of these anxieties as well as to pit the teachers' organizations against each other. Solidarity was crucial.

One thing came out clearly: strength under the pressure of a strike did not depend on age, teaching style, or the organization one belonged to. A factor that did seem to have an effect on the teachers' attitudes was their own family background. Those who came from working-class backgrounds and had seen parents and relatives on strike in the past showed the others how to act. This shifting of traditional patterns caused people who had never paid attention to one another or thought they had nothing to learn from each other to begin to communicate.

The strike lasted for six weeks. Then an arbitration committee was agreed upon, and the teachers went back to work pending a final agreement. The committee returned a report which restored only a part of what had been taken away from the teachers. However, the teachers were too tired and demoralized to go back on strike; they weren't confident in their leadership, which had assured them that the committee would return a report favorable to the teachers. They voted to accept the committee report at the same time that the school board warned that next year teachers would have to be fired. Clearly, the teachers in Berkeley will have to face the issue of going out again.

The situation is not unique to Berkeley. Many of us will have to face the possibility of being on the picket line in the next few years, and it is important to share experiences. Perhaps the best way to conclude this discussion is to quote Dan Peletz, who described some of his experiences and reactions this way:

> It is necessary to figure out some guidelines for my own behavior in a highly unusual situation. For the most part, I continue to rely on those values that govern my behavior during more normal circumstances. I don't intentionally harass people when there's no strike on, and I'm not intentionally harassing anyone now. I don't make a practice of calling people names, and I haven't started. I would not in any way hassle another regular staff member

who decided to go into school. I respect each person's right to make his or her own decision, and a decision to go in must be a very painful one, indeed.

I wrote three or four songs and shared them, and if they offend, so be it. I stayed as honest as I know how to be in writing them, and I'll stand by them. My anger and frustration needed a vent, and I chose to write songs.

I've spent a lot of time talking to friends all over the district, many of whom I haven't seen in ages. And one of the great benefits of the strike is that every staff member on the line is feeling a great sense of connectedness, that somehow we all relate to one another and are all in the same boat.

Where do we go from here? This level of tension cannot be maintained, a fact which is obvious to everyone. Either we go back to work and admit defeat (which few people I talk to have any intention of doing) or the struggle will be escalated. It's all very new, but I feel good about what we're doing. I'm proud to stand up for what I believe, and I'm confident we will prevail.

POSTSCRIPT

WHAT POWER SHOULD TEACHERS HAVE?

Constitutional rights, professional rights, and professional power are educational issues which touch those involved at deep personal levels. The quality of a teacher's professional life is determined in major ways by the decisions and actions taken in these realms. The growing strength of teacher organizations provides an avenue for the assertion of ideas related to policy matters, but the crucial test lies in the direct relationships among teachers, school officials, parents, and students. It is in these relationships that true professionalism becomes manifest.

Chronicles of the development of teacher organizations can be helpful in understanding the present situation. Some sources are: Edgar B. Wesley's *NEA: The First Hundred Years* (1957), William Edward Eaton's *The American Federation of Teachers, 1916–1961: A History of the Movement* (1974), and Timothy Stinnett's *Turmoil in Teaching: A History of the Organizational Struggle for America's Teachers* (1968).

Professional and organizational assertiveness during recent years is bringing about a changing image of the teacher. Some books that attempt to describe the changes are: Myron Brenton's *What's Happened to Teacher?* (1970), which examines the limits of professionalism; Ronald G. Corwin's *Militant Professionalism* (1970); *The New Professionals* (1972) by Ronald Gross and Paul Osterman; *The New Teacher: Changing Patterns of Authority and Responsibility* (1973) by G. Louis Heath; and *Power to the Teacher: How America's Educators Became Militant* (1976) by Marshall O. Donley, Jr.

Two other interesting perspectives are presented in Dan Lortie's *Schoolteacher: A Sociological Study* (1975), which offers the informative results of an extensive survey of teachers, and Robert Dreeben's *The Nature of Teaching,* which contains a provocative segment on professionalism.

The fact remains, regardless of certain gains in general teacher power, that a professional life characterized by deadly routine, the following of orders and directives, and exclusion from participation in policy-formation and other serious matters has a debilitating effect on teachers. There is a similar effect upon students who work under like conditions, and this is the topic of the final issue of Part 2.

ISSUE 12

WHAT RIGHTS DO STUDENTS HAVE?

In "Schools for Scandal—The Bill of Rights and Public Education (*Phi Delta Kappan*, December 1969), Ira Glasser states, "there are only two public institutions in the United States which steadfastly deny that the Bill of Rights applies to them: one is the military and the other is the public schools." The recognition of the authoritarian nature of compulsory schooling is not new (Willard Waller's 1932 *The Sociology of Teaching* provides a classic portrayal of student oppression and alienation), but the past two decades have been marked by widespread expression of concern over students' rights.

Early consciousness-raising in the recent wave of analyses of the experiences of children and youth was provided by such works as Paul Goodman's *Growing Up Absurd* (1956), Edgar Z. Friedenberg's *The Vanishing Adolescent* (1959), and John Holt's *How Children Fail* (1964). The late 1960s and early 1970s produced more radical calls for action against authoritarianism in the schools, chronicled in such books as *Young Radicals: Notes on Committed Youth* (1968) by Kenneth Keniston, *The Student as Nigger* (1969) by Jerry Farber, *Our Time Is Now* (1970) by John Birmingham, and *The Soft Revolution: A Student Handbook for Turning Schools Around* (1971) by Neil Postman and Charles Weingartner.

A 1969 statement by an activist group, the Montgomery County (Md.) Student Alliance, shows the spectrum of student concerns. The group listed, among others, the following detrimental conditions: the school system is based on fear; schools put a premium on conformity and blind obedience; schools compel students to be dishonest; schools destroy the eagerness to learn; schools cause feelings of resentment and alienation; and the school atmosphere stifles self-expression and honest reactions. More recently, a 1974 federal government report (James S. Coleman *et. al.*, *Youth: Transition to Adulthood*) found a lack of school and total community commitment to the problems of alienated young people who see few opportunities for obtaining practical and worthwhile skills.

During the 1970s the protest movement and the moral arguments regarding student rights combined in a search for legal guidelines concerning the civil and human rights of the young. Guy Leekley, in one of the following selections, distinguishes among the various types of claims communicated by students to school authorities and examines the nature of the authorities' obligations regarding such issues as free speech, dress codes, and fair hearings. In his analysis Leekley draws on a number of court decisions which contributed to the development of guidelines, such as *Tinker v. Des Moines Independent Community School District* and *Ordway v. Hargraves.*

The Hon. Mary Kohler, in the accompanying article, grants that young people have won some procedural safeguards through various legal actions but observes that their rights as human beings extend much further, into areas not clearly protected by the law and certainly not manifested in usual social practices. She includes among these rights protection from protectors who wave the banner of "child welfare" while in reality contributing to further oppression. "If the choice is ultimately between what is least detrimental to the child and what is least detrimental to the adult," she states, "I profess a bias in the child's interest."

Both the Leekley and the Kohler statements address some prevalent practices of parents and schools that can block the full human development of the young. Leekley calls for greater clarity in understanding and resolving rights conflicts; Kohler proposes extensive social action to reverse the conditions that lead to such conflicts.

GUY LEEKLEY

LEGAL BASIS FOR RIGHTS CLAIMS

A traditional controversy in Anglo-American political and social life has revolved around the questions of who is to be included in the protection of civil rights and how broad should be the range of that protection. Arguments and conclusions regarding rights have generally been formulated in quite different ways by those who look at the issues from the various viewpoints of law, politics, or philosophy. Whatever the approach or prescription, however, until quite recently the mainstream arguments assumed that the population to be protected by "rights" was composed of adult, white males. The perimeters of the protected group have been gradually expanded during this century, but it was not until the 1960s that claims by students of rights against school authorities began to be recognized and enforced by American courts.

In the last decade the number of court decisions that have supported student claims of rights in relation to their schools has increased considerably. Knowledge of this increase sensitizes students to the possibility of seeking protection against excesses of authority and tends to encourage claims of the right to be so protected. As this new dimension is added to the general ferment of school life, every element involved—courts, teachers, parents, students, and school administrators—must learn to distinguish among various kinds of claims that students might make and must generally develop an understanding of the nature of these claims. In order to increase that understanding, we will need to determine what a student means when he makes such a claim, and we will have to examine some judicial decisions to see what has happened when claims of student rights have been tested in the courts.

This analysis of the nature of such claims should not be confused with studies that have been made by philosophers and political scientists of the concept of "rights." Claims by students of rights, and the response of school officials and courts, are forms of human interaction that have become important enough to deserve close inspection. As was pointed out in a recent study of children's rights, "The term *rights* is commonly used in a quasi-legal or moral sense to identify 'something to which one has a just claim.' Such a

Continued on p. 190

Hon. Mary Kohler

RIGHTS EXTEND TO HUMAN CONCERNS

Children constitute one of the largest and most vulnerable minority groups. They have no voice in the political process. They participate directly in no lobbies on their own behalf. At a time when they are particularly weak and easily intimidated and manipulated, their rights are particularly vulnerable to infringement, perhaps at least as often as not by those who declaim that they act in the children's regard.

The spate of recent court decisions (*In Re Gault* and others) has brought into question the view of the state as *parens patriae*—the benevolent protection of the vulnerable child. And whatever the procedural safeguards won, there are entitlements of children that go much further—the right to protection against neglect, abuse, poverty, discrimination, or degradation. Especially when rights are infringed upon in the name of rehabilitation or treatment, the latter must in fact be benevolent and therapeutic, not merely avoidance or shunting aside of the problem, to say nothing of incarceration or imprisonment.

So far these entitlements are only unachieved aspirations. We have still to develop the means and mechanisms to assure them. The experience of the past makes it clear that neither fine laws nor benevolent administrators are sufficient. Children's rights at law are only a prologue to a delineation of those specific rights that control the well-being of our children. So far the purely legal focus has left unexplored the whole area of "pre-court" rights, in which the child is often a victim of those whom society has designated as his protectors—parents, guardians, teachers, physicians, and lawyers. Thus I am concerned here with precourt rights and those rights beyond the ken of the court; I am concerned with the problem of who protects the child from his protectors, who guards against the guardians.

Much of the law now governing the relationship between parent and child relegates the child to little more than the status of a chattel. Parents are described as having "property" rights in children. Children's economic interests are made subservient to those of the parent in almost every instance. Legal concepts of parental control and legal requirements of parental consent

Continued on p. 197

(Leekley, cont. from p. 188)
definition connotes that rights are a given or pre-existent entity, inherent in nature, embodied in tradition, or incorporate in law, which one can demand or assert. This popular understanding of what constitutes rights does little to explain where rights originate, who may exercise rights, or how rights are secured and maintained." Such an explanation of what it means to seek positive recognition of a right does not depend on the determination of the validity of any particular rights; that determination would be a legal or moral issue. Here we are limiting ourselves to the study of the meaning of a specific form of communication among students, administrators, and other interested parties—a claim on the part of students that they have rights, and the responses to that claim. This inquiry is worthwhile because an improved understanding of the nature of this form of communication will result in more effective communication, which, in the arena of human relations in the schools, is sorely needed.

As we turn to claims on behalf of students that they have rights, we notice that they are actually claims directed toward school authorities, who generally have the power to control their actions, limit their freedom, or provide desired goods and services. It is an assertion that they have an obligation to act, or to refrain from acting, in certain ways. In another sense, the claim is also being directed at judicial authorities who have the power to restrain or coerce school authorities. The student is claiming that the judiciary has a duty to see to it that obligations of the school officials are fulfilled. The issues that must be considered in support of this second sense have to do with the court's jurisdiction over the question and the court's authority to enforce its decisions regarding actions of the school officials.

This discussion will be limited to an analysis of the first sense of the claim (directed to school authorities) and will leave a treatment of the second sense (directed to the judiciary) for a more specifically legal context.

The analysis of claims as they are directed to school authorities is presented in two parts. The first part attempts to show how the assertion of a claim for student rights indicates that an obligation is being demanded of the school authorities. The remainder of that part consists of an examination of the various kinds of obligations for which a school official might be held responsible. The conclusion is that the nature of a particular student rights claim can be determined by identifying the nature of the corresponding obligation.

The second part attempts to show that all claims for student rights are based on an appeal to an existing rule, which, if enforced, would require the school authorities to perform the claimed obligation. This is followed by an examination of the range of rules to which appeal might be made and demonstrates how the nature of the claim depends on the scope of the particular rule on which the claim is grounded.

Throughout this analysis reference is made to adjudicated legal cases in which questions regarding student rights were tested, thus illustrating the variety of claims that can be raised and the responses with which they have been met.

THE NATURE OF THE OBLIGATION

To see how claims of rights on behalf of students imply the assertion that school authorities have a certain obligation due to the students, we need only consider the form and manner in which such claims actually arise in the school setting. It would be typical, in these times, to find a group of high school students speaking to their principal or school board to the point that the student body had a right to the provision of their own area of free speech, or to the elimination of all dress or appearance codes, or to the assurance of a fair hearing in the case of a threatened suspension of a student. In each of these examples, if the administration were to agree that such a right existed, it would be admitting to the existence of a duty to perform certain actions, or to refrain from acting in certain ways. It is also clear that, in response to a refusal by the administration, the students might be able to convince a judge to enforce their claim, in which case the administration would be required to meet the obligation implied by the claim. Thus the question "What rights do the students have?" can be rephrased in terms of the presence of obligations that are being demanded of the authorities and the means by which those demands might be enforced. Whether it is termed a "right" or a "duty," the attempt is to articulate a particular kind of relation or interaction between students and the school administration.

A way of determining the kind of right that is being claimed by students is to classify its corresponding obligation or duty. Looking at the first example suggested above, we can see that the claim for a right to an area for free speech really implies two different obligations. The students first wish to require the administration to provide space and facilities and second to make sure that the administration will not interfere with their activities in this area. These obligations are quite different from each other. The one is an obligation to do something and provide something. The other is an obligation not to do something, an obligation to refrain from acting.

In the example of students claiming a right to attend school without the restrictions of a dress or appearance code, we see again that the corresponding obligation would be to restrain from interfering with the appearance of the students.

When students claim the right to a fair hearing, the emphasis in the corresponding obligation is that the administration should proceed in a certain prescribed manner. This category of obligation can, of course, be clearly distinguished from obligations to do something and from obligations to restrain from interfering with student actions or appearance.

These are the three categories into which claims of students rights can be organized by distinguishing among the kinds of obligations entailed by the various claims. Each of these categories will be examined more closely and will be illustrated by actual court cases.

The Obligation to Refrain from Interfering

When we examine school situations where students are claiming a right to act or speak freely, or a right to be left alone, the corresponding obligation they are asserting is the obligation to refrain from interfering with that speech, action, or appearance. The most important litigation in that category is the *Tinker* case, where high school students in Des Moines had been suspended for refusing to remove arm bands worn in a silent demonstration in opposition to the Vietnam war. The issue was whether the school authorities had a right to interfere with such a demonstration. The students claimed that their silent demonstration was protected by provisions of the First Amendment against state infringement on free speech.

In the *Tinker* case the students were successful in gaining support for their claimed right. The Supreme Court ordered the school officials not to interfere with the peaceful demonstration, essentially finding an obligation to refrain, which corresponded with the student claim of a right to act freely in this endeavor.

In 1969, soon after the *Tinker* decision, the case of *Scoville v. Board of Education of Joliet Township High School* was decided by a federal court of appeals. Several high school students had been expelled upon a determination that they were guilty of "gross disobedience and misconduct" after they had published "objectionable" material in their underground newspaper. The students claimed that this interference violated their constitutional rights and that the school authorities should be enjoined from action in the matter. The court of appeals agreed. "We conclude that absent an evidentiary showing, and an appropriate balancing of the evidence by the district court to determine whether the Board was justified in a 'forecast' of the disruption and interference, as required under *Tinker*, plaintiffs are entitled to the declaratory judgment, injunctive and damage relief sought."

What principle seems to underlie the reasoning in these cases involving student claims that a right of free action has been violated? The above cases show that the courts are resting on the classical libertarian position that one can insist on noninterference by the state in personal actions or speech as long as others are not harmed or seriously disrupted. It is important to note that in the face of such a claim, it is up to the officials to prove that their interference was justified by the reasonable forecast of such disruption.

The students in the *Tinker* case argued that they deserved the same constitutional protection that had been enjoyed by some elements of our society since the passage of the Bill of Rights. As indicated in the Constitution, those protections are the right of "persons." We should note that a constitutional amendment was required to include in the category "persons" those people (presumably the adult males) in our society who had been slaves and those races whose skins are not white. It took another amendment to establish that the class of "persons" also included adult women, at least to the extent of allowing one of the prerogatives enjoyed by that class (the right to vote). There has been no such amendment allowing non-adults the protections afforded to "persons," but that appears to be the effect of the *Tinker* decision.

The Obligation of Performance

In our example of students claiming a right to be provided an area for free speech, they were not only insisting on a right to act freely in that area, but they were also claiming a right to be provided adequate space and facilities. The obligation that students were here attempting to require of the school authorities was, therefore, one to provide something or to give something to the students. They were saying that they have a right to receive something, which corresponds to an obligation to provide something. In other words, the students insisted on a right of recipience which corresponds to an obligation of performance.

A number of other student claims can clearly be classified in this category of right and obligation, for example, a claim to access to certain information or a claim to be provided an education. A case involving the former situation arose in Maine, where in 1968 a student claimed that he had a right to be shown the recommendations that his high school officials were writing about him and sending to college admissions offices. The court agreed with the student and required the high school to make the recommendations available to him.

The case of a student claiming the right to an education has risen in a variety of forms in courts across the country. A good example is the *Ordway* case (1971) where school officials in Massachusets informed a high school senior that she could no longer attend regular classes because she was pregnant and unmarried. The administration was operating under a rule that provided that "whenever an unmarried girl enrolled in North Middlesex Regional High School shall be known to be pregnant, her membership in the school shall be immediately terminated." The student claimed that she had a right to be provided an education and that her pregnancy did not constitute a valid reason for depriving her of that right. After reviewing the evidence and the arguments, the court concluded its opinion in these words:

> In summary, no danger to petitioner's physical or mental health resultant from her attending classes during regular school hours has been shown; no likelihood that her presence will cause any disruption of or interference with school activities or pose a threat of harm to others has been shown; and no valid educational or other reason to justify her segregation. . . .
>
> *It would seem beyond argument that the right to receive a public school education is a basic personal right or liberty.* Consequently, the burden of justifying any school rule or regulation limiting or terminating that right is on the school authorities [italics mine].

The basic authority on which this court relied was the *Tinker* case, "where the Supreme Court limited school officials' curtailment of claimed rights of students to situations involving substantial disruption of or material interference with school activities." This is a very broad interpretation of the *Tinker* case and appears not to notice that the nature of the right claimed in *Ordway* is quite different from that claimed in *Tinker.* In *Tinker* the students were not raising the question of whether they had a right to an education, since they would have objected to any other form of punishment or curtailment as well as to expulsion. In the *Ordway* case, the student did not argue that her right to get pregnant was being curtailed. She argued that her pregnancy was not an adequate justification for curtailing her right to be provided an education. . . .

The Obligation to Proceed in an Appropriate Manner

All claims for student rights that are not characterized as claims for the right to recipience or the right to free action will fit the category of claims for the right to due process. These claims arise out of situations where the school administration is taking an action that seems to pose some threat to students, and the students claim that they deserve due process. The corresponding obligation on the part of the administrators is that they should proceed in their action in a certain specified manner that is clearly fair to all parties.

A typical example of this form of claim to rights on behalf of students is presented by the case of *Jones v. Gillespie* (1970). Here a ninth-grade student was suspended from school for taking a ten-cent box of cookies from a fellow student. The student claimed that he had a right to a hearing prior to suspension and that this right had been denied. Another way of stating the student's claim is that the authorities had an obligation to include a fair hearing as part of their response to his alleged misconduct. The court in *Jones v. Gillespie* accepted, and applied to the public school context, the proposition that due process requires a hearing whenever substantial rights of individuals are affected by government action. Once the student could show that substantial rights were threatened (presumably his right to an education), the burden was on the school to show that this was an emergency that did not allow time for a hearing. This the school failed to show. The court decree ordered that

> defendant School District shall establish, by written regulations, effective procedures to ensure conformity to the aforesaid provisions of this decree, and defendant *School District, shall, in the preparation of such regulations, consider matters including but not limited to: formation of the hearing committee, notice by the principal to the committee, time, place, notice to the student, right to counsel, evidence to be considered, form of hearing and appeals therefrom, and consequences of failure to hold a hearing within five days.* Such regulations shall be effective no later than September 30, 1970 [italics mine].

The burden of justifying the fact that correct procedures were not followed falls on the school as soon as a student can show that the procedure constituted a substantial threat and that due process was not followed. It is important, therefore, to determine what is going to count as a substantial threat. The *Madera* case in New York gives an indication of the kind of school procedure that might not be considered a substantial threat to the student. There a fourteen-year-old boy had been suspended by his principal for behavior problems. According to New York School Board rules a guidance conference is required during the period of suspension to bring together parents, teachers, counselors, and others in an attempt to resolve the conflict. The rule specifically denies student or parent the opportunity to have present at this conference an attorney representing them. Madera claimed that not allowing counsel at this conference violated his right to due process. The U.S. Court of Appeals did not agree. It found that the possible outcomes of the conference did not pose a threat serious enough to the student to warrant his attorney's being present. The student's claim to this right was, therefore, not enforced. . . .

THE SCOPE OF THE RULE

. . . We have attempted to distinguish among various categories of claims for student rights according to the character of the obligations implied by those claims. We shall now examine the nature of these claims by analyzing the rules to which they appeal. One way of understanding the importance of rules to the claim for every type of right is to remind ourselves of the manner in which enforcement of those claims is sought.

We can assume that a claim of a right is made by students, or on behalf of students, because of a desire to see the corresponding obligation either agreed to by the school officials or enforced by the judicial and executive branches of government. The process, in our society, for gaining enforcement of such a claim in the courts is to argue that the official actions of the school officials are governed by rules, that something in those rules requires the obligation that one is demanding, and that the officials are not abiding by those rules. One identifies the rule, argues that the school is bound by that rule, and then shows that his case falls within that rule.

It is not necessary, however, to look to the enforcement process in order to determine the importance of the nature of rules in claims for student rights. Once it is clear that rights and obligations are two ways of talking about one relationship, we see the importance of understanding the different categories of obligations. We also realize that what we mean by "obligation" is behavior that is prescribed by rules. Whenever we talk about obligations, we always have a rule in mind, and if the rule points to a beneficiary of the obligation, we say that the beneficiary can successfully claim a right. At the time such a right is claimed, appeal is made to what seems to be the appropriate rule. If logical categories can be found by which those rules can be organized, we will have available another framework by which to analyze claims for student rights.

The characteristic of our system of rules that seems likely to produce the most useful set of categories is the fact that some rules are created by a small number of people simply to govern relations among them, other rules are created to govern relations among larger groups of people, while some rules have to be created to regulate rulemakers. When we have identified and characterized the various categories in this range of rules, we will be able to ask of any claim to rights the scope of the rule with which it identifies itself.

Rules of the narrowest scope are those created by individual parties to regulate ways in which they interact with each other. These rules are contract relations, and in our society such privately created rules are generally upheld and enforced by courts if the parties to the contract had the authority to create rights and obligations among themselves. Quite often students will base a claim of right on what they take to be an agreement or contract with school authorities. For example, students in a particular high school may feel that because of an agreement with their principal they can claim the right to be provided a smoking lounge. Even if the students could produce evidence of that agreement, the question would be raised as to whether the principal had legal authority to enter into the agreement.

Next wider in scope to private contracts are those rules at the statutory level. They directly regulate the official actions of school administrators. A common form of claim would be an attempt to show that statutes created a specific obligation on the part of school administators and a corresponding right on the part of the students and that the administrators were not conforming to the rule.

An example of this form of claim is the case of *Jones v. Gillespie,* which resulted from a widespread practice of suspending high school students for indeterminate periods without a prior hearing. The student claimed a right to a hearing when threatened with a suspension of five days or more. In support of this claim, the student appealed to a rule at the statutory level, a section of the school code that dealt in an ambiguous manner with the question of suspension. The court upheld the student's reading of the statute. Thus, we can classify this as a claim of a right to due process that is grounded in a rule at the statute level.

The set of rules that governs the actions of legislatures is next in scope; these constitutional rules authorize and limit the scope of the statutory rules. This level of rules is most often associated with claims for student rights. When a claim is based on a rule at this level, the student is saying that not only do the actions of the administrator violate the rule, but so also does the statute that requires or allows the offending administrative action.

In the *Scoville* case the high school students asked the court to require that school officials not interfere with the students' publication of an "underground paper"; they were claiming a right to free action. To support their claim they relied on a rule from the constitutional level, the protection of free speech granted in the First Amendment. They were successful in this claim because the judge could turn to the *Tinker* decision, which had ruled that the Constitution required school officials reasonably to forecast "substantial disruption or material interference" before they could interfere with student communications.

The rules with the broadest scope in our system are the moral rules of the community. Students will at times feel that a moral rule exists on which they can base a claim, in spite of the fact that neither contracts, statutes, nor Constitution support such a rule. One example of this is the occasionally successful attempt by students to gain community support for their claim to their own smoking lounge.

Another example is the *Ordway* case, where the pregnant, unmarried student was attacking both her expulsion and the school board rule that required her expulsion. One might expect that such a rule would have been attacked on grounds that it discriminates for no good reason and that it violates the Equal Protection clause of the Constitution. But here the student was not simply claiming a right to be left alone, a claim she could have supported by appeal to a rule at the constitutional level. She was claiming a welfare right to be provided an education. It is clear from the language in the court's opinion that the student succeeded in an appeal to the level of rule higher than the Constitution, the moral rules of the community. Recall the language of the judge: "It would seem beyond argument that the right to receive a public school education is a basic personal right or liberty." We have already seen that this is not a constitutional right. . . .

SUMMARY

We have examined the nature of claims for student rights by analyzing the categories of rules on which such claims might be grounded. Students making claims, or those who must respond to those claims, will be able to communicate more effectively if they can share an understanding of the underlying nature of the claim. Are the students asserting that the administration should refrain from acting, that it should act in providing goods and services, or that they should proceed with threatening procedures in a fair and orderly manner? Are the students claiming that the obligations stem from a contract agreement they have with the administration? Or do they look to a broader, statutory rule that they feel proscribes the official actions they find offensive? Do they turn to the Constitution to support their objection to the action, or inaction, of the administrators? Or are they seeking the broadest possible base of support in the attitudes of the community?

At this point it might be helpful to enumerate the advantages gained by organizing claims for student rights according to the categories developed in this chapter.

1. The categories allow the person or institution against whom the claim has been made to determine the nature of the obligation demanded of him, and they provide the student a means of becoming clearer about his own claim. It may even be that claims of rights by students would be accepted more often by school officials if they recognized the demanded obligation as one already accepted by their school, or by other schools.

2. Each category of claim is based on a somewhat different principal or rule, which an individual claim would have to invoke before it could gain support or enforcement. It is important to recognize the basis in principle of the particular claim with which one is faced.

3. The nature of what a defending school district is going to have to prove varies from category to category, as does the question of who has the burden of defending his position in a disagreement over a claimed right.

The cause of much confusion in responding to the possible claims of student rights is the lack of clarity regarding the distinctions detailed in this chapter. It is to be hoped that the habit of applying the framework developed here will result in speedier and more effective resolution of conflict.

(Kohler, cont. from p. 189)

leave the child little opportunity for self-determination. The time has come for re-examination of such fundamental issues as the extent to which a child is entitled to seek medical and psychiatric assistance, birth-control information, and even abortion without parental consent or over parental opposition. The desirability of subjecting children to the stigma of juvenile-court proceedings merely because their conduct does not seem to accord with parental standards of governability should be the subject of careful study.

A SERIOUS COMMITMENT TO CHILDREN

Divorce, child-custody, and adoption laws and regulations, while paying obsequious obeisance to the "welfare of the child," are often—advertently or not—the means for playing out adult interests, the venting of adult anger, the serving of adult convenience, the fulfillment of adult desires. A serious commitment to children calls for a re-examination of the laws, statutes, ordinances, rules, and regulations governing marriage, divorce, custody, support, paternity, adoption, dependency, guardianship, and property rights in order to bring some clarity and coherence to a confused and often contradictory whole and to ground these policies and procedures in the primary of the child's interests.

Even though the state compels a child to attend school, his ability to attend, to be cared for, and to be given access to school are depressingly subject to considerations of color, sex, race, class, physical condition, or behavior. No child should be excluded, expelled, or suspended from such services for more than a few days unless alternative provisions for his education are available and arranged.

The rights children have in school—and out—are not those which have to be earned, but are ones whose exercise is their privilege even if they have poor judgment, are ill-informed or ill-mannered, or have contributed little or nothing to their class, school, or society.

If the choice is ultimately between what is least detrimental to the child and what is least detrimental to the adult, I profess a bias in the child's interest. I see the exercise of this preference as a means of interrupting the transmission of conflict and pathology from one generation to the next. The well-nurtured child is most likely to be the nurturing parent. We must also ask to what extent the right to be wanted, in an affectionate sense, is undercut and interfered with by our tendency toward violent resolution of conflict, both internationally and domestically.

One cannot simply assume that persons who father and mother a child are adequately prepared to be parents, to have wanted children. The opportunity for children to serve (as volunteers or workers) in a day-care program or other child- and youth-serving activity can be an important means of observing behavior and learning patterns at various ages; it provides the ideal preparation for parenthood.

It is, in a sense, to state no more than a truism that this (and any) nation's most precious natural resource is its children. To state this truism is not, however, to affirm that we have always acted in keeping with it. Nor is it to assume that the current tension in our society permits us the capability and the will so to act. From the legal point of view, we seem still to be in need of such drastic action as a new constitutional amendment, for example, to establish that all other constitutional amendments apply to young people as well as to their elders. From the extra- and supra-legal point of view, we must first acknowledge the right of all children and their families to respect and dignity. And before that can happen we must be ready to protect every child and his family from social institutions that are abusive, even when well meaning. We must free ourselves of threat of domestic and foreign turmoil if the inequities of hierarchies based on race, sex, and class are to be effectively engaged. The rights of children can, in the final analysis, be attained only in a society whose institutions, public and private, are open and humane.

At this point it is possible only to offer guidelines for evaluating current practices and developing strategies for their improvement. New approaches are needed, not simply the modification and expansion of current practices and services. We have to develop and support sound options based upon the following principles:

> The birth, growth and developmental needs of children and their families must be met as these needs are manifested among children at different ages, in differing sequences and patterns, in differing circumstances.
>
> The needs of all chilldren must be met regardless of socioeconomic status, race, sex, or residence.

Both the family and the society share the responsibility for meeting these needs. The responsibility of the child—self-discipline, respect for others, full development—that is necessary for the child's development results from the family's and society's responsible behavior toward him.

Services must be equal—in access, control, and quality—without regard to the financial circumstances of the family. They must be tailored to the needs of the individual and delivered by persons and institutions fully and directly accountable to the individual recipient and the community of which he is a part.

AGAINST TYRANNY OF SERVICES

In the active pursuit of the conditions to facilitate the development of the child into an adult able both to influence and to adapt to society, emphasis must be placed upon the design and establishment of opportunities, not the creation of a tyranny of services. In so doing it must be assured that the availability of the service not become a requirement for its utilization.

A system of multiple sources of support and protection would seem more likely to assure the expression of children's rights. Those persons and institutions—parents, school, social-welfare agency, public official, governmental unit—charged with the duty of promoting, protecting, and implementing the rights of children must be held legally accountable for their failures and deficiencies in so doing. A variation on this point is to make it a positive obligation of all school personnel and others who have authority over students to take specific steps to protect the students' exercise of their legal rights. Citizen complaint suits could be brought in cases of dereliction.

Persons and agencies need to be established and charged with the obligation of seeking the enforcement of the rights of children. Various forms are possible—ombudsman, child advocate, enlarged access to counsel, etc; perhaps some combination of these and other means may be best. In addition, ways must be developed to involve the children themselves in protecting their own rights.

BASIC RIGHTS

The categorization of rights that follows is neither unique nor original, as one can see by comparing the basic rights listed both in the Children's Charter of the White House Conference of 1930 and the Joint Commission on Mental Health report *Crisis in Child Mental Health: Challenge for the 1970s.*

The Right to Grow In a Society That Respects the Dignity of Life, Free of Poverty, Discrimination, and Other Forms of Degradation

Children must have the opportunity to live and grow in a society free of war and ever-present threats of war, a society that demonstrates its commitment to its children by wiping out hunger, poverty, racism, and sexism—in other words, a child must have the opportunity to live in an ordered world, a world in which there is an opportunity to anticipate the consequences of action, the effect of effort.

The Right to Be Born a Wanted Child

We define a wanted child as a child who is wanted, in an affectionate and nourishing sense, on a continuing basis by at least one adult—a child who can feel that he is, and will continue to be, valued by those who take care of him.

It is well known that there are unwanted pregnancies that result in wanted children; that there are wanted pregnancies that result in unwanted children. The child who is wanted begins life under conditions that favor his development. Nevertheless, his parents will need various kinds of assistance and services in order to sustain his healthy growth and development over time and through the vicissitudes of life. Particular emphasis must be placed on developing psychological supports and tangible services on a neighborhood and community basis.

For those who wish to prevent a pregnancy, there should be easy accessibility to information on contraception and family planning. Abortions should be available; they should be neither prohibited nor compelled. The parent who brings a child into the world and discovers he does not want him should not be forced or shamed into keeping him. There should be available nurturing adults who become the real parents of the child whose biological family is unable to take care of him. Ritualistic adherence to the biological or blood tie has frequently led the law to preclude the child's having an opportunity to be wanted.

The financial incapacity of the new parent should not, as it too frequently does, preclude the assurance of continuity of adequate, nourishing care of the child. Laws should assure financial and other tangible supports so that adults can fulfill the parental role. The arbitrary categorizing of the non-biological parent as a "foster" parent, which carries with it vulnerability to interruption and discontinuity of the relationship, could be largely alleviated through changes in existing laws and policies. When children's institutions or other group-care settings need to be available, they must be so staffed as to ensure closeness with, and continuity of care by, significant adults.

All pregnant women, regardless of their class, location, or marital status, must have adequate nutrition, excellent prenatal care, and skilled delivery, in order to ensure healthy children. Our technical skills and economic capability make such care possible.

All newly delivered mothers should be under the care of specially trained nursing personnel; and paraprofessionals trained to the needs of mothers, fathers, and children should be made available to help parents with home and child on an ongoing basis. The services of these paraprofessionals can be supported, as needed, by those of nurses, social workers, and physicians.

Taking the concept of a wanted child seriously also requires us to find ways, without intruding upon the rights of adults, to identify unwanted (i.e., very poorly nurtured) children as early as possible in order that their opportunities to grow and develop in a healthy way may be ensured. Although the interests of the parents as well as those of the child must be safeguarded, we leave many children too long in a desperate situation in their own families. Our capacity to identify maternal depression and early mother-child alienation, for example, means that we cannot in good conscience, and must not, permit psychotic children and depressed parents to develop when we know and can provide the cure via intervention by paraprofessionals with professional consultation.

Other children, we take out of their families too soon. By "too soon" I mean we take children away from their families without having mobilized the kinds of help that might enable the family to maintain or reconstitute itself, and the parents, through such help, to function adequately as parents. In temporary placements and in foster care we are often confronted with a similar problem. Frequently we must ask at what point the biological parent has, in a psychological sense, lost his status as a real parent. The law must come to recognize that "foster" parents can become "real" parents.

To take the concept of being a wanted child seriously requires re-examination of many of our current policies with regard to compulsory education, the concept of truancy, schools for boys and girls under juvenile proceedings, etc. If these were examined in terms of what it means to be a wanted child, there is reason to believe we would modify or reorder many of our ideas about such "solutions."

The Right To Grow Up Nurtured By Affectionate Parents

Here we see an instance of the interconnection between the first rights we have set forth: if a parent is degraded by society or if the absence of birth-control or abortion facilities results in an unwanted child, the likelihood of the child's growing up nurtured by affectionate parents is sharply diminished.

The special possibilities for natural parents to play a nurturing role should not blind us to the possibility, if the child's best interests call for it, that this role may by played by one or more other adults. This possibility should not be hampered by the stigmatizing of "foster parents" or the tenuousness and lack of permanence that today too frequently are made inherent in foster-home or other, similar placements.

Child-centered divorce laws should be required to ensure that the welfare of children of the marriage is primary. This would mean that the capacity for nurturing and loving of the child that is required for child development would determine the parent most capable of exercising custody. It would also mean that when parents were using the child against each other, the court would provide a nurturing and loving foster home and an adoptive family, under continuous professional supervision. Here anticipatory guidance of new parents would be provided to ensure an optimal environment for the child.

One of the most effective ways to help young people experience closeness and affection in preparation for marriage is through group projects. Group projects, beginning in the fourth and fifth grades, that involve children in the practice of participatory democracy in the classroom, where they assess their own learning and teaching and gather data and make recommendations on issues of major concern to their community (e.g., better housing, pollution control, safety measures in the streets, multiple use of school plants for community functions) teach children how to obtain facts, evaluate them, and come to rational, workable conclusions. Such preparation for responsible citizenship is essential. Older children can act as resource persons and guides to resource materials and thus enhance the relationships between age groups. Such close involvement around actual problem-solving experience in the schools and community brings about mutual respect, a sense of warmth, closeness, and regard for the contributions of others. . . .

Disruption of the family and weakening of the family structure and bonds of affection should rarely be permitted. Child-centered criminal and civil law would not, as happens now, remove parents from their families for minor crimes and misdemeanors, i.e., failure to pay parking fines, rents, etc. The court would be enjoined to consider the primacy of the family and be obligated to strengthen it in any consideration of punishment for minor crimes or misdemeanors. Opportunities to make restitution by meaningful weekend work designed to clean up and beautify the environment should be considered by courts as more beneficial than imprisonment to the defendant's learning citizen responsibility and parental responsibility. In some instances conjoint work projects with teen-agers in the family may enhance family unity and decrease criminal tendencies, especially if other opportunities to maintain one's job and do it more effectively are part of the court's injunction, as is current in some county courts.

When parents have been imprisoned, maintenance of some degree of stability in family ties requires the utilization of liberal visiting privileges or provision of live-in situations in order for the mother to care for small infants, as is currently the practice in some modern institutions. Similarly, the effect upon children should be a factor in the implementation of the Selective Service laws.

The Right To Be A Child During Childhood And To Have Meaningful Choices In The Process of Maturation And Development And A Meaningful Voice In The Community

Too-early forcing of choices, too-quick labeling and categorizing of children, and all-encompassing and permanent record-keeping and stigmatizing rob the child of the opportunity to be a child, the right to play, investigate, explore, relate, test, try out, experiment, rebel. The balance between gathering and recording information about the child, his activities, feelings, and attitudes as a means of aiding and abetting his growth and the very same activities as a means of stigmatizing, categorizing, labeling, and shunting the child into one or another "track" is too tenuous to allow mere expression of good intent or goodwill to justify such activities. Continuing attention needs to be given to how and by whom such information is collected, by whom and for what purposes it is used, and for how long and in what way it is maintained. Prevention of abuse is promoted by openness concerning the existence of such records, access to them by the party concerned, opportunity to comment upon and challenge particular items, and positive legal sanctions to assure their non-harmful use.

A child has the right to learn through trial and error, to try a variety of educational experiences, and, if necessary to fail without acquiring stigmas or labels that carry the force of a continuing burden. Laws and police practices, school regulations, and social welfare agency procedures must not stigmatize children as criminals, deviates, or disruptors.

In a rapidly changing, pluralistic society we have a vital need to help children learn flexibility, openness, tolerance of others, capability for leadership, and capacity for living with the dissonance and differences made inevitable by technological change. The right of children to such an upbringing faces us squarely with the need for basic respect for differences through respect and understanding of minority groups. We must not only allow and enable minorities to preserve their heritage as a basis for stability of children but we must, more importantly, be committed to their self-determination and economic security of having parents who know their origins and can communicate them and thus provide the heritage and history that offer the flexible stability so necessary for meaningful change and ready adaptation to solving new problems. This requires a new and flexible educational system, ready to help children learn flexibility and problem-solving, unlike today's rigid schools.

Children raised in their own culture and capable of valuing it, seeing their parents as dignified and significant adults, are secure enough to make free choices about their own future. They need assurance of a decent standard of living themselves in every setting to choose the best values of each world and to love and provide security for their own children.

Future shock, with resulting apathy and immobilization, occurs primarily in children and adults whose heritage and relations with their parents have been insecure, who have shrunk from involvement and feared commitment, since they had no parental and adult models to follow.

We must provide:

(*a*) self-determination through community control of the institutions that serve the citizens and development of indigenous community participation and leadership in these institutions;

(*b*) a culturally relevant education in the family, related to the values of the family, to reinforce self-esteem and a positive self-image;

(*c*) models of effective parents through economic security and a meaningful voice in decisions that affect the parents' lives. Such parents are the living embodiment of the history and culture of their people and are able to give their children a sense of continuity, security, and free choice about how they will live their lives and rear their own children.

The Right To Be Educated To The Limits of Individual Capacity and Through Processes Designed to Elicit Them

Children learn best by active involvement, by doing, experiencing, engaging. Children have a right to learn through participation in making the decisions that affect their lives and in significant tasks of sharing and being of service. They develop social responsibility as participating citizens. They have a right to guidance from models whose love and concern are expressed in ways that lead to self-reliance, self-discipline, and self-realization.

Too often, education stifles the spirit of inquiry, curiosity, experimentation, creativity. These are qualities that must be nurtured and encouraged.

A child has a right to learn through trial and error, to try a variety of experiences. Educators and others with responsibility for the child's education are obliged to use their observations on behalf of the child, to help him use his talents in ways most satisfying to him and most useful to society. . . .

The Right To Societal Mechanisms To Make The Foregoing Rights Effective

Schools, welfare agencies, police and courts, and mental-health and health institutions are all enmeshed in undermining individual and social differences and abusing their clients' rights through a system of non-service or, at best, brutalized service, as black, Indian, Spanish-speaking, and Oriental adults and children can all testify. To prevent further alienation, social institutions must be controlled and directed by those whom they are to serve. Inherent here is our commitment to meaningful employment and a decent standard of living for all

American citizens. Only under such conditions can social institutions actually reflect the citizen's concerns and needs in a changing scene.

Most observers would agree that our present system falls short of this standard and that

> service delivery arrangements are geared more to professional and field needs than to those of children;
>
> we deal with crises more than prevention;
>
> we reach only a fraction of the population in need and, all too often, with too little, too late;
>
> we know that problems often begin in infancy, yet we develop programs that intervene after this critical period.

To establish systems that carry out our stated commitment to children, we need to revise the basis upon which services are offered, provide instruments and agents who act on behalf of children, bring those to be served into the governance of programs, and train and utilize new personnel.

Individuals, agencies, and public bodies providing services to fulfill children's rights must be legally accountable for their performance. Such a recommendation has consequences for malpractice liability, sovereign immunity, the defenses of legislative domain, and professional standards and practices. . . .

Child-advocate services should be established to assert children's rights. Such services must be accessible and available to every child, able to operate effectively within the context of each of the institutions that impinge upon the life of the child—schools, courts, police, child-care agencies, etc. Such advocates should seek redress through both individual "casework" approaches and more general social action. Such an advocacy service should include both local and national components: what is called for is both a national "Office of Child Advocacy," operating at the highest governmental level as an advocate and inside "lobby" on behalf of children, and local child-advocate services responsive to a local constituency.

We have often limited those who may serve children by arbitrary and irrelevant standards regarding formal training, credentials, etc. The experience over the past several years in the utilization of paraprofessional workers in schools, health and welfare agencies, courts and counseling programs, etc., argues for a broadening of the definition of those who can and should serve.

Training must also provide for understanding the contingencies of any professional's or paraprofessional's actions on the child's next stage of development and their effect on the integrity of the family. Thus teachers, judges, and medical personnel must be aware of their importance and impact on the child and family and of how their behavior serves as a model of adult behavior for the child. . . .

Training of adolescents to serve children in various paraprofessional roles not only is excellent paraprofessional experience but also enables the child to learn from a person near his age and to model himself after a peer. . . .

Sufficient paraprofessionals and trained volunteers, including parents and older children, can provide individual attention. Nurse practitioners and trained paraprofessionals can provide individualized well-child care and refer sick children to physicians. Our failure to take extensive action in this direction means we do not care to do what is possible for the health, mental health, and well-being of all children.

POSTSCRIPT

WHAT RIGHTS DO STUDENTS HAVE?

The principles that children are not only entitled to be heard but that they can best determine what is in their self-interest seem to be emerging from the legal and professional dialogue concerning the rights of children and youth. There is a discernible trend away from official unilateral decisions toward decisions based on much wider considerations.

Components of this movement away from a totalitarian school atmosphere are described in a number of recent publications, including *Growing Pains: Uses of School Conflict* (1974) by John P. DeCecco and Arlene K. Richards; *Student Rights and Discipline* (1975) by Edward T. Ladd, with John C. Walden; *The Civil Rights of Students* (1975) by David Schimmel and Louis Fischer; "Child Advocacy: The Next Step," *New York University Education Quarterly* (Spring 1976) by Donald N. Bersoff; and *The Children's Rights Movement* (1977), edited by Beatrice Gross and Ronald Gross. The latter volume contains articles by some of the foremost scholars in the field of childhood, among them Uri Bronfenbrenner, Margaret Mead, Robert Coles, Thomas Cottle and Lloyd deMause.

These works concern the problems of physical abuse and mental torture of children, environmental effects on growth and well-being, violations of privacy and due process, discriminatory exclusion, and the lack of options within the present schooling process. A consistent theme trailing through many of these books is that if increasing self-management responsibility is to be granted to the young they must be better prepared for it. A clear message is that the schools must become places in which the young learn to choose and to take responsibility for their choices.

Many issues remain unresolved in the realm of the rights, responsibilities, and opportunities of students. Perhaps most basic to all is the issue of the right *not* to go to school. This issue serves as the initial point of departure in the final part of this book.

David Attie

PART III

How Can Education Be Improved?

ISSUE 13

SHOULD COMPULSORY SCHOOLING BE ABOLISHED?

The argument between advocates of formalism and "structure" and advocates of informalism and "freedom" perhaps reached its zenith in the 1970s. With the publication of Ivan Illich's *Deschooling Society* in 1970 a new point of view was added to the dialogue regarding the ways to improve educational quality: to improve education, eliminate schools.

According to Illich, compulsory, government-controlled schooling treats knowledge as a commodity, deadens the individual's will to learn, and establishes an artificial structure for "success" which socially damages those who are unable to take advantage of the system. He further contends that "the whole enterprise of formal education is based on the false assumption that learning will be assured, maximized, and made more efficient if it is administered by specially prepared professionals in a special place at a prescribed time according to a preconceived plan to a group of children of a certain age."

To replace compulsory schooling, Illich suggests the formation of "learning networks" which would provide "convivial access" to tools, techniques, and services. He envisions communities in which people of all ages would come together to exchange skills and ideas, assisted by widely expanded reference services. In such an atmosphere, learning would be real rather than artificial, and people would be evaluated on the basis of what they know and can do rather than by the number of years of schooling completed.

Illich's detractors feel that his ideas are an invitation to chaos, that he offers no constructive educational theory, and that the poor, with whom he obviously sympathizes, will be further disadvantaged because of access difficulties. In a particularly sharp attack ("Illich's De-schooled Utopia," *Encounter*, January

1972), Sidney Hook contends that Illich's "absurd extremism warrants little attention from anyone endowed with a normal common sense."

But the deschooling viewpoint *has* gained wide attention. It has prompted a renewed concern about a basic and difficult question: What is our warrant for determining what children, youth, and adults shall learn and how they shall learn it? The root issue is the right of government to intervene in people's lives.

Historically, compulsory schooling has been justified in a variety of ways—parental inability to educate their offspring, a social need to elevate the level of moral behavior, the need to maintain the social and economic order, the desire to widen opportunities for social mobility, the need to acculturate an immigrant population, and the need for a vehicle for passing on the cultural heritage and "civilizing" the young. The residue of these and other justifications forms the "hidden curriculum" which Illich and his followers see as manipulative. Michael Katz (in "The Present Moment in Educational Reform," *Harvard Educational Review,* August 1971) finds that many people have arrived at the position that "the attempt to teach patriotism, conventional morality, or even their opposite in a *compulsory* public institution represents a gross violation of civil rights."

Along with the problem of intervention goes the issue of whether schooling can be shaped to make justified intervention worthwhile. Illich explains in the following selection why he feels schooling is unreformable. Some leaders of the reform movement—John Holt in particular—have indeed drifted toward the deschooling thesis. Others feel that Illich's campaign is based on faulty assumptions and that internal reform of the schools is still possible. The following selection by Philip Jackson represents the latter point of view.

Ivan Illich

WE MUST DISESTABLISH SCHOOLING

Two centuries ago the United States led the world in a movement to disestablish the monopoly of a single church. Now we need the constitutional disestablishment of the monopoly of the school, and thereby of a system which legally combines prejudice with discrimination. The first article of a bill of rights for a modern, humanist society would correspond to the First Amendment to the U.S. Constitution: "The State shall make no law with respect to the establishment of education." There shall be no ritual obligatory for all.

To make this disestablishment effective, we need a law forbidding discrimination in hiring, voting, or admission to centers of learning based on previous attendance at some curriculum. This guarantee would not exclude performance tests of competence for a function or role, but would remove the present absurd discrimination in favor of the person who learns a given skill with the largest expenditure of public funds or—what is equally likely—has been able to obtain a diploma which has no relation to any useful skill or job. Only by protecting the citizen from being disqualified by anything in his career in school can a constitutional disestablishment of school become psychologically effective.

Neither learning nor justice is promoted by schooling because educators insist on packaging instruction with certification. Learning and the assignment of social roles are melted into schooling. Yet to learn means to acquire a new skill or insight, while promotion depends on an opinion which others have formed. Learning frequently is the result of instruction, but selection for a role or category in the job market increasingly depends on mere length of attendance.

Instruction is the choice of circumstances which facilitate learning. Roles are assigned by setting a curriculum of conditions which the candidate must meet if he is to make the grade. School links instruction—but not learning—to these roles. This is neither reasonable or liberating. It is not reasonable because it does not link relevant qualities or competence to roles, but rather the process by which such qualities are supposed to be acquired. It is not

Continued on p. 212

From pp. 11–19 and 22–23 in *Deschooling Society* by Ivan Illich, Vol. 41 of the World Perspective Series edited by Ruth Nanda Anshen.

Philip W. Jackson

DESCHOOLING? NO!

The criticism of schools is a profitable pastime, as a visit to our local bookstore or a glance at the current issue of almost any of our most widely circulated magazines will quickly show. There, in volume after volume and article after article, some of our most well-schooled and well-read journalists, novelists, academicians, ex-teachers, and just plain critics describe the evils of our educational system and discuss what should be done about them. The quality of the writing and the sharpness of the criticism vary from one author to the next, but the overall tone is one of uniform dissatisfaction with things as they are.

Despite the up-to-the-minute freshness of much of this writing, the fact that many people seem to be unhappy with current educational practices is not exactly new. Our schools have long been the target of critics from all walks of life. Moreover, it would be surprising if this were not so, given the centrality of schooling in the lives of our citizens and the complexity of the institution designed to perform this important service.

What *is* new in the current situation is a marked increased in the amount of criticism, reflecting a corresponding growth in the size of the critics' audience. What is also new and even more important in the current scene is a marked radicalization of the critics' proposals for change.

Until quite recently, the desirability of schools and of compulsory attendance by the young were more or less taken for granted by friend and foe alike. The aim of both, even of those who were must unhappy with the status quo, was not to do away with schools as we now know them, but somehow to improve their operation.

Now from a growing number of writers—including such prominent critics as Ivan Illich, Everett Reimer, John Holt, and the late Paul Goodman—the message is that improving what we presently have is not enough. Today's schools, so the argument goes, have outlived or outgrown their usefulness. They are institutional dinosaurs that should either be hunted down or allowed to sink of their own dead weight into the swamps of academia.

Continued on p. 217

From *Today's Education,* November 1972. Reprinted by permission of *Today's Education* and the author.

(Illich, cont. from p. 210)
liberating or educational because school reserves instruction to those whose every step in learning fits previously approved measures of social control.

Curriculum has always been used to assign social rank. At times it could be prenatal: karma ascribes you to a caste and lineage to the aristocracy. Curriculum could take the form of a ritual, of sequential sacred ordinations, or it could consist of a succession of feats in war or hunting, or further advancement could be made to depend on a series of previous princely favors. Universal schooling was meant to detach role assignment from personal life history: it was meant to give everybody an equal chance to any office. Even now many people wrongly believe that school ensures the dependence of public trust on relevant learning achievements. However, instead of equalizing chances, the school system has monopolized their distribution.

To detach competence from curriculum, inquiries into a man's learning history must be made taboo, like inquiries into his political affiliation, church attendance, lineage, sex habits, or racial background. Laws forbidding discrimination on the basis of prior schooling must be enacted. Laws, of course, cannot stop prejudice against the unschooled—nor are they meant to force anyone to intermarry with an autodidact—but they can discourage unjustified discrimination.

A second major illusion on which the school system rests is that most learning is the result of teaching. Technique, it is true, may contribute to certain kinds of learning under certain circumstancs. But most people acquire most of their knowledge outside school, and in school only insofar as school, in a few rich countries, has become their place of confinement during an increasing part of their lives.

Most learning happens casually, and even most intentional learning is not the result of programmed instruction. Normal children learn their first language casually, although faster if their parents pay attention to them. Most people who learn a second language well do so as a result of odd circumstances and not of sequential teaching. They go to live with their grandparents, they travel, or they fall in love with a foreigner. Fluency in reading is also more often than not a result of such extracurricular activities. Most people who read widely, and with pleasure, merely believe that they learned to do so in school; when challenged, they easily discard this illusion.

But the fact that a great deal of learning even now seems to happen casually and as a by-product of some other activity defined as work or leisure does not mean that planned learning does not benefit from planned instruction and that both do not stand in need of improvement. The strongly motivated student who is faced with the task of acquiring a new and complex skill may benefit greatly from the discipline now associated with the old-fashioned schoolmaster who taught reading, Hebrew, catechism, or multiplication by rote. School has now made this kind of drill teaching rare and disreputable, yet there are many skills which a motivated student with normal aptitude can master in a matter of a few months if taught in this traditional way. This is as true of codes as of their encipherment; of second and third languages as of reading and writing; and equally of special languages such as algebra, computer programming, chemical analysis, or of manual skills like typing, watchmaking, plumbing, wiring,

TV repair; or for that matter dancing, driving, and diving.

In certain cases acceptance into a learning program aimed at a specific skill might presuppose competence in some other skill, but it should certainly not be made to depend upon the process by which such prerequisite skills were acquired. TV repair presupposes literacy and some math; diving, good swimming; and driving, very little of either.

Progress in learning skills is measurable. The optimum resources in time and materials needed by an average motivated adult can be easily estimated. The cost of teaching a second Western European language to a high level of fluency ranges between four and six hundred dollars in the United States, and for an Oriental tongue the time needed for instruction might be doubled. This would still be very little compared with the cost of twelve years of schooling in New York City (a condition for acceptance of a worker into the Sanitation Department)—almost fifteen thousand dollars. No doubt not only the teacher but also the printer and the pharmacist protect their trades through the public illusion that training for them is very expensive.

At present schools pre-empt most educational funds. Drill instruction which costs less than comparable schooling is now a privilege of those rich enough to bypass the schools, and those whom either the army or big business sends through in-service training. In a program of progressive deschooling of U.S. education, at first the resources available for drill training would be limited. But ultimately there should be no obstacle for anyone at any time of his life to be able to choose instruction among hundreds of definable skills at public expense.

Right now educational credit good at any skill center could be provided in limited amounts for people of all ages, and not just to the poor. I envisage such credit in the form of an educational passport or an "edu-credit card" provided to each citizen at birth. In order to favor the poor, who probably would not use their yearly grants early in life, a provision could be made that interest accrued to later users of cumulated "entitlements." Such credits would permit most people to acquire the skills most in demand, at their convenience, better, faster, cheaper, and with fewer undesirable side effects than in school.

Potential skill teachers are never scarce for long because, on the one hand, demand for a skill grows only with its performance within a community and, on the other, a man exercising a skill could also teach it. But, at present, those using skills which are in demand and do require a human teacher are discouraged from sharing these skills with others. This is done either by teachers who monopolize the licenses or by unions which protect their trade interests. Skill centers which would be judged by customers on their results, and not on the personnel they employ or the process they use, would open unsuspected working opportunities, frequently even for those who are now considered unemployable. Indeed, there is no reason why such skill centers should not be at the work place itself, with the employer and his work force supplying instruction as well as jobs to those who choose to use their educational credits in this way.

In 1956 there arose a need to teach Spanish quickly to several hundred teachers, social workers, and ministers from the New York Archdiocese so that they could communicate with Puerto Ricans. My friend Gerry Morris announced over a Spanish radio station that he needed native speakers from Harlem. Next day some two hundred teenagers lined up in front of his office, and he selected four dozen of them—many of them school dropouts. He trained them in the use of the U.S. Foreign Service Institute (FSI) Spanish manual, designed for use by linguists with graduate training, and within a week his teachers were on their own—each in charge of four New Yorkers who wanted to speak the language. Within six months the mission was accomplished. Cardinal Spellman could claim that he had 127 parishes in which at least three staff members could communicate in Spanish. No school program could have matched these results.

Skill teachers are made scarce by the belief in the value of licenses. Certification constitutes a form of market manipulation and is plausible only to a schooled mind. Most teachers of arts and trades are less skillful, less inventive, and less communicative than the best craftsmen and tradesmen. Most high-school teachers of Spanish or French do not speak the language as correctly as their pupils might after half a year of competent drills. Experiments conducted by Angel Quintero in Puerto Rico suggest that many young teen-agers, if given the proper incentives, programs, and access to tools, are better than most schoolteachers at introducing their peers to the scientific exploration of plants, stars, and matter, and to the discovery of how and why a motor or a radio functions.

Opportunities for skill-learning can be vastly multiplied if we open the "market." This depends on matching the right teacher with the right student when he is highly motivated in an intelligent program, without the constraint of curriculum.

Free and competing drill instruction is a subversive blasphemy to the orthodox educator. It dissociates the acquisition of skills from "humane" education, which schools package together, and thus it promotes unlicensed learning no less than unlicensed teaching for unpredictable purposes.

There is currently a proposal on record which seems at first to make a great deal of sense. It has been prepared by Christopher Jencks of the Center for the Study of Public Policy and is sponsored by the Office of Economic Opportunity. It proposes to put educational "entitlements" or tuition grants into the hands of parents and students for expenditure in the schools of their choice. Such individual entitlements could indeed be an important step in the right direction. We need a guarantee of the right of each citizen to an equal share of tax-derived educational resources, the right to verify this share, and the right to sue for it if denied. It is one form of a guarantee against regressive taxation.

The Jencks proposal, however, begins with the ominous statement that "conservatives, liberals, and radicals have all complained at one time or another that the American educational system gives professional educators too little incentive to provide high quality education to most children." The proposal condemns itself by proposing tuition grants which would have to be spent on schooling.

This is like giving a lame man a pair of crutches and stipulating that he use them only if the ends are tied together. As the proposal for tuition grants now stands, it plays into the hands not only of the professional educators but of racists, promoters of religious schools, and others whose interests are socially divisive. Above all, educational entitlements restricted to use within schools play into the hands of all those who want to continue to live in a society in which social advancement is tied not to proven knowledge but to the learning pedigree by which it is supposedly acquired. This discrimination in favor of schools which dominates Jencks's discussion on refinancing education could discredit one of the most critically needed principles for educational reform: the return of initiative and accountability for learning to the learner or his most immediate tutor.

The deschooling of society implies a recognition of the two-faced nature of learning. An insistence on skill drill alone could be a disaster; equal emphasis must be placed on other kinds of learning. But if schools are the wrong places for learning a skill, they are even worse places for getting an education. School does both tasks badly, partly because it does not distinguish between them. School is inefficient in skill instruction especially because it is curricular. In most schools a program which is meant to improve one skill is chained always to another irrelevant task. History is tied to advancement in math, and class attendance to the right to use the playground.

Schools are even less efficient in the arrangement of the circumstances which encourage the open-ended, exploratory use of acquired skills, for which I will reserve the term "liberal education." The main reason for this is that school is obligatory and becomes schooling for schooling's sake: an enforced stay in the company of teachers, which pays off in the doubtful privilege of more such company. Just as skill instruction must be freed from curricular restraints, so must liberal education be dissociated from obligatory attendance. Both skill-learning and education for inventive and creative behavior can be aided by institutional arrangement, but they are of a different, frequently opposed nature.

Most skills can be acquired and improved by drills, because skill implies the mastery of definable and predictable behavior. Skill instruction can rely, therefore, on the simulation of circumstances in which the skill will be used. Education in the exploratory and creative use of skills, however, cannot rely on drills. Education can be the outcome of instruction, though instruction of a kind fundamentally opposed to drill. It relies on the relationship between partners who already have some of the keys which give access to memories stored in and by the community. It relies on the critical intent of all those who use memories creatively. It relies on the surprise of the unexpected question which opens new doors for the inquirer and his partner.

The skill instructor relies on the arrangement of set circumstances which permit the learner to develop standard responses. The educational guide or master is concerned with helping matching partners to meet so that learning can take place. He matches individuals starting from their own, unresolved questions. At the most he helps the pupil to formulate his puzzlement since only a clear statement will give him the power to find his match, moved like him, at the moment, to explore the same issue in the same context.

Matching partners for educational purposes initially seems more difficult to imagine than finding skill instructors and partners for a game. One reason is the deep fear which school has implanted in us, a fear which makes us censorious. The unlicensed exchange of skills—even undesirable skills—is more predictable and therefore seems less dangerous than the unlimited opportunity for meeting among people who share an issue which for them, at the moment, is socially, intellectually, and emotionally important.

The Brazilian teacher Paulo Freire knows this from experience. He discovered that any adult can begin to read in a matter of forty hours if the first words he deciphers are charged with political meaning. Freire trains his teachers to move into a village and to discover the words which designate current important issues, such as the access to a well or the compound interest on the debts owed to the *patron*. In the evening the villagers meet for the discussion of these key words. They begin to realize that each word stays on the blackboard even after its sound has faded. The letters continue to unlock reality and to make it manageable as a problem. I have frequently witnessed how discussants grow in social awareness and how they are impelled to take political action as fast as they learn to read. They seem to take reality into their hands as they write it down.

I remember the man who complained about the weight of pencils; they were difficult to handle because they did not weigh as much as a shovel; and I remember another who on his way to work stopped with his companions and wrote the word they were discussing with his hoe on the ground: "*agua*." Since 1962 my friend Freire has moved from exile to exile, mainly because he refuses to conduct his sessions around words which are preselected by approved educators, rather than those which his discussants bring to the class.

The educational matchmaking among people who have been successfully schooled is a different task. Those who do not need such assistance are a minority, even among the readers of serious journals. The majority cannot and should not be rallied for discussion around a slogan, a word, or a picture. But the idea remains the same: they should be able to meet around a problem chosen and defined by their own initiative. Creative, exploratory learning requires peers currently puzzled about the same terms or problems. Large universities make the futile attempt to match them by multiplying their courses, and they generally fail since they are bound to curriculum, course structure, and bureaucratic administration. In schools, including universities, most resources are spent to purchase the time and motivation of a limited number of people to take up predetermined problems in a ritually defined setting. The most radical alternative to school would be a network or service which gave each man the same opportunity to share his current concern with others motivated by the same concern. . . .

Both the exchange of skills and matching of partners are based on the assumption that education for all means education by all. Not the draft into a specialized institution but only the mobilization of the whole population can lead to popular culture. The equal right of each man to exercise his competence to learn and to instruct is now pre-empted by certified teachers. The teachers' competence, in turn, is restricted to what may be done in school. And, further, work and leisure are alienated from each other as a result: the spectator and the worker alike are supposed to arrive at the work place all ready to fit into a routine prepared for them. Adaptation in the form of a product's design, instruction, and publicity shapes them for their role as much as formal education by schooling. A radical alternative to a schooled society requires not only new formal mechanisms for the formal acquisition of skills and their educational use. A deschooled society implies a new approach to incidental or informal education.

Incidental education cannot any longer return to the forms which learning took in the village or the medieval town. Traditional society was more like a set of concentric circles of meaningful structures, while modern man must learn how to find meaning in many structures to which he is only marginally related. In the village, language and architecture and work and religion and family customs were consistent with one another, mutually explanatory and reinforcing. To grow into one implied a growth into the others. Even specialized apprenticeship was a by-product of specialized activities, such as shoemaking or the singing of psalms. If an apprentice never became a master or a scholar, he still contributed to making shoes or to making church services solemn. Education did not compete for time with either work or leisure. Almost all education was complex, lifelong, and unplanned.

Contemporary society is the result of conscious designs, and educational opportunities must be designed into them. Our reliance on specialized, full-time instruction through school will now decrease, and we must find more ways to learn and teach: the educational quality of all institutions must increase again. But this is a very ambiguous forecast. It could mean that men in the modern city will be increasingly the victims of an effective process of total instruction and manipulation once they are deprived of even the tenuous pretense of critical independence which liberal schools now provide for at least some of their pupils.

It could also mean that men will shield themselves less behind certificates acquired in school and thus gain in courage to "talk back" and thereby control and instruct the institutions in which they participate. To ensure the latter we must learn to estimate the social value of work and leisure by the educational give-and-take for which they offer opportunity. Effective participation in the politics of a street, a work place, the library, a new program, or a hospital is therefore the best measuring stick to evaluate their level as educational institutions.

(Jackson, cont. from p. 211)

The aggressive brashness of such a charge, with its not-so-subtle promise of a good old-fashioned free-for-all between defenders of our schools and their attackers, is bound to generate excitement and to bring out crowds of onlookers. And, clearly, the school-is-dead argument has done just that. Its proponents appear on talk shows, testify before Congressional committees, are given front-page space in Sunday magazine sections, and are even in demand as speakers at educational conventions!

For those of us who work in these allegedly dead or dying institutions, living, as it were, like parasites ecologically tied to the fate of our dinosaur hosts, there is the serious question of what to do in the face of such allegations. Should we simply ignore them and get on with our work? Should we pause to reply? Might we, in a more hopeful vein, actually learn something from those who would have us go out of business and, armed with that new learning, return with even greater strength and deepened conviction to the task at hand? In my judgment, there is something to be said on behalf of each of these alternatives.

At first glance, the strategy of simply ignoring the deschoolers does seem a bit foolhardy, if not downright stupid. It brings to mind images of Nero with his legendary fiddle or of ostriches with their heads stuck in the sand.

How dare we ignore the enemy veritably clamoring at our gates? The answer, in part, depends on how serious we judge the threat to be, a judgment that requires a detailed examination of the critics' charges. If Rome is *really* burning or if the ostrich hunters are *really* nearby, then larger numbers of us had better turn from whatever we are doing and consider what should be done about the disturbance. This involves becoming critics of the critics, so to speak, an alternative about which more will be said later.

But even if the threat is real, the fact remains that we do have schools that have to be run as best we know how. No matter what the future holds, millions of students and the public at large are counting on us to perform those duties for which we are being paid. Teaching, if it is done well, and school administration, if it is done at all, are full-time jobs, requiring almost all the available time and energy of those who engage in them.

What with daily classes, preparing lessons, grading papers, attending meetings, consulting with parents, and all the other things he is expected to do, there is not much time left for the average teacher to man the barricades, even if the will and ability to do so were strong.

And most school administrators are in a similar fix. Even as I write this, during the final days of my summer vacation, I realize that it is a great luxury for me to have the time to turn my attention to what critics are saying about our schools and to compose, however sketchily, a reasoned reply. Next week, the demands of school administration will descend with a dull thud, and I will look back on this moment and this activity with a feeling akin to nostalgia.

The truth is that most of us who work in schools are (or should be!) too busy to be more than casually engaged in listening to the school-is-dead critics or in responding to what they say. Teaching is a serious undertaking, as is the job of administering a school.

If those who are engaged in these pursuits take their work seriously, they often find little time for anything else. Yet, there may be teachers and administrators who, for a variety of reasons, have energy and time to spare, or there may be persons from other walks of life, such as university professors, who feel sufficiently incensed to take arms, as it were, against a sea of troubles.

Theirs is the strategy of countercriticism or, if you prefer, counterattack. Fortunately for those of us who are interested in preserving our school system, the writings of most critics reveal weaknesses that seriously damage the force of their argument. The most blatant of these is surely to be found in the demagogic style that characterizes so much of the school-is-dead literature. The tone throughout is strident and at times borders on hysteria.

We are told that our present schools are little more than prisons or concentration camps for the young. Teachers (*all* teachers, presumably) are depicted as mindless and inhumane, and administrators are described as pigheaded and petty tyrants whose main purpose in life seems to be to keep the halls clean and the cafeteria running smoothly. Students, poor things, are crushed by their exposure to these horrible conditions and leave school much worse off than when they entered—with psyches destroyed, spirits sagging, and minds devoid of any true knowledge. It is enough to make the blood boil, which is precisely the intended effect of the authors who write in such a style.

It does not require much analytic power to discern the emotionalism and propagandistic aims of such prose. Hopefully, even the casual reader will take these qualities into account as he judges the critics' case. What does require closer analysis is the detection of flaws in the critics' logic or the scantiness of the evidence they present. Also, more than a casual reading is required to reveal deficiencies in the historical perspective of those who criticize today's schools and in the reasonableness of the alternative proposals they put forth.

Let us consider one or two quick examples of what such an analysis might yield.

Take, for instance, the following statement by John Holt that appeared in a recent issue of *Harper's Magazine* in an article entitled, significantly enough, "The Little Red Prison."

"Thus, as more people learn in school to dislike reading, fewer buy books from bookstores and borrow them from libraries. The bookstores close and the libraries cut back their services, and so we have fewer places in which people outside of school can have ready access to books. This is just one of the ways in which too much school works against education."

A grim picture, indeed. It makes a person want to run out and buy or borrow a couple of books while they are still to be had! But we must ask: It is true? *Are* more people learning to dislike reading in school? Is the sale of books *really* declining? Are libraries across the nation cutting back their services because of a shortage of interest in their wares? The answer, as all the statistics on publishing and library usage clearly indicate, is emphatically "No!"

Or take another instance, this one chosen almost at random from Ivan Illich's book, *Deschooling Society.* In attempting to analyze what he calls "the phenomenology of school," Illich offers his readers the following gem of syllogistic reasoning:

"School groups people according to age. This grouping rests on three unquestioned premises. Children belong in school. Children learn in school. Children can be taught only in school. I think these unexamined premises deserve serious questioning."

Indeed they do, Mr. Illich. But so does the logic by which the premises are said to lead to the conclusion: "School groups people according to age." We can begin with the assumption that Illich was referring not to the system of grades by which students customarily are grouped *within* school, but rather to the fact that children go to school and adults, for the most part, do not. School, in other words, segregates children from adults. Fair enough, but how does that fact "rest" on the premises? And, further, are the premises themselves seriously held by a significant segment of our population, including, incidentally, our professional educators? Who among us seriously believes that children can be taught only in school?

Other instances of illogic or scant evidence or unreasonable assumptions are easy to come by in the writings of the deschoolers, but these two will have to suffice as illustrations of the kind of detailed criticism that must surely come if we are to take such writings and the proposals contained within them seriously. Some of this countercriticism is already beginning to appear in print, and more is bound to be written.

The chief danger in focusing on flaws in the deschoolers' argument is that such a strategy may blind us to the strengths that are also there. In our zest to prove them wrong, in other words, we may overlook the extent to which the critics are right. And, let's face it: There *is* basis for concern about what our schools are doing and how their operation might be improved. Perhaps, contrary to what John Holt contends, more and more students are not being taught to dislike reading by their school experience, but a goodly number *are,* and we should be worried about that.

Obviously our high schools are *not* the concentration camps that some critics would have us believe, but many students within them do feel constrained and bridled by their experience, and that fact should trouble us.

Certainly the vast majority of our teachers and school administrators are *not* the mindless and unfeeling creatures depicted by some of the less responsible attackers of our schools, but too many of them *are* halfheartedly engaged in what they are about, more concerned with the benefits of their position than with the services they perform. We cannot rest easy so long as this is true.

The list could be extended, but the point is already obvious: There is serious work to be done within our schools.

This brings us to the third and last of the alternative responses educators might presumably take in the face of the deschooling argument. The first was to ignore the critics and get on with our work. The second was to expose weaknesses in the critics' argument, to counterattack, so to speak. The third is to learn from the critics, not simply by having them reinforce our awareness of our schools' shortcomings, but by seeing where their efforts fall short of perfection and by trying to avoid similar pitfalls as we go about trying to improve our schools. Two such shortcomings are worthy of mention and serve well as examples of lessons to be learned from those who would bring lessons, as such, to an end.

As I study the contemporary critics of our schools, it becomes increasingly evident to me that most of them are animated more by a sense of what is *wrong* with our present system than by a conception of what education is all about and how it might proceed. They lack, in other words, a vision of the good in educational terms. What they are *against* is more evident than what they are *for.*

This same tendency, incidentally, is also apparent within the ranks of professional educators as they impatiently work to reduce the abrasiveness of schooling without pausing to give sufficient thought to the educational purpose of the institution. I plead as guilty as the rest in yielding to the natural appeal of such a tactic. After all, it is easier to put oil on squeaky wheels than to ask about where the vehicle is headed in the first place and to ponder the necessity of a change in direction. The danger, of course, is that by so doing we may create a smoothly running machine that is moving in the wrong direction or not at all.

And this is precisely the likelihood we face if we only ask: What is wrong with our schools and how can we correct those faults? In answering such questions, we may indeed produce conditions in which students and teachers are happier and more contented than is presently true, but will those happier and more contented people still be students and teachers in the educational sense of those terms?

Our goal, in other words, cannot simply be to eliminate the discomfort of schooling, though certainly there is much that should be eliminated. Nor can it even be simply to provide environments in which students are learning things they *want* to learn—a favorite image of many of the romantic critics. It must be to create environments—institutions, if you like—in which students are being educated, a different matter entirely.

This last point deserves elaboration, for it contrasts nicely with one of the major premises in the deschooling argument. Many of the more radical critics are fond of reminding their readers that education involves more than schooling—that it can occur in the absence of teachers and courses and classrooms and all of the paraphernalia that we have come to associate with formal schooling. The same argument, incidentally, has recently been adopted as the slogan of several not-so-radical researchers and professors of education who use it to justify turning their attention away from schools and toward other institutions and agencies within our society that perform an educative function.

Now no one can dispute the truism that reminds us of differences between the concepts of education and schooling. Perhaps such a reminder needs to be presented more frequently and more forcefully today than in the past. But there is another truism that needs to be stated with equal force, for it often seems to be overlooked by friend and foe alike. It is that education, in addition to being more than schooling, is also more than learning.

John Dewey, more than any other educator with whom I am familiar, understood supremely both of the cautions to which I have now made reference: that the foundations on which to build a new and constructive view of schooling cannot simply be a reaction to the ailments of our present system and that education involves much more than letting students "do their thing" even when the latter results in significant learning.

Disturbed by the excesses of the reform movement carried out in his name, Dewey pointed out:

"There is always the danger in a new movement that in rejecting the aims and methods of that which it would supplant, it may develop its principles negatively rather than positively and constructively. Then it takes its clew in practice from that which is rejected instead of from the constructive development of its own philosophy."

And, in my judgment, this seems to be precisely what today's would-be reformers are doing. They are saying, in effect, "Here are the features of schooling that are unpleasant. Let us, therefore, make the absence of those features our goal in the design of alternate forms of schooling." The missing element, of course, is a conception of what the process of education leads *toward,* and this can only be supplied by an ethic and a psychology which are conjured in a coherent philosophy or *theory* of education.

The closest today's critics seem to come to such a conception is their insistence on individual choice and their celebration of man's natural curiosity and his desire to learn. Apparently, if unfettered by institutional constraints, the human spirit will spontaneously seek and achieve those ends that schools are designed to serve. Such is the hope, at any rate. Nor are the critics alone in holding to this belief. Even within our schools themselves a number of persons who call themselves educators seem to be arguing for such a hands-off policy.

Again, it is Dewey who blows the whistle of alarm better than most. Almost 50 years ago he wrote:

> There is a present tendency in so-called advanced schools of educational thought . . . to say, in effect, let us surround pupils with certain materials, tools, appliances, etc., and then let pupils respond to these things according to their own desires. Above all, let us not suggest any end or plan to the students; let us not suggest to them what they shall do, for that is an unwarranted trespass upon their sacred intellectual individuality since the essence of such individuality is to set up ends and aims.
>
> Now such a method is really stupid. For it attempts the impossible, which is always stupid; and it misconceives the conditions of independent thinking. There are a multitude of ways of reacting to surrounding conditions, and without some guidance from experience these reactions are almost sure to be casual, sporadic, and ultimately fatiguing, accompanied by nervous strain. Since the teacher has presumably a greater background of experience, there is the same presumption of the right of a teacher to make suggestions as to what to do, as there is on the part of a head carpenter to suggest to apprentices something of what they are to do.

Coming from as mild-mannered a man as Dewey, those are strong words indeed. Yet the fact that they are as applicable today as when they first were written suggests that the message they contain remains unheeded by many educational critics both inside and outside the schools. And, I suspect, a major reason why this is so is because to take Dewey's admonition seriously would entail an enormous amount of work and thought on the part of everyone connected with schooling.

It is no easy task to keep our educational purpose in mind while carrying out our day-to-day responsibilities in classrooms and administrative offices; in short, to blend theory and practice. To achieve that end requires nothing less than that each of us, again in Dewey's words, be "possessed by the spirit of an abiding student of education."

Such is the challenge that lies before us if we are to learn from our critics to sidestep some of the pitfalls into which they themselves appear to have fallen. Only then will we truly be able to respond with conviction to those who would claim that schools are passé. Moreover, if we are to avoid a tone of defensiveness and apology, our conviction must be voiced in the language of educational purpose. This means more than empty slogans cloaking an absence of thought, but, rather, a lively and tough-minded discourse that means what it says, that changes as schools change, and that mirrors the reality within them.

Our schools are neither dead nor dying, but neither, unfortunately, are they marked by a degree of vitality and energy that befits the grandeur of their mission. Paradoxically, and even ironically, the writings of those who would bury us may well stimulate such an infusion of new life.

POSTSCRIPT

SHOULD COMPULSORY SCHOOLING BE ABOLISHED?

The improvement of social institutions has been a dominant theme of the 1960s and 1970s. Because any improvement must arise from a critique of existing conditions, the analysis of institutional shortcomings has been particularly penetrating during this period. The radical critique demanding complete and immediate reform has received the most attention, but it has been accompanied by conservative and middle-of-the-road critiques as well.

John Gardner's *Self-Renewal: The Individual and the Innovative Society* (1964) described a basic cultural pattern: the necessity in a reasonable and dynamic society of accepting dissent and criticism, without which the society is bound to become stagnant and authoritarian. Theodore Roszak's *The Making of a Counter Culture* (1969) and Charles A. Reich's *The Greening of America* (1970) portrayed the value of divergent forces, particularly those associated with youth, in vitalizing society.

In the field of education, this theme has been played out in both theoretical formulations and practical experimentation. At the theoretical level, for example, Adam Curle portrays, in his *Education for Liberation* (1973), a movement from the competition, exploitation, and manipulation of the existing system to a cooperative, empathetic, humanitarian counter-system. In *The Pedagogy of the Oppressed* (1970), Paulo Freire describes the oppressiveness of culture and social institutions and suggests a critical and liberating dialogue in education through which the "banking concept" of teachers doling out selected knowledge would be replaced by a "problem-posing" approach in which teachers and students are coinvestigators.

At the practical level, innovations such as Philadelphia's Parkway Program and the development of the *Yellow Pages of Learning Resources* and similar tools have altered the usual conception of schooling. Such programs and tools allow many learning activities to occur outside the confines of the traditional school building and place the learner in a more responsible role.

"The Greening of the High School," a report sponsored by the Ford Foundation and the Institute for Development of Educational Activities (I/D/E/A), concludes that school should be a *place,* but it must be an *active, human* place, a "social scene" filled with learning tools and private spaces. How this "place" can be further defined is explored in the following pieces by Carl Bereiter and Robert Hutchins.

ISSUE 14

ARE THERE VIABLE OPTIONS TO SCHOOLING?

The general critique of compulsory public education during the past decade has left the impression that the system is at best mediocre. Student motivation is often lacking, achievement measures show a continuing decline, and the high school diploma is seen by many as meaningless. Efforts to reform the process of education, while sometimes successful in creating more liveable settings, too often have been inefficient, anti-intellectual, and permeated by fads and gimmickry.

The argument over which direction to pursue in order to resolve current difficulties has boiled down to a reanalysis of the meaning of education. In *Must We Educate?* (1973) Carl Bereiter calls for a pause from asking how society can educate its children better while we consider whether society should educate its children at all.

For Bereiter, to "educate" implies a profound influence on the overall development of a young person which goes far beyond mere functional relationships such as those involved in baby-sitting and training. Bereiter concludes that, because this developmental influence is unavoidably authoritarian, especially in the lives of young children, public schooling should be limited to skills training.

Sharing Ivan Illich's concern about the effects of schooling, Bereiter sees the monopolistic credentialing power of the schools as a serious threat to individual freedom of choice and personal responsibility. According to Bereiter, the schools should focus on basic skills and, beyond that, should provide a range of optional activities and unprogrammed resources through which the young may develop their talents.

The Bereiter analysis and the Illich critique attempt to shatter the mythology of schooling which has become cemented in the American consciousness. Similarly, in "The Seven Deadly Myths of Education and How They Mangle the Young," (*Psychology Today,* March 1971) Dwight W. Allen attacks the following educational myths:

1. Children are stupid until teachers make them smart.
2. Rationality must strictly control the emotions and the body.
3. There is one perfect way to solve a problem.
4. Knowledge is sacred, certain, and fixed.
5. Learning takes place in school and nowhere else.
6. Education is a mechanical rather than an organic process.
7. Teachers are interchangeable parts rather than unique individuals.

On the other hand, Robert M. Hutchins does not accept such demolition efforts—in fact, he refuses to treat many of these points of attack as "myths." He campaigned relentlessly against those who conclude that schools make little difference in people's lives and against those who feel that the schools are primarily social control devices. Hutchins contends that any abandonment of tax-supported, universal, free, compulsory education will lead to disaster.

While he sees some of the faults in present schooling that are cited by the harshest of critics, Hutchins refuses to accept the argument that schooling has lost its value. If the evaluation is limited to the attainment of economic advantage alone, then perhaps the schools have at least partly failed. But this is a far too narrow basis for judgment, Hutchins contends; the schools are still a major vehicle of mental and ethical development and as such must remain within the fabric of social institutions. In the selections included here, Bereiter summarizes his modified-deschooling position, while Hutchins offers his justification of schooling and directly attacks Bereiter's stance.

Carl Bereiter

ALTERNATIVES MUST BE FOUND

In no other institution of our society are the ideal and the reality so far apart as they are in education.

The ideal. The teacher is a sensitive monitor of the child's entire process of growth and development, entering into it in manifold ways, never to hamper, but always to encourage and guide development toward the fullest realization of the child's potentialities. There are other educational purposes (such as a nation's need for technically trained manpower), but no other ideal comes close to all-around acceptability in a free society, and with increasing prosperity and secularity we should expect that other educational purposes will drop out of competition with this ideal. Thus, when we speak of education in America we speak of one ideal, shared by almost all educators, even though they differ as to how it should be pursued.

The reality. Two to three dozen captive children are placed in the charge of a teacher of only modest intellectual ability and little learning, where they spend approximately six hours a day engaged in activities that someone has decided are good for them. In the course of 12 years they acquire a certain amount of worthwhile skill and knowledge, but only on the rarest occasions, if at all, do they encounter anything even remotely resembling the kind of teacher-pupil interaction prescribed as ideal.

It is time to question the ideal

The ideal of humanistic education—"that education in which the primary function of the schools is to cultivate the 'independence' of each 'individual' and to develop each person to the fullest"—has been with us since ancient Greece. Today, it is accepted as virtually beyond question. Educators occasionally accuse one another of holding conflicting ideals, but this is mere mud-slinging. Every scheme for educational reform is an attempt, whether misguided or not, to bring reality closer to the humanistic ideal.

Perhaps the humanistic ideal cannot be questioned on ideal grounds, but it can be questioned on practical grounds. The question may be phrased as follows:

Continued on p. 228

From "Needs of Elementary and Secondary Education in the Seventies: A Compendium of Policy Papers," General Subcommittee on Education of the Committee on Education and Labor, House of Representatives, 91st Congress (1970).

Robert M. Hutchins

THE SCHOOLS MUST STAY

The great campaign against the American public school has now reached the stage of overkill. It is impossible to believe that anything new can be added to the attacks already delivered, for the schools have been assailed from every conceivable direction, with every conceivable motive. The coalition against them is such as to suggest that the one thing on which our people have reached unanimity is the evils of our system of public education. The coalition is a strange one, because the critics would not agree with, or even speak to, one another on any other subject. Softhearted revolutionaries and hard-headed businessmen join in arguing that the public schools should be abolished. A critic is now regarded as moderate if he proposes merely that the system be instantly, drastically, and thoroughly reformed. Everybody wants to have education available. Everybody wants it paid for by taxes. But nobody has a kind word for the public school, the institution that only the other day was looked upon as the foundation of our freedom, the guaranty of our future, the cause of our prosperity and power, the bastion of our security, and the source of our enlightenment.

The signs of overkill are not merely that the critics are repeating themselves. Some of them are beginning to question solutions advanced by members of their own groups, such as the abolition of all schools whatever. Recoiling from this proposal, questioners have asked what problems it would solve. They have gone on to point out that poverty, slums, racial discrimination, disorganized families, disease, injustice, and television would remain and have thus inferentially let us know that, if the schools are bad, or if children do not learn in school, or if they have a hard time there, some of the fault may lie with the community and the environment in which children live rather than only with the schools.

Other critics appear to be preparing for a strategic withdrawal. Some of those who have told us schools are prisons and teachers tyrants are now hinting that some schools are joyous and some teachers humane. Others who led us to believe that all we had to do was to follow the whims of children now

Continued on p. 234

Reprinted with permission from *The Center Magazine*, a publication of the Robert Maynard Hutchins Center for the Study of Democratic Institutions, Santa Barbara, California.

(Bereiter, cont. from p. 226)

> Is it better to approximate the humanistic ideal as best we can, regardless of how far we fall short, or is it better to pursue some other ideal more in keeping with the limits imposed by reality?

This is a type of question that is all too seldom asked in the social sphere, although it is common in the industrial sphere, where, for instance, the ideal of producing a machine that will last forever is frequently supplanted by the ideal of producing a machine that will give maximum value per unit of cost. This type of question has recently begun to be asked in the social sphere by members of the "Third World," particularly by members of the Centro Intercultural de Documentacion. As these social thinkers see it, underdeveloped countries have taken North American institutions and technologies as their "ideals" and have strived to approximate them as closely as possible, whereas, in view of the very limited economic resources of these countries, approximations to North American models are likely to be so remote as to be seriously dysfunctional and greatly inferior to institutions and technologies based on models suited to the economic and social realities of the countries involved. This line of reasoning is directly applicable to American education, which has the same problem of resources too limited for the model it tries to follow.

Talent as the limiting factor in education

During the seventies it should become clear that lack of money is not the primary factor accounting for the great discrepancy between the educational ideal and reality. If we are unwise, we may learn this lesson through bitter experience. We may invest heavily in electronic and paraprofessional aides in order to free teachers to carry out humanistic education, only to find that they cannot do so any better than they do now. We may extend schooling down into earlier childhood, only to discover that we have spread the supply of competent teachers more thinly than before. We may increase teacher salaries only to find that the quality of teachers remains the same. We may increase the attractiveness of school buildings, equipment, and materials, only to find that students become increasingly disaffected. If, on the other hand, we are wise, we may foresee these results and channel our resources into other kinds of provisions for children that will yield greater social benefits, even though the benefits are not ones that we can properly call educational.

At the bottom of these dismal predictions is the simple premise that humanistic education calls for a supply of teacher talent that cannot possibly be met on the scale for universal education. Educational philosophers, when expounding their particular version of humanistic education, are always ready to admit that the talent required for teachers to bring it off is of a very high level. They seem to feel, however, that the talent can be produced by exhortation, and enormous amounts of educational ink go each year into resounding calls for greatness. If what is required ideally is something more than a Socrates, what is required for even a reasonable approximation is something not much less. Rousseau, who deserves first credit for re-establishing the humanistic ideal in the modern world, was less optimistic:

> How can a child be well educated unless by one who is well educated himself? Can this rare mortal be found? I do not know.

The humanistic educator must be continually aware of the growing edge of the child's intellect and character. He must be exceedingly resourceful in seizing upon opportunities of the moment to turn them to educational account. To help the child learn, he must not only know what the child is to learn but know it so thoroughly that he can choose just the right question or demonstration or activity at just the right time. He cannot work from a prepared curriculum but must invent as he interacts with the child. He must at once be a good model and someone who does not force the child to be like himself or as he would like himself to be.

I could go on listing attributes, but let us try to jump from qualitative requirements to ones that can be quantified, realizing that much is lost in the process. It would stand to reason, I think, that a minimum requirement for such an educator—a bare minimum, indeed—would be an IQ of 115. Those who would object that some very clever people will earn IQ scores of less than this ought also to agree that their number will be offset by people of higher IQ who are not so clever. By this requirement we limit the potential teaching population to a sixth of the total work. The other requirements, which have more to do with personality, are not so easily quantified, but we might reasonably judge that no more than half of the people who meet the intelligence requirements would possess the other personal characteristics needed to function adequately as humanistic educators. This reduces the potential supply of educators to a twelfth of the labor force.

Projections of census totals for the labor force and the student population (including those in post-secondary education) into the seventies indicates that about two-thirds as many people will be in school as will be working. Therefore, if everyone who had the minimum talent to teach did teach, we should have a teacher-pupil ratio of one-to-eight. This ratio would be scarcely sufficient to carry on the kind of teacher-pupil interaction required for personalistic education, which is ideally a one-to-one operation. But, of course, we cannot expect that all or even most of the people who could teach would teach, since the qualifications are ones that also fit an increasing number of other careers (including careers in education other than teaching).

Thus, if for no other reason, humanistic education must fail on grounds of a simple shortage of talent. This shortage, moreover, is one that cannot be remedied by any immediate action. Conceivably, better education would produce more people qualified to educate, but such improvement could only come about slowly over generations of students, and for all we know the trend may be downward rather than upward. Educational technology may relieve the teacher of many burdens—it might even be able to take over entirely the teaching of specific skills and knowledge—but what remains for the teacher is the very kind of creative person-to-person activity for which talent is most wanting.

Proposals for reform of the educational system, far from promising to alleviate the strain on talent resources, almost invariably call for more teachers of more exalted calibre. This is [as] true of traditionalist schemes for a return to basic disciplines as it is of radical schemes for the abandonment of definite curricula. It could not be otherwise, for they are all efforts to bring practice closer to the ideal of humanistic education. We must apply to them Daniel P. Moynihan's dictum that "systems that require immense amounts of extraordinarily competent people to run them are not going to run."

The humanistic ideal does more harm than good

Thomas F. Green has claimed that, while educators almost universally claim to be pursuing humanistic education, what they do in reality is not concerned with developing individual potentialities but with training individuals to meet the needs of other institutions in the society. It is no doubt true that what the public mainly expects of the schools is not the development of individual potentials but the teaching of socially useful skills—such as the three R's—and that the schools cannot avoid being responsive to this expectation. I believe it is incorrect, however, to infer from this that the commitment of educators to a humanistic ideology has no practical consequence.

In the first place, the humanistic commitment of educators has an effect—largely negative—on how they carry out their elementary training functions. In teaching reading and arithmetic, for instance, educators do not simply look for the most effective methods of achieving performance criteria. They tend to prefer, on ideological grounds, methods which seem to entail creativity, freedom of choice, discovery, challenges to thinking, democratic processes, and growth of self-knowledge. Moreover, they strive continually to win recognition for these values as more important than objective performance criteria.

In the second place, training in socially required skills does not begin to take up the entire school day. If schools restricted themselves to such training and attempted to do it as efficiently as possible, the school day might have to be only a third as long as it is now, and school costs could be lowered accordingly. Thus it is the addition of many other high-flown purposes, drawn from the humanistic ideal, that serves to justify the vast amount of time and money devoted to schooling and to motivate such costly proposals as year-round schooling and the extension of public education down into the early childhood years.

In the third place, educators are continually pressing for reforms that serve humanistic purposes in education. Nongrading, the open-plan school, the language experience approach, individualized instruction, and innovations of this sort are all reforms which would have the effect of shifting emphasis off training in elementary skills. Indeed, as these approaches come to be assimilated to common educational thinking, it becomes impossible to tell one from the other, because they all consist largely of reassertions of established tenets of humanistic education. And they all involve unrealistic requirements of teacher talent.

In the fourth place, humanistic values subtly infect the ways pupils and teachers are evaluated. Even if correctness and docility are still the attributes most consistently rewarded in students, there is a tendency for the less imaginative, insightful, or independent students to be regarded as failures; and such students are bound to get the message. Such students are put in a very agonizing position, since they are being condemned for failure to learn things that are not actually being taught. Teachers also tend to be evaluated and to evaluate themselves on how well they promote humanistic goals. Since these goals cannot be achieved, teachers are demoralized. Many of them are fine people and could be quite competent in training, but humanistic ideology often forces them to denigrate their own strengths.

This brings us to the last and most ignominious way in which humanistic ideology interacts with the training function of schools. It is that mechanisms of training are applied not only to the skill-learning purposes for which they are appropriate but also to other, humanistically based purposes for which they are radically unsuited. The result is pseudotraining—ritualistic behavior that has the appearance of training but does not produce any of its desirable results. In social studies, science, and literature, teachers will often claim to be helping students to develop deep understanding, thinking abilities, attitudes, interests, and values. Lacking any definite ways of promoting such development, however, they fall back on memorization, lecture and exhortation, tasks that amount to no more than busy work, and endless practice. Even activities that are less mechanical, such as discussions, "projects," experiments, themes, and field trips, are robbed of what intrinsic merits they might have by efforts to turn them to educational account. Discussions become mealymouthed, ill-timed, and pointless; projects become mere copy work; experiments turn into dull problems or the following of recipes; themes become exercises in grammar; and field trips become holidays.

Most of what is so tedious, unprofitable, phony, and "irrelevant" in schooling is done not in the name of training in basic skills but in the name of the highest-sounding humanistic objectives. Radical critics of education find this anomaly perverse, and seem to think that if only educators could get their values straight they would do better. But the anomaly is built into the very structure of mass education. Most teachers cannot educate in the humanistic sense, and of those who can, few are able to do so even sporadically under the pupil loads they bear.

Current movements away from education

Under the impulse of humanistic ideology, many schools are moving away from the kind of pseudo-training I have described to a type of program in which the pupil is free much of the time to do what he wants. In practice, societal demands for training are usually still recognized, but only limited portions of the day are devoted to meeting them. Individual development is seen as something that will occur pretty much by itself, and the teacher's main job is to refrain from obstructing it. One of the more recent trends is to get away from confining children to school at all, allowing them to pursue their interests in the community at large.

To the extent that development is truly left up to the child, this type of program amounts to the abandonment of humanistic education in favor of a more simplistic faith in nature. However, these types of programs carry if anything an even heavier burden of educational purpose than existing ones. As a result they are even more unrealistic and potentially harmful. The following are some of the disadvantages of this educational approach:

1. Expectations of personal growth in such areas as creativity and understanding are heightened, while the teacher is provided with even less that she can do to bring it about. This can induce a

feeling of helplessness in teachers and failure in students.

2. The teacher is expected to monitor the growth process in subtle and unspecified ways, thus to function fully as a humanistic educator, which few teachers are talented enough to do.

3. Since the entire program is carried out under the auspices of the school system, it is continuously vulnerable to pressure from a public which expects something quite different from its schools.

4. The laissez-faire approach is frequently generalized to areas of skill training, where it will likely lead to a deterioration in achievement.

5. A concern to make activities educational is likely to lead to limiting the options open to children and to corruption of activities which they might otherwise enjoy.

6. Such programs are costly, not only because of the need to provide a greater variety of facilities and materials, but also because more teachers are required to supervise children when they are all engaged in different activities. When educational programs are extended into the community there are added costs from the greater demand for community facilities, while teacher costs increase even further.

7. Providing an optimum environment is something that professional educators are not necessarily the best qualified people to do. An enormous variety of specialized talents are applicable, and there is no reason why the utilization of these talents should be centralized. Moreover, as a public institution the school system is barred from partisan, sectarian, or controversial activities that ought to be available to children under a truly open program.

Why not abandon the effort at humanistic education altogether?

I have argued that current and proposed methods of carrying out humanistic education through the schools only make a mockery of it, and that such education is impossible to achieve on a mass basis. Current movements away from education, however, suggest a logical next step. It consists of the following changes:

1. Restrict the responsibility of the schools entirely to training in well-defined, clearly teachable skills. This should require only about a third of the cost in money, personnel, and time that schooling costs now. What would be lost would be largely good riddance, and with exclusive concentration on training the schools could probably do a much more efficient and pleasing job of it than they do now.

2. Set children free the rest of the time to do what they want, but in doing so get them out from under the authority of the schools. Provide more economical forms of custodial care and guidance, as needed, and do it without educational intent.

3. Use the large amount of money thus saved to provide an enormously enriched supply of cultural resources for children, with which they can spend their newfound free time. These resources may reflect humanistic values to the fullest, but they should not carry any burden of educational intent, in the sense of trying to direct or improve upon the course of personal development. They should simply be resources and activities considered worthy in their own right.

4. Do not restrict children to these publicly sponsored activities. Maintain an open cultural market, in which proponents of diverse activities may compete to attract children to them.

This proposal has, I believe, all of the genuine advantages of the current movements toward freer, more humanistic education, while avoiding the seven faults noted above. In addition it has the potentiality of enriching the cultural life of our communities in ways by which all citizens would benefit—by increasing the supply of cultural resources, some of which would be of value to adults as well as children, and also by freeing young people to pursue activities through which they could contribute their talents to society.*

If humanistic education existed, it would be a shame to lose it; if it could exist we should try to achieve it. When I discuss with people this proposal to abandon pursuit of humanistic education, I am repeatedly met with personal anecdotes about the one teacher in a person's school career who changed his life, who opened up to him a vision of what he could become and started him on the road to becoming it. These single events are taken as sufficient to offset all the dross that filled most of their school days and to justify the continued, largely futile pursuit of the humanistic ideal of education. To this argument I would only reply that such rare encounters, which are indeed the essence of humanistic education, are more likely to occur in a system where children are free to seek their own contacts in the cultural world.

Suggestions for governmental action

1. There is already considerable support for research on the improvement of training in basic skills. This should continue, and be made freer than it is now of ideological obstructions. There is considerable pressure from educational ideologues to suppress training research that does not conform sufficiently to humanistic educational expectations. It should be recognized that such expectations are irrelevant to the training function of schools. There should be special encouragement of research which seeks to extend the range of what is actually teachable. Thinking skills, for instance, are not now teachable to any significant extent, but some of them might be.

2. Support programs of teacher training that develop training skills. Most teachers receive no relevant training of any kind; they only learn *about* teaching and *about* children. If schools are to train, teachers must learn how to do it, and this is something that ordinary teachers could learn.

3. Support the development of new kinds of cultural opportunities for children, to take the place of schooling. This type of development should not be done predominantly by educators, and supervision of it should probably not be in the hands of the Office of Education, since it is not an educational undertaking. Various agencies concerned with arts, sciences, recreation, and communications should be empowered to support such work on the part of creative people from all walks of life.

4. Model programs along the lines set forth in the preceding section should be instituted to work out the numerous problems and to explore the numerous possibilities associated with the disbanding of a century-old institution and the creation of a new way of serving the nation's youth.

* I have in mind such possibilities as theater, music, and journalism produced by young people and youth participation in social action and scientific activities.

(Hutchins, cont. from p. 227)

want to make sure we understand that a curriculum, with teachers in charge, is required.

On the side of the hard-headed businessmen, the voucher plan sponsored by the Office of Economic Opportunity contains so many restrictions on free enterprise and so much governmental control that it cannot be looked upon with much favor by the free-enterprise economists who were its principal sponsors at the outset. And those who announced that performance contracting, by which commercial corporations take over teaching and are paid for "results," was the remedy for the inefficiency of the academic bureaucracy are now rebuffed by their erstwhile advocates in government.

Whether or not the campaign against the schools subsides, it will leave traces for years to come. The wrecks of bond issues and proposals for tax increases for the schools are scattered all over the landscape. What is more significant, the value of universal, free, compulsory education, supported by taxes and controlled by the political community, has been called in question for the first time in American history. If we cannot give a clear answer we may take irreversible steps downhill. So we should try to answer. The political community should be required to justify the prolonged detention of children in an educational system.

Many of the negative criticisms of the public schools are justified, though some of them are stated in somewhat intemperate language. Nobody who has attended an American public school will deny that it is afflicted with boredom, authoritarianism, bureaucracy, inefficiency, and ineffectiveness. It always has been. But it is now much more expensive than it ever has been. It includes a higher proportion of the population than ever. Success in school and getting credentials to prove it are thought to be indispensable to social mobility; and we have discovered that the school, contrary to our expectations, does not provide it. We have learned that socio-economic status and family attitudes and background impose constraints upon the child that the school seems powerless to overcome.

The question is now raised whether the educational system has much or, indeed, any effect, whether it has any function except a custodial one, whether it does much of anything except keep children out of worse places until they can go to work. Some critics suggest, in fact, that any place the child wanted to go would be better than school, where he is "imprisoned" against his will. The slogan of one recent book is, "Let Our Children Go," and one of the authors intimates that truancy offers the only hope of salvation to the rising generation.

What has happened to the purposes for which the schools have been thought to exist? In recent years these purposes have been the material and social improvement of the individual and the establishment and maintenance of self-government in the community. The first of these, helping the individual get ahead, has suffered at the hands of scholars who have shown that family background and attitudes and the influences of the earliest years may make it almost impossible for schools as we have known them to help the individual get out of the station in which he was born. Evidence of another, but no less disturbing, kind has been piling up that the whole idea of getting a better job by getting more credentials may be absurd.

If educational credentials turn out to confer no benefit on the individual who acquires them, and none on the firms that employ those who hold them, the question arises whether schooling confers any practical benefits at all, and, if it does not, why the costly and elaborate system should be maintained. If your object in going to school was to get ahead, and you did not get ahead, why should you have gone? Why should others go?

Adam Smith's and John Stuart Mill's concern with the development of the individual as a human being, saved from stupidity, ignorance, and torpor, able to carry on a rational conversation, conceive elevating sentiments, form just judgments, and use his mind has passed through various stages of degradation until nothing is left but an exhortation to acquire a piece of paper, however meaningless, the magical powers of which as a passport to a brighter future seem to be declining. Insofar as the schools have cooperated in building up the impression that years of schooling confer economic advantage in proportion to their number, the schools could expect to suffer from the rage and disappointment of those who put in the years without reaping the advantage.

A school is truly public if it belongs to the public and if its aim is to form and maintain the public. As Werner Jaeger put it in *Paideia,* education is the deliberate attempt to form men in terms of an ideal. The aim of the American public school originally was to form men as independent, self-governing members of a self-governing community. That community was as wide as each of the thirteen original states. After the passage of the Fourteenth Amendment, it became as wide as the nation, in the sense that the states were not permitted to violate national standards in any of their important activities, of which education was one. That the political community extends beyond the boundaries of the state is evident in the judicial regulation of education in the states and in congressional appropriations for support of education, which are becoming commonplace.

The growth of technology is shrinking the planet at such a rate that we must already think of a world community, no matter how far off a world political community may be. Hence it is alarming that American educational discussion either omits the community from consideration entirely or refers to it only in a dwarfed and trivial form, as the selfish interest of neighborhoods, groups, or classes. Such a redefinition of the community is defensible only if its self-centeredness is mitigated as it would be in the context of a carefully worked out theory of decentralization or subsidiarity, in which each smaller unit made its contribution to and carried its share of the burdens of the whole. As Senator J. William Fulbright has said, "The essence of any community—local, national, or international—is some degree of acceptance of the principle that the good of the whole must take precedence over the good of the parts."

A large, conspicuous, elaborate, expensive institution on which the hopes of a nation have been pinned cannot hope to escape attack in a period of national distress unless it can show that it has intelligible purposes and that it is achieving them. The American educational system cannot make the required demonstration. This is not altogether the fault of the schools. The failure of educational philosophy reflects the failure of our philosophy in general. It is not the schools that make their purposes, but the people who control them. For example, credentialism is not the fault of the schools but of parents and employers. The unfortunate new definition of community did not originate in the schools but in the propaganda of those who wished to use them for their purposes. . . .

Let us accept all we have heard about genetic limitations, those imposed by socio-economic status, family background, parental attitudes, the conditions of the earliest years of life, together with those brought to bear by the neighborhood, the home, and television—in short, all the waves of every sort that beat upon the child from birth on and even before. We cannot assume that all these forces are permanent or that they leave irreversible effects. If society is bad, and hence a bad educator, let us by all means struggle to improve it, and let us not imagine that we can do so solely by improving the educational system. If we have no philosophy in general because we do not know what we want, or our philosphy is defective because we want the wrong things, let us try to straighten ourselves out; and let us recognize that we cannot do this solely by straightening out our educational system. The limitations within which an educational system operates are severe. It is a means of accentuating and perpetuating accepted values, not of raising a nation by its own bootstraps into a different and better world. This is true of any system of education under any form of government.

Education takes a long time.

No matter what an educational system does, it is not in our time going to get rid of war, disease, poverty, slums, or crime. Its contributions, if any, to the elimination of these and other plagues, will be indirect, through helping people learn to be as intelligent as they can be.

It may be that in many countries such an aim for an educational system would be impossible. In some the sheer magnitude of the task would be too much for the nation's resources. In others helping people to become intelligent may be contrary to public policy: the state may want people to have technical skill—to be efficient, rather than intelligent. It may not want them to think or to exercise critical judgment. Such a country may produce experts of every kind, including experts in indoctrination, called teachers. But the system of "educational" institutions it has will be dedicated to training, rather than education. Education is a process of civilization. To this end it aims at intellectual development. It excludes indoctrination. Educated people may also be trained, and trained people may be educated, but the two objects can be confused only at the risk of failure to achieve one or both. Since training is usually easier, and more easily measureable, than education, it is usually education that suffers from the effort to combine them.

The United States may be a bad society: it is certainly far worse than it ought to be. Its educational system reflects the atmosphere of crass materialism and anti-intellectualism in which it operates. But the people of this country have some commitments that may make it possible for education to take place, even in schools maintained by taxes and controlled by political entities. . . .

Ways must be found to break the lockstep, the system by which all pupils proceed at the same pace through the same curriculum for the same number of years.

The disadvantages of small schools can be overcome by building them in clusters, each with somewhat different courses and methods and permitting students to avail themselves of anything offered in any one. This is an extension of the idea of dual enrollment or shared time, which now exists everywhere, and which allows students in one school to take advantage of what is taught in another, even if one of the schools is private and the other public.

Variety in the methods and curriculum is one way of breaking the lockstep. Another is allowing the student to proceed at his own rate of speed. Under the present system the slow learner is eventually thrown into despair because he cannot keep up, and the fast learner is in the same condition because he has "nothing to do." If we are to have a graded curriculum, we can overcome some of the handicaps it imposes by substituting examinations for time spent and encouraging the student to present himself for them whenever in his opinion he is ready to take them.

It is self-evident that if a course of study is designed to provide the minimum requisites for democratic citizenship, nobody can be permitted to fail. If, then, the basic curriculum is revised as proposed above, so that it is limited to studies essential to the exercise of citizenship, it follows that grades would be eliminated and with them the invidious distinction between winners and losers. If parental attitudes are, as the Plowden Report intimates, profoundly influential in producing this distinction, then the grading system makes the children pay for the sins of their parents. We have reason to believe that everybody is educable. The rate and method of education may vary; the aim of basic education is the same with all individuals, and the obligation of the public schools is to achieve it with all. On this principle, if there is failure, it is the failure of the school, not of the pupil.

I take for granted the adoption or adaptation of many of those reforms about which so much noise has been made of late. The critics of the schools have performed a public service in calling attention to shortcomings that can be repaired by keeping them in mind and working on them. Interest, for example, can be restored to schooling without coming to the indefensible conclusion that whatever is not immediately interesting to children should be omitted from their education. About some other matters the elementary and secondary schools can do little or nothing.

They cannot do much to change parental attitudes, though they should certainly try by keeping in touch with the families of pupils. They can do nothing about the socio-economic status or the slum environment of the children in their charge. The present efforts in pre-school education have a trifling effect in improving the conditions of the earliest years in the lives of slum children. The schools can do nothing about the high taxes that infuriate their no-nonsense, hard-headed critics. They can see to it that money is not wasted, but the definition of waste depends upon an understanding of the purpose of the activity and the best methods of accomplishing it. For example, I would say that buying uniforms for the school band was a waste of money, even though they were bought after competitive bidding, whereas buying good books for the library was not, even though they were not required by the curriculum.

The purpose of the activity is the

crucial question. The purpose of the public schools is not accomplished by having them free, universal, and compulsory. Schools are public because they are dedicated to the maintenance and improvement of the public thing, the *res publica;* they are the common schools of the commonwealth, the political community. They may do many things for the young: they may amuse them, comfort them, look after their health, and keep them off the streets. But they are not public schools unless they start their pupils toward an understanding of what it means to be a self-governing citizen of a self-governing political community.

Since the preceding essay originally went to press in the spring of 1972 the attack on the public schools has continued unabated. In general what the critics seem to want are private schools supported by taxes. The community is to pay the bills. Children or their parents are to decide what, if anything, is to be taught, learned, or done.

So the conclusion of Christopher Jencks's book, *Inequality*, is that schools should be pleasant places for children. Because one child's pleasure is another child's poison, schools should vary according to the preferences children display. Why the power of the state should be invoked to compel children to enjoy themselves remains obscure. If a child and his parents agree that he has a better time at home than he has at school, why should he not stay home? If he and his parents have no interest in education, and if the community has no interest in having him educated, why not give up education altogether?

This is in effect what Carl Bereiter advocates in an article in the *Harvard Educational Review,* called, in all seriousness, "Schools Without Education." I can understand him only as proposing the abandonment of all institutions he would regard as educational.

To Mr. Bereiter education is "the deliberate development of human personality, the making of citizens. . . . Schools cannot cease to be places where intellectual growth and personality development go on, but they can cease to be places where an effort is made to direct or shape these processes. . . . Parents typically educate, and it is my contention . . . that they are the only ones who have a clear-cut right to educate."

If parents are the only ones who have a clear-cut right to educate, the interest of the community in education or in "the making of citizens" is at best unclear. Bereiter, like Jencks, favors voucher plans that would enable parents to decide how tax dollars would be spent on their children.

He proposes to retain schools, apparently compulsory, for two purposes: child care and training in reading, writing, and arithmetic. If parents have the only clear-cut right to educate their children, one would think they would have the only clear-cut right to determine what care their children had outside the home, or indeed whether they needed any at all. If compulsory education is unjustifiable, compulsory child care seems less so. These problems are apart from the difficulty that even the most self-restrained baby-sitter is bound to give way once in a while and try to influence the child, thus invading the forbidden field of education. . . .

Reading, writing, and arithmetic are the essential tools of education. They have other uses, but a parent unconcerned about education might feel that he did not want his child to waste much time acquiring them. If education is the exclusive territory of the parent, his conclusion on reading, writing, and arithmetic, should have great weight.

Since reading and writing, if not arithmetic, are certain to have an educational effect, depending on what is read and written in learning to read and write, training in these activities comes dangerously close to the process that parents, and parents only, have a right to direct.

Mr. Bereiter says, "The need for training arises from the incompleteness of normal experience." This is precisely the way the need for education arises. To intimate that the normal experience of a slum child does not teach him arithmetic, whereas it does "make a citizen" out of him is to display a lamentable ignorance of the facts of life. Consider the implications of Bereiter's recommendation that after training is completed, we should "then simply provide enough resources in the environment that the child can put the skills to use if he feels inclined."

The conclusions of Jencks and Bereiter are based on the proposition that schools make no difference. The logical result would be to abolish them or at least any compulsion to attend them. This would also be the result of the opposite argument, advanced by Joel H. Spring, that schools make too much difference. In his book, *Education and the Rise of the Corporate State,* the community is the villain. It uses the schools as an "instrument of social control," to fit the young into the established social, economic, and political structure. The power of the school is enormous, and it must be broken in order to achieve democracy, which means, "freedom to choose one's own goals and the opportunity to develop one's own life-style."

Whereas Jencks and Bereiter ignore the community and make light of schools as ineffective, Spring thinks of the community as the modern Medusa and finds the schools all too effective in her service. He cannot stand "socialization." Neither can I, chiefly because I do not know what it means. When it appears, as it often does, to be synonymous with Carl Bereiter's definition of the purpose of education, making citizens, it seems sensible enough.

According to Spring: "The solution is not to change the goals and direction of socialization and social control. This is impossible. As long as the public schools take responsibility for the socialization of the child, social adaptation to the institution becomes inevitable. . . . The only possible solution is to end the power of the school." If "socialization" as Spring uses the word can be equated with "education" as Bereiter uses it, then the way to end the power of the school is to restrict its educational efforts along the lines Jencks and Bereiter propose. This would mean that the community would have no interest in what went on in the schools.

The novel definition of democracy put forward by Spring, freedom to choose one's own goals and the opportunity to develop one's own life-style, leads to the conclusion, as much by what it omits as what it contains, that there can be no such thing as a democratic community anyway. A community of any kind must impose some limits on the freedom to choose one's own goals and develop one's own life-style. Those who talk about a community at all, even those who refer to it in the most high-minded, disinterested, and (it seems to me) reasonable way, play a consistently fiendish role in Spring's book. One shudders to think what his opinion of Aristotle would be. He remarked in the *Politics,* "The state . . . is a plurality, which should be united and made into a community by education."

There is no easy way by which a political community can make itself better. It seems doubtful that it can do so by leaving education, "the making of citizens," to chance. The whims of children are unreliable guides and the vagaries of parents not much better. There is some evidence that compulsory schooling came into existence to rescue children from their families, and neglect and exploitation by parents are visible in every American city. Jencks and Bereiter write as though they had been brought up in Scarsdale or Winnetka. Even in these oases, rich with all the promises of the Muslim paradise, "fair like the sheltered egg," I have encountered parents whose interest in the education of their children seemed spectacularly misguided. One such, at the time a power in Chicago business, told me he wanted his son to go to Yale so he could get into the Yale Club of New York.

How do we change the status quo? If I understand the authors discussed here, they hold we can do nothing about it through educational institutions. Jencks and Bereiter believe these institutions can make no difference. Spring says the same thing: they can do nothing but sustain the existing order. What would happen if the schools or compulsory attendance at them were abolished and "the making of citizens" were left to parents? The status quo would be maintained—or would deteriorate.

This must be so because those who had the power would start with all the advantages, and their children would end with them. The restraints now placed on snobbishness and exclusivity, on racial, social, and economic prejudice, would disappear and any idea of the common good would vanish into thin air.

But perhaps there is nothing in that idea, or in the idea of community, anyway. Since there is no space for argument, I shall have to content myself for the moment with the assertion that man has never been able to live without the community and that, if he is to live well, he must try to make the community as good as it can be.

The American political community is based on the notion of the continuous engagement of all the people in dialogue about their common concerns. I am aware of the obstacles, ranging from secrecy in government to monopoly in the mass media, that make this dialogue an ideal rather than a reality. I am also aware that an educational system operates within severe limitations. It is limited by the background and ability of its pupils and the environment in which they live. It is limited by the prejudices of taxpayers. It cannot proclaim a revolution and survive.

But to proclaim rededication to basic American principles, to announce a commitment to prepare the rising generation for that dialogue which it should carry on, to enunciate the reasons why the rising generation should be prepared, and to work out the methods by which it could be is within the scope—and I hope the competence—of American educators.

American citizens have an awful responsibility: they have to try to understand the world. Of course the public schools cannot provide this understanding. But statistics showing the dubious results of our present efforts will not convince me that it is impossible to formulate an educational program in this country that will make a difference in the degree of understanding the citizen achieves.

POSTSCRIPT

ARE THERE VIABLE OPTIONS TO SCHOOLING?

Schooling (viewed basically in terms of the status quo) and deschooling (viewed mainly as a complete reconsideration of the function of organized instruction) are polar opposites. But, just as Bereiter modifies Illich's position and both Hutchins and Jackson recognize the imperfections of the status quo, so most thinkers move toward a middle ground of reschooling or reformed schooling. The final segments of this book explore some representative thinking on public school reform, the reform of higher education, and the prospects for future educational improvement.

Besides the impact of the variety of views presented by critics, apologists, and reformers in recent years, large and powerful professional organizations and philanthropic groups have become increasingly critical (and sometimes self-critical) and have moved into the vanguard of school improvement. The National Education Association (NEA), the American Federation of Teachers (AFT), the Ford Foundation, the Carnegie Foundation, the American Council on Education, and the Association for Supervision and Curriculum Development (ASCD) must be counted among such organizations whose messages often penetrate to the classroom level.

An example of such a potential reform influence is ASCD's widely distributed 1975 yearbook, *Schools in Search of Meaning,* edited by James B. Macdonald and Esther Zaret. This book analyzes the real and assumed barriers separating educational ideals and good intentions from actual classroom practices. The yearbook focuses especially on the relationship between school activities and social structure, grappling with questions that are essential to any reform thinking, including:

—What is the role of schooling in society?

—How do schools affect human relationships?

—How do schools relate to the interests of specific social groups?

—What is needed in order to disclose the political realities of schooling?

—Where might educators look for alliances in the task of restructuring both schools and society?

—What is the nature of education that is liberating rather than dominating?

A number of these essential matters are treated under the next issue by co-authors Harvey B. Scribner and Leonard B. Stevens, who position informed parents at the center of the needed reform alliance, and co-authors Samuel Bowles and Herbert Gintis, who reflect much of the ASCD yearbook message in their insistence that economic reform is a prerequisite to true educational reform.

ISSUE 15

CAN TRUE REFORM BE ACCOMPLISHED?

In changing times, schools must change—or perish. In this century there have been periodic thrusts to improve schooling by making its procedures more scientific, by making its atmosphere more humane, by reducing its formality, by diminishing its indoctrination function, by developing technology-based instructional approaches. But often these attempts to improve the quality of education are constrained by social and political realities, by outmoded teacher preparation, by public resistance, and by an incomplete understanding of the attitudinal and valuational effects of social change.

As Philip W. Jackson pointed out in his 1968 *Life in Classrooms,* regardless of the extent of reform measures the average school is often mired in trivial activities and pettiness. Problems remain today which have plagued organized education for years: the lack of student motivation, the predominance of artificially fragmented approaches to knowledge, a lack of truly individualized instruction, a pace-pressure which discourages many learners, a tendency on the part of schools to sort and label students, an adherence to an outmoded evaluation system, and the persistence of age-, race-, ethnic-, and sex-stereotyping.

Some recent efforts to deal with these many continuing practical reform problems include the following: *Making New Schools: The Liberation of Learning* (1971) by Joseph Turner, *The School Book: For People Who Want To Know What All the Hollering Is About* (1973) by Neil Postman and Charles Weingartner, *How To Change the Schools* (1970) by Ellen Lurie, Ray Rist's *Reconstructing American Education* (1972), John Goodlad's *The Dynamics of Educational Change: Toward Responsive Schools* (1975), Mario Fantini's *Public Schools of Choice* (1974), *Learning Environments* (1975) by Thomas G. David and Benjamin D. Wright (eds.), *Competency-Based Education: A*

Process for the Improvement of Education (1976) by Gene E. Hall and Howard L. Jones, and Nat Hentoff's *Does Anybody Give a Damn?* (1977).

Although the fervor for radical changes which was spawned by the ideas of Paul Goodman, John Holt, and Ivan Illich may be receding, the proliferation of exploratory ideas for improving education (as attested to by the above citations) indicates that the reform struggle will continue in the 1980s. In "Strategies for Educational Reform" (*Teachers College Record,* September 1974), Eli Ginzberg identifies some crucial targets of educational reform:

1. student boredom and purposelessness
2. student floundering at all levels of schooling
3. persistence of opportunity gaps for the poor, the rural, and minority-group youth
4. increasing voter rejection of tax increases
5. lack of clarity in defining the school's role in transforming society
6. lack of firm evidence of the value of large governmental expenditures for educational improvement
7. the current surplus of educated manpower in this country

James S. Coleman's report, *Youth: Transition to Adulthood* (1974), also deals with these concerns, and counsels that the linkage between schools and the working world must, through career education programs and work-study opportunities, be maximized.

Exploring the theme of searching for appropriate reform strategies, the following selections reveal the complexity of the issue. The first selection examines the reform ideas of Ivan Illich, Charles Silberman, and Mario Fantini and charts a course for further action. The second analyzes the social and economic realities which are central to the accomplishment of any true reform, and in the process evaluates Illich's propositions.

Harvey B. Scribner
and
Leonard B. Stevens

THE PUBLIC MUST LEAD THE WAY

What is the hope for school reform? Is reform possible any more?

Ivan Illich[1] says that we should not waste time hoping (or working) for the reform of schools. Instead we should get on with the business of abolishing them. Schools are empty of education, full of ritual, his argument goes. Therefore, for the sake of the young and a better society, schools should be disestablished. No more compulsory education. No more formal education. Ban the diploma. Prohibit discimination on the basis of accumulated education. Create informal networks, and share our skills and knowledge by mutual consent and for mutual benefit. The Illich vision is of a deschooled society.

The Illich critique of schooling and the way credentials are offered is incisive and on target, but its ultimate conclusion is not persuasive. Schools may be places of empty ritual, but it is difficult to generate much hope that informal "learning webs" would not be susceptible to comparable ills, not least of which might be their domination by established elites, professional or otherwise. Diplomas, degrees and other credentials may be means of discriminating, but it is reasonable that their elimination would be followed quickly by the creation of other instruments of marking and sorting people; schools may justify class systems, but they did not create them. The problems of the world are mostly other than educational—hunger, violence, tyranny, prejudice, poverty. It is difficult to envision how such problems would recede if schools were disestablished; it is easy to foresee things getting even worse. The Illich theory fails to answer two basic questions: In what ways would the world be a better place without schools? How would the young be better off?

A second and more important critic, Charles E. Silberman,[2] has another view of schools and school reform. The hope, he says, is to recognize that schools do not have to be bad. The cause of bad schools is "mindlessness," his theory goes, and when schools are bad, two sets of people get hurt: the children and the teachers. The Silberman critique of schools rests in part on this teacher-as-victim concept. School reform thus has two outcomes: the

1. See his *Deschooling Society*.
2. Author of *Crisis in the Classroom: The Remaking of American Education*.

Continued on p. 246

Samuel Bowles and Herbert Gintis

ECONOMIC REFORM IS NEEDED CONTEXT

The 1960s and 1970s, like other periods of social dislocation in U.S. history, have spawned a host of proposals for restructuring the educational system. In response to the struggles of blacks, women, Chicanos, and other oppressed groups for a more just share of the economic pie have come proposals for racially integrated schooling, compensatory education, open enrollment, voucher systems, and other reforms aimed at creating a more equal educational system. In response to job dissatisfaction, a growing sense of powerlessness among even the relatively privileged, and the spread of a do-your-own-thing youth culture, reformers have offered the open classroom, unstructured learning environments, the open campus, pass-fail options, and other changes directed toward a more liberating educational experience. Some have proposed that we do away with schools altogether and carry on the task of education in decentralized and voluntary skill exchanges, reference services, and "learning webs." Some of these proposals go little beyond social tinkering; others are quite radical. Most of the proposals have existed in some form for at least half a century; a few are genuinely new. Some have been proferred in the hopes of preserving the status quo; others embody distinctly revolutionary objectives. Many modern progressive educators have seen a more equal and liberating school system as the major instrument for the construction of a just and humane society.

The reader will not be surprised to find that we are more than a little skeptical of these claims. The social problems to which these reforms are addressed have their roots not primarily in the school system itself, but rather in the normal functioning of the economic system. Educational alternatives which fail to address this basic fact join a club of venerable lineage: the legion of school reforms which, at times against the better intentions of its leading proponents, have served to deflect discontent, depoliticize social distress, and thereby have helped to stabilize the prevailing structures of privilege.

Schools and educational reforms play a central role in the reproduction of the social order. Yet this need not be the case. The character of reform

Continued on p. 250

(Scribner and Stevens, cont. from p. 244)
liberation of teachers, and the improvement of educational opportunities for the young.

Silberman is not the usual critic; he likes teachers. "To read some of the more important and influential contemporary critics of education—men like Edgar Friedenberg, Paul Goodman, John Holt, Jonathan Kozol—one might think that the schools are staffed by sadists and clods," Silberman wrote in *Crisis in the Classroom,* an enormously popular and widely praised book.[3]

> But teachers *are* human. . . . If they appear otherwise, it is because the institution in which they are engulfed demands it of them. . . . If placed in an atmosphere of freedom and trust, if treated as professionals and as people of worth, teachers behave like the caring, concerned people they would like to be. They, no less than their students, are victimized by the way in which schools are currently organized and run.

There are an enormous number of decent, capable professionals in the schools of America. They exist in virtually every school. And the best are, as Silberman says, crushed or chased away by the worst of schools, the worst of administrators, and the proliferation of petty rules.

The explanation, however, is incomplete. The trouble with Silberman's explanation is that it falls short of the entire story, and what is omitted is at least as significant as what is there. If most teachers are "decent, honest, well-intentioned people" with an inherent concern for the young, one must presume that they are also reasonably intelligent, reasonably skilled and endowed with a certain amount of perception. And if so many schools are so badly run that they victimize teacher and student alike, the question is: What are the teachers doing about the bad situation? Are teachers so intimidated and controlled by their supervisors and principals that they are fearful to lift a finger in protest? Have teachers come to feel that it is not their place to question school practices that they view as harmful to children? Why aren't more teachers in revolt against repressive schools and incompetent principals? Why aren't more teachers allied with students and parents in protesting inequitable policies and unjust rules? Why do so many teachers speak of "my children"—but do not speak up against schools that they know are numbing so many of the young? We recall the comment Archibald Cox made about the many fine young men in Washington who found it impossible to say No to their superiors in the Watergate era. One wonders how many fine men and women are teaching in schools that are harming students—and failing to speak or act against the harm they see. The Silberman explanation seems to imply that teachers have no capacity to take a stand to protect the young.

The Silberman theory of teachers as powerless victims of bad schools also falls short of reality in a second respect—its failure to recognize the power of organized teachers, and to analyze the ends toward which this power more than occasionally is used. Teacher organizations frequently oppose reforms that might improve schools and would help

3. The book, among its other awards, received the John Dewey Award of the United Federation of Teachers of New York City. The empathy of Mr. Silberman for teachers no doubt was a major factor, since teachers have been notably negative toward other critics of schools. The acceptability of *Crisis in the Classroom* is one feature that distinguishes it from the rest of the body of literature that criticizes schools and schooling—the book was acceptable to professional and layman alike.

children. During our time in New York City, the United Federation of Teachers fought against decentralization of the school system, opposed expansion of teacher licenses for bilingual teachers, opposed efforts to liberalize the licensing system for teachers and other professionals; and worked in the state legislature for bills to restrict the counseling of students to licensed guidance counselors (and thereby prevent classroom teachers from counseling students), to impair reorganization of the central school headquarters by mandating retention of several powerful central bureaus. During the same time, organized teachers opposed state legislation to permit commercial driving schools to teach students how to drive, to establish parent councils with the right to observe teachers in the classroom, to allow schools to be open on weekends, to make teacher tenure subject to periodic renewal.

The Silberman thesis stops short of the more abrasive conclusion that teachers do have to bear some of the responsibility for bad schools—to the extent, first, that they may fail as individuals; but more to the extent, second, that they allow their organizations, union or otherwise, to work politically to block and impair school reforms. Do the medical professions have a responsibility to help make the nation's health-care systems more rational and more equitable? Have they had no political role in blocking or slowing down reformist proposals?

Charles Silberman is not an apologist for bad schools; he is an extremely important advocate of better schools, and he has added his considerable weight to the task of school reform. Nor, as should be equally needless to say, do we subscribe to any brief that would diminish the right of teachers to organize, lobby, campaign and bargain, to influence public opinion, and take stands on matters of public importance, including the endorsing of candidates for public office. But Silberman's critique, valuable for its vision of schools as humane institutions in a humane society, puts them in a political vacuum. They are not, and never have been. Silberman tells us little about the politics of reforming schools; and without such an understanding, schools are not likely to be changed very much.

A third critic, Mario D. Fantini,[4] has looked at school reform and emerged with an attractive concept—"public schools of choice." Families would select the kind of schools they want for their children. It is a kind of voucher system. But is it realistic to believe that, as Fantini says, this sweeping reform can come about through "a politics of cooperation" that brings together "the thousands of people of good will, both in and out of our public schools, who are really motivated by what is best for children?" And can we believe that such an ambitious plan for the refashioning of American education could be achieved without a real loss of power for professionals and a commensurate gain for parents in such matters as control, governance and prerogative?

Fantini's dream is this: "Teachers, students, parents, administrators can work together if they feel that their own rights are not being preempted." But is it not precisely the point that some existing "rights" will have to be "preempted" if a system that now withholds power and influence from parents and the young is to be made over? Can there be "public

4. Author of *Public Schools of Choice: A Plan for the Reform of American Education.* We urge its readers to give special attention to the book's appendix, which contains an exchange between Fantini and Herb Kohl, a rather well-known school critic. It is a revealing exchange on the politics of school reform.

schools of choice" without changing most if not virtually all existing ways of conducting school business? Would this not preempt or revise many prerogatives that professionals now enjoy? What serious reforms can these people of good will discuss, plan and implement which do not preempt someone's "rights?" Where a "right" would be preempted, would this mean the plan in question would be scrapped so that no one of good will would be offended and walk away? Is this not a formula for no reform, or reform only of the harmless variety to which no one of consequence would object?

Fantini concedes that his notion of cooperative politics "may appear to be naive." We are forced to agree, even though we are attracted to his schools of choice. It is not merely a matter of separating those of good will from those of ill will. The problem is that professionals of good will have their own agenda to follow. That agenda, rhetoric aside, takes precedence over the reforming of schools; indeed, it often conflicts with reform ideas.

What, then, is the hope, what is the strategy of reform? No one can imagine the shapes and forms that schools and education will take in a generation. But there are some goals that we should be heading for.

We can assume that such areas as how schools are organized, how they are governed, whom they employ, how students enter and leave and re-enter, how education is defined, how opportunities are guaranteed will be subjects of debate, and should be targets of reform. We should strive for flexibility of policies, in contrast to policies that restrict and contain.

We can assume, given the new legitimacy of pluralism, that diversity will be a powerful theme in future educational policy. We should work to increase the interest in alternatives in education—specifically, alternatives within the public-education sector. The demand for choices has already begun to make itself felt. The notion of "public schools of choice" would have been unthinkable just a few years ago; now the idea is taken seriously. We should encourage the trend to deliberately send students out of school for the sake of their education—into internships, apprenticeships, work-study, "city as school" and "parkway" programs—and push it downward to include younger children. We can assume that the education of parents and other adults will be of more concern, not less. The wildest schemes we can dream up now may seem quaintly conventional before the turn of the century. We should look for policies that encourage the creation of "wild" schemes, and give them the chance to be tried. The greater risk is to do only that which is safe.

We can assume, and hope, that the public will insist on more direct accountability from its schools, and that parents will demand more of a direct role in the governing of schools. We can assume that professionals will not take the parents' challenge lightly. Indications are that the public treasury will be less able to give schools all the money they say they need. And because parents and legislators will demand more concrete evidence of results, schools will seemingly be in the position of being asked to do more with less. It's not an altogether unreasonable demand, given the historical reticence and inability of schools to close out failing efforts as a way of saving money for promising ideas. But schools and school leaders will tend to see it that way.[5]

Are schools preparing for the future? Are they asking questions of fundamental consequence to the lives of the young? Are they consciously making themselves more flexible institutions—questioning old practices, looking with honest skepticism on old restraints and old limits, reaching out for parents, stretching old definitions of education, taking down old barriers between home and school and classroom and world, asking the universities for assistance in the creative design of new visions of school? As they build each new annual budget, do they weigh the existing ways of spending money with the same scrutiny that is given to proposed new ways? Are they restudying the words and recommendations of their critics in search of clues as to how they might relate more productively with students and parents, and teachers as well? We leave it to parents to judge their own schools. By our standard of judgment, the great majority of schools—though there are notable, refreshing, exciting exceptions—cannot see the future yet, because they are looking behind.

The hope for the reform of the public schools rests with the public, especially parents.[6] Parents must believe they are capable of governing schools, able to select teachers and principals, worthy of making the decisions as to how their children will be educated. Parents have been trained that it is not their place to question educational practice, that it is inappropriate for them to be critical and discontented. The role of the good parent is part of the legend: to be supportive, to be helpful, to rally other taxpayers in support of schools, to belong to the P.T.A., to make sure the young stay in school, to come to graduation ceremonies. Parents have yet to take their ultimate role, their ultimate responsibility: to control their schools as a piece of their government.

The day will come, we hope, in some communities, small and large, when parents will say to the professionals they employ, "This is what we want for our children. Don't tell us the reasons it can't be done. Tell us how to do it. Or give us a better idea." Should the school board choose to respond that the parents' wishes cannot be fulfilled, because of this contract or that understanding, because of this policy or that regulation, and indicate its unwillingness to act, the parents at least will know where the problem is. They will know that they are not as represented as they may have thought. They will know, too, that their rights and their children's rights have been bargained or given away by their own representatives.

5. We hope it is clear that we are not suggesting that public education ought to get less financial support. It ought to get more. The point is that money alone, without serious reforms, will not make schools that are worthy of the young.

6. Throughout this book we have argued for parent participation in the control of schools. The conservatism and traditionalism inherent in the views of a great many parents do not dissuade us from this basic recommendation. The public, we feel, has been taught to think about schools in traditional, conservative, uncreative ways by school leaders who, over the years, have tended to be conservative, traditional and professional-oriented themselves. With little opportunity to participate in educational planning and decision-making, the public has little reason, indeed, not to believe what it is told. We would submit that the more the leaders in education talk about the need for more professionals, more new buildings, more discipline, separate schools for "disruptive" children, the dangers of "radical" reforms, et cetera, the more the public will reflect these opinions in the polls that ask the public what it thinks about schools. Further, we would submit that the more parents and other citizens participate directly and consistently in school decision-making, the more they will be exposed to the failure that goes on in the name of education, the more they will make their own conclusions as to causes and solutions, and the more the public's opinions on schools will become enlightened and creative.

15. CAN TRUE REFORM BE ACCOMPLISHED?

How refreshing it would be to see families picking and choosing the days on which they send their children to school, days that make sense to them and fit the family schedule; to see children treated and learning as individuals, each following a personally tailored program of study; to see older children and young adults of high-school age systematically guided by their schools into educational work experience, internships, apprenticeships, community service and research, all outside the walls of school; to see all students of all ages paired for regular periods of tutoring and mutual aid; to hear students and their parents intelligently discussing which teachers to select in the coming session, knowing that the choice is theirs; to watch boards of education discovering human-size space for learning in vacant houses and commercial buildings, and lease it instead of building yet another massive schoolhouse; to witness, perhaps, an intensely troubled urban high school making sensible plans for its own renewal and reorganization by taking the risk of stopping classes while students and teachers work together on a plan; to find parents of each school electing their own governing boards to control their school; to read in the newspaper a routine announcement of diplomas awarded to persons long past school age, on the basis of competence acquired and demonstrated external to schools; to see a state guarantee twelve years of education to all its citizens, including those who "save" some of their allotted years for later in life.

If the class of professionals has higher priorities than reform, if school boards tend to be less than aggressive in protecting the public's interests and in representing the young who but the parent can be expected to take the lead in the reformation of schools? Who is more appropriate to lead? At the bottom line the citizenry is responsible for its own institutions; and the public, when aroused and informed, has a powerful reform capacity, far transcending that of professionals, school boards, or even critics.

This is the hope: that the public will become aroused and enlightened and that their necessary leadership will come forth. This would be the first step toward creating systems of public education that are worthy of the young. Difficult as it may be, the first step could prove to be nine tenths of the journey.

(Bowles and Gintis, cont. from p. 245)

depends, not only on the content of the reform itself, but on the programatic context in which the reform is advocated and the process by which it is won as well. Many of the above proposals could be welded into a powerful and progressive program. Such a program would have as its overriding objective the ultimate dismantling of the capitalist system and its replacement by a more progressive social order. Yet its most immediate objectives would certainly include many of those espoused by today's social reformers. The unifying theme of a program of revolutionary reforms is that short-run successes yield concrete gains for those participating in the struggle and, at the same time, strengthen the movement for further change. In the context of a general strategy for social change, we include proposals for a more equal and less repressive education as revolutionary reforms.

Revolutionary school reformers must recognize, and take advantage of, the critical role of education in reproducing the economic order. It is precisely this role of education which both offers the opportunity for using schools to promote revolutionary change and, at the same time, presents the danger of co-optation and assimilation into a counterstrategy to stabilize the social order. Nothing in our analysis suggests that equal schooling or open education is impossible in the U.S. But we are firmly convinced that, if these alternatives are to contribute to a better social order, they must be part of a more general revolutionary movement—a movement which is not confined to schooling, but embraces all spheres of social life. . . .

FREE SCHOOLS

Why saddle our youth with the burden of authoritarian schools? Why ought the better part of a young person's days pass in an atmosphere of powerlessness, of demeaning and dictatorial rigidity, perpetual boredom, and behavior modification? Why, in a democratic society, should an individual's first real contact with a formal institution be so profoundly anti-democratic?

Many people have been asking these questions in recent years. Whence the birth of a new movement: free school reform. With a heavy intellectual debt to such venerable thinkers as Paul Goodman and Abraham Maslow, a host of poignant interpreters and critics of modern education have emerged in the past decade with creative alternatives to the dismal countenance of the school. Ranging from the personal diaries of George Dennison, James Herndon, Herbert Kohl, and Jonathan Kozol through the programatic writings of John Holt to the full-fledged social analysis of Charles Silberman, the ideas and strategies of these critics have left scarcely a person involved in education untouched and unmoved.

Indeed, who but the reactionary or ill-informed could disagree with the ideal of liberated education? Evidently no one. Indeed the politics of free schools and open classrooms have made strange bedfellows. Ex-hippies and well-to-do suburbanites; refugees from the radical student movement and editors of *Fortune* magazine, T-group psychotherapists, and the Secretary of the U.S. Department of Health, Education and Welfare; and from various other segments of the political spectrum educational liberators find themselves united by a common vision: a democratic, cooperative, and unstructured education—a vision of schools that promotes rather than retards personal development.

Almost too good to be true! Indeed, we believe that the perception of unity of purpose and clarity of vision is profoundly illusory. The illusion has taken the reform movement some distance. But at a price: failure to develop a realistic analysis of the class basis of educational repression and a viable long-range strategy to combat it. We believe that these deficiencies may be overcome—indeed, as they are in the recent writings of Kozol, Graubard, and other radicals in the movement, for example—and that the free-school movement can be transformed into a powerful progressive force. What this requires is the development within the movement of an analysis which rejects any notion that schools are independent of society, an analysis which places schools concretely in their social and economic context. The unavoidable outcome of such an analysis, we believe, is a commitment to the transformation of the capitalist economy as the guiding principle of a revolutionary program for a liberated education.

We will argue for a rejection of the present free-school movement's economics, its philosophy, and its politics. Our critique of the implicit economics of the movement is exceedingly simple and flows directly from the analysis presented [here]. The educational system trains people to take positions in economic life by patterning its own social relationships after those of the office and factory. Thus, the repressive aspects of schooling are by no means irrational or perverse but are, rather, systematic and pervasive reflections of economic reality. By itself a liberated education will produce occupational misfits and a proliferation of the job blues. It will not by itself contribute to a freer existence because the sources of repression lie outside the school system. If schools are to assume a more humane form, so, too, must jobs.

This economic reality has implications for the philosophy of education: The free-school movement must develop an educational philosophy which recognizes that a liberated educational system must prepare youth for democracy and participation in economic life. This educational philosophy—in order to avoid the failures and distortions of earlier Progressive movements—must be revolutionary and egalitarian. Here we find the prevalent ideology of free school reform, with its emphasis on the abolition of authority and its ideal of the unsullied flowering of the child's "true inner self," to be barren and naively individualistic. Democracy—particularly economic democracy—involves both authority and an intrinsically social consciousness on the part of individuals. Above all, socialism involves the will to struggle as well as the capacity to cooperate. A realistic educational philosophy must reflect this.

A further shortcoming of the free-school movement concerns the manner in which it treats (or, to be more precise, ignores) its own class composition. Its supporters among teachers, students, and parents are drawn from a rather limited and privileged segment of the population. Yet the movement has presented its ideals as universal; it has remained puzzled by its lack of acceptance by other social groupings—among which oppressed minorities and the traditional working class are only the most obvious. One political error in this approach is to orient strategy uniquely around gaining recruits to its ideology, rather than recruiting within itself while developing working alliances with other classes and groups which have distinct immediate needs and objectives. A revolutionary transformation and democratization of economic life clearly requires united action of diverse social groups and classes—e.g., minority groups; white- and blue-collar, and technical workers; public sector employees; and the women's movement. Each of these groups has specific and diverse immediate educational needs and aspirations. It is hardly surprising that the educational liberation movement must also take the form of a cooperative (not to say conflict-free) alliance among groups. What is valid and just for one, may be irrelevant—at least here and now—for another. This leads to a fundamental strategic error in a movement which does not recognize its class basis: By treating its ideas as universally valid and by ignoring its emergence as a particular sociohistorical event, the educational liberation movement loses perspective on the social forces which gave rise to it and which may promote or hinder its further development. . . .

But what does all this imply for educational change? What is the potential of the free-school movement both to achieve a more humane education and to contribute to the radical transformation of the structure of economic life? As in the case of egalitarian reforms, our evaluation must be ambiguous.

There is a considerable potential for the assimilation of the free-school movement into a program for the streamlining and rationalization of the advanced capitalist order. The new corporate organization itself requires a shift in the social relationships of education. Direct discipline and emphasis on external rewards, characteristic of the assembly line and the factory system, have given way for a major segment of the work force to motivation by internalized norms characteristic of the service and office worker. Cooperative rather than individually competitive work relationships are increasingly emphasized. Entrepreneurial capitalism, which brought us the chairs-nailed-to-the-floor classroom, has given way to corporate capitalism. It may belatedly usher in the era of the open classroom, minimization of grading, and internalized behavior norms contemplated for at least a century by so many educational reformers. Thus the free-school movement contains elements thoroughly consistent with the modern corporate capitalist imperative for the "soft" socialization of at least a substantial minority of the workers: whence the strange coalition of corporate and political leaders with free school "radicals." The very rhetoric of educational liberation—genuinely put forth by radicals—can quite easily become the concrete practice of recasting much of the school system into the mold of advanced corporate capitalism. As in the case of its inspirational progenitor, the Progressive Movement, the ideology of educational liberation can become a tool of domination.

Yet the revolutionary potential of the free-school movement is substantial. While much of the rhetoric and results of free schooling will be easily assimilated by the modern corporate and state bureaucracies, much of it will be difficult to digest. Young people, whose dominant experiences in school have been cooperative, democratic, and substantially participatory, will find integration into the world of work a wrenching experience. Students emerging from genuinely free schools already know that hierarchical organization is not the natural, best, or only form of productive human relationships.

But it takes more than personal discontent and job blues to create a movement capable of transforming the structure of society. The incompatibility of the antiauthoritarian and spontaneous ethic of the free schools with alienated labor, by itself, hardly provides the basis for a revolutionary politics. Some turn to drugs and self-indulgent consumption, some to counterculture, some seek a back-to-the-earth or craft solution, and others develop a personally and politically destructive self-hatred and cynicism.

The potential revolutionary impact of the free school movement will depend not so much on its capacity to create miniutopias in our schools as on its ability to create an awareness among its participants of why the ideals of the movement cannot be generally realized. To be an effective tool for human liberation, free schools must create, not a temporary and privileged oasis of freedom, but an understanding of oppression and how to fight it in capitalist society. Lacking a political understanding of their predicament, graduates of free schools may well attribute their discontent to their own failings, to human nature, or to the inevitable requisites of production. Yet a politically radical free-school movement could well provide a seed bed for revolutionaries. The content as well as the process of free schooling has an important role to play. The free-school movement must go beyond life-style radicalism and a preoccupation with educational form and begin to teach the tools of liberation. Much depends on the development of a political self-understanding by the movement itself. . . .

DE-SCHOOLING

The most drastic recent proposal for education, and one with a growing number of adherents, is that schools be abolished. The popularity of this idea owes much to an eloquent and incisive book, *De-Schooling Society* by Ivan Illich. In it, Illich confronts the full spectrum of the modern crisis in values by rejecting the basic tenets of progressive liberalism. He dismisses what he calls the "myth of consumption" as a cruel and illusory ideology foisted upon the populace by a manipulative bureaucratic system. He treats welfare and service institutions as part of the problem, not as part of the solution. He rejects the belief that education constitutes the great equalizer and the path to personal liberation. Schools, says Illich, simply must be eliminated.

Illich does more than merely criticize; he conceptualizes constructive technological alternatives to repressive education. Moreover, he sees the present age as revolutionary because the existing social relationships of economic and political life, including the dominant institutional structure of schooling, have become impediments to the development of liberating socially productive technologies. Here Illich is relevant indeed, for the tension between technological possibility and social reality pervades all advanced industrial societies today. Illich's response is a forthright vision of participatory, decentralized, and liberating learning technologies, and a radically altered vision of social relationships in education.

Yet, while his description of modern society is sufficiently incisive, his analysis is, we believe, inadequate, and his program, consequently, is a diversion from the immensely complex and demanding political, organization[al], intellectual, and personal demands of revolutionary reconstruction in the coming decades. . . .

Educational reformers commonly err by treating the system of schools as if it existed in a social vacuum. Illich does not make this mistake. Rather, he views the internal irrationalities of modern education as reflections of the larger society. The key to understanding the problems of advanced industrial economics, he argues, lies in the character of its consumption activities and the ideology which supports them. The schools, in turn, are exemplary models of bureaucracies geared toward the indoctrination of docile and manipulable consumers.

Guiding modern social life and interpersonal behavior, says Illich, is a destructive system of "institutionalized values" which determines how one perceives one's needs and defines instruments for one's satisfaction. The process which creates institutional values insures that all individual needs—physical, psychological, social, intellectual, emotional, and spiritual—are transformed into demands for goods and services. In contrast to the "psychological impotence" which results from institutionalized values, Illich envisages the "psychic health" which emerges from self-realization—both personal and social. Guided by institutionalized values, one's well-being lies not in what one does but in what one has—the status of one's job and the level of material consumption.

Illich's model of consumption manipulation is crucial at every stage of his political argument. But it is substantially incorrect. First, Illich locates the source of social decay in the autonomous, manipulative behavior of corporate bureaucracies. However, as we have argued, the source must be sought in the normal operation of the basic economic institutions of capitalism which consistently sacrifice the healthy development of work, education, and social equality to the accumulation of capital and the requisites of the hierarchical division of labor. Moreover, given that individuals must participate in economic activity, these social outcomes are quite insensitive to the preferences or values of individuals, and are certainly in no sense a reflection of the autonomous wills of manipulating bureaucrats or gullible consumers. Hence, merely ending manipulation while maintaining basic economic institutions will affect social life only minimally.

Second, Illich locates the source of consumer consciousness in the manipulative socialization of individuals by agencies controlled by corporate and welfare bureaucracies. This institutionalized consciousness induces individuals to choose outcomes not in conformity with their real needs. Yet a causal analysis can never take socialization agencies as basic explanatory variables in assessing the overall behavior of the social system. In particular, consumer consciousness is generated through the day-to-day activities and observations of individuals in capitalist society. The sales pitches of manipulative institutions do not produce the values of commodity fetishism, but rather capitalize on and reinforce the values and anxieties derived from and reconfirmed by daily personal experience in the social system. In fact, while consumer behavior may seem irrational and fetishistic, it is a reasonable accommodation to the options for meaningful social outlets in the context of capitalist institutions. Driving an oversized car may be one of the few experiences of personal power available in a world of alienated labor and fragmented community. Owning a late model convertible probably does enhance one's love life, or at least provide a substitute for one. Therefore the abolition of addictive propaganda cannot liberate the individual to "free choice" of personal goals. Such choice is still conditioned by the pattern of social processes which have historically rendered individuals amenable to "institutionalized values." In fact, the likely outcome of demanipulation of values would be no significant alteration of these values at all.

Moreover, the ideology of commodity fetishism reflects not only the day-to-day operations of the economy. It is also a necessary condition for the profitability of capitalism as a system in the long run. Commodity fetishism motivates men and women to accept and participate in the system of alienated production, to peddle their (potentially) creative activities to the highest bidder through the market in labor, to accept and participate in the destruction of their communities, and to bear allegiance to an economic system whose market institutions and patterns of control of work and community systematically subordinate all social goals to the criteria of profit. Thus, the weakening in institutionalized values would, in itself, lead logically either to unproductive and undirected social chaos or to a rejection of the social relations of capitalist production along with commodity fetishism.

Third, Illich argues that the goal of social change is to transform institutions according to the criterion of nonaddictiveness, or left-conviviality. However, since manipulation and addictiveness are not the sources of social problems, their elimination offers no cure. Certainly, the implementation of left-convivial forms in welfare and service agencies—however desirable in itself—will not counter the effects of capitalist development on social life. More important, Illich's criterion explicitly accepts those basic economic institutions which structure decision-making power, lead to the growth of corporate and welfare bureaucracies, and lie at the root of social decay. Illich's criterion must be replaced by one of democratic and participatory, control over social outcomes in factory, office, community, schools, and media.

If sources of social problems lay in consumer manipulation of which schooling is both an exemplary instance and a crucial preparation for future manipulation, then a political movement for de-schooling might be, as Illich says, ". . . at the root of any movement for human liberation." But if schooling is a preparation for work and a central aspect of the reproduction of the social relationships of production, the elimination of school without the transformation of economic life would inevitably lead to a situation of social chaos, but probably not to a viable mass movement toward constructive social change. In this case, the correspondence principle simply fails to hold, producing, at best, a temporary breakdown in the social fabric, if elites can find an alternative mode of work socialization, or ultimately fatal, if they cannot. . . .

CONCLUSION

Many of the reforms discussed in this chapter are feasible within the context of present-day U.S. society. There are also a host of others of great interest we have not discussed. Some, like local control of schools, would extend to urban areas some of the privileges of the relatively class- and race-homogeneous suburbs. At the same time, however, local control would further the fragmentation of working people. Others, like educational vouchers which would offer parents a fixed sum of money per child to spend on education any way they see fit, might equalize educational resources and foster the proliferation of alternative educational settings. All would, with hard work, have the effect of improving, to some degree, the future lives and present comforts of our youth. As such, they are desirable indeed. However, we have argued that none, within its own framework, is capable of addressing the major problems facing U.S. society today. None utilizes the full potential of the educational system for contributing to social change. Only revolutionary reforms, we believe, have this potential. Implicit in the need for such reforms is the understanding that educational change must contribute to a fundamental democratization of economic life.

POSTSCRIPT

CAN TRUE REFORM BE ACCOMPLISHED?

Scribner and Stevens call for an aroused and informed citizenry to take responsibility for the quality of its schools and to use its potentially powerful reform capacity. Theirs is a plea for a shift in the locus of power from education officials to parents and students.

Bowles and Gintis find that reform efforts typically lack staying power and cohesiveness because of their tendency to overlook the most important factor in the maintenance of the status quo, namely the economic system and the prevailing social order. A reformed and humane school, they contend, will not prepare the young for an unreformed and inhumane society.

Scribner and Stevens require a parental revolution; Bowles and Gintis require a social revolution. As different as the approaches might be, each involves a movement toward democratic participation. Movement in this direction, combined with an increasing awareness on the part of education professionals of curricular alternatives, could initiate true reform at the practical level.

Evidence of such awareness within the profession is emerging, as both theorists and practitioners examine more closely the qualitative aspects of the social relationships within educational settings. William Pinar's 1975 "Sanity, Madness, and the School" (in *Curriculum Theorizing: The Reconceptualists*) illustrates this sort of emerging analysis. He uses the images and metaphors of the schooling process to explore the concrete effects of socialization on the individual. His analysis reveals, among others, the following subjective effects:

—hypertrophy or atrophy of fantasy life
—division or loss of self to others via modeling
—dependence or arrested development of autonomy
—loss of self-love through criticism by others
—thwarting of affiliative needs
—weakening of capacity for self-direction
—estrangement from self

Such effects lead to a form of madness in which the individual becomes alienated from personal reality. We graduate, Pinar concludes, credentialed but crazed.

The reform movement of the coming decades may well go beyond the search for physical, organizational, and ideological alternatives to conventional schooling to include the more profound considerations of the rescue of human individuality from the increasingly crushing effects of technology and bureaucracy.

ISSUE 16

WHAT DIRECTION FOR HIGHER EDUCATION?

The 1828 *Report of the Yale Faculty* reasserted the value of the standard liberal arts curriculum for training of the intellect and elevation of the spirit. In his 1869 inaugural address Harvard president Charles W. Eliot proclaimed the virtues of electives, variety, and individualization. There has been an abiding conflict over curriculum in the field of higher education ever since. In American colleges and universities the latter view has ascended, in some quarters to strange heights, and we find ourselves once again searching for "the idea of a university."

In the 20th century, the curriculum debate was rekindled by Thorstein Veblen in *The Higher Learning in America: A Memorandum on the Conduct of Universities by Businessmen* (1918) and set ablaze by Robert Maynard Hutchins in his Yale lecture series under the same general title. Hutchins at that time found the universities to be engaged in three basic activities—externally funded research, vocational certification, and social accommodation—which he felt often detracted from the real purpose of higher education. He also found an erosion of standards in the lower schools which forced 70 percent of the nation's colleges to offer remedial English and to provide an amazing array of "hilarious" courses requiring minimal intellectual effort.

In *The Learning Society* (1968), Hutchins expressed a deep concern about the tendency, not just in America but on a worldwide basis, toward universities' loss of autonomy as intellectual communities. He feels that as colleges and universities become more and more a part of a nationalized education industry their function as centers of independent thought and criticism will be obliterated. Hutchins finds himself at odds with fellow educator Clark Kerr, who, in *The Uses of the University* (1963), seeks to reconcile the many modern purposes of higher education under a new conception: the multiversity. (An amusing inside portrait of this new phenomenon is drawn by Nicholas von Hoffman in his 1966 *The Multiversity: A*

Personal Report on What Happens to Today's Students at American Universities.)

Jacques Barzun, too, has been a determined critic of the path taken by modern institutions of higher learning. In *The American University: How It Runs, Where It Is Going* (1968), he returns to the argument that a university "should be and remain One, not Many, singular not plural, a republic, not an empire." In this critical work Barzun offers 68 general and specific suggestions for improving higher education, among them that the faculty, which is the university, must convey at every turn what education is; the slogan throughout the university must be SIMPLIFY; survey courses should be replaced by short courses with a minimum of class time expenditure; we must recognize that ostentatious research comes from lust for prestige, on the part of faculty members and departments.

Beyond this sort of curricular and organizational criticism, recent years have seen a growing volume of radical commentary on the nature of higher education. Paul Goodman's *The Community of Scholars* (1964), Theodore Roszak's *The Dissenting Academy* (1968), and Harold Taylor's *Students Without Teachers: The Crisis in the University* (1969), launched a line of criticism which questioned the place of higher education in American society. Taylor insists, for instance, that administrative expediency has segmented the lives of students and created barriers between teaching and learning. He also feels that the general education curriculum spawned by Harvard, Chicago, and Columbia has provided a model for locked-in studies by locked-in students that has been emulated across the nation.

Two strong attacks on higher education are presented in the selections which follow. Arthur Pearl, touching on most aspects of college education, sees potential for making a difference in the quality of society but feels that there is a present lack of purposefulness beyond vocational training and regards most "reforms" as trivial innovations. Caroline Bird contends that college education simply does not live up to expectations and is losing its value in contemporary life.

Arthur Pearl

UNIVERSITIES NEED REALISTIC PURPOSES

The call for change in the American university ranges today from non-negotiable demands to polite requests, and from complete exchange of power to some minor tinkering with the curriculum. Every college and university is prideful of its willingness to innovate. And yet what has all this noise and activity achieved? Not very much; and the little that has been changed isn't even desirable.

The need for fundamental change in the university is obvious. Both outside and inside its hallowed halls the evidence fairly shrieks out at us. In the outside world there are mounting unresolved problems that threaten man's survival, and the university provides neither the men nor the ideas for solving them; worse yet, there is not even a promise that solutions will be forthcoming. Not unrelated to this is the nonsensical struggle for power that goes on within the university in which various factions, distinguished only by their lack of qualification to lead, joust for hegemony. To make matters worse, the majority in the university ignores both the outside concerns and the internal upsets, and continues business as usual. The majority would have you believe that their indifference reflects maturity. In truth, they are the walking dead—the zombies whose condition is ascribed in the horror flicks to voodoo. Now we know better. They are merely well-educated, conformist students, teachers and administrators.

The main failing of the university is that it has become an alien institution: it does not relate itself to anything of importance. Its processes are corrupted because the university itself is not pertinent to man's tenuous hold on life. At rock bottom the university is alien to nature, and as a consequence it is also alien to any defensible world of work, politics, culture and individual growth.

Now at a crossroads, the university faces a classical dilemma. Because it is out of phase with external realities the university has established internal structures and procedures that are as resistant to change as those established by an advanced schizophrenic as a defense against the threats of reality. The geography, the logistics, the normative behavior, the tolerance of ways of life,

Continued on p. 262

From "The More We Change, the Worse We Get" by Arthur Pearl. Reprinted with permission from *Change* Magazine, Vol. 2, No. 2 (March-April 1970). Copyrighted by the Council on Learning, NBW Tower, New Rochelle, New York 10801.

Caroline Bird

WE NEED ALTERNATIVES TO COLLEGE

"The fellowship of educated men" is an informal organization, but the piece of paper that attests membership in that company is a reliable passport to jobs, power, and , as one older Ivy League graduate put it, "instant prestige."

The reason is embarrassing. In our supposedly classless society, the diploma is our class distinction. By giving it to everyone, egalitarians hope somehow to make everyone upper class.

This is plain speaking. The proponents of college for all, the employers who prefer college graduates, and the mothers who "want the best" for their children don't like to think of themselves as snobs. That's why the language in which they discuss college is murky and the reasoning strays.

"He might be handicapped some time in some way if he didn't have a college degree," a mother will say. "He can go. He can get in. We have the money. And since there's nothing better for him to do right now anyway—well, why shouldn't he go?"

And then comes the father with the vocational clincher: "Maybe he won't need college to do the kind of job he'll probably want, but he'll need a degree to *get* it in the first place.". . .

What these people are saying, in a very polite and often oblique way, is that the tone of voice and language of an educated man implies a superiority that commands attention. The "educated" man "communicates" better not so much because he speaks more articulately or even because he has something more relevant to say, but because people—subordinates, associates, customers—listen to him more respectfully.

Instant operational prestige with strangers, the words and accents that make traffic cops believe your side of the story. This is one of the practical benefits of sounding educated, and it has very little to do with what is learned in expensively equipped classrooms or libraries. Very frequently it's what employers and parents are really buying for the price of a college education, and some are frank to admit it. One parent we interviewed hoped, rather vaguely, that a college education would be a "business and social asset" to his

Continued on p. 268

(Pearl, cont. from p. 260)
the admission policies, the evaluative systems, the content and sequence of courses, the hiring practices, the promotion system, the access to funds, the financial support of students, the administrative apparatus, the relationships of students with employers and recruiters, the "experimental' innovations"—all become mechanisms to insulate the university from outside influences, regardless of their urgency. The university system, moreover, with all its convolutions, impedes change because the organization itself has a vitality which enhances and extends itself with the Parkinsonian vigor of a metastasizing cancer. No wonder some critics of the university conclude that the only hope lies in a restart of the university, after it is destroyed. This conclusion is not greeted enthusiastically by most university teachers and administrators. As one of them, I too shy from the ultimate solution, but not because I find anything to defend in the contemporary form of the institution. Rather, I fear that its replacement would look god-awfully similar to that which was ostensibly destroyed.

Man has tinkered with ecological balance nearly to the point of no return. The equilibrium between death and birth has been seriously disrupted. The population of the world, now calculated to be in excess of three billion, is projected to double again in thirty-seven years. The resources necessary to sustain life are being depleted. Pollutants are ravaging our air and water resources. The most fertile land is being covered with concrete. The university has not only failed to help solve our ecological crises, it has contributed significantly to them: technology, one of education's most prized contributions, is the major polluter and destroyer of life-sustaining resources. Related to the problems of the ecological equation is the deflection of energy to anti-human activities; the most obvious examples are war and racism. In both of these areas, the university's record is similarly dismal: the scientists' most significant accomplishment of the twentieth century was the creation of the super-weapon. If the university, as an institution, has been involved in any major peace-making activities, that activity must stand as one of the best-kept secrets of all times.

Because we are a credential society, because we portion out wealth, prestige and status disproportionately to those who successfully complete a formal education, the university has become the primary vehicle for the maintenance of racism. The precious few numbers of poor minority youth who obtain degrees camouflage the university's apparent true function, which is to help maintain the current inequitable distribution of power and wealth. The continued existence of poverty, the developing of "behavioral sinks" in the inner cities where overcrowding and dilapidation contribute to the degeneration of human relationships, the muddling of our attempts to build model cities—all reflect the failure of the university and its self-proclaimed scholars to come to grips with major social problems. Even some ecologists fail to appreciate the extent to which war, racism, poverty and urban blight relate to the environmental crisis.

Consider that minorities are asked to join with the rest of us and limit population, but they are also told that their political impotence is caused by their lack of numbers. Minorities are asked to join in the common cause of survival, but they are also told to be content with a barely livable existence, and for God's sake, don't get militant about it. War and threat of war preclude international cooperation on population growth and preservation of the environment; war and threat of war destroy and pollute, divert enormous power resources and manpower into wasteful activity, and energize nations to stimulate population growth. Poverty destroys hope, and without hope there is no concern for the future. Seeing no future, we see no point in taking the time or the trouble to prevent population growth. The mess of the metropolis impedes rationality in family planning, but also is profligate in the use of energy resources and devastating in the matter of pollution.

Leadership and ideas are needed to solve all such problems, and every aspect of university life is to some extent involved. The involvement should pervade university concerns with work, politics, culture and human competence. But functioning as it does, the university (and its advertised innovations) is guilty of malfeasance, misfeasance and nonfeasance. To illustrate, the student government at the University of Oregon recently asked the faculty at that institution to approve a one-week moratorium on business as usual to permit discussion of the responsibilities of colleges and universities to help eliminate the ecological crises. The students requested that every department justify its activities in the context of man's survival. After some extensive and acrimonious debate over procedure, one of the more esteemed science professors arose and in stentorian tones dismissed the request, proclaiming that it was absurd for a department of romance languages, for example, to justify itself ecologically. The sad thing is he thought he had said something profound.

The university is primarily in the business of vocational training. It turns and tailors the student to meet the specifications of the business, medical, legal, educational and engineering industries. The procedures used reinforce all prevailing prejudices and deny opportunity to the poor and the nonwhite. But the reinforcement of racism is, perhaps, not the university's primary evil; it is conceivable that even more devastating is the low level of competence that results from the process. In the end, the credentialed professional is either palpably unable to perform (trained incapacity, as in the case of the teacher in the ghetto), or he has deceived himself and others that he possesses the requisite skills (delusional competence, as in the case of the teacher in the suburbs).

Every aspect of professional training suffers from inertia. Neither the training nor the profession relates to physical or human ecological problems. The university trains in obsolete procedures for a world which long since has gone out of existence. Lawyers are unable to deal with anomic responses to legal statutes or with the argument that justice takes precedence over law and order; and they are unable to deal with the fact that a world unable to provide adequate food, water and air for its people cannot possibly develop a stable pattern of law. Medical doctors are unprepared to treat chronic diseases associated with an urban ecology. Social workers become completely unraveled when they confront anything not explainable by generic casework theory. Businessmen are so taken with their discovery of group dynamics that they forget that the economic theory on which they pin their enterprise is puerile.

The university responds to the challenges of training for work by offering curriculum "innovation." Field placement is the most prevalent and exalted of these reforms. Earlier and earlier in their college careers, students are paroled from campus and placed in schools, in welfare and probation offices, in recreation departments, in local and federal government, and in business and law offices. The practice is justified on the grounds that the student thus is tethered to reality, learns the ropes and as a consequence becomes a better trained, more valuable practitioner.

But both logic and evidence suggest that field placement only serves to initiate the prospective employee into the ritual of the system. Ever more efficiently he becomes a frictionless cog in a well-oiled bureaucratic machine totally removed from problems of livability. The student is trained to be just as bad a probation officer as the current group of bad probation officers, because he is going to be trained by them. The tenuous commitment to humanistic principles that school teachers evince in their pre-service training evaporates soon after they get on the job. The police cadet in the academy displays more respect for laws of evidence and the rights of the accused than he manifests after he is in the squad car—his partner, the senior officer who wises him up, educates him to forget all the mickey mouse crap he learned in the academy. The supervisors in the employment and parole offices do much the same thing. Why doesn't the university ask what it can do to help the student retain the little good which derives from a university association after he gets into the field?

To withstand the pressures to conform, incipient professionals must be a tougher, smarter breed of animal than those currently mass-produced. Innovation must be directed toward developing persons who can change the system, not reinforce it. Nevitt Sanford, among others, has become so disheartened that he doubts whether there is enough gumption in publicly subsidized educational institutions to even try to develop such leadership. James Ridgeway suggests that the corruption of the university by military and business is so complete that its staff and administration are perfectly willing to prostitute their limited talents for the loot derived by serving the system. (I think he treats my colleagues much too kindly. They are not prostitutes. From what I know of them, they will gladly *give* their favors away.)

The university has the capacity to produce change-agents. To be sure, there is risk in the venture; but since the ruptures in the university are becoming increasingly apparent and because there are more adventurous students on campus, true innovation in training for work is possible. It would require that professional preparation be far more "educational" than it is now. Professionals must be much more theoretical. They must have an ideology. They must know what a *good* world of work would look like, and subsume under that the service they provide. They must have a theory of change in which strategies and tactics are specified. They must verify the efficacy of their theory through case study, simulation and field test. They must use the broadest issue of man's survival as the star by which to steer.

University innovation in the realm of work preparation is piddling at best; the university is even more derelict in the area of work planning. Work in this country is not determined by plan. Systems develop which need manpower, and away they go. Large numbers of persons are not allowed to participate in the design; many others obtain little gratification from the work itself. Products and services produce comfort for some, but many are unable to become effective consumers. The concept of a free market was clouded by monopoly and collusion, which eliminated competition. There was, and is, much to criticize about the system, simply in terms of distribution of wealth and concern for the human being, but even these considerations pale beside the considerations of ecology.

The basic work systems developed by this society can no longer be tolerated because they are wasteful. Our number one product is pollution. We subsidize industry to pollute even more. We generate pollution by depleting our power resources. We build, ship, warehouse, display, advertise and sell products we should never have produced in the first place. We don't need a society which doubles its electrical output every ten years: we need a society which discourages people from using electricity to cut a turkey or open a can or shave; we need houses which provide convenience and livability and at the same time conserve energy. We cannot afford to employ millions to build automobiles which are the primary polluters not only of air but also of space.

If people are not going to work in industries dedicated to waste, then where shall they work? How will new industries develop? What will be *their* logistics? The university has not even begun to ask such questions, let alone teased out any answers. Indeed, the university is the greatest single obstacle to new thoughts about work. It is not merely that new ideas are ignored in the university; worse, the ideas are forbidden. At the University of Oregon, for example, a curriculum committee is resisting inclusion of course numbers which would permit community colleges to offer new career training that could be transferred to the university. Inclusion of these courses would in no way affect standards. It would neither hinder nor hamper any existing irrelevancy. It would cost the university no money. But at this moment, after months of haggling, the curriculum committee is adamant against even this tiny change.

In a modern, complex, overcrowded world, change is political. Everything done in the university is political. The curriculum committee operates politically, so does the admissions committee, the space committee, the search committee for a new dean, the committee which selects the search committee to search for the new dean. Everything revolves around political consideration. Everything that happens outside of the university and which affects the university is baldly political. (Any faculty member who doesn't believe that after what has gone on in California doesn't really deserve his status.) And any change, either within or without the university, in the direction of ecological validity will require political action, will demand the mobilization of power.

For the first time in the history of any nation, our colleges and universities have the potential power to make a difference. The power is both in numbers (there are in the United States at least nine million students and faculty members) and in strategic position (every enterprise in the country depends upon the university). It is no longer possible even to go to war without relying on the brains of the university to design sophisticated weaponry. If united, the university is in a marvelous bargaining position, and yet it refuses to exert its force. Worse yet, it fails to debate, discuss, analyze or study the legitimate uses of its power to produce change. In almost all its activities, the university is either anti- or non-intellectual, and nowhere does it demonstrate this more clearly than in the area of politics. If the university-based scholar enters politics at all, he prefers to be an Iago, planning and scheming for or against the administration he serves, rather than to be a leader and state unequivocally the principles for which he is prepared to fight.

An ecologically valid world would require new kinds of political decision-making. The current system is too turgid and too chaotic. Too many groups are forced into powerlessness, and with no possibility for them to gain power through coalition. The university must begin to provide leadership for political growth. Because of the enormity of the problems facing us, the arguments in favor of totalitarian efficiency may be hard to resist. If the university reneges in its obligation to help make democracy work, democratic principles undoubtedly will be a casualty of our increasingly complex world. Since it is hardly possible to have an ecologically valid world—or an ecologically valid university—in a totalitarian society, we must struggle for new models of effective politics based firmly on democratic principles. Most particularly, we must build a system based on respect for individual rights.

The university should represent a model democratic community. It could, and should, develop a political structure which would be the beachhead for larger political entities. Its political system should be consistent with every concern for livability. It must reject dehumanization through bureaucratic intransigence and racism, provide alternatives to the wastage of a war mentality, and provide for the sharing of power among all concerned. It should be accountable to outside forces and influence, and it should show how it is possible to unite in an effort to gain things for which there is consensus. That kind of innovation does not exist. Instead, we display our shabby student governments and other mockeries of viable political practices, which some people have the audacity to call innovation.

Another aspect of logical university innovation in the arena of politics is the development of leadership consistent with democratic principles. We should be able to develop leadership which respects diverse and pluralistic populations, which holds itself accountable to all groups over which it presides, which willingly negotiates with the opposition, which treats grievances on merit, which recognizes that conflict is inevitable and thus is not traumatized by its existence, which recognizes that in a rapidly changing society all rules are means, not ends, and therefore are subject to change as the world changes. That type of development—that kind of innovation—is not taking place in the university either.

The most trivial and traditional means of teaching are called "innovations." One of the most popular ones for undergraduates takes the form of performance goals and programmed learning. These "innovators" take for themselves the mantle of science. They claim for themselves a toughmindedness, they argue that the university has gone to hell because it is aimless, and as remedy they propose performance goals. But there is no accountability in their "system." The goals cannot be justified. They accept all that is now being taught as valid, and claim only that they can teach it more efficiently. The goals consist of test passing; they feel they have accomplished something if they improve the efficiency of memorization of names and dates: their concern is "right answer" learning.

Anything based on such a behavioral goal does not belong in the university. It is intellectually stultifying. Leave it perhaps for a six-week training program run by the Department of Labor, but remove it forever from university curriculum and admit that there *are* no Right Answers. If we do not begin with that assumption, we can only hinder the university. For our ecological problems inform us that all which we do, we do wrong, and that we need to struggle for entirely new answers.

Another alleged innovation is the honors college—the curricular invention by which we provide a few select persons with an enriched and diversified education. We allow them options not available to other students. We give them unique independence and unmatched choices. Yet still the fare is limited. The university cafeteria is simply not very diversified: the "honors" student is offered spinach or broccoli. And where the university offers only garbage, the choice is even more restricted. In short, there is no independence in independent study if all the choices are worthless.

The university is involuted. Its students, who come from restricted environments and limited experiences, are further restricted and limited because they are allowed to interact only with each other. The university as a whole lacks sufficient stimulation from minority groups and other populations with diverse experiences. But bad as that is in the university, it is worse in the honors college, whose students mingle only with each other. Thus is prevented even limited personal contact with the problems of black people and the social ecology of the ghetto, or Mexicans and the social ecology of the barrio, or what happens to people when they are crowded more and more into less and less livable space. At best, the student in the honors college gets the information which is emitted from a sanitized computer. If racism is a major problem in our society, and if it is related to the question of survival, then the bias in higher education could be the disease which destroys us all. The honors college, protector of our academic elite, may provide more of a problem than a solution. The "elite" is distinguished because it is whiter, more middle class and more restricted in background than any other group in the university. "Honors" college is a misappellation.

Why don't we require all our students to write a different scenario than Paul Ehrlich provides in his book, *The Population Bomb?* Ehrlich predicts that the future will bring either atomic war or a series of local calamities—famine, local wars, things of that nature—which would reduce the world population from three and a half billion to a billion and a half. Every student should try to write his own scenario, basing it on what he knows about economics, psychology, sociology, social organization, theater, art, music, literature, etc. Once we begin to direct student attention to such major problems, perhaps we will begin to eliminate our bickering.

The world as currently constituted distorts character and personality, and people who are unable to live harmoniously with themselves or their neighbors distort even further their physical and social environment. The university has the obligation to develop areas of interpersonal and intrapersonal competence, to test out its theories, and to develop experiments based on them. The most logical place to begin is in the university itself. But no such innovation is taking place.

The university has an obligation to update personality theory. Today there is preoccupation with obviously outdated mechanistic learning models and psychodynamic theories. At the practical level, the university not only fails to develop model living communities, but is itself becoming a "behavioral sink." It is overcrowded, bureaucratically organized, fragmented, depersonalized and computerized. At yet another level—the level of leadership development—the university has failed even to identify the attributes of a person: the intellectual, social, communicative, emotional characteristics which are necessary if we are to move from where we are now to where we must go to survive.

Leadership in the university is similar to that exemplified by the captain of a luxury liner who, after five or six days at sea, told the passengers: "I've got some good news and bad new. The bad news is that we are lost, we haven't any idea where we are, our electronic compass is broken, we've lost radio contact with the mainland, because of overcast conditions we can't use celestial navigation—we are hopelessly lost. Now for the good news: We are two hours ahead of schedule." The trouble with the university is that it is aimless. It can justify itself only because it has not specified goals. (As it says in the Talmud, if you do not know where you are going, all roads will get you there.)

Because the university has reached no consensus as to its purpose, the delusion that it has gotten someplace is easily believed. Because it has lost its sense of direction, because it survives to exist and exists to survive, because it generates leadership through perverted politics, because it prefers to model its leaders after the mayor of Chicago rather than to provide leadership for the city of Chicago, all those things which are called innovations in the university are trivia. And since the world and its problems worsen every minute, the more we change, the worse we get.

(Bird, cont. from p. 261)

son for the rest of his life. A woman student hoped that college would enable her to "carry on a conversation with her husband's boss when he came to dinner."

The more secure of the old-fashioned college professors are often daring enough to admit that their renowned liberal arts is "really" a "finishing school" to "hone the sensibilities" of gentlemen who can afford to pay the high price of these intangible and largely ornamental benefits. Some of them think it's a joke that employers set such store by the right accents. Although it's good form, these days, to sound apologetic about it, they are quick to admit that they aren't teaching students anything practical. They are teaching "attitudes" and "approaches" and providing "broad, general background" for "making decisions." Their graduates have no specific skills. They are being trained not to do the dirty work but to get other people to do it.

The notion of the executive as "gentleman" has been incorporated into management science. He gets other people to do things. He knows how to motivate, how to lead, how to get others to do what he wants them to do. If he pitches in and works with the "men" he's a confessed failure.

The "gentleman" of an earlier era led by virtue of his birth. In the nineteenth century power was open to those with "personal magnetism," like Napoleon. In a supposedly egalitarian society like ours, there must be another route, one open to all.

We have said that higher education is the legitimate road to power and have enshrined in its curriculum and its environment the diversions and tastes of the powerful. College has taught large numbers of people to read books, buy art, attend concerts, go to Europe, visit museums, play tennis, savor wine, and cope with menus written in French. It costs a great deal of time and money to acquire these amenities, and, though many are happy with the bargain, real power remains as closely held as ever. Very few of the new art collectors, for instance, have anything to say about zoning regulations, interest rates, income tax provisions, nominations of candidates for elective office, the acquisition policies of museums, and the Ford Foundation's choice of research projects, to name a few examples of real power. The people who make these ground rules are the same old people who were born to do it.

No one likes to say it out loud, but in America we have cruelly deluded the lower middle class into thinking that they can gain access to power by studying, informal classes, the arts, amusements, concerns, sentiments, and conventions of the "gentlemen" who are the successors if not the descendants of the "gentlemen" who inherited power along with their land. . . .

The inference that college makes a person "better" has become credible because college graduates do better on almost every measurable test that can be devised. It's hard to name anything desirable enough to test for that isn't more apt to go to those who check "sixteen plus" years of schooling on surveys. The college educated are healthier, wealthier, happier, wiser, and morally superior in every way to those who haven't been to college.

As for health, they live longer, and, although they go to the doctor more often, they are out sick less. They are less apt to have nervous breakdowns, and less apt to report symptoms of psychological distress, such as dizziness and headaches, but more apt to consult a psychiatrist if they feel they need one and more apt to profit by psychotherapy once they undertake it.

As for wealth, they have more assets and are better paid both in dollars and in psychic income. Not only do they like their work more than the less educated, but they are more apt to value it for intrinsic interest or social value rather than pay or prestige. It's nicer work, too: safer, cleaner, steadier, physically easier, with longer vacations, more fringe benefits, and more chance for advancement.

They are happier. They have fewer divorces. They have fewer babies. Although more introspective and concerned about their relations with others, they get more pleasure from them and have a greater sense of well-being and satisfaction. They are more confident and optimistic about their own outlook and the national economy, too.

They are wiser in all things both great and small. They test out more "open, flexible, critical, objective, and nonjudgmental."

They are more internationalist, more opposed to war, military spending, and the personal possession of firearms. They are more liberal on social issues, more apt to blame society than the criminal, to favor abortion and male sterilization, and to accept marriages between black and whites, Protestants and Catholics, or Jews and non-Jews. They are more inclined to support lowering the voting age and giving birth control pills to teen-age girls. They are more likely to vote for higher school taxes, even when they are paying private school tuition for their own children.

The list is long, but could easily be extended. Some of the items were collected by Stephen Withey for the Carnegie Commission on Higher Education, and, although he was careful not to claim too much for them, the message is unmistakable: send everyone to college and everyone and everything is bound to get better.

During the 1960s we doubled the number of young people attending college, and everyone and everything seemed to get worse. The most charitable conclusion is probably correct: College has very little, if any, effect on people and things at all. Now, in the 1970s, the false premises are easier to see:

1) College doesn't make people intelligent, ambitious, happy, liberal, or quick to learn new things. It's the other way around. Intelligent, ambitious, happy, liberal, quick-learning people are attracted to college in the first place. Going to college in hopes of being like them, if you are not, is like playing tennis to look like the tennis-playing rich. It doesn't work.

2) Colleges can't claim much credit for the learning experiences that really change students while they are there. Jobs, friends, history, and most of all the sheer passage of time has as big an impact as anything even indirectly related to the campus. Something that happened during a summer is so frequently the most significant learning experience a student can cite that it is tempting to wonder whether the best thing colleges do is to provide young people with unstructured time off.

3) Colleges have changed so radically that a freshman entering in the fall of 1974 can't be sure to gain even the limited value added reported in studies made during the middle 1960s. While we don't know what the new impact will be, all indications are that it will be considerably less than in the past. . . .

Sweeping changes will be needed to rescue reluctant students from the academic youth ghettoes, where their futures are controlled by a self-perpetuating and largely unaccountable professoriate, and restore them to full participation in the mainstream of American life. Attitudes won't change until institutions—and their funding—are restructured on some new premises:

1) High-school graduates have the same right as older people to take responsibility for their own lives in their own way without special privileges or "protection"; and 2) Professors should be stripped of the political, economic, and social power they now wield over young adults and stick to teaching whatever it is they

actually know to anybody anywhere who really wants to learn it.

Both premises sound reasonable enough until you see where they lead. Then they sound outrageously revolutionary. When you begin to spell out specific proposals, the consequences are easier to see.

1) We might fund—and so legitimize—all the ways in which a young person can get what students have told us are the real benefits of college: getting away from home, living on their own, making friends different from themselves, exploring knowledge, trying a field of work, training for a job, growing up. The most direct way to be independent, or "adult," as students say, "is to pull your own weight, and the simplest way to do that in our society is to earn your own living. For that, a young person needs a job—something that needs doing for its own sake, whether or not it is paid and whether or not it is directed to a lifetime career.

This means taking money away from colleges where young people are demeaned by the "make-work" of academia and investing it in the "real" work and learning students would choose if it were available. We need—and not especially for the development of any particular group—enough people to tidy up and patrol the streets, answer all the patient bells in hospitals, coach the slow learners in grade school, talk with the troubled, the suicidal, and the drug addicted, run down all the complaints of consumers, put all the library books back on the shelves, answer all the mail Congressmen get, haul in groceries for citizens physically unable to push supermarket carts, deliver the mail, and do all those small but essential services that keep a society civil.

A lot of these activities simply don't pay and are going to have to be funded out of taxes. Let the money come right out of the appropriations now being spent by institutions of higher education, and then allocate it on a formula which takes into account not only the need for service, but how many people would like to render it. (Services which are needed but hated, such as garbage collection, should be allowed to rise to their market wage which, in a well-run economy, will be high enough to warrant radical new labor-saving systems. This is coming anyway and will need no special legislation.)

The new jobs to be created should not be specially tailored for young people or designed in any way as learning opportunities. The professoriate will have to keep its pedagogical hands off. The jobs will be open to, and attract, other members of our society now arbitrarily excluded on the basis of age, sex, or some other irrelevant circumstance such as retirement or specialization in an obsolescent field. For the sake of everyone's self-respect, we must avoid creating a new age- or sex-segregated job ghetto.

2) Some of the money withdrawn from the colleges should, especially at the outset, be spent on pilot demonstrations and explorations of specific alternatives to college. This is the philosophy of a report entitled "Youth: Transition to Adulthood," made by the Panel on Youth of the President's Science Advisory Committee chaired by James S. Coleman of Johns Hopkins University. The committee recommended a pilot program of disbursing vouchers to students equivalent in value to the cost of four years of college that could be applied toward a wide range of skill-training programs as well as higher education.

One area for exploration would be extension of the present system of apprenticeship to many more occupations than are now covered by our state apprenticeship regulations. We could also experiment with new, more open and more flexible ways for beginners to learn on the job. Instead of funneling money into vocational schools, which have to spend a lot of money to create the working conditions under which students can learn to cook or repair cars or run machines, we ought to use that money to encourage employers to hire and train beginners on the job, and the tax rebates or subsidies should be awarded on a system of accounting which recognizes the high cost of supervising the inexperienced.

3) We ought to explore a national service plan that would require or permit all young people to spend at least a year of their lives serving their country in a capacity over which they had some choice. This would give them a chance to get away from home and give them opportunities to mature, to work, and perhaps to make a real contribution of time and labor to some of our most pressing problems. It's not an easy solution, and it could easily cost more than college.

To many people "national service" sounds as coercive as the draft it was originally intended to replace. The Task Force on the Draft and National Service of the White House Conference on Youth of 1971 recommended against a compulsory program, but a Gallup poll of 1973 showed a majority favoring one year of required military or nonmilitary service for all males.

4) Pilot projects might be funded to explore a nationally supported program for making widely available some of the alternatives invented to dropouts and stopouts. One that deserves a second look is the time-honored system of sending a young person to live and work with another family. During the Middle Ages, gently bred young people were farmed out to the castle to work as pages or ladies-in-waiting and learn "manners." In contrast to the public schools which replaced it, this informal apprenticeship did not segregate the young, did not put them under the control of a schoolteacher class, and afforded them the self-respect of self-support. At worst, they did "real" work actually needed or wanted by someone else. The practice of sending a daughter to work in a neighbor's house rather than help her own mother helped to make the domestic arts socially respectable in Scandinavian culture.

5) Present colleges and universities should be returned to the teaching and learning activities for which they were founded by shedding the power they now exercise over access to jobs and social prestige. While administrators are essentially empire builders, most good professors would welcome a system which would insure them smaller classes of students interested in learning for its own sake.

Higher education should be treated like any other consumer product. Those who enjoy studying for its own sake should get no more subsidy for this amusement than those who like to ski, nor should this choice confer on them any special fringe benefit of power or prestige.

For starters, we might follow the recommendation of the Committee for Economic Development and target financial aid directly to students rather than allow institutions of higher education to dole it out. This would not only reduce the temptation to use the money to aggrandize the college or its special programs, but it would make all institutions compete with each other to meet the real needs of students—as they are perceived by the students, and not as they are defined by administrators, bureaucrats, and educational experts. . . .

6) In order to reduce the stranglehold of academic values, if not the professoriate, on the future of the young, we must take aggressive steps to decredentialize employment. Fairness to applicants and efficiency both require that jobs go to the candidates most competent to perform the duties actually required. The first step would be to separate the licensing of lawyers, doctors, teachers, and other professionals from the influence of the professional schools which prepare candidates for licensing examinations.

Schools could cram their students for examinations, but their graduates would not automatically be licensed, nor would a diploma be required in order to take the examination. This would keep the professional schools honest because they would have to compete with other ways of acquiring the competence tested by the licensing examinations. Competitive channels for acquiring professional competence would make the professions accountable to the public. It would, for instance, be harder for law and medical schools to perpetuate as "professional ethics" practices which result in the padding of bills, the provision of unnecessary services, and the withholding of information patients and clients have a right to know.

In the mid-1970s, a number of states were working on a system that would get better teachers into classrooms than the present system of licensing all graduates of accredited schools of education. In New York State and in Pennsylvania plans were under way to require all candidates for a teacher's license to demonstrate their competence in the actual classroom.

7) Laws forbidding discrimination in employment on the basis of race, religion, sex, and age should be amended to prohibit discrimination on the basis of educational status, too. This may, in fact, be the law of the land right now, since the 1971 Griggs decision of the Supreme Court declared it unlawful to require for employment a qualification which rules out any particular group unless that qualification can be shown to predict performance on the job.

Personnel administrators shudder when they imagine what a strict application of this principle would do to their employment practices. The awful truth is that there has been very little "validation" of employment tests to see whether they do, in fact, sort out those best able to perform on the job. According to Marvin Dunnette, a personnel test specialist at the University of Minnesota, the situation is even worse: most employers don't really know how to describe competence, much less test for it.

Removal of the diploma as credential will force employers to think through how work is really done and what kinds of people are really needed to do it. . . .

8) Open learning to all comers, of every age and educational status, by offering courses at times and places convenient to anyone in the community who wants to take them. Substitute a gigantic network of adult education for the present age-segregated (and, in some cases, sex-segregated) programs which aim in part at least at sociability and personal development.

Schools would offer whatever anyone wanted to learn. This would return control of the curriculum to the students instead of forcing them to consume whatever schools think they should have. Offerings would include recreational courses, such as gourmet cooking, and professional courses, such as certified public accounting for people in mid-career who need it as well as beginners. Young and old, employed and still to be employed would learn together, each student bringing his or her own contribution and taking according to his or her own need. Teachers who have taught mixed classes say that the discussions are more meaningful when fueled by varying inputs.

9) In order to make learning available to people when they need it, we should adopt the proposal of the Carnegie Commission to guarantee all high-school graduates two years of postsecondary education they can take any time in their lives.

10) To break the lockstep which incarcerates so many nonacademic young people in school, the National Commission on the Reform of Secondary Education has proposed lowering the school-leaving age from sixteen to fourteen. This would free younger teen-agers for alternative forms of learning or job training, much of which, of course, would have to be provided by new programs.

11) The personal development and social experience provided by residential schooling should be extended to students of all ages as well as both sexes in order to provide a more diverse, more natural, and more rewarding experience for all. Teen-agers are not the only citizens who can profit by the shelter of a campus environment. Older people, particularly those in mid-career, frequently need "time to think" in an uncommitting but stimulating setting. For maximum benefit, both old and young would stay on campus only as long as they continued to feel that the campus experience was rewarding. Consequently, colleges would not be able to count on controlling their students for an arbitrary period of four years and they would have to adapt financially, intellectually, and logistically to consumer preferences.

12) Stop making young people carry the burden of social reform. We have assumed for so long that education can solve social ills ranging from race prejudice to poverty that we unwittingly saddle our children with the burdens adults won't shoulder themselves. Busing school children is less threatening to adults than desegregating housing. And as Christopher Jencks points out in his book *Inequality,* universal higher education is a clumsy and expensive way to help the poor. If we want to redistribute wealth, it would be simpler, cheaper, and fairer to tax the rich and give money to the poor, rather than do it hypocritically and indirectly by offering "equal opportunity" to win credentials in a loaded academic setting which serves to legitimize class distinctions.

POSTSCRIPT
WHAT DIRECTION FOR HIGHER EDUCATION?

Higher education in the United States is immensely diverse, and its complexities are often perplexing. Because of this diversity and complexity, ideas for the reform and improvement of colleges and universities are extremely difficult to bring to realization. In order to obtain a comprehensive understanding of the problem, one must turn to a wide range of sources which supply historical data, critical perspectives, and accounts of successful experimentation.

In addition to the works mentioned in the introduction of this issue, the following sources contribute to the understanding that is essential to constructive action. Historical information and interpretation may be found in *American Higher Education: A Documentary History* (1961), edited by Richard Hofstadter and Wilson Smith; *The Higher Learning in America: A Reassessment* (1968) by Paul Woodring; *The Academic Revolution* (1968) by Christopher Jencks and David Riesman; Alain Touraine's *The Academic System in American Society* (1974); the 1973 report of the Carnegie Commission on Higher Education, *The Purposes and Performance of Higher Education in the U.S.: Approaching the Year 2000; The University: The Anatomy of Academe* (1976) by Murray G. Ross; and Nathan Pusey's *American Higher Education, 1945–1970: A Personal Report* (1978).

Among those books providing critical perspectives on the social and political realities of higher education are Joseph J. Schwab's *College Curriculum and Student Protest* (1969); *Neutrality and Impartiality: The University and Political Commitment* (1975), edited by Alan Montefiore; *Professors, Unions, and American Higher Education* (1973) by Everett C. Ladd and Seymour Martin Lipset; John D. Millett's *New Structures of Campus Power* (1978); and Geoffrey Wagner's critique of open admissions, *The End of Education* (1976).

Experimental approaches to college-level learning and organizational structure are described in Laurence Hall's *New Colleges for New Students* (1974); Eric Ashby's *Adapting Universities to a Technological Society* (1974); the 1973 report of the Commission on Non-Traditional Study, *Diversity by Design; Academic Transformation: Seventeen Institutions Under Pressure* (1973), edited by David Riesman and Verne A. Stadtman; and Walter Perry's *The Open University: History and Evaluation of a Dynamic Innovation in Higher Education* (1977).

Whatever alternatives and reforms emerge from the current financial crunches, questionable standards, and increasing loss of autonomy, it seems a good bet that higher education will in the future move toward greater use of technologized information retrieval and toward deeper concentration on a variety of modes of inquiry and analytical perspectives.

ISSUE 17

WHAT IS THE HOPE FOR THE FUTURE?

Educators need to ask: What am I doing now to improve the quality of my students' future lives—ten, twenty, fifty years from now? If the future were predictable, the task would certainly be simplified. But the best we have to go on are expert projections, extrapolations from current trends, some knowledge of emerging forces of change—in other words, some educated guesses.

Futurism itself is a growth industry. A widening spectrum of projections is being offered by Alvin Toffler, Herman Kahn, Robert Theobald, Marshall McLuhan, Daniel Bell, R. Buckminster Fuller, Herbert J. Muller, Isaac Asimov, and scores of others. The importance of this is not that one prediction may actually come true, but that the entire effort focuses our attention on the future, makes us more alert and less subject to shock and unpreparedness, and allows us to exert influence which might indeed have a shaping effect on future developments.

In the field of education, George Leonard, Donald Michael, Harold Shane, Patrick Suppes, Robert Bundy, John Goodlad, Peter Drucker, and Kenneth Boulding stand out among those who feel that a future orientation is vital to the process of constructive change. Daniel Bell points out in *The Coming of Post-Industrial Society: A Venture in Social Forecasting* (1973) that while in former times the schools were the central organizers of experience and the primary codifiers of values, now, with the vast spread of communication media, more education takes place outside of schools, which, in turn, have become more specialized and vocational. Taking this observation into consideration, Neil Postman and Charles Weingartner, in *The School Book* (1973), conclude that the school as a medium of communication and a source of information is bankrupt. They predict that as the financial bind on schools becomes increasingly tight in the near future the inefficiency and obsolescence of the present form of schooling will become more visible. They contend that electronic media has not been successful in classrooms but they hold hopes that a relocation of electronic educational systems, to 24-hour learning centers that can be activated on demand like neighborhood laundromats, would prove to be efficiently attuned to the times.

Isaac Asimov emphasizes in his works that the problems of the coming decades can be solved only by technology. Patrick Suppes carries this theme to a consideration of technological possibilities in the enhancement of the educational process. In the following selection, Suppes examines such prospects as localized learning centers, truly individualized instruction, and home-based learning. Although he sees many exciting possibilities along these lines, Suppes cautions that we need far more sophisticated understanding of the processes of learning and instruction, human motivation, and the factors involved in concentration.

Suppes' concern about a diminishment of spontaneity and instinctive responses between learner and electronic media is shared by John Goodlad. Seeing schooling still as the primary hope for the development of individual human potential, Goodlad charts a series of future reforms which he feels are needed in order to update the concept of school. These changes include a movement toward a lifelong approach to education; an emphasis on "phases" rather than specific levels; a move from fragmented subject matter to studies unified by the types of thinking involved; and creation of a learning environment offering instructional teams of professionals, paraprofessionals, and peers, and emphasizing self-instruction and self-evaluation. Goodlad details his school of the future in the following article.

Patrick Suppes

TECHNOLOGY CAN LEAD THE WAY

Although I do not claim to have a scenario of the future, I would like to describe some alternative scenarios of technological possibilities for the school of the future. Since I think the best way to begin to talk about the future is to look at the past, I would like to review briefly what I consider to be the four most important technological innovations for learning and teaching of the past. The first innovation, which goes back to our most ancient civilizations but is associated especially with Greek and Hellenistic times, is the introduction of manuscripts and written records for the purpose of teaching—not books, of course, but the papyri, or other forms of writing for the purposes of communicating knowledge and ideas. This, itself, was a big step forward and, as in the case of all introductions of technology, there were objections to it. An excellent reference and a beautiful phrasing of the objections can be found in Plato's *Phaedrus.* Socrates asserts that "only in principles of justice and goodness . . . taught and communicated orally for the sake of instruction . . . is there clearness and perfection and seriousness." When the teacher no longer directly talks to the student but hands the student something to read and contemplate in written form, the tone and personality of the spoken word have been lost. So already at the introduction of a technology we would consider absolutely essential to education, we have a natural and important objection. We will find that true for the introduction of all technologies in education, and I mention it because it gives us historical insight into what it means to make a change.

The second technology is the advance from individually written manuscripts to the production of books. It may be recalled that Gutenberg's Bible was printed in the West in 1452; there had been an introduction of block printing in China and Korea a couple of hundred years earlier, but from the standpoint of our perspective today, the important thing is that it was not until the end of the eighteenth century, over three hundred years later, that there was any serious use of books in schools. Again, the important point is that the

Continued on p. 280

From "The School of the Future: Technological Possibilities" by Patrick Suppes, in *The Future of Education: Perspectives on Tomorrow's Schooling,* edited by Louis Rubin for Research for Better Schools, Inc., Philadelphia

John I. Goodlad

PERSONALIZED EDUCATION IS POSSIBLE

. . . Only occasionally and sporadically do specific external interventions make much difference in the massive enterprise of reconstructing the schools. We can develop new proposals; we can have program planning and budgeting systems; we can contract for instruction; but in the final analysis the school must change itself. This is the only legitimate argument for decentralization. It provides the school with a clear mandate to change itself. Mere decentralization will do little unless the responsibility, the authority, and the accountability for changing the school are vested in the responsible parties in that school. And I use the term "school" to mean people—the people connected with each individual school: the principal, the teachers, the children, the parents, and anyone else the school wishes to bring in. These people must be given the freedom and the authority necessary to diagnose the condition of the school, to come up with plans for action, and to take those actions. This is their educational mandate and they must be held accountable for their response to it.

This sounds very much like what we have wanted all along—for the principal and the staff to be responsible for their own school and to collaborate with the children and the community in devising a viable, interesting, and potent educational program. But is it really? How much more comfortable to let George do it. How much more comfortable to watch with smug satisfaction George foundering on the rocks of inadequate conception. But when he fails, who is going to be George the Second? In this moment of truth we must not go into our schools as mere managers. We must go in as educational leaders, aware that we need new skills and secure in the premise—not afraid of it—that the buck stops here.

The critical question we have to confront is: "What kinds of schools do we need for our children?" If we have no idea of where we are going, if we have no answers to the basic questions of schooling, how can we lead? There can be no excuses. If 50 percent of the teachers changed schools last year, if the children are undernourished and undermotivated, these facts are part of the condition,

Continued on p. 288

From "The Child and His School in Transition," by John I. Goodlad, *National Elementary Principal,* January 1973.

(Suppes, cont. from p. 278)

spirit of the technology, a technology for education that all of us recognize as an essential ingredient today, took over three hundred years to spread into the schools. Furthermore, even with the introduction of this technology, teachers had to rely mainly on the traditional oral methods, because the books were so poor from a pedagogical standpoint. A good example of this would be the teaching of elementary mathematics in the nineteenth century. Even though books were available, they were not successfully introduced or successfully used in even so universal a subject as the teaching of elementary mathematics, especially elementary arithmetic. The printing of books, then, is the second technology.

The third technology, which follows closely upon the introduction of books in the western world, is the introduction of schools. It is easy to trace the development of grammar schools in England and Western Europe in the fifteenth and sixteenth centuries, and it is important to note that school enrollment was not widespread during these times. The concept we have today of universal mass education, a concept that has in fact been adopted throughout the world, is one that is quite recent historically. Two hundred years ago it would have been considered idiotic, an act of lunacy, to talk about educating all of the people. Even as recently as one hundred years ago, John Stuart Mill despaired of ever having an educated general populace; at that time the concept of the equivalent of, say, a high school education for the general public was not accepted or thought possible. In 1870 in the United States, less than 2 percent of the age population graduated from high school. Thus the idea of universal education at the elementary and secondary levels, as we now conceive it, is one of the most revolutionary and radical changes in the history of the world. It is also very recent.

The fourth technology is the use of tests for evaluation, selection, and so forth. Tests do not necessarily follow in time the other three technologies I have already mentioned. In China, for example, which has the longest continuous history of systematic tests, there were no general schools associated with the extensive development of examinations for the selection of mandarins. These tests began in about the twelfth century and were abolished only at the fall of the empire at the end of the nineteenth century. Thus there were seven hundred years of continuous development and use of tests in China, although there are no serious data, particularly of a statistical kind, about the results. It is sometimes said, and I think correctly so, that the use of tests from a systematic and scientific standpoint, especially the study of the properties of tests as technological instruments, is indeed a twentieth-century technology. I do emphasize, however, that we have a long historical tradition of testing, and it is a tradition separate from the introduction of books and from the introduction of schools.

Of these four technologies—the introduction of written records, the introduction of books, the introduction of schools, and the introduction of tests—none had been in any way adequately forecast or outlined at the time it was introduced. Of course, a few individuals foresaw the consequences and had something to say about those consequences, but certainly the details of the use of any of these four technologies had not been adequately foreseen. I am certain that the same thing will be true of technologies now developing for use in the future, and so I do not want to appear confident that what I say is a correct scenario for the future.

Before I turn to the issue of the technology and education of the future, I would like to comment on the configuration of schools. I have mentioned, and I want to emphasize again, the very recent and historically very transient character of schools. It is a phenomenon in a general sense of the last hundred years in the most developed parts of the world, and a phenomenon of the last thirty years (that is, since World War II) in the underdeveloped parts of the world. Now, an important question for the future is this: In fifty years or one hundred years, will we abolish schools? Will we deliver into the home, or into small neighborhood units by technological means all curriculum and instruction? Further, will the wish of the individual, the family, the parents, or the neighborhood group be such that they will not want their children in school, but rather want them at home or in the neighborhood? I think the answers to these questions are not easy to predict or to foresee. This does not mean that schools will disappear in twenty years or in thirty years, but what will happen one hundred years from now . . . is indeed difficult to tell.

A second general remark before I turn to some details is that the same forecast may be made for books. The importance of books that we have felt for several hundred years, since the beginning of the Renaissance, and that has been associated with the development and education of an informed citizenry, may once again fade away. I think that all of us, at least those of my age, have seen this already in the case of young students. Some recent studies have indicated that the cultural reference points for the younger generation are no longer to be found in books, or in current novels, but television. A reflection of this is mirrored in that popular program "All in the Family"; conversations between the characters of that program frequently refer to other TV programs, for example, "Marcus Welby." So what we shall see in the future may be a still more substantial decrease in the importance of books, and I will come to some of the reasons as I go along.

Now for the other two technologies. In the case of tests, I think again that in the future this classical technology will decrease in importance. I believe that tests will decrease in importance because we will have the technological means to keep a much more satisfactory and much more detailed record of the learning of individual students. Thus our inferences about the performance of students and their capabilities for taking next steps will depend upon a much more substantial record, a much better basis of inference than we have in current tests. So once again, I can see the technology of tests fading away and not having the importance it has had in the past.

Finally, what about the written record? The written record will undoubtedly continue to have importance, but I think that when it comes to teaching, the objections found in Plato's dialogue to the cold and neutral written word as opposed to the warm and friendly voice of the teacher will once again be heard and felt as serious objections. What I am saying is that in starting to think about the future, we can forecast obsolescence or semiobsolescence for all of the great technologies of the past—and that is proper and appropriate.

REORGANIZING FOR TOMORROW'S SCHOOLS

School Size

Now let me turn to aspects of the school of the future. I shall break my remarks into two parts: the first contains organizational remarks and the second contains intellectual remarks about the tasks ahead of us in making use of the technology that will be available. The first organizational remark has already been touched on, namely, the question of what we are going to seek in terms of the nature and size of schools. The consolidated high school, developed in this century and the instrument of mass education in the United States, will go down historically as one of the most important institutional innovations in twentieth-century education. Still it is not at all certain that the large high school will be around one hundred years from now. We may prefer to have schools of one or two hundred students that have a kind of intimacy and localness that the large high schools of today do not have. Now although it may be easy for me to say, "Yes, I am certain that will happen," such a remark would be foolish because I do not know this for sure, and the basis for prediction is not solid or firm. I do know that such a case can be made, because we shall have the technological resources in the use of television and its successors, especially in the use of computers, to bring into a small school of one hundred students, either elementary or secondary, all of the intellectual resources and all of the teaching resources that we now associate with the large high school. Any decision about the size of the school of the future will therefore be a social rather than an intellectual one.

One of my reasons for caution in predicting these alternatives for the future can be seen in the example of the junior high school son of a colleague of mine who read those suggestions and responded with, "Who would want to go to a school with only one hundred students?" I think that this remark is a proper and pointed warning that merely because we have the technology, and thus the possibility of having small and intimate schools, it does not mean we will have them or that students will want them. Still, the possibility is there, and I put it forward as an issue for the future—that the size of schools is neither a technological problem nor an intellectual problem in terms of delivery but rather a social problem. What is the optimal size? We do not know, but hopefully we shall be finding out in the future.

Home-Based Learning

The second topic closely related to the issue of the decentralization of schools is the issue of home-based learning. How much education will we take directly into the home? This raises the issue of another technology that I could have mentioned when I spoke of technologies already developed—namely, television, or more generally, radio and television. No one in 1930 could have adequately forecast the astounding impact of television on the modern world. Because of its enormous success, it is reasonable to say that the next step forward will be to bring all the educational background, all the teaching and curriculum that a student will want, directly into the home via television. And, in the only slightly more distant future, there will also be computer terminals. For example, in my own work at Stanford, we are in the process of putting individual computer terminals in the homes of a selected group of highly gifted children so that the children can work at home on material that goes beyond what they are getting in school and that they are more than able to take on, given their unusual abilities. What we do not know, in any broad sense, is how much the young student, the high school student, or the adult continuing his education will want to do at home, or how much learning will take place at home, as opposed to how much will take place in some kind of institutional setting. Still, this will be a central issue for the school of the future, now that we have the technological possibilities available to us. My own prediction is that we will have some kind of mix. Once we have the possibility, there will be a swing toward the home as the place in which learning takes place, that is, the place where the student stays and engages in learning, even though the exact configuration is simply not easy to see at the present time. Already today there is no comparison between the technological precision and sophistication of the color television set and the simpler and cheaper computer terminals. The color television set is a much more complicated and much more delicate instrument. Still we find color sets in a high proportion of the homes, and it is fair to say that we could install millions of the simpler computer terminals for interactive learning in the home, if that were what the population as a whole desired. We do not know the answers to these questions yet—they have not been explored—but we shall be finding them out. The point here is that getting the instrument into the home is not a technological problem; rather the problems are how to use it and how to find out whether people want to use it once it is there.

Curriculum Standardization

A third main topic concerning the organization of the school of the future, one that is a broader cultural and intellectual problem, is the issue of diversification versus standardization of the curriculum. Let me deal first with standardization. One aspect of standardization is standardization across countries. For example, an area in which I have worked for many years is the teaching of elementary mathematics. At the present time there is such enormous uniformity throughout the world in the approach to the teaching of elementary mathematics, especially in the content of the curriculum, that the same curriculum can be found everywhere in the world. Thus there has been a standardization that seemed unlikely half a century ago. We can, of course, find such standardization in the teaching of advanced scientific topics, such standardization, in fact, that in developing countries a large portion of courses in advanced science are taught in English because so many textbooks and publications are in English. As the resources of various countries become greater, we will need to face the issue of whether to continue on this world trend toward standardization, or toward Americanization, as our friends in other lands like to think of it. Such a decision will have a highly significant impact on education and what we plan for the education of the future.

The other side of the issue is diversification. The standard stand-up lecture with thirty or fifty or two hundred students is in the long run obsolescent. Nevertheless, the question remains, regardless of whether we talk about the second graders or the twelfth graders in a community, as to whether they should be studying the same material. Should we require that they all learn some reasonable level of reading skills, or, in the case of more particular subjects, that they all have some knowledge of culture and history of their regions and of the national units and of the world? Again, we can use technology in order to have a degree of individualization that was simply not possible in the past.

Although we shall have the option to permit substantial diversification in what students learn, we shall still have to think through what is the appropriate level of such diversification. Thus, for the school of the future, the technological possibilities of letting each student go his or her own way will be available, and what we will need to know is how far we want to travel down such a path. A favorite theme of American education—at least since John Dewey established the laboratory school at the University of Chicago in the 1890's—is that we should individualize instruction according to the needs and capabilities of the individual student. However, it is not clear to what extent we should let students pursue matters of individual interest. It is sometimes expressed as a romantic idea that students will come out all right if they are permitted to pursue their interests as they wish, but I know of no serious evidence that indeed students will come out all right. What kind of constraints we need is an important question for the future. . . especially since the possibilities of so much diversification are open to us.

Availability of Higher Education.

Finally, concerning the problems of organization, I want to talk about level of education. I recently had an intense debate with my friend Fritz Machlup, who is critical of broad-based higher education. In his view, higher education, in its real sense, should be restricted to the 15 or 20 percent of the population who have "real" learning ability and who show unusual intellectual aptitude for learning. Without going into that debate now, I want to state that I strongly disagreed with his view. I have mentioned the despair felt by John Stuart Mill about the prospects of ever having the mass population in a democratic society educated and informed, but I think Mill would have been happy at the level of information and competence possessed by American society at the present time. In terms of information processing, in terms of knowledge of the world, in terms of capacities for learning, our society's general competence contrasts greatly with that of the society in England in which Mill lived one hundred years ago. Thus I continue in my own predilections to be optimistic about the future. Mill despaired for his society, but I do not despair for ours. As far as I can see, the long historical trend has led upward since the time of Plato. Of course, we may have a downturn, and many doomsayers think that we shall, but it seems to me that the long-term trend will continue, and that trend will lead to a future in which we shall reach for ever higher levels of education for the general population.

A hundred years ago it was unthinkable that the mass of the population in any country of the world would complete twelve years of public education. A hundred years before that it was unthinkable that the mass of the population would complete four years of education. And a hundred years before that it was ridiculous to think of very much education for any but a small elite. Now it is certainly true that societies can develop along the lines of a totally elitist philosophy and be enormously successful, and I am not so naive as to think that could not happen again in the future. For instance, the prime example of such an elitist society, the one that I consider the most important intellectual center of the world historically, was Alexandria, founded in 322 B.C. by Alexander and taken over in the seventh century by the invading Arabs. In that intervening 1,000 years more was accomplished that was of intellectual importance than in any other city in the history of the world in terms of science, technology, and culture—from the invention of the organ to the development of mathematics to the beginnings of literary criticism. And that society sat in Egypt speaking Greek, rather than the language of the population around it, and still brought about the education and intense development of culture for a foreign minority of a very small size. So it is possible that that might be the picture for the future, although I think, as does Bell, it would be surprising and not consistent with the long-term trend.

Looking at the years following the despairing picture of John Stuart Mill a century ago, and then projecting ahead one hundred years from the 1970's to the 2070's, I see no reason not to think that we will be at about the level of a master's degree for the mass of the population, and two hundred years from now at the level of a Ph.D. for the mass of the population. Already we are close to having everyone at the level of a college education. In other words, I predict that if we are able to continue the trends now under way, and if we do not reverse them, society will consist almost exclusively of highly educated, highly trained, sophisticated professionals. That, to me, is the simplest and most straightforward extrapolation from the past, and I shall be happy to argue with those who consider it too optimistic, even though in general I am skeptical of anyone's ability to make detailed predictions. I might add that from the standpoint of education and from the standpoint of cost, this does not represent so great a change as the change that took place between 1870 and 1970 in this country, from the time when only 2 percent of the population graduated from high school to the current time when about 40 percent of the eligible population graduates from college.

THE INTELLECTUAL PROBLEMS OF TECHNOLOGY

At this point I would like to discuss some of the intellectual problems involved in learning how to use the available technologies deeply and well. I have already mentioned the intellectual problem of individualization and the difficulties inherent in determining the degree of individualization desired, but I believe we will be making a deep thrust for some time to come for an ever-increasing degree of individualization in instruction. . . .

To give focus to my comments on the technologies of the future and the intellectual problems of using them, I shall mainly restrict myself to computers—not capriciously, but because the issues we can expect to deal with in the case of the computer subsume the issues we will face from other media, especially television. The use of video tape and the selection of appropriate segments of instruction will be under computer control, so that general media questions rightly fall within my general discussion of computers.

Computers That Talk

Let me break this discussion of intellectual problems into four parts that will take us back through some of the earlier technologies. The first problem is simply that of talking. What does it take to get a computer to talk? The fact is that the technical issues are already pretty well in hand. Perhaps the reader saw on television "The Forbin Project?"—a movie about two large computers in the Soviet Union and the United States getting together to dominate the world. To the cognoscenti who have seen that movie, let me make a casual remark about talking. A technical criticism of the movie is that the two very large and sophisticated computers were conducting only one conversation at a time. Already in our computer system at Stanford we have eighteen channels of independent simultaneous talk and the computer talks independently and differently to eighteen students at the same time. So you see, we have the capacity for the computer to talk. What we need, however, is better information about what is to be said. For example, when I serve as a tutor, teaching one of you, or when one of you is teaching me, intuitively and naturally we follow cues and say things to each other without having an explicit theory of how we say what we say. We speak as part of our humanness, instinctively, on the basis of our past experience. But to satisfactorily talk with a computer, we need an explicit theory of talking.

Computers That Listen

The replacement of the written record, the kind of record that was objected to in Plato's *Phaedrus,* can be available to us in the talking computer. The other side of that coin which Socrates also emphasized, or should have emphasized, concerns listening, and that is the second problem of this discussion. It is a much more difficult technical problem. The problem of designing a computer that can listen to a student talk is much more difficult than having a student listen to the computer talk. However, the problems are solvable. For example, we just completed our first experiments with ten-year-olds talking to the computer in order to give answers to elementary mathematical problems. Our current exercise, to give you a sense of where we are in a classical curriculum, is spelling over the telephone. We call the student at home and give him five or ten minutes of spelling lessons. During this period he spells orally and the computer tries to recognize what he has spelled. This recognition problem has proved to be difficult but not impossible operationally.

That is where we are now, but the effort to solve this problem is already under way in many parts of the world. One hundred years from now, or fifty years from now, there is no doubt that computers will be listening at least moderately well. Certainly they will be listening as well as an inattentive tutor. And, once these talking and listening capabilities are available, we will seriously be able to respond to Socrates to say, "Yes, we agree, especially in teaching the young child, let's not have so much of the written record; let's have more talking and listening."

The Use of Knowledge

The third part of my discussion concerns the problem of understanding the knowledge base. To have an effective computer-based system of instruction, we must transcend mindless talking and listening and learn to understand and use a large knowledge base. For example, if we were simply to require information retrieval from a knowledge base, it would be relatively simple in the near future to put the entire Library of Congress in every elementary school. The capacity to store information is increasing so rapidly that we will be able to store much more information than could ever possibly be used.

A different and more difficult question is how to get the sizable knowledge base to interact with the student. As we come to understand how to handle such a knowledge base, the school computer of the future should be able to answer any wayward question that the student might like to ask. Moreover, as we all know, once a student uses such a capability, he will have a strong tendency to pursue still further questions that are more difficult and more idiosyncratic. It will, I think, be wonderful to see how children interact with such a system; in all likelihood, we will see children give to learning the high degree of concentration and the sustained span of attention they now give to commercial television.

There is one related point I want to emphasize. From the very beginning of school, students learn quickly the "law of the land" and know they should not ask questions the teacher cannot answer. This task of diagnosing the limitations of teachers begins early and continues through college and graduate school. So, once we have the capacity for answering out-of-the-way questions, it will be marvelous to see how students will take advantage of the opportunity and test their own capacities with a relentlessness they dare not engage in now.

Need for Theories of Learning and Instruction

The fourth problem, and in many ways the least-developed feature of this technology, is the theory of learning and instruction. We can make the computer talk, listen, and adequately handle a large knowledge data base, but we still need to develop an explicit theory of learning and instruction. In teaching a student, young or old, a given subject matter or a given skill, a computer-based learning system can keep a record of everything the student does. It can know cognitively an enormous amount of information about the student. The problem is how to use this information wisely, skillfully, and efficiently to teach the student. This is something that the very best human tutor does well, even though he does not understand at all how he does it, just as he does not understand how he talks. None of us understand how we talk and none of us understand how we intuitively interact with someone we are teaching on a one-to-one basis. Still, even though our past and present theories of instruction have not cut very deep, it does not mean that we have not made some progress. First, we at least recognize that there is a scientific problem; that alone is progress. One hundred fifty years ago there was no explicit recognition that there was even a problem. There is not stated in the education literature of 150 years ago any view that it is important to understand in detail the process of learning on the part of the student. Only in the twentieth century do we find any systematic data or any systematic theoretical ideas about the data. What precedes this period is romance and fantasy unsubstantiated by any sophisticated relation to evidence. So at least we can say that we have begun the task.

CONCLUDING NOTE

To conclude, I want to reemphasize that the four points I have mentioned are intellectual matters, not problems of hardware or of technology in a narrow sense. Understanding talking is a general problem of intellectual investigation for humans as well as for computers. The same is true of listening. Accessing a data base and using it properly constitute a general intellectual problem. Having a theory of instruction and having a theory of learning are general intellectual and scientific problems. Finally, let me say what I said at the beginning—I am skeptical of predicting the future. When I sketched the four technologies of the past, I emphasized that none had been predicted in detail. I think that this is true also for all the powerful and sophisticated technologies of the future I have discussed here. Only God knows what learning and teaching will look like one hundred years from now. Five hundred years from now is beyond the imagination.

(Goodlad, cont. from p. 279)

part of the reality we have to deal with.

What kind of school would I like to build? The first question I have to ask is: "What do I mean by school?" I hope I no longer mean a place children spend from 9:00 to 3:00 in little boxes arranged side by side down an aisle, where they sit in rows all day and listen to a teacher expound or raise questions. For the future we have to think of school as a concept, not a place—not that physical plant, not those ten or twenty or thirty little boxes. We have to think of school as a concept of developing human potential for the sake of both the individual and society. It is a concept that leads to utilizing all possible resources—people or things, wherever they may be, in or out of school, at any time of day. It is a concept of guiding learning, not just from 9:00 to 3:00, but twenty-four hours a day.

What shall be the prime goal of my school? If I had to sacrifice every single function or goal but one, my goal would be thinking. My school shall be a thinking school. Man is the time-binding, space-binding animal, so far as we know the only creature capable of linking himself with all men, of all time, in all places. The basis of compassion, the basis of affect, is thought. When we treat another person unkindly, we are not thinking about his lot in life, his particular situation, his needs. Behind a great deal of our talk about affect and sensitivity is the realization that we have the ability to use our minds effectively and clearly in a whole range of situations involving our behavior toward others. Working with the individual must help him learn to deal in more rational, thinking, ways with his fellow man.

I want my school organized into phases—not grades—of three to four years each to permit family grouping. Perhaps this organization could be made to coincide with Erik Erickson's eight ages of man; at any rate, three-, four-, five-, six-, and maybe seven-year-olds would be together, and so on. One reason for multi-age grouping is that every child should have the experience of being both the youngest and the oldest in a group. This is a very important developmental opportunity, and one that we have ignored in our traditional, graded schools. Into each phase of schooling would come 25 to 30 percent of the children each year, and 25 to 30 percent would move on to the next phase—not all at the same age,of course, but according to their readiness. My phases are organized around three to four year groupings because it takes time to achieve any important function in life. It takes time to diagnose the individual's achievement, potentialities, problems, and how we can help. In the usual September to June rat race, there simply is not time for this diagnosis.

Each of the phases in my school will be guided by a team, and not just a team of fully qualified teachers. There will be some fully qualified professionals, paid much more than any fully qualified professional today. And there will be paraprofessionals, aides, volunteers—maybe dentists, lawyers, artists, folk singers, and the like—all part of the team, contributing bits and pieces of time. In the school I envision, everybody is a teacher—even the children.

Each of these phases of schooling will have its own unique function; that is, in addition to learning to think, which will be the prime focus of the entire school, some other major function will be stressed. For example, the early childhood phase (from three to six or four to seven) will be a period of self-transcendence. It will not be a time to learn to read or write (although most children will) but a time to transcend oneself, a time to come to grips with oneself as a person, to find out what kind of person one is. It will be a time to begin to move beyond the self—through fantasy, through parallel play, through working with many different kinds of materials—to a true identification with other people. The literacy of learning to transcend the myopia of selfhood in developing an identification with other human beings I place much higher than the literacy of learning to read and write, and if that literacy is not attained early in life, I am not sure that it ever will be.

We will assure that during this period of three or four years every single child will develop a unique talent—some aspect of music or of art, some craft, some sport, some academic subject. It does not really matter what this talent may be, but the child must learn the rigor that goes with it. The process of acquiring a talent and developing the discipline that goes with it transfers to many other things. Show me a child who feels potent because he can do one thing well, and I will show you a child who will tolerate a lot of things that are not very meaningful, a child who is better equipped to deal with life's complexities.

How shall the children in my school be grouped? Rather than trying to achieve homogeneity—we have spent most of this century trying to get homogeneous groups, and we have failed hopelessly—why don't we just turn the coin over and strive for heterogeneity? Let's put the children together *because* they are different. One kind of difference is expressed through multiage grouping, another through a wide religious, ethnic, and racial mix. One way to help achieve this mix is a highly sophisticated kind of busing that will get the youngsters to the educational opportunities that are right for them, in each case grouping children who will indeed learn to work together and understand each other. The future depends heavily on that understanding.

How shall the children be taught in my school? Mostly by peer groups. One of the problems in individualizing instruction is that we have not faced the possibility of how much youngsters can learn from one another. The older children can teach the younger ones, and the younger ones can teach the older ones. The younger child will see what subsequent periods of development are like by living daily with older children.

In my school children will be taught also by adult models, people who not only talk about a skill but also demonstrate it. There will be someone who can play the guitar or the flute, someone who can take a piece of clay and shape it, someone who can form sentences into an exciting story.

These adults will not necessarily be certified; many of them will be volunteers, and they can be brought into the team as part of the instructional process. In many instances the children will go to planned educational laboratories where the teacher will be hard at work on a particular creative task, and the children will join in and become part of it, learning from the adult model. Sports have proved to be a great model for young people in this country and a great means of upward mobility. But why only sports? Why not bring models into the school in every phase of endeavor? Why not take the children to the models so they can see what it is they want to do?

In my school the child will have a great deal of self-selection, but he will be accountable for his choices. If he encounters difficulties, he will be able to get help to keep him moving ahead rather than becoming discouraged and failing. And there will be much talk: "What would happen if we did so and so?" Reading and writing will emerge out of much of this talk, and ideas will be taught through every possible medium. We will think and dance about it, dance and think about it. We will think and construct, construct and think. Think and write, write and think. Look at it and think about it. We will use every conceivable way to develop a single concept, a single skill, a single idea.

How shall the children in my school be classified and evaluated? Of course there will be no grades or report cards, no external rewards of that kind. But there will be performance evaluation. Someone who can both perform and understand will sit down with the child and help him see his strengths and weaknesses and what areas need improvement. The standard will be the child's progress in relation to a criterion. If you are going to learn to play baseball, these are the things one learns. How are you doing in relation to the performance criteria?

There also will be comprehensive assessments. Pupil, teacher, parents, and specialists will sit down together periodically to talk about how the child is doing. And there will be a different kind of educational voucher plan. At various times in a child's development, he will have a number of vouchers, not worth a nickel in money, but worth educational time—a voucher for art or a voucher for math with which the child "buys" the richest sources encompassed by the concept of school.

But my school is really only a transition to the school of 2001, a twenty-four-hour-a-day school that will reach out to all children and youth with all of the educational resources and facilities available. In the school of 2001 there will be many roles for teachers, from counseling, to coordinating a team, to preparing materials, to preparing a televised lesson.

Because we will spend the next thirty years developing the school we would like to have, some other changes are going to be taking place in society. One of the most profound of these has to do with communication, especially public television. The time is only a short way off when we will be able to plug into forty or fifty channels of public television. Through a television network we can begin to talk about the strengths and the values in which we believe, as a people. We can show the actions and institutions that support our beliefs, and we can expose those that deny them.

Another change that will come about is a rejuvenation of the inner city so that the school no longer carries the burden currently carried by busing and other devices. The cities will be rejuvenated from the core outward. I see no alternative but a destruction of the inner city as we know it now and the replacement of the slum, the broken-down buildings and the broken-down morale, with a cultural/ educational center of museums, art galleries, libraries, theaters, and the like surrounding a central green space. To the green belt at the periphery will be added the green belt at the center, with cultural activities surrounding it and the city progressing outward from there.

In the center there will be no housing for families, but there will be housing for adults. Their lives will be richer because they can walk to the theater, to the museums, to the galleries, and the like, without having to depend on driving automobiles. There will be housing for managerial services, for artists, and for visitors —speakers and entertainers who can enjoy the cultural life of the city while they are there. The inner cultural center will be common land, accessible to all for cultural and educational purposes and managed not by a superintendent of schools, but by a commissioner of cultural affairs who is responsible for the whole. And into it will come children.

Private vehicles will be prohibited in the center of the city; moving belts and battery operated minibuses will move us about without cars. And there will be a free, nonpolluting rapid transit system, radiating like the spokes of a wheel into the outlying areas.

Residential communities and green belts will be scattered along the spokes of the transit wheel, and distributed along these transportation networks will be educational and cultural facilities of all kinds. Children will move back and forth between home and education and cultural facilities on fast-moving trains. Everyone will be bused, in effect.

The educational districts will be cone or wedge shaped, starting from the center and fanning outward, so that the entire gamut of housing will be represented in the tax structure of each district. We will no longer have the problem of the cost of education increasing across the board while financial support for education increases unevenly because of different tax bases in different communities. Each district will contain a full array of educational services, provided by schools in the old sense, and by industry, civil agencies, and the like, financed from both state and local resources. (The cultural hub will be financed by the federal government).

The sophisticated system of busing will permit children from one school to "buy" with their vouchers the kind of educational enrichment, the kind of educational opportunities that simply cannot be provided through our present staffing plan. Multisensory terminals will be available in various centers, certainly in every school. The terminal will do more than educate a child; it will print out all of the cultural activities available at any time, any day, any week. Similar smaller devices will be used in the home, and once again the home will become a learning center.

And clearly there will be a different kind of teaching staff: a core of highly prepared professionals and a whole array of others, some who do not plan on a teaching career, others moving up to fully professional status.

While we are putting together the ingredients of our new school, we cannot assume that the rest of the world will stay as it is today. Everything I have described here has been designed somewhere already, and some cities—such as Atlanta, with its transportation system—are already moving in these directions.

The school we know today will evolve so as to be scarcely if at all recognizable. But this is not a process of deschooling. It is a process of making education out of our entire lives, of making a oneness out of all the modes of communication that impinge upon us. The process will take two related functions:

1. The realization and fulfillment of an individual identity, the development of individuals who are able to participate in all of the richness that lies ahead.

2. Self-transcendence and the adaptation of selfhood to those practices of disciplined cooperation demanded by the fact that no person, no nation, is or can be an island unto itself.

We must transcend self and develop a mankind perspective, or there may be no twenty-first century man.

POSTSCRIPT

WHAT IS THE HOPE FOR THE FUTURE?

As indicated in the introduction to this issue, the study of the future is occupying more and more attention in the field of education. Among the most widely read books and anthologies featuring studies and speculations on alternative futures are: Robert Bundy (ed.), *Images of the Future: the Twenty-first Century and Beyond* (1976); John I. Goodlad, *Facing the Future: Issues in Education and Schooling* (1976); John I. Goodlad *et.al., The Conventional and the Alternative in Education* (1975); Richard W. Hostrop (ed.), *Foundations of Futurology in Education* (1973) and *Education. . . .Beyond Tomorrow* (1975); Louis Rubin (ed.), *The Future of Education: Perspectives on Tomorrow's Schooling* (1975); Harold Shane, *The Educational Significance of the Future* (1973); Alvin Toffler (ed.), *Learning for Tomorrow* (1974).

The Toffler volume explores the psychology of the future, the black child's image of the future, tomorrow's curriculum today, educating scientists for tomorrow, and futurism and the reform of higher education. Many of the writers represented in the above volumes, especially Shane and Goodlad, would agree that, paraphrasing Goodlad, the learner of the future must have the freedom to learn what he or she needs to learn in his or her own way at his or her own rate in his or her own place.

The present reality in schooling, however, seems to militate against such a future. The insistence on highly regimented instruction controlled by behavioral objectives, the current mania regarding test results and teacher accountability, and the campaigns for proficiency in functional skills and curricula geared to career goals, if taken as the be-all and end-all of the educational process, appear to point to a more confining future for most learners.

How would you respond to the concerns raised by Suppes and by Goodlad? What kind of school would you like to fashion? What sort of future would you like to create?

CONTRIBUTORS

Editor

JAMES Wm. NOLL is an associate professor at the College of Education, University of Maryland. He received his BA in English from the University of Wisconsin, an MS in Educational Administration from the University of Wisconsin, and a PhD in Philosophy of Education from the University of Chicago. He is a member of the American Educational Studies Association, the National Society for the Study of Education, and the Association for Supervision and Curriculum Development.

Dr. Noll is co-author of *Foundations of Education in America,* and his articles have appeared in several education journals. He has served as academic editor for *Annual Editions—Readings in Education,* 76/77 and 77/78 editions.

Authors

JAMES A. BANKS is professor of education at the University of Washington, Seattle. Among his major works are *The Sociology of Social Movements, Black Self-Concept* (with Jean Dresden Grambs), *March Toward Freedom: A History of Black Americans,* and *Teaching Strategies for Ethnic Studies.*

CARL BEREITER is professor of applied psychology at The Ontario Institute for Studies in Education in Toronto, Canada. He is author of *Teaching Disadvantaged Children in the Pre-school* (with Siegfried Engelmann) and *Must We Educate?* (his 1974 book which elaborates upon the ideas excerpted in this book).

CAROLINE BIRD is an author and researcher who has taught at Russell Sage College and Case-Western Reserve University. Besides *The Case Against College,* she has written *The Crowding Syndrome, Enterprising Women,* and a book on the depression, *The Invisible Scar.*

SAMUEL BOWLES is professor in the Department of Economics at the University of Massachusetts. He is co-author of *Schooling in Capitalist America: Educational Reform and the Contradictions of Economic Life.*

JEROME S. BRUNER is Watts Professor of psychology at Oxford University and former director of the center for Cognitive Studies at Harvard University. Among his many works are *The Process of Education, On Knowing, Toward a Theory of Instruction, The Relevance of Education,* and *Beyond the Information Given.*

ROBERT F. BUNDY is an educational planning consultant, writer, lecturer, and futurist. He has edited a book entitled *Images of the Future* and has written a number of provocative articles, among them "Social Visions and Educational Futures."

The late JAMES BRYANT CONANT was president of Harvard University between 1933 and 1953 and subsequently served as U.S. ambassador to the Federal Republic of Germany. His writings include *The Citadel of Learning, The American High School Today, Slums and Suburbs, Shaping Educational Policy,* and *My Several Lives.*

JOHN DEWEY (1859–1952) was probably America's foremost philosopher and a leader in the field of education. While associated with the University of Michigan, the University of Chicago, and Columbia University, his voluminous work included *How We Think, Human Nature and Conduct, Democracy and Education,* and *Experience and Education.*

CLIFTON FADIMAN is a writer, editor, and radio and television performer who has been associated with the *Encyclopedia Britannica* and the Council for Basic Education. His works include *The Lifetime Reading Plan* (recently revised), *Ecocide—and Thoughts Toward Survival* (with Jean White), and *In the Midst of Life.*

MARIO FANTINI is dean of the School of Education at the University of Massachusetts, Amherst. He is the author of *The Disadvantaged: Challenge to Education* (with Gerald Weinstein), *Community Control and the Urban School, Decentralization: Achieving Reform* (with Marilyn Gittell), and *What's Best for Children?*

ROBERT M. GAGNÉ is a professor in the Department of Educational Research at Florida State University, Tallahassee. His major works are *The Conditions of Learning* (the third edition of which appeared in 1977), *Principles of Instructional Design* (with L.J. Briggs), and *Essentials of Learning for Instruction.*

HERBERT GINTIS is a professor in the Department of Economics at the University of Massachusetts, Amherst. He is co-author of *Schooling in Capitalist America: Educational Reform and the Contradictions of Economic Life.*

MARILYN GITTELL is professor of political science at the Graduate Center, City University of New York. Besides *Decentralization; Achieving Reform* (with Mario Fantini), she is the author of *Local Control in Education* (with others) and *School Boards and School Policy.*

NATHAN GLAZER is professor of education and social structure at Harvard University. Co-author of *The Lonely Crowd* and *Beyond the Melting Pot,* he has written *The Social Basis of American Communism* and *Affirmative Discrimination* and has co-edited *Cities in Trouble, The American Commonwealth,* and *Ethnicity: Theory and Experience.*

JOHN I. GOODLAD is professor of education and dean of the Graduate School of Education at UCLA. A charter member of the National Academy of Education, he has written *The Dynamics of Educational Change,* and *Facing the Future: Issues in Education and Schooling,* and is co-author of *Toward a Mankind School: An Adventure in Humanistic Education.*

The late PAUL GOODMAN was a writer, educator, and social critic who became a major theorist of the educational reform movement of the 1960s. Among his books are *Growing Up Absurd, Utopian Essays and Practical Proposals,* and *Compulsory Mis-education.*

PATRICIA ALBJERG GRAHAM is Warren professor of history of American education at Harvard University and recently served as director of the National Institute of Education. A former vice-president of Radcliffe College, she is the author of *Progressive Education—From Arcady to Academe* and *Community and Class in American Education 1865–1918.*

The late ROBERT M. HUTCHINS was chancellor of the University of Chicago, co-compiler of *The Great Books of the Western World,* and director of the Center for the Study of Democratic Institutions. Among his books are *The Higher Learning in America, The Conflict in Education in a Democratic Society,* and *The University of Utopia.*

IVAN ILLICH is an educator, social critic, and director of the Center for Intercultural Documentation in Cuernavaca, Mexico. He served as a Catholic priest in New York and Puerto Rico and was vice-president of the University of Santa Maria in Ponce. He has written *De-schooling Society, Tools for Conviviality, Energy and Equity, Medical Nemesis,* and *A History of Needs.*

PHILIP W. JACKSON is Shillinglaw distinguished service professor of education at the University of Chicago and former chairman of the Department of Education and dean of the Graduate School of Education there. He has written *Creativity and Intelligence* (with Jacob W. Getzels), *The Teacher and the Machine,* and *Life in Classrooms.*

CHRISTOPHER JENCKS is professor of education at Harvard University, where he has been associated with the Center for Educational Policy Research. He is co-author of *The Academic Revolution* and *Inequality: A Reassessment of the Effect of Family and Schooling in America.*

HOWARD KIRSCHENBAUM is co-director of the National Humanistic Education Center in Saratoga Springs, N.Y. He has written *Wad-Ja-Get?: The Grading Game in American Education, Advanced Value Clarification,* and *On Becoming Carl Rogers.*

HERBERT KOHL is an educator and writer who is presently co-director of the Center for Open Learning and Teaching in Berkeley, California. A columnist for *Teacher* magazine, he is author of *36 Children, The Open Classroom, Half the House, On Teaching,* and *Growing with Your Children.*

LAWRENCE KOHLBERG is professor of education and director of the Center for Moral Education at Harvard University. He has written many articles based on his research into the relationship of cognitive growth and ethicality and has compiled a volume entitled *Essays on the Philosophy of Moral Development.*

MARY KOHLER is a judge who is Chairperson of the National Commission on Resources for Youth, a New York City-based action group founded in 1967 for the purpose of identifying and utilizing talents of young people. She is co-author of *Children Teach Children: Learning By Teaching.*

GUY LEEKLEY is professor of law and associate dean at Northern Illinois University. In addition to his contribution to *Schooling and the Rights of Children,* Dr. Leekley has written "The Nature of Claims for Student Rights," and "Anglo-American Law in the Multicultural School."

LEON LESSINGER is superintendent of the Stockton (Calif.) Unified School District. His works include *Every Kid a Winner: Accountability in Education* and *Accountability: Systems Planning in Education.*

ORLANDO PATTERSON is professor of sociology at Harvard University. He is the author of *The Sociology of Slavery, Die the Long Day, Ethnic Chauvinism: The Reactionary Impulse, The Children of Sisyphus,* and *An Absence of Ruins.*

ARTHUR PEARL is professor of education at the University of California, Santa Cruz, where he has served as chairman of the Committee on Education. He is the author of *The Atrocity of Education* and numerous articles on issues in higher education.

MAX RAFFERTY is dean of the School of Education at Troy State University in Alabama and is a former superintendent of public instruction in the state of California. He has written *Suffer, Little Children, What They Are Doing to Your Children, Max Rafferty on Education,* and *Classroom Countdown: Education at the Crossroads.*

CARL R. ROGERS is a former professor of psychology and psychiatry at the University of Wisconsin who is now associated with the Center for Studies of the Person in La Jolla, California. Among his books are *Client-Centered Therapy, On Becoming a Person, Freedom To Learn, Becoming Partners: Marriage and Its Alternatives,* and *Carl Rogers on Personal Power.*

PETER SCHRAG is a writer and editor who has been associated with *Saturday Review, Change,* and *Social Policy.* He has also been a lecturer at the University of California at Berkeley and is author of *Voices in the Classroom, Village School Downtown, Out of Place in America, The End of the American Future, Test of Loyalty,* and *Mind Control.*

HARVEY B. SCRIBNER is a former superintendent of schools, state commissioner of education, and New York Public Schools chancellor who now teaches at the University of Massachusetts, Amherst. He is co-author of *Making Your Schools Work.*

ALBERT SHANKER has been president of the American Federation of Teachers (AFL-CIO) since 1974 and president of the United Federation of Teachers, New York City, since 1964. He is author of numerous articles on educational issues.

B.F. SKINNER is professor emeritus of psychology at Harvard University. His major works are *Science and Human Behavior, Walden Two, The Technology of Teaching, Beyond Freedom and Dignity, About Behaviorism, Particulars of My Life,* and *Reflections on Behaviorism and Society.*

LEONARD B. STEVENS is an educational policy specialist at the University of Massachusetts, Amherst. He was special assistant to Harvey B. Scribner when the latter was Chancellor of the New York school system and wrote *Making Your Schools Work* with him.

PATRICK SUPPES is professor of philosophy, statistics, education, and psychology at Stanford University. He has co-authored *Computer-Assisted Instruction* and has written *Studies in the Methodology and Foundations of Science* and *Probabilistic Metaphysics,* Volumes 1 and 2.

INDEX